Importing Diversity

Inside Japan's JET Program

DAVID L. McCONNELL

University of California Press

<small>BERKELEY</small>   <small>LOS ANGELES</small>   <small>LONDON</small>

University of California Press
Berkeley and Los Angeles, California

University of California Press, Ltd.
London, England

© 2000 by the Regents of the University of California

Library of Congress Cataloging-in-Publication Data

McConnell, David L., 1959–
     Importing diversity : inside Japan's JET Program / David L.
McConnell.
          p.   cm.
     Includes bibliographical references (p.   ) and index.
     ISBN 0-520-21635-0 (alk. paper).—ISBN 0-520-21636-9
(pbk. : alk. paper)
     1. Educational exchanges—Social aspects—Japan.   2. JET
Puroguramu.   3. Multicultural education—Japan.   I. Title.
LB2285.J3M33   2000
370.117'0952—dc21   99-38465
                                                         CIP

Manufactured in the United States of America

08   07   06   05   04   03   02   01   00   99
10   9   8   7   6   5   4   3   2   1

Dedicated to the memory of Jackson Bailey, whose scholarship, values, and commitment to intercultural exchange served as an inspiration for this study

Importing Diversity

Contents

Preface

"Show us some leadership, Japan!" This refrain, perhaps more than any other, sums up Japan's predicament in the waning years of the twentieth century. Having completed one of the most dramatic economic turn-arounds in recorded history, Japan nonetheless continues to suffer from an acute image problem within much of the international community. The Gulf War vividly demonstrated the widespread persistence of skeptical attitudes about Japan's motives. After contributing $13 billion to the war effort, Japan was roundly criticized for its "checkbook diplomacy." While the challenge facing Japan is articulated differently by different observers, all pose the same underlying question: How has Japan been able to gain so much economically without experiencing a comparable rise in its international standing?

The usual answer, at least in part, is that for all its overseas connections, Japan still largely lacks a sense of participation in the larger world. Japan's intense feelings of isolation and exaggerated sense of uniqueness are increasingly criticized by the rest of the world as barriers to business and by Japanese themselves as embarrassing social handicaps incommensurate with Japan's growing status as a world economic leader. Thus, at a time when pluralist nations around the world are struggling to integrate their ethnically diverse populations, Japan is under intense international pressure to solve the opposite problem: to "create diversity" and to acquaint its insulated people with foreigners at the level of face-to-face interaction.

In 1987 the Japanese government decided to address this problem via a different tack: drop thousands of college graduates primarily from Western countries into public secondary schools and local government offices in every corner of the nation. With an annual budget approaching $500 million, the Japan Exchange and Teaching (JET) Program is now the centerpiece of a top-down effort to create "mass internationalization." Eclipsing in magnitude even such highly regarded exchange programs as the Fulbright Program and Peace Corps, this effort has been proclaimed by Japanese officials as "the greatest initiative undertaken since World War II related to the field of human and cultural relations."[1]

This book examines the struggle for cultural and educational change in contemporary Japanese society through the lens of the JET Program. It asks what happens when a country known the world over for its organizational efficiency tackles the thorny issue of coping with diversity. What is the political symbolism and social reality of "internationalization" in a society structured on modes of social relations very unlike those in most Western countries? What are the powers and limitations of the Japanese state in facilitating top-down change? How does the JET Program chart a course between the sincere desire of the Japanese to raise their status within the world community and the deep-rooted sense of separateness still felt by many Japanese today? Relying on two years of fieldwork in Japan from 1988 to 1990 and four follow-up visits between 1993 and 1999, I explore these and other questions.

While the topic of Japan's integration with the rest of the world has received much attention of late, there appears to be little consensus on the subject. Indeed, mutually opposing views carry the day. On the one hand, we often hear that Japan has something akin to a culture of resentment toward foreigners, as if the entire country were engaged in a concerted and well-orchestrated effort to keep them out. Media reports targeting the "dark side" of Japan perpetuate this image of a country of reactionaries: highly placed policymakers who regularly drop racial slurs, Ministry of Education officials who ruthlessly censor textbooks, politicians who are unable to come to grips with Japan's militaristic past, bureaucrats who stubbornly cling to the status quo, and company executives who, in collusion with Ministry of International Trade and Industry officials, go out of their way to make it difficult for foreign companies to do business in Japan. In this view, Japan has changed little over the past century. It remains a "closed society" at heart, and the current internationalization campaign is little more than a smoke screen to divert attention from the country's true nationalistic interests.

On the other hand, a competing set of images stress the many changes that Japan has made during the postwar period. According to this model, Japan's similarities with other industrialized countries now far outweigh its differences. The history of postwar Japan can be read as the triumph of urbanism over rural life, corporations over family-owned shops and farms, bread and meat over rice and fish, mass media over the oral tradition, and meritocracy over ascription. In other words, there has been a steady, if gradual, movement toward Western forms and meanings. Efforts at internationalization in virtually all sectors of Japanese society clearly testify to the importance the Japanese place on changing their institutions and practices. In this view, it is unrealistic to expect Japan to change overnight; but it is assumed that given time and proper guidance, Japan will gradually open itself up to the rest of the world and free itself of bias.

Which of these two views is accurate? Is Japan a closed society or not? Or do either-or characterizations oversimplify the reality of the situation? To answer these questions requires a detailed ethnographic study based on careful observation. Therein lies the rationale for this study.

It has been said that the best way to find out how something works is to kick it and see whether it kicks back. The foreign participants in the JET Program disrupt the accustomed routines in Japanese schools and communities in countless ways, intentionally and unintentionally. By examining both the diversity and the regularities in Japanese responses to these reform-minded youth, I hope that we can acquire a more accurate and nuanced understanding of Japan's struggle for global integration in the Heisei era.

Acknowledgments

Thirteen years have passed since I first began this project, and I have had the good fortune of being accompanied at various stages of the journey by many wonderful people. Mentors, colleagues, friends, and family provided me with unselfish and sustained support, for which I am deeply grateful.

My interest in education and internationalization in Japan dates back to the early 1980s, when I was an undergraduate at Earlham College. I want to thank the late Jackson Bailey as well as Nelson Bingham for first opening my eyes to the potential self-knowledge to be gained through the study of Japanese culture, and for nurturing that interest both professionally and personally ever since. Nancy Rosenberger, my first mentor in Japan, was largely responsible for cultivating my interest in examining Japanese education through the lens of anthropology.

The research project itself could not have been accomplished without the kindness and support of many people. In Japan, this work was entirely dependent on the generosity and goodwill of officials in the Ministries of Education, Home Affairs, and Foreign Affairs. I am especially grateful for the cooperation of the senior Japanese staff and the program coordinators at the Council of Local Authorities for International Relations (CLAIR), the national-level administrative office for the JET Program. At the prefectural, municipal, and local school levels, I am indebted to the many Japanese administrators, teachers, and students, as well as the foreign participants on the JET Program, who so willingly shared their time and insights with me. Apart from the few individuals who are on public record as playing a role in the start-up of the JET Program, or who have consented to having their real names used, all of the above collaborators must remain anonymous, as they were promised. (In the text, full names indicate real names, and all others are pseudonyms.)

Throughout the initial two years of research in Japan, Caroline Yang and her staff at the Japan-U.S. Education Commission went far beyond the call of duty to lend a helping hand whenever possible. Tetsuya Kobayashi, my mentor at Kyoto University, extended kindness at every opportunity. He introduced me to many key people and generously included me in his own research project on English teaching in Japan. Wada Minoru was instrumental in shaping my understanding of the role of the Ministry of Education in the JET Program, and I deeply appreciate the patience and good humor with which he put up with my nagging questions for nearly ten years. Sugimoto Hitoshi gave selflessly of his time to assist me in translating many documents, and Tachibana Masaru was instrumental in arranging many important interviews.

During my doctoral studies in anthropology and education at Stanford University, Harumi Befu shepherded me through the dissertation process with wisdom and patience. David Tyack, Ray McDermott, and John Meyer also contributed substantially to the project. Merry White, Susan Pharr, Carol Gluck, and John Montgomery helped me sharpen my focus on the big issues during a one-year postdoctoral fellowship at the Program on U.S.-Japan Relations at Harvard University.

I owe a special debt of gratitude to Thomas Rohlen. Possessing a rare combination of compassion and perspective, he has been a source of inspiration for this project from start to finish. I dare say I have learned more about things Japanese from Tom than from any other single person.

Many other people have taken the time to share ideas and encouragement at various stages of the endeavor: I am especially grateful to Catherine Lewis, John Singleton, Richard Rubinger, Gerald LeTendre, Steve Nussbaum, Edward Beauchamp, Marc Ventresca, Nancy Sato, Becky Erwin Fukuzawa, Diane Musselwhite, Brent Gaston, Tsuneyuki and Kiyomi Ueki, Fumiko Arao, Robert Clayton, Buffy Lundgren, Angela Joyce, and Midori Kuno Hasegawa.

For contributing monetary assistance to support this research project, I wish to thank the Fulbright Program of the Japan-U.S. Education Commission; the Japan Fund of the Institute of International Studies at Stanford University; the Spencer Foundation of the Woodrow Wilson National Fellowship Foundation; the Program on U.S.-Japan Relations and the Pacific Basin Research Center at Harvard University; the College of Wooster's Henry Luce III Fund for Distinguished Scholarship; the Great Lakes College Association's Japan Fund; and the Northeast Asia Council of the Association for Asian Studies. A one-semester leave received from the College of Wooster in the fall of 1995 was invaluable in facilitating work on an initial draft of the book.

The editing process benefited from the valuable input of several persons. First and foremost, I want to thank Robert Juppé, Jr., for his tireless and inspirational commitment to this project. Bob not only shared his unique perspective on the JET Program with me during the time of fieldwork but also spent dozens of hours writing out lengthy and insightful comments on an earlier draft of the manuscript. Scott Olinger, too, provided detailed commentary on the same draft based on his long association with the program. The very existence of such thoughtful alumni who care deeply about the long-term prospects of the JET Program is striking testimony to its considerable influence.

Laura Driussi at the University of California Press was indefatigable in her support of the project as it moved through the complex maze toward publication. Her patience, wisdom, and good humor all shaped the final product in important ways. Sheila Levine and Scott Norton were of great help as well, and I received superb editorial assistance from Alice Falk. Special thanks are also due to three anonymous reviewers for their helpful suggestions. All errors of fact and interpretation, of course, remain my own.

Any project of this magnitude is ultimately dependent on the goodwill of family members, and my grandparents, parents, and parents-in-law have contributed their time and moral support as well as substantive suggestions. A special thanks to my father-in-law, Jack Love, for giving so generously of his time and talent to help fashion the attic office in which the final stages of this manuscript were written. My children Brennen and Alaina have contributed to the book in their own way, asking probing questions such as "Daddy, what is data?" and "Are you ever going to be finished with that thing?" Last but certainly not least, my wife Cathy has been a constant companion, critic, and confidante throughout the entire journey. At various stages of the project, and always when it was most needed, she has offered wisdom, reassurance, perspective, and impatience. For all these contributions, and especially for her uncommonly good judgment, I am truly grateful.

List of Acronyms

AET   Assistant English teacher: any of the JET Program participants from the United States, United Kingdom, Canada, Australia, Ireland, or New Zealand assisting in English teaching in Japanese secondary schools

AJET   Association of JET Participants: a group established by the JET Program participants in 1987 as a support group and as a lobby to influence Japanese government officials who administer the program

ALT   Assistant language teacher: any of the JET participants who assist in teaching a foreign language in Japanese secondary schools

BET   British English Teaching Scheme: one of the immediate predecessors of the JET Program, for British youth

CIEE   Council on International Education Exchange: the New York–based administrative office for the MEF Program from 1976 to 1986

CIR   Coordinator of international relations: any of the JET participants who work in prefectural or municipal offices rather than schools; they are solely under the authority of the Ministry of Home Affairs

CLAIR   Council of Local Authorities for International Relations: the administrative office of the JET Program under the control of the Ministry of Home Affairs

ETC   English teachers' consultant: the ALTs' supervisor, who works for boards of education (usually a career teacher temporarily posted to the board of education before becoming a vice-principal)

JET   Term used to refer to any of the foreigners participating in the Japan Exchange and Teaching Program

JETAA   JET Alumni Association

JTL   Japanese teacher of language: a member of the Japanese staff who teach any foreign language in secondary schools

MEF   Mombushō English Fellows Program: one of the immediate predecessors to the JET Program, for Americans

SEA   Sports exchange advisor: a member of the category of JET participants inaugurated in 1993 to bring professional athletes from select countries to teach in Japanese schools and communities

1 Japan's Image Problem
Culture, History, and Global Integration

The challenge facing Japan is evident and enormous. . . . Japan
urgently needs to change its pattern of interaction with the world,
since the consequences of Japan's past and present self-centered
behavior are being felt. . . . The passive, receptive role Japan still
plays in the international arena is now obsolete, and the burden of
change rests with Japan.

> James Abegglen, cross-cultural consultant,
> in "Japan's Ultimate Vulnerability" (1988)

The greatest single problem the Japanese face today is their
relationship with other peoples. . . . Japan naturally is much
admired but it is not widely liked or trusted.

> The late Edwin O. Reischauer, former U.S. ambassador
> to Japan, in *The Japanese Today* (1988)

Over the past decade a fascinating social experiment has been quietly un-
folding in schools, communities, and local government offices throughout
Japan. Conceived during the height of the U.S.-Japan trade war in the mid-
1980s, the proposal for the Japan Exchange and Teaching (JET) Program
was first presented as a "gift" to the American delegation at the "Ron-
Yasu" summit in 1986 between U.S. President Ronald Reagan and Japanese
Prime Minister Yasuhiro Nakasone. At considerable expense, the Japanese
government would invite young people from the United States and several
other English-speaking countries "to foster international perspectives by
promoting international exchange at local levels as well as intensifying
foreign language education."[1] After a weeklong orientation in Tokyo, participants would be sent to local schools and government offices throughout
the country. At a time when conflict about economic policy seemed never-
ending, the JET Program would provide tangible evidence of good faith efforts being taken to open up the Japanese system at local levels and to rec-
tify the imbalance in the flow of goods and personnel.

Three ministries—Jichishō, Mombushō, and Gaimushō—were charged
with administering the program jointly. The Ministry of Home Affairs

1

(Jichishō) gained overall control of the program, including the budget, and quickly formed an administrative agency to oversee implementation. The Ministry of Education, Science, and Culture (Mombushō) was charged with providing guidance to offices of education and local schools regarding the team-teaching portion of the program. The Ministry of Foreign Affairs (Gaimushō) would recruit participants through its consulates overseas. Job types for participants were divided into two major categories. The first, assistant English teachers (AETs) based in public secondary schools or offices of education, would make up more than 90 percent of all participants; their primary duties would involve team-teaching communicative language classes with a Japanese teacher of English.[2] Those in the second category of participants, coordinators of international relations (CIRs), were to be placed in prefectural or municipal offices, where they would assist in a variety of international activities in their area.

On 1 August 1987, less than a year after the initial press release, the first group of 848 college graduates from the United States, Britain, Australia, and New Zealand arrived at Narita Airport outside Tokyo; they were greeted with an extraordinary degree of media hype and with red-carpet treatment.[3] These "foreign ambassadors," as they were called, were wined and dined at a five-star Tokyo hotel during a weeklong orientation. Their arrival was covered by all the major newspapers and television networks in Japan. The governor of Tokyo and cabinet ministers from the sponsoring ministries attended the opening ceremony. Speech after speech by top government officials stressed the select nature of the foreigners chosen to come to Japan and exhorted them to shoulder an important part of the responsibility for Japan's internationalization. As one American participant recalled, "We were treated like stars and really felt special."

But the concept of internationalization, so easy to agree on when kept abstract, began to break down as soon as the reform-minded college graduates were dispatched to public secondary schools and local government offices throughout Japan. Accustomed to being in the racial majority in their own cultures, many were surprised at being thrust into a fish bowl where they were subject to stares and much scrutiny. Others were shocked when prefectural offices began sending them on a one-shot basis to dozens of schools, where they were wheeled out like living globes in classroom after classroom. The realities of entrance exams and the poor conversational abilities of many Japanese teachers of English left most feeling underutilized at best and intentionally misled at worst. By the third year of the program, burnout and cynicism had become rampant, and the informal grapevine among foreign participants was abuzz with the dark view that the government was using JET participants as mere window dressing.

On the Japanese side, prefectural administrators complained bitterly, if privately, about the extra work and indigestion created by daily interactions with unpredictable foreigners. Seminars on "how to team-teach" spread like wildfire around the country; virtually overnight, publication of step-by-step guidebooks on how to host an ALT became a cottage industry.

To compound the expectations gap, a number of serious incidents—ranging from participants being sexually harassed to driving drunk to committing suicide (see chapter 3)—shook program morale during the early years. In the first year more than 90 percent of foreign participants joined together to press Japanese officials for improvements in program policy, and in virtually every prefecture a group of participants crusaded vocally against their treatment. As corporations attempting joint ventures have often discovered, when people with radically different cognitive frameworks are thrown together in a common enterprise, they may produce little more than the breakdown of trust.

Furthermore, as the program unfolded in its second and third years, there was no shortage of domestic and foreign critics second-guessing the government's intentions. "Teacher Torture," screamed the *Tokyo Journal*. "Apathy Rampant in JET Program," proclaimed the *Japan Times*. "Japan Pulls in Welcome Mat with Racial Insensitivity," charged another article, which featured the experiences of an African American JET participant. The *San Jose Mercury News* warned darkly, "The Japanese government is spending millions to create potential enemies . . . which is exactly contrary to what it intended to do."[4] Almost overnight the JET Program had become a political football for critics of all stripes.

But ten years later, when the dust had settled and expectations had been adjusted, the JET Program was being touted by Japanese officials and foreign participants alike as one of the most successful policies in the postwar era. By 1999 the JET program had grown to nearly 6,000 foreign participants each year, and there were more than 20,000 alumni. The number of participating countries had grown to ten for the assistant language teacher (ALT) position; and thirty-six provided CIRs and filled a newly created category, the sports exchange advisor (SEA). With an annual budget of almost $500 million, the JET Program now stands as a massive investment in resources and effort.

More important, ALTs are now based in nearly a third of the nation's 16,000-plus public secondary schools and make regular visits to virtually every one of them. This complex, top-down intervention was accomplished with no formal resistance from the Japan Teacher's Union, which has opposed virtually every other major Ministry of Education initiative in the postwar period. Given the received wisdom in the United States that top-down reforms rarely reach the classroom, the receptivity of the Japanese system to such changes appears nothing short of phenomenal. Meanwhile, CIRs have been placed in every prefectural office in Japan; the new target is to place a foreign participant in every one of Japan's more than 3,000 municipalities (*shichōson*).

The satisfaction of foreign participants as well has markedly improved. Nearly 95 percent of JET participants say they would recommend or strongly recommend the program to a friend. The rate of participants who return home prematurely has fallen from a high of 3.1 percent in 1987 to less than 1 percent a year by 1997, and many more participants now are extending their contracts beyond the initial year.[5] Moreover, the program's effects are lasting. There is an increasingly active JET Alumni Association with branches in all participating countries, and alumni are flocking to graduate programs and jobs in a variety of Asia-related fields. Emblematic of the high status the program has gained was the presence of a JET table and a JET speaker at a Tokyo luncheon for President Clinton during his Japan summit in April 1996.

In the fall of 1996, government officials coordinated a gala set of events to mark the tenth anniversary of the program.[6] The target number of foreign participants had been officially raised to 6,000, and the mood among officials in each of the sponsoring ministries was optimistic. One Ministry of Home Affairs official, likening JET to a "reverse Peace Corps," remarked, "Considering how conservative local governments in Japan are, to get them to open their doors to foreigners was quite a feat. It's probably not an understatement to say that the JET Program is one of the most unusual revolutions in world history."[7]

WHY STUDY THE JET PROGRAM?

The JET Program is worth examining in detail; apart from its large scale and apparent success, it is a significant test case for top-down internationalization in a historically insular society. To be sure, there is no shortage of studies on the topic of Japan's global integration. Yet much of this writing suffers from what might be called a "yardstick approach." That is, Japan's progress in internationalizing tends to be measured against a set of standards derived from Western sensibilities. The implicit assumption is that

Japan must change and that it must follow a comprehensive list of prescriptions along lines dictated by Western countries. Not surprisingly, Japan never seems to make the grade. Rather than set out on the futile quest for some "true" definition, I view "internationalization" as a social and political construct. Much like a historian wishing to examine different meanings of "democracy" in different societies, I assume that the term is multivocal, with different associations and meanings for the Japanese hosts than it has for the foreign participants.

Moreover, those studying Japan's global integration almost always focus on the analysis of discourse among intellectuals, politicians, media specialists, and social elites. Few studies have attempted to show how internationalization is defined through the implementation of a policy, thereby acquiring a form that is independent of the perspectives of any one group of people. The JET Program transforms a buzzword into a reality, for the myriad decisions regarding program structure and policy, the ways Japanese define and handle problem cases, their efforts to integrate the foreign participants into schools and communities—all these make concrete (even if in unintended ways) the concept of internationalization.

The JET Program comes at a time of tremendous change and uncertainty for Japan. With the end of the cold war, and spurred by dissatisfaction over Japan's role in the Gulf War, foreign allies are questioning whether Japan can fulfill the high expectations for leadership that have come with her new global role. At home, the death of the Showa emperor, domestic political shakeups, and the prolonged recession have fueled calls for a new era of openness and a new generation of leaders.[8] At the same time, the bureaucracy is increasingly under fire from all quarters for its staunch conservatism, its insularity, and its refusal to challenge the status quo. For some, Ronald Dore's 1979 observation, that "the Japanese elite is full of people whose main reaction to the outside world is to wish it would go away," still rings true.[9] We are told that while bureaucratic guidance was instrumental in engineering Japan's modernization effort, these strategies are now outmoded. Incapable of inspiring human creativity, bureaucrats become paralyzed in new situations in which the goals are unclear and the means of implementation ambiguous—in short, when there is no model to follow.

Because the JET Program is a top-down initiative that spans the entire range of administrative levels in Japan, it is ideally situated as a window for assessing the power and limitations of the state to foster change. On the one hand, the centralization of policymaking—the ruling triumvirate of

Liberal Democratic Party leaders, senior bureaucrats, and senior managers of Japan's major enterprises—has long been taken for granted.[10] The defining feature of Japan's political economy is held to be a close relationship between government and business, an image epitomized in "Japan, Inc." In education as well, while the political significance of the so-called reverse course (the systematic dismantling of many Allied Occupation reforms) is hotly debated, the reality of recentralization, whether welcomed or not, is rarely questioned. But, on the other hand, some scholars have recently begun to criticize what they call the "myth of centralization." John Haley argues that the power of the bureaucrats has been vastly overestimated; their negotiations may influence the outcome of a policy, but they neither command nor control it. Steven Reed has discovered a relatively high degree of local discretion and autonomy in high school education policy, and Leonard Schoppa paints a complex picture of interaction among Ministry of Education officials and external actors—including the ruling and opposition party leaders, businesses, universities, local educational administrators, and the teacher's union—in the formulation of educational policy.[11] Thus government does not, as a monolithic entity, simply impose its will; every policy follows a unique course and grows out of specific conditions. Most of this chapter describes the historical and cultural context in which the JET Program began, as well as the approach used here to study it.

A case study of this program enables us to assess the tensions, inconsistencies, and gaps (or lack thereof) in the implementation process. Drawing on Thomas Rohlen's framework for analyzing postwar educational politics, I view each administrative level as a distinct sociocultural subsystem with its own set of priorities and its own manner of participating in a top-down intervention.[12] Each institutional level differs along such dimensions as the relevance of ideological concerns or outside pressure, the nature of internal partisan politics, the distribution of formal authority, and institutional worldview. Like playing a game of three-dimensional tic-tac-toe, implementing the JET Program involves both horizontal and vertical tensions and cleavages.[13]

At the national level, lateral tensions were virtually ensured by the administrative arrangement in which three government ministries with different goals and methods—Home Affairs, Education, and Foreign Affairs—were charged with oversight. The story of the start-up of the JET Program is thus replete with examples of backroom negotiations and turf battles between the internally focused and externally oriented ministries that were implementing it. Chapters 2 and 3 explore these dimensions of the JET Program. I conclude that it is in achieving the Ministry of Foreign

Affairs' goal—the idea of JET as a cultural exchange program designed to enhance foreign understanding of Japanese society—that the program has enjoyed such surprising success (see chapter 6). The structure and form of the JET Program make the most sense when viewed as a vehicle for creating sympathy for Japan among young people in select Western countries.

As the concept of internationalization moves from the corridors of the sponsoring ministries through prefectural offices to local schools and classrooms across the nation, it is reinterpreted; the program takes a form determined by the expectations and objectives—the particular social environment—operating at each level. The pressure to succeed is most intense at the national level. Prefectures and municipalities, by contrast, walk a fine line between wanting to appear receptive to a major government initiative and having to respond to school-level demands as well. The reactions of prefectural administrators to the JET Program are examined in detail in chapter 4.

It is in the schools themselves that the fit between internationalization and local priorities becomes most problematic. The most important functions of Japanese secondary schools are to prepare for high school and college entrance examinations and to maintain social order. The stress is on propriety and organizational maintenance, and judged by these standards, the foreign participants often behave quite poorly. Chapter 5 examines the diverse reactions of Japanese school-based personnel to the JET participants—how assistant language teachers are placed in schools and integrated (or not integrated) into daily social routines; how Japanese teachers respond when the ALT upsets the accustomed routine, either intentionally or unintentionally; and the creative ways in which teachers reconcile the desire to be "good citizens" and support the mandate for internationalization with the equally strong desire to protect local interests.

The final level to be considered (also in chapter 5) is that of the classroom, where classes are conducted together by the JET participants and the Japanese foreign language faculty. Unlike most educational top-down interventions, this one is almost impossible for teachers to ignore: it walks, talks, and even talks back. Precisely because the instruction provided by the JET participants represents a potential threat to accepted norms and standard methodologies, team-teaching has become one of the most controversial aspects of the JET Program. Yet many Japanese teachers have worked hard, with mixed results, to incorporate the ALTs into their overall teaching plan.

By paying attention to the historical, political, and administrative dimensions of program policy and to how the program has changed over time, my analysis provides an important counter to the myth of Japanese homogeneity. During the course of my fieldwork I met Japanese teachers and administrators who viewed the foreign participants as much-needed medicine for an outdated system as well as those who viewed them more like a virus whose potentially deleterious effects had to be controlled at all costs. Perhaps less surprisingly, the JET participants as well were an extremely varied group. In addition, the learning curve for Japanese hosts and JET participants alike was very steep; the program today differs in some important ways from its incarnation in the late 1980s. Chapter 6 assesses the current state of the program, now past its tenth year, and chapter 7 briefly speculates on its future.

An account of Japan's struggles to come to grips with diversity ultimately forces those of us in other countries to confront our own debates over multiculturalism. In the epilogue I examine the form of the debate over integration versus pluralism in the United States when viewed in the mirror offered by Japan. What are the similarities and differences between Japanese approaches to internationalization and American responses to cultural and linguistic pluralism? How does individualism, and the corresponding emphasis on choice and informality, shape the ideology and practice of multiculturalism in the United States? It is my hope that through juxtaposing the Japanese experience with at least one other case, we can gain insight into some of these questions.

THE WEIGHT OF HISTORY

At first glance the JET Program appears to be a noteworthy example of the government going against the grain of a long history of tightly regulating the flow of personnel across its borders. Centuries of self-imposed isolation appear suddenly to end as nearly a half billion dollars in public tax money is spent on importing thousands of foreigners. Yet closer inspection of Japan's history reveals a broad mixture of cosmopolitan influences that belie the stereotype of the isolated island nation. Indeed, Japan has been in the business of "internationalizing" for the better part of its history. The JET Program even has a remarkable historical precedent. In the early Meiji period roughly 3,000 "hired foreigners" (*oyatoi gaikokujin*) were brought over to assist in Japan's modernization efforts, sometimes with salaries ten times greater than those of their Japanese counterparts.

Where else but in Japan can we imagine a government going to such extraordinary lengths to invite foreigners to come and internationalize the entire country as a matter of national policy? Over the past decade, we have become accustomed to hearing about the profound difficulties of deploying public policy to integrate diverse populations. In countries throughout Africa and Asia, where colonial rulers formed nation-states with little regard for preexisting ethnic boundaries, public schooling has become a flash point for conflict over language and culture policy. Closer to home, the debate over bilingualism in Quebec has threatened to literally tear Canada apart, and the United States is embroiled in ongoing controversies over affirmative action and bilingual education. When the process of integration is largely driven by politics, it is usually marked by divisive and bitter public debate: social attachments based on language, race, religion, and custom come into direct conflict with government policies aimed at creating a unified state and a national identity.

In a few places, however, the boundaries of the modern state more or less coincide with boundaries defined by language, race, and ethnicity. In such "folk nations," where the population has a relatively high degree of homogeneity, the more problematic issue is global integration, which is largely driven by economics. The teaching of English in Scandinavian countries, for instance, has been crucial for the integration of their citizens into the world economic community. The case of Japan belongs in this latter category.

Pendulum Swings

The image of Japan as a historically exclusivist society does not hold up on closer examination. Analyses of blood types suggest that populations from the Asian continent were involved in forming the Japanese people as recently as early historic times; the tropical nature of Japan's early architecture points to southeast Asian influence. Moreover, the process of deliberately importing foreign ideas and objects has been going on for quite some time. Alternating with periods of contraction and isolation have been times, most notably in the eighth and nineteenth centuries, when Japanese have rushed to embrace foreign influences. The pattern of Japan's interaction with the outside world is perhaps best characterized as a series of pendulum swings, with each era of openness followed by conservative reaction. Underlying this dynamic is a profound sense of ambivalence and insecurity about Japan's status in the world.

Japan's cultural debt to China is huge: in the span of several hundred years Japan acquired the foundations for its political institutions, its literary system, the Confucian code of ethics, literature, architecture, and Buddhism. Between 607 and 839 there were seventeen full-scale Japanese missions to China, each comprising crews of 200 to 600 persons, including painters, scribes, musicians, priests, doctors, and military personnel.[14] It was during this period that the term *ryūgakusei* (overseas student) was coined, with the initial meaning "bearer of enlightenment from the lands beyond the sea."[15]

So ornate and colorful did imported Chinese culture appear that for a while it made everything about the indigenous culture seem drab and inconsequential. Even today, visitors to the Buddhist temples of Nara and the Shinto shrine at Ise grasp this contrast immediately. The Chinese method of inspiring awe was to clear out a broad open space and erect spectacular temples, complete with giant gilded buddhas and ornate pagodas. But at Ise the most sacred place is precisely the least obvious in location and the simplest in structure. For a while, native Shinto cosmology appeared completely overmatched by the color and flair of Chinese imports. What could possibly be awe inspiring about a rock in running water? Even indigenous food seemed boring next to Chinese dishes.

Over time, however, anxiety about loss of native culture grew, and its superiority began again to be vigorously asserted. This ambivalence was captured in the popular slogan of the times, *wakon kansai* (Japanese spirit, Chinese technology), which stressed the importance of importing Chinese knowledge without upsetting indigenous traditions. In addition, much of what had been imported from China was domesticated and remolded in the Japanese context, thus establishing what was essentially a new cultural system that blended elements from both. For instance, in the ninth century Chinese characters were simplified into the *kana* syllabaries used to represent Japanese syllables phonetically. Syncretism is also evident in the transformation of Buddhism; it lost its otherworldly focus to recognize religious significance in secular life and to emphasize activities within a concrete social nexus.[16]

After a long period of feudalism during which Chinese influences underwent further change, the early sixteenth century saw the beginnings of European influence in Japan in the form of Christianity, European languages, and Western technology. Following the return of four Japanese voyagers from Europe, a Western craze set in: even the shogun Hideyoshi Toyotomi and his retainers frequently wore Portuguese-style dress. But in the early seventeenth century, under the shogun Tokugawa Ieyasu, the tide shifted dramatically; by 1636 the death penalty was prescribed for any Japanese caught trying to visit the outside world. The official policy of seclusion (*sakoku*) was to last for over two centuries.

Unquestionably, the insularity that developed during the *sakoku* period can still be felt today. Yet two important points bear mentioning. First, the Tokugawa policy was a purely practical measure aimed at consolidating political power; it cannot be used as evidence of innate Japanese xenophobia.[17] Second, the Chinese and Dutch traders were allowed into the artificial port in Nagasaki, enabling the government to continue to pick up foreign technical and commercial information. For example, at Nagasaki officers of foreign ships were routinely questioned about Chinese capacities for agriculture and for silk production.[18] By 1740 two of the shogun's retainers were studying Dutch, and between 1764 and 1789, there was a "Dutch craze" (*Rampeki*) among the merchant class. Temple schools (*terakoya*) developed during this period, and the view that Western learning was quite appropriate for practical matters, though not for acquiring wisdom and virtue, became widespread.[19]

Meiji Japan Awakes to the World

In their fervor for Western things during the early Meiji period, the Japanese seemed determined to compensate for any attitude of reaction against the rest of the world that had emerged in two hundred years of self-imposed isolation in the Tokugawa period. In a surprisingly short time, English replaced Dutch as the primary medium by which Western ideas and technology were imported. Japanese individuals who had for various reasons been marooned overseas now returned to a very positive reception and sometimes considerable power. In 1856 an Institute for the Investigation of Barbarian Writings (Bansho Torishirabe-dokoro) was set up, thus beginning a systematic borrowing of ideas and institutions from the West. The Iwakura mission, which included many senior government officials, was sent to the United States and Europe in 1871 to renegotiate Japan's international status; a less formal purpose, as W. G. Beasley explains, was to "assess the civilization of the West, with a view to adopting those parts of it which would be of value to Japan."[20] Some of Japan's best and brightest were sent abroad for longer periods before taking up positions of influence. Mori Arinori, for instance, returned from many years in England and the United States to become minister of education. So impressed was he with Western cultures that at one point he officially advocated that Japanese be abolished and English be made the national language.

In retrospect, several features of cultural borrowing in early Meiji Japan stand out. Japanese were able to incorporate foreign technology with impressive speed, largely because of the high level of education and literacy of the general population, and particularly of workers in the industrial sector, by the end of the late Tokugawa period. Moreover, the cultural borrowing had become extremely selective. As Beasley notes, seventh-century Japan seemed "backward" in every respect compared with China, but late Tokugawa Japan had achieved remarkable heights in poetry, painting, music, and religion and chose to focus on Western scientific skills and technology. In that focus, the Japanese relied on what Rohlen calls "alert objectivity," the ability to scan one's external environment in order to grasp the essence of other social and technological orders.[21] One result was that Japanese borrowing from Western countries displayed remarkable eclecticism. For example, in the field of education Meiji leaders molded a system which resembled that of France in its organization, the United States in its curriculum, and Germany in its theoretical rationale. It was during the first two decades of the Meiji period that the Japanese government hired, at considerable expense, thousands of Western "experts." Some of these technicians and teachers gained considerable influence, and for a while, in the early Christian institutions of higher education, imported texts were used and English was the medium of instruction. The slogan "Boys Be Ambitious," offered by one of these imported *ōyatoi* and inscribed on the gate to Hokkaido University, has now motivated several generations of Japanese youth.

But even this early catch-up period was closely linked to a larger national purpose, especially to national defense. The modernization policy was sometimes described by the Japanese as "using the barbarian to control the barbarian."[22] As a result, Japanese officials took a very pragmatic stance toward the *ōyatoi*; Hazel Jones argues that they were actually treated as "live machines," their humanity overlooked in the rush to appropriate their skills.[23] When Japanese officials were satisfied that enough information had been provided, the *ōyatoi* were asked to leave. While this treatment clearly frustrated some of the *ōyatoi* themselves, it provides important insights into how Japanese approach learning from abroad. Japan's intense preoccupation with borrowing seems to be matched only by its drive for mastering what has been appropriated. In the early Meiji period the heavy reliance on cultural adoption and foreign teachers and technicians did not lead to permanent dependence on foreign sources. A combination of humility and willingness to be placed in the position of learner, on the one hand, and national pride and purpose, on the other, proved astonishingly effective in the push for modernization.

By the 1880s, however, enthusiasm for Westernizing was ending. The Meiji oligarchs were increasingly humiliated by their treatment at the hands of the countries they tried to emulate. It had begun with the unequal treaty negotiated in 1858 by the American consul, Townsend Harris, under the threat of naval power: foreign traders in Japan were protected by their own military forces and the extraterritorial privilege of trial by their own judges under their own laws, and at the same time the tariffs that Japanese could levy on Western imports were limited. After the turn of the century, resentment was heightened by the failure to secure a clause on racial equality in the Versailles Treaty and by the continued discrimination against Japanese in U.S. immigration laws; the Japanese felt unwelcome in the community of nations. Reaction against foreign influence took several forms; for example, the Imperial Rescript on Education explicitly linked education with providing glory to the emperor, and the folk religion, Shinto, was harnessed to the goals of state building and the legitimation of the emperor.[24] The waging of "the Greater East Asian War" obviously represented the culmination of this nativist sentiment.

The Postwar Period

Defeat in World War II marked the beginning of another swing in public opinion away from nationalism and toward democracy. Progressive reform of Japan's constitution, its political system, its education system, and its land policy, as well as dissolution of the large financial conglomerates (*zaibatsu*) and encouragement of unionization, were all goals of General Douglas MacArthur's temporary government. Yet because implementation of many of these reforms was left to Japanese, and because the advent of the cold war led Occupation authorities to concentrate on rebuilding Japan as an ally, many were reversed after the Occupation forces left. For instance, local boards of education, which were to be elected under Occupation guidelines, were made political appointments. But there was no backlash; instead, a series of gradual and moderate changes took place.

Despite such reversals, the war is today nearly universally rejected as having been immoral. This has created a profound ambivalence about the use of nationalistic symbols in contemporary Japan. Debates about the emperor's responsibility in the war, which surfaced in the media following Hirohito's death in 1989, made it clear that the imperial institution does not unequivocally symbolize national unity. Sometimes the Japanese flag and the anthem are questioned, as neither of them is mentioned in the constitution. While the Ministry of Education has decreed that the flag be raised and the national anthem sung at all official school ceremonies, compliance has not been universal.[25] Finally, official visits by the prime ministers to Yasukuni Shrine, where the souls of all soldiers who died for the country in wars are cherished as sacred, have been very controversial; they are seen as a sign of resurgent militarism by Japan's Asian neighbors, who suffered greatly at Japan's hands. Thus the major symbols of national identity—the imperial household, the flag, the anthem, and national monuments—were largely discredited by World War II.[26]

After the war, the focus of Japan's global articulation shifted from military expansion to economic recovery and then growth. Yoshida Shigeru, a prewar diplomat and postwar prime minister, came up with the formula that has served as Japan's national policy virtually to this day. Japan would ally itself with the United States, which would take over all defense functions and allow Japan to concentrate on its economy. In return, Japan would accept American leadership in foreign policy. As Yoshida said, "If you like the shade, be sure to find yourself a big tree." By most accounts, these efforts have paid off handsomely. Today Japan boasts the second-largest GNP in the world, and its corporations are household names around the globe; it is the world's largest donor of foreign aid; its education system is widely praised for producing uniformly high levels of academic achievement and social order. Many Japanese cite the publication in 1979 of Ezra Vogel's best-seller, *Japan as Number One*, as evidence that they had finally achieved prosperity. Rather than the emperor system or military might, the Japanese economic system, particularly its community-oriented aspects, had now become the principal symbol of national pride. Japan's alacrity in equaling and surpassing Western countries is all the more astonishing given its relative lack of technical and material advantages in the mid–nineteenth century. Japan can truly lay claim to being the dark horse of the twentieth century's peacetime competition.[27]

EDUCATIONAL REFORM AS THE SOLUTION
TO INTERNATIONAL PRESSURE

As it has emerged as an economic power, Japan—with its relatively homogeneous population and sense of isolation—has faced an acute problem of global integration. Western countries have protested with growing vigor what they perceive as the closed nature of Japanese society and Japan's refusal to play by the rules of the international liberal trading order. Foreign pressure on Japan to take concrete measures to liberalize the country and to reform what is seen as a feudalistic value system has been a political constant during the past few decades.

On the one hand, contemporary Japanese society ranks quite high on most "objective" measures associated with the term "internationalization." Overseas investment is flourishing, and more and more countries are doing business in Japan. Every year millions of Japanese travel abroad, and almost all American and European books of any importance are translated into Japanese. A great deal of attention is given to foreign language learning: most Japanese youth study English for at least six years. The Japanese have a great propensity for importing foreign loanwords, and a typical person knows thousands of *katakana* words that are derived from English. Today few nations are more acutely conscious than Japan of living in a global environment, and the Japanese appetite for foreign goods and ideas shows no signs of abating.

On the other hand, critics have observed that evidence of a closed mindset is not hard to find; in fact, there appears to be a direct connection between Japan's forging of international linkages and the rise at home of national introspection and the search for roots.[28] Even in the early postwar years, the archaeological excavation of a site from the Yayoi period (300 B.C.E. to 300 C.E.) enabled many Japanese to repair their wartorn national identity with the comforting knowledge of an unbroken 2,000-year history of rice cultivation.[29] Since then, the boom in nostalgia and *furusato* (consciousness of native place) can be read as indicating a search for an "authentic" past in the face of new and unpredictable challenges.[30] Takie Lebra points out that the increasing number of intercultural marriages has provided fodder for private detective agencies that screen job and marriage candidates for purity of background. Similarly, David Titus notes that the more contemporary Japan accepts influences from the outside, the more the entity called "emperor" is sought after as a symbol of Japanese community and uniqueness.[31] As the homogenizing framework of the world system presses closer, cultural identity is fostered and intensified.[32]

One of the most striking manifestations of this national introspection in the postwar period is the surging popularity of a genre of quasi-academic and popular literature known as *nihonjinron* (literally, "theories of Japanese culture"), in which authors have attempted to define their country's uniqueness.[33] In much of this literature, race, language, and culture become synonymous, resulting in what one Japanese critic calls a "unitary ethnic nation, intolerant of alien elements, constitutionally unable to accept the existence of different kinds of Japanese."[34] Dependency (*amae*), hierarchy (*tateshakai*), and left brain orientation have all been suggested as defining features of "Japaneseness." Some politicians have taken these ideas to extremes—for example, making the outrageous claim that the Japanese intestinal tract is unable to digest foreign-grown rice. Sales of books in this vein have skyrocketed almost in parallel with Japan's rising economic penetration overseas; any decent bookstore in Japan now has a shelf devoted to the genre.

These writings have been harshly criticized by Western writers who view *nihonjinron* as the worst kind of pseudo-scientific enterprise. In fact, the phrase "*nihonjinron*-like portraits" is now widely used among Japan specialists as a put-down of analyses of Japanese society that perpetuate the homogeneity myth and stereotypical pictures devoid of diversity. So eager are critics to unmask the "real" interests that lie behind *nihonjinron*, however, that they largely ignore the public's huge appetite for these books. Clearly, the message of *nihonjinron* is welcome to many Japanese.

Moreover, a strong sense of separateness and a concomitant arm's-length approach to global integration have some benefits. A feeling of cultural uniqueness, reinforced by a shared language, makes it easier to achieve internal compromises and sustain a decent society without the skewed income distribution that plagues some industrial democracies.[35] In addition, *speaking* English and feeling comfortable in personal meetings with foreigners are not necessarily prerequisites for being able to read technical manuals and acquiring the know-how for conducting concerted export drives.

Yet foreign criticism and pressure simply will not disappear. In recent years, Japan's success at integrating foreigners into domestic institutions has increasingly come to be seen by outside critics as its litmus test of internationalization. A global economic power such as Japan, they say, should open itself to foreign peoples and learn how to be more comfortable with the Other, both at home and abroad. Indeed, it can be argued that this lack of a certain fellow feeling with the rest of the world is at the root of many of the problems facing Japan in the late twentieth century. In the United State, for example, most of the criticisms that media, politicians, and scholars have leveled against Japan center on relations in trade, but others address the domestic treatment of minorities.

Though U.S.-Japan trade friction has eased somewhat in the late 1990s, for most Americans the bilateral relationship is summed up in the conflict over annual trade surpluses, which hovered around $50 billion for much of the 1980s. With this imbalance came a sudden anxiety about "losing" to a competitor, and some critics complain that the Japanese are not playing fair. Pointing to the failure of many Japanese firms with U.S. operations to integrate into local communities, they question not only the companies' business practices (e.g., reliance largely on Japanese suppliers) but also their commitment to racial and gender equity (offering as a case in point the notorious April 1996 lawsuit against Mitsubishi alleging sexual harassment). Conversely, they argue that a variety of nontariff barriers within Japan—the rigid and complex distribution system, the time-consuming system of patenting, the presence of industrial groups (*keiretsu*) that obstruct free competition, and bid rigging in industries such as construction—make it practically impossible for foreign competitors to succeed there.[36] And the charge that the Japanese attempt to win economically at all costs carries over to analyses of foreign policy. Japan has been criticized both for its persistent refusal to link politics and economics (e.g., Japan was one of the last countries to suspend business dealings with the apartheid regime in South Africa) and for the strongly commercial orientation of its foreign aid.[37]

Even on the level of personal contacts, Japanese are criticized for preferring package tours over arrangements that might bring them into informal contact with foreign people. And their behavior at home has fallen under still harsher criticism. Japan's increasing visibility internationally has exposed to the world the persistent fissure between dominant and marginal groups, the latter including in particular Koreans (who make up nearly half of the relatively small number of foreign residents in Japan) and *burakumin* (long-ghettoized descendants of the outcaste class of the feudal period).[38] Foreign suspicions about Japanese prejudices have only been heightened by a series of highly publicized racial slurs by prominent Japanese officials. In 1986 Prime Minister Nakasone Yasuhiro connected the presence of minorities in the United States to declining American intelligence levels, and before the decade's end two cabinet officials were quoted making remarks critical of blacks in particular.[39]

Images do matter, and try as she might, Japan simply has not been able to shake the perception that the country as a whole is intolerant of diversity. The very strengths on which Japan's economic success was built have become liabilities as the country is drawn further into a global environment. How, then, to raise Japan's status in the eyes of the international community without completely sacrificing the familiar modes of social relations that have served the nation so well?

In the mid-1980s, numerous policy prescriptions were proposed and implemented, but some argued that these national-level fixes would not seriously address the underlying problem. If arm's-lengths strategies of global integration were no longer tenable, then "mass internationalization" was crucial to continued economic progress. Though more and more people were traveling and living abroad, these individuals still constituted only a small part of the population. Japan's leaders began to see the exam-oriented educational system as a major barrier to internationalization. In

March 1980 the Ministry of International Trade and Industry (MITI) issued a report blaming the system for failing to produce the creative and in-
ternationalist workers necessary to meet the coming economic challenges.
Business organizations have also been loud in their criticism of Japan's
one-track school system and its failure to open itself up to diversity. Japanese education, long viewed as an asset in fueling Japan's domestic transformation, has recently come to be seen as a potential hindrance in meeting the challenges of the new world order.

American views of Japanese education have undergone a similar change.
For a long time Americans were largely indifferent to Japanese education,
but in the early to mid-1980s interest surged as Japan's economic success
was linked to its highly educated and disciplined workforce. Several scholars published influential books arguing that broad public support for education, the social organization of schooling, and culturally specific approaches to child rearing and discipline were the foundation of Japan's
educational successes.[40] Popular media sung the praises of Japan's schools
as models of academic achievement and warned of the follies of ignoring
the educational accomplishments of our major economic competitors. Influential American educators such as Diane Ravitch signed on for whirlwind tours of Japan's schools, returning home to exhort their colleagues to
consider the merits of the Japanese approach. While liberals applauded the
egalitarian streak in Japanese schooling, pointing out that Japan did a much
better job than the United States in raising a large proportion of its population to high levels of achievement and making them part of the social
order, conservatives praised the streamlined core curriculum and noted the
many ways in which "family values" undergirded the system. The overall
sentiment was that American educators, parents, and the general public
had much to learn from the Japanese.

But dissenting voices emerged: another set of popular and academic accounts purported to reveal "the dark side of Japanese education," to quote
the subtitle of Ken Schoolland's 1990 book, *Shogun's Ghost*. Rather than
portraying Japanese education as possessing a desirable difference, these
reports decried its uniformity, inflexibility, and closed nature. The images
offered were poignant if predictable: narrow-minded administrators
caught in the deadly grip of the "diploma disease," Ministry of Education
officials who ruthlessly censored textbooks, discrimination against Korean
and *burakumin* minorities, "returnee children" who were bullied by their
teachers and peers, adolescents driven to suicide or "school refusal syn-
drome" by exam pressures, the relentless *kyōiku mama* (education mothers) who pushed their children to do well on the entrance exams, and the

limited options for learning-disabled children. A 1995 *New York Times* article went so far as to claim that Japanese schools are "assembly lines that press students into the same shape," likening their atmosphere to that of a military academy.[41]

While some of these critiques were clearly based on myths and not reality, others could not be dismissed so lightly. As a whole, they suggested that whereas American educators begin by assuming that all children are different, Japanese teachers and administrators begin from the opposite position; and the notion that all children are basically the same creates enormous pressure to conform to a cultural center. In this view, Japanese education is a closed system that allows little room for deviance and few second chances. In several areas, Japanese education has deservedly been taken to task; many criticisms relate to its insularity.

Nationalistic Textbooks

State control over textbooks in Japan can be traced back to the late 1800s; as one historian explains, "the government promulgated the Imperial Rescript on Education . . . to bring to the education system the same system of thought control that had been instituted in the army."[42] Textbook revisions to promote new government policies were frequent up to and during World War II. Although Occupation reforms after the war gave schools discretion in choosing textbooks, the Ministry of Education moved in the 1950s and 1960s to expand its power over their authorization. Today, two advisory bodies in the Ministry of Education—the Council on Textbook Authorization and Research and the Curriculum Council—exert firm control over textbook content.

Social studies and history textbooks have proved most controversial. A 1982 media report claiming that the Ministry of Education had requested that Japan's military activities in Asia in the 1930s be described as an "advance" rather than an "invasion" drew harsh international criticism; even though the report was later found to be inaccurate, the whitewashing of textbooks is still widely seen as symptomatic of a deeper reluctance to acknowledge the Nanking Massacre and other war atrocities. But textbooks are more generally purged of materials that may be critical of the government's position and are thus characterized by a bland neutrality on hotly contested social and political issues. Teruhisa Horio points to one case in which the Ministry of Education failed to approve a well-respected work of literature because it did not use the official onomatopoeic word for a river's sound: "We can only conclude from this that the Ministry's inspectors feared that the children might get the idea that it was all right to play with the national language in ways which would encourage them to think of it as something belonging *to them* rather than as something whose use is controlled by the State *for them.*"[43] More recently Ienaga Saburo, a professor emeritus at the now-defunct Tokyo University of Education (currently Tsukuba University), won a 1997 ruling in favor of his claim that the government abused its discretionary powers when it ordered him to remove from his textbook a reference to live human experiments conducted by the Imperial Japanese Army's Unit 731 in northern China during World War II.[44]

Treatment of "Returnee Children"

The overseas migration of Japanese subsidiaries in search of cheaper labor and profitable markets has given rise to another vexed educational issue: children returning to Japan after extended stays in other countries. These children, known as *kikokushijo* (returnee children), are often pressured by teachers and peers to give up the cognitive and behavioral styles they had learned abroad. While such treatment is by no means universal—in certain schools these children are seen as a cultural asset—*kikokushijo* are likely to feel they must keep a very low profile, and many have serious problems readjusting. During the 1970s and 1980s most scholarly and popular accounts portrayed these children as victims of the closed nature of the school system and the tenacity with which cultural boundaries are maintained in Japan.[45] The titles and subtitles of books on the returnee children (e.g., "Life in Between" and "Can They Go Home Again?") suggested that returnees occupied a liminal category; and familiar expressions such as *gaikoku hagashi* (peeling away the foreignness) were seized on as manifestations in the schools of Japan's ideology of blood.

Roger Goodman's revisionist analysis seems to have marked a turning point of sorts in the dominant views of these children.[46] Goodman argues that it is misleading to compare the returnee children with Koreans or *burakumin,* because they are actually the vanguard of a new social elite. As the children of power brokers in Japanese society, the returnees—unlike other minorities in Japan—can expect as adults to find significant employment opportunities. Goodman's analysis was followed by a number of articles pointing out the special provisions for returnee children who compete for university slots and discussing the resentment such "privileged treatment" creates among other students. Yet a closer reading of Goodman's study reveals that even he recognizes the considerable ambivalence many Japanese feel toward these children. Moreover, his analysis is based primarily on data from one special school for returnees; those returning to schools without support systems in place continue to face strong pressure to give up the patterns of speech and behavior that they learned abroad.

The "Education Gap"

Another area that has received increased attention of late is the imbalance in educational exchange. In 1997, for every American going to Japan, twenty Japanese were studying in the United States.[47] While a lack of interest and language ability on the part of American students may be partly to blame, Japan has long been criticized for the low numbers of foreign students that its universities accept. Drawing parallels with Japan's trade surplus, critics argue that this gap is symptomatic of the self-centered and narrowly instrumental approach taken by Japanese schools toward the issue of global integration. The United States has opened up its educational institutions to Japanese students, so the argument goes, and thus expects reciprocal treatment.

The system of support in Japan for foreign students, the large majority of whom come from Asia, is poorly developed. For example, high prices and landlords who refuse to rent to foreigners can make good housing hard to find. One longtime observer claims that the role of foreign students in Japanese universities resembles that of imported laborers.[48] For their part, Japanese faculty and graduate students privately complain about the burden of caring for foreign students who aren't sensitive to the norms of reciprocity and tend to follow codes of local behavior only when doing so is in their best interest.

Sensitive to criticism in this area, the Ministry of Education embarked on a series of steps to import diversity and create more parity in educational exchange. In 1983, shortly before the advent of the JET Program, the ministry drew on the example of France and began a "100,000 Foreign Students Plan," hoping to meet that goal by the turn of the century. Through the early 1990s the program reached its annual target every year, but since 1994 the pace of growth has slowed considerably and the target now appears impossible to reach. Searching for a solution to the slowdown in growth and to the Asian background of the overwhelming majority of foreign students, the Ministry of Education in 1996 created a new category of scholarships, which in effect pay American and European students to study in Japan.

Foreign Language Education

Perhaps no other aspect of Japan's education system has been so sharply criticized for its insularity as the teaching of foreign languages. Although oral English had been held in high esteem during the early Meiji period, by the early twentieth century Japanese interest in learning foreign languages—particularly spoken English—had declined. The rise in nationalism led many foreign teachers to be replaced by native-born Japanese who were not always very proficient in spoken English. During the same time, the Japanese system of higher education took on an increasingly pyramidal structure, funneling the most capable students into a few elite schools; the keen competition that resulted only magnified the importance of the entrance exams. This, in turn, affected the way English was taught at the precollegiate level, and soon English became a means of sorting students rather than a basis of communication.[49]

Worsening relations with the West and the popularity of continental European fiction also contributed to a revulsion against spoken English and a perception that English was a language for businessmen. This too encouraged a return to the "translation method"—that is, an almost sole reliance on written texts—by which Chinese had been appropriated nearly a thousand years earlier. Inazo Nitobe conveys the prevailing sentiment:

> For the Japanese . . . the advantages of studying foreign languages are of a higher and more intangible nature than are the so-called "practical" benefits. In some ways the most valuable advantage lies in its "unpractical" aspect, namely, in its hidden and unutilitarian effect on the mind. . . . The age of Chinese classics is gone and with them the severe disciplinarian. His place is taken now by the English grammar, which with manifold rules and exceptions to rules, with its mysterious orthography and esoteric idioms, exacts of the neophyte the most strenuous use of his reason and memory, together . . . with unbounded admiration for the people who have mastered its intricacies.[50]

Thus two schools of thought developed on teaching the English language, one emphasizing cultural enrichment through reading of literature and the other stressing communication for international business. Nitobe comments, "Japanese teachers make no secret of their utter incompetence in oral intercourse; it is not expected of them. In fact, there is a deplorable propensity to boast of colloquial ignorance."[51] For most of the twentieth century the translation and literature school has been dominant, but there has always been a small but vocal minority of teachers calling for an emphasis on the practical dimensions of English communication.

Today, in sharp contrast to the highly politicized debates over bilingual and multicultural education in the United States, there is virtually no opposition in Japan to the *idea* of teaching English. All junior high students study a foreign language for three years, and most continue it for three more years in high school. Private English *juku*, or after-school classes catering to students who want to learn to speak, are a multimillion-dollar business in Japan. Yet language teaching in the Japanese public school system has continued to be harshly criticized on several grounds. Some object to the domination of one language: foreign languages are technically electives in Japan, but English has become almost mandatory. And because the approach emphasizes rote and grammar—much as Latin was long taught in American schools—students gain little sense of a living language. The six years invested in the study of English thus yield meager returns. It is not uncommon for students' conversational abilities to decline from the eighth grade on. The American linguist Roy Andrew Miller minces no words: "What are potentially the most valuable years for foreign-language learning are totally wasted in the course of hour after dreary hour in the English classroom with Japanese teachers, most of whom drone away in Japanese explaining the grammar and pronunciation of a language that they themselves have rarely even heard and certainly cannot speak."[52] Masayoshi Harasawa concurs: "Of all the countries in the world where English has been taught on a nationwide scale, Japan seems to me about the least successful. . . . On balance, our English teaching has become a disastrous failure."[53]

Most Japanese would agree; indeed, the notion has become a part of Japanese perceptions of their own national character. The lament that almost all students, despite going through six to ten years of English instruction, remain unable to hold the most basic conversation with a native speaker is heard from Japanese in all walks of life.[54] Former Prime Minister Takeshita, who himself had been an English teacher, was especially fond of poking fun at the poor state of English education in Japan, often at his own expense. Though private English conversation schools (*eikaiwa gakkō*) have thrived in direct proportion to the exam emphasis in the English curriculum in the public schools, there has been an increasing feeling that the public secondary schools themselves must do more to promote the acquisition of English conversational skills.

The education system, and foreign language instruction in particular, thus seems to be an area ripe for reform. Moreover, educational reform has been identified as vital to successful internationalization—however that is understood. To be sure, Japanese hold deeply ambivalent attitudes toward internationalization.[55] For much of its history Japan has been content to pursue global integration primarily through arm's-length strategies. These included training an elite to act as go-betweens with the outside world, educating a general population to digest foreign languages and foreign ideas from a distance, and on occasion even importing a few technicians and teachers. Rather than pursuing global integration through exporting ideology, personnel, and educational services (via such institutions as the Peace Corps or the British Council), Japan has preferred to pursue selective integration through importing ideas, technology, and, to a more limited degree, people. But now Japan is being asked to go beyond appropriating skills and knowledge to transforming its entire value system. What foreign criticism amounts to is a demand that the Japanese reconstitute themselves and their society so as to make them more compatible with international norms and institutions. Reforms—driven both by external pressure and by domestic calls for change—thus also need to address the persistent image of Japan as a self-centered and parochial society. The JET program is one response.

With the end of the cold war, the rise of multinational corporations, and the development of increasingly sophisticated communications technologies, every nation is in the process of adapting to an increasingly global world. Yet while we hear much about global homogenization and the need to cultivate a more global outlook on life, we often fail to recognize that cultural, political, and historical particulars lend each nation its own manner and style of participating in the new world order. The Japanese approach to global integration is distinctive but by no means unique, and we ignore it at our own peril. Now that Japan has emerged on the world scene, and Japanese corporations, residential communities, and tourist circuits have sprung up in our own backyard, the issue of how Japanese cope with diversity has become more immediate and urgent. An analysis of how Japanese respond to the foreign participants on the JET Program can reveal the human side of Japan's struggle to come to terms with the profound changes that one society has undergone in the past few decades.

METHODOLOGY

The sheer breadth and scope of the JET program made the traditional anthropological practice of participant observation highly problematic. Arriving in Japan in late summer of 1988, I was bewildered to find that the JET Program could not be isolated in one geographic location or even in one spacially bounded organization, like a company or a school. At the national level alone, the principal actors included the three sponsoring ministries, the administrative office called CLAIR, the embassies of the participating countries, and the Japanese consulates abroad.[56] To these structural complexities must be added the realities of implementation as the JET Program unfolded in dozens of prefectures, hundreds of district boards of education, and thousands of secondary schools across the country.

I was thus forced to modify the worn-out model of culture as an isolated, bounded entity characterized by internally consistent norms and behavior. While I did not completely jettison the idea that Japanese responses to the JET Program were culturally patterned, I assumed that alongside the dominant forces promoting integration were those that reinforced differentiation and fragmentation.[57] I also assumed that the numerous external linkages in the JET Program had a significant capacity to shape internal policy forms. Finally, I knew I had to take into account how the JET program was historically situated. In short, I needed a methodology that encompassed not only multilevel linkages and internal contradictions but also the evolution of the JET Program over time.[58]

My solution was to use an eclectic approach to gather as many kinds of data as possible over a ten-year period. Most of the intensive fieldwork was completed during two years of on-site research in Japan from 1988 to 1990, but I returned for a month each in the summers of 1993, 1995, and 1996 and for a week in 1999. Having served as an assistant English teacher in junior high schools in Iwate Prefecture in 1980 and 1983 to 1985 in two similar but smaller programs, I had firsthand experience working in a municipal board of education and team-teaching English in secondary schools; I also had good conversational Japanese.

Initially, I decided to anchor myself in one locale in order to focus on one prefectural board of education and its downward linkages. I received a crucial introduction to the prefectural administrators in charge of the JET Program from my Fulbright sponsor. These two men, one an English teacher temporarily assigned to the board of education and the other a career civil servant, were more helpful than I ever could have expected. They arranged for me to attend all prefectural orientations, seminars, and team-teaching workshops related to the JET Program. They also set up short visits to five district boards of education and twelve secondary schools in the prefecture. Most important, they arranged for me to conduct regular visits to a high school that had recently been chosen as a base school for a British JET participant. I visited twice weekly for three months and for another six months less frequently. I spent the entire day at the school on each visit and was able to observe many team-taught and solo English classes and to interview Japanese students and teachers. I also was able to acquire a variety of written materials on hosting the ALT.

At the same time that I was relying on these formal channels, I also made informal contact with numerous JET participants as well as Japanese teachers of English. Usually interviews took place in a coffee shop, and I guaranteed anonymity. Documentation thus includes field notes from observations of thirty-two team-teaching workshops and classes and notes or audiotapes from interviews with sixty-five foreign participants, fifty-four Japanese teachers of English, and thirty-five Japanese students.

I was able to take short trips to other prefectures and to Tokyo to obtain an overview of the program. At first, I found negotiating access to Ministry of Education and CLAIR officials and gaining permission to observe national-level conferences quite difficult; a general ministry policy forbids any outside research on the JET Program. I met several Japanese researchers who had been turned down by CLAIR and heard that CLAIR officials had become incensed when a foreign researcher distributed a survey at a conference even though they had denied him permission to do so. My own relative success was aided by letters of introduction to key officials in CLAIR and the sponsoring ministries from Caroline Yang, then at the Fulbright Commission, and from Mike Smith, then dean of the School of Education at Stanford University. By far the most crucial introduction, however, was provided by my mentor, Tetsuya Kobayashi. In fact, Kobayashi-sensei was a personal friend of Wada Minoru in the Ministry of Education, and his phone call to CLAIR was instrumental in opening doors there as well. "You must thank Professor Kobayashi," I was told by a CLAIR official years later. "He is a very powerful person."

I interviewed officials at the Ministries of Education, Home Affairs, and Foreign Affairs who were connected with the program on several occasions during the initial fieldwork period and again during my 1993 and 1995 visits. In ten visits to CLAIR, I interviewed twelve ranking officials of CLAIR's managerial staff and fifteen of the "program coordinators" (JET Program alumni working in CLAIR) to learn their vantage point on forming and enacting program policy. The follow-up visits were particularly useful for examining the learning curve of the Japanese administrators and for systematically tracing the continuities and changes in program policies over time.

Several other vehicles for data collection also proved quite fruitful. I attended the weeklong Tokyo orientation for new JET participants in 1989, two midyear conferences for ALTs in 1989 and 1990, and two "renewers' conferences" in 1990 and 1993 for JET participants who were extending their contracts. I also interviewed the JET liaisons in the German, Canadian, and American embassies in Tokyo as well as several knowledgeable professors in Japanese universities. To gain insight into the selection process, I participated in a half-day orientation for new JET participants at the San Francisco consulate in 1988 and was fortunate to be able to serve on the selection committee for new JET participants in Boston in 1991. I interviewed a handful of Japanese and American officials at each of these consulates as well as several other members of the selection committees.

Finally, CLAIR officials provided me with numerous in-house surveys, documents, and manuals that have been produced over the program's ten-year history. These include copies of most monthly newsletters sent by CLAIR to program participants, copies of the *JET Journal* and the *CIR Report* (a quarterly compilation of short essays written by the foreign participants and their Japanese hosts), orientation manuals for new JET participants, programs for midyear and renewers' conferences, the newsletter published by the JET participants' "support group," internal surveys, and the monthly newsletter sent by the Ministry of Home Affairs to all local government bodies. I have also collected international, national, and local newspaper articles about the JET Program since its inception. Taken together, these documents provide a wealth of information from which to reconstruct the history and evolution of the program.

In short, I used the techniques of both the anthropologist and the historian to provide a realistic portrait of the JET Program that captures not only the diverse perspectives of its many participants but also the larger whole to which they all contributed. As with any study, there are limitations that must be acknowledged. As an outsider, I found it difficult at times to elicit anything beyond the knee-jerk response that Harumi Befu has so aptly captured: "To internationalize is fashionable and good, and not to do so or to resist doing so is a sign of the backwardness of a country bumpkin."[59] On numerous occasions, particularly when I was visiting public offices for the first time, I was given only the version of the JET Program designed for public consumption. Yet I am confident that I was often able to get beyond the official, or *tatemae*, version. By guaranteeing anonymity, by meeting with people at neutral places, by tagging along at drinking parties whenever possible, and by nurturing a set of relationships over the entire thirteen-year period of research, I was able to obtain relatively frank opinions and accounts. In this regard, the extended time frame of the study clearly worked to my benefit. I was frequently able to locate individuals, now in new posts, who had played key roles in implementing JET; removed in space and time from those responsibilities, they were now able to talk more freely.

Three methodological limitations bear particular mention. First, I must apologize to readers of other nationalities for the American slant to this account. At the time when I did much of my interviewing, Americans made up nearly three-quarters of all JET participants; moreover, I was unable to visit Japanese consulates outside the United States and thus my data on the selection process in other countries are much thinner than I would have liked. My own positioning as a middle-class Anglo-American has undoubtedly colored my analysis in subtle ways as well, though I have made a concerted effort to highlight differences among JET participants both between and within nationalities. Second, this book focuses heavily on the ALT (assistant language teacher) component of the JET program rather than the CIR (coordinator of international relations) or SEA (sports exchange advisor) components. While there are significant similarities among these, there are also important differences, and the complex roles of the CIR and SEA in local government are among the many topics that merit further study. And third, the book emphasizes conflict resolution and policy formation during the early years of the JET Program. In part, this emphasis is simply a function of the time at which I conducted most of my research; however, there are also strong theoretical reasons for it. The formative period of the program deserves a closer analysis because that is when most of the current policies were being hammered out; thus, it is when differences among the actors were thrown into highest relief. Nonetheless, I do not mean to slight the many ways in which Japanese and JET participants have worked together since those early years to create new projects beneficial to Japanese society, for it is in these cooperative activities that the program's lasting impact will be felt.

The primary emphasis in this book is on the *process* of "internationalization" in Japan rather than an evaluation of the JET Program per se. Put simply, I seek to understand how the JET Program evolved and how that form is a product of the historical, social, and political contexts in which the program is embedded.[60]

Nevertheless, the one question that I was asked over and over again during the course of my fieldwork is, Does the JET Program work? Obviously, the answer depends on one's perspective. Judged by different criteria, the JET Program can look either wonderfully impressive or horribly bad. In the course of the book, we will encounter cultural preoccupations, foreign pressures, political maneuvering, and bureaucratic decision making: these may or may not satisfy anyone as demonstrations of "internationalization" or the "failure of internationalization." As we will see, many of the foreign participants believe that what goes on in JET is not internationalization, while most Japanese officials believe that it is. Rather than seeking some absolute judgment, I examine how program outcomes are treated by participants on all sides. Are there demands for measurement? What kind?

What criteria do the various parties involved in the JET Program use in evaluating the program?

I must stress that my intent is not to discredit the JET Program or anyone associated with it. Rather, this book is an account of what happens when everyone does their best. Through exploring the difficulties encountered on all levels by all participants, Japanese and foreign, during the initial phase of what was essentially a crash course in internationalization, I aim to show how particular actions are sensible products of complex cultural, political, and historical forces. Before leaping to judgments about whether the JET Program is good or bad, let us first understand the reasons why the program came to be the way it is.

2 The Solution

Top-Down "Grassroots Internationalization"

Frankly speaking, the purpose of the JET Program was never focused on the revolution of English education. The main goal was to get local governments to open up their gates to foreigners. It's basically a grassroots regional development program.

A Ministry of Home Affairs official

Our main hope for the JET Program is to increase understanding of Japanese society and education among youth in the participating countries.

A Ministry of Foreign Affairs official

If Japanese students and teachers improve their communicative competence in English, then they have become more internationalized. This is the goal of the JET Program from the point of view of our ministry.

A Ministry of Education, Science, and Culture official

The previous chapter sketched the broad historical context within which the key policymakers began to stress the goal of raising Japan's international standing. Yet the presence of deep-seated cultural assumptions about social relations and exclusivity suggests that an "away-with-frontiers" internationalism will not come easily to the Japanese. The social, cultural, and historical barriers to a broader formulation of Japan's national purpose are truly formidable, and many Japanese understandably find the expectation that Japanese culture must change both perplexing and threatening. Yet Japan has a long history of adaptation to changing environmental realities, and the perception is widespread that substantive change is inevitable if Japan is to maintain its economic gains of recent decades.

This chapter examines the behind-the-scenes process of policy formation and the conflicting ministerial goals that became enmeshed in the JET Program. At the national level, political maneuvering dominates: from the very moment the idea for the JET Program was conceived, its administrative structure and implementation were affected by competing goals and rivalries between the inward- and outward-looking ministries that were directly charged with its oversight. In moving from its conception to a system of national-level administration, a relatively straightforward and appealing idea became subject to the political complexities of forming a coalition of diverse actors.

AN UNLIKELY SPONSOR: THE MINISTRY OF HOME AFFAIRS GOES INTERNATIONAL

Oddly enough, the story of the JET Program begins in the Ministry of Home Affairs (Jichishō). Literally the "Ministry of Self-Government," the agency is ostensibly concerned with local administration, fire protection, and tax affairs. Why would this ministry, which in 1987 was by almost any definition one of the least "international" ministries in Japan, take control of a program to import foreigners primarily for the purpose of teaching English in public secondary schools?

The question is all the more interesting because prior to and during World War II, the old Home Ministry (Naimushō), first established in 1873, was the nation's most powerful administrative institution. It was in charge of virtually anything related to maintaining control of the nation's population—local government, the police, religion, civil engineering, even the people's thoughts. In fact, local boards of education and the Ministry of Education, Science, and Culture itself were run by officials of the Home Ministry. Not surprisingly, the Home Ministry was hardest hit by the Occupation purge, with 60 percent of its top officials removed. It was then broken up into the separate Ministries of Home Affairs, Construction, Labor, and Health and Welfare and the Police Agency. After a brief period as a special agency, it renewed itself in 1960 as Jichishō, with a much narrower mandate focused on supervision of prefectural and municipal governments.

By the 1980s, however, Home Affairs had achieved a remarkable comeback. Its former bureaucrats occupied roughly one-third of the prefectural governorships, as well as prominent positions in municipal government. This ministry had also become quite popular among graduates from prestigious universities who sought careers in local or national politics, for it had the reputation of allowing aspiring politicians and bureaucrats to move up quickly in their careers. Karel van Wolferen even argues that by the late 1980s Home Affairs had become the chief rival of the Finance Ministry as a domestic power broker.[1]

Nevertheless, the involvement of the Ministry of Home Affairs with overseas projects of any kind had been virtually nil. Why in the mid-1980s would it suddenly decide to get on the bandwagon of internationalization? The interest of this ministry in "going international" must be viewed in the context of the rise of regionalism in Japan and the delicate balancing act required to simultaneously promote this trend and ensure a coordinating role for itself. While every ministry in Japan has some relationship with local governments, for Home Affairs those governments are its client group. This role often pits it as the advocate for local interests against other ministries. Yet as a central ministry itself, Home Affairs stands atop the system of local public administration in Japan.[2]

This dual, even contradictory, role as both proponent and coordinator of local autonomy necessitates a continual search for new avenues to ensure its continued leverage vis-à-vis local governments. In 1988 Home Affairs engineered and administered the *ichioku furusato* (one million for hometowns) policy attributed to former Prime Minister Takeshita: the onetime deal provided each municipality in Japan with one million yen, no strings attached, to promote local development. In addition, as the agency charged with promoting regional development and local autonomy, Home Affairs has long promoted a campaign against *ikkyoku shuchō*, or the concentration of resources in Tokyo.

In the 1970s and 1980s, however, local governments throughout Japan began vigorously pursuing overseas contacts and establishing international exchange programs. Of course, some local governments had formed independent ties with foreign cities much earlier. Prefectures and municipalities along the Japan Sea coast, for example, have a long history of trade relations with Korea and China. But the movement to cultivate links outside a national framework has been driven in recent years by the boom in sister-city relationships. While these were often superficial connections designed to give prefectural and municipal officials an excuse for traveling abroad, they nevertheless represented independent contacts with foreign entities. Some of Japan's bigger cities, such as Yokohama, now have ten or more sister cities all over the world. Moreover, with the increase in the numbers of returnee students, foreign students in Japanese universities, resident foreigners, and participants in various overseas exchange programs, many prefectural governments in the 1980s created an entirely new administrative section for the oversight of international issues: the international relations division (*kokusai koryūka*) within the prefectural office.

The effect of these local initiatives was to force the Ministry of Home Affairs into an uncomfortable and unfamiliar role. Accustomed to providing top-down guidance to local governments, officials found themselves mere bystanders. In addition, when local governments did approach them for guidance on international matters, they found it frustrating to have to rely exclusively on the Ministry of Foreign Affairs and their overseas offices to be their eyes and ears abroad.

Going international was therefore a logical next step, and in 1985 the Ministry of Home Affairs established an advisory board (*kokusaika iinkai*) to research ways in which its international profile could be enhanced. The composition of the committee was itself an admission of the ministry's lack of experience in this area. In addition to several ministry officials, it included Okawara Yoshio, former Japanese ambassador to the United States; Eto Shinkichi, the former president of Asia University; and William Horsley, a BBC correspondent. Based on the deliberations of this committee, the Ministry of Home Affairs released a report in July of 1985 titled *Plans for International Exchange Projects*, which mapped out a variety of possible projects for local governments, including sister-city relationships and exchanges of local government personnel.

But it was the improvement of English language skills among local government personnel that the board particularly stressed. Its chairman, Tsuchiya Yoshiteru, a former vice-minister of home affairs who became governor of Kagoshima Prefecture, recalls: "When I was in the Ministry of Home Affairs, the government as a whole was making great efforts to encourage international relations, and local governments were beginning to expand the initiatives begun at the national level. . . . But the main barrier to local governments opening their doors to foreigners was English deficiency and that made us realize the necessity of introducing real English over and above the foreign language education provided by the Ministry of Education."[3] Eto concurs: "The advisory council was concerned with many different things, including sister-city exchanges, but I remember that Mr. Horsley and I strongly and repeatedly asserted that local middle school English education should be changed, and this educational problem was very well understood by the Ministry of Home Affairs."[4]

The push for better English language instruction was given added impetus when a handful of prefectural governors approached the Ministry of Home Affairs about the possibility of expanding the small English teaching programs that the Ministry of Education was then running in public schools. Hyogo Prefecture's governor, for instance, was considering an ambitious plan to place a native speaker of English in every public high school in the prefecture; Kumamoto Prefecture also wanted to markedly increase the profile of conversational English in public schools. But these local requests were being stymied by the Ministry of Education, which refused to allocate money for anything more than incremental increases in its current programs.

While the idea of improving communication-oriented English looked good on paper, enormous barriers stood in the way of implementation, including internal resistance within the Ministry of Home Affairs, the problem of funding, and the fear of being accused of encroaching on the turf of the Ministries of Education or Foreign Affairs. In the mid-1980s, Nosé (pronounced No-say) Kuniyuki was a career official in Home Affair's secretariat (a catchall department for high-priority projects); he was charged with drawing up plans for specific programs based on the recommendations of the advisory council:

> I remember when I first made the original proposal for the JET Program in early 1985, my boss turned it down because the jurisdiction of our ministry was primarily domestic affairs. He said we had absolutely no experience with international policies, and that it was something Foreign Affairs should do. At that time my proposal was to establish an exchange program for people in local government offices; it was closer to what became the CIR [coordinator for international relations] category in the JET Program. My idea back then was that municipalities rather than prefectures should play a role in international affairs. I thought that local governments should start to open their gates. We had lots of meetings with mayors and talked about a lot of different options; but unfortunately, at that time there were not many cities and towns who would accept a foreigner.[5]

Nosé and his co-workers then toyed with the idea of sponsoring foreign youth to teach English in public schools, but this time their superiors raised the objection that such a program would be a clear violation of the Ministry of Education's jurisdiction.[6] It was looking more and more likely that the idea for JET was doomed when help suddenly came from an unexpected quarter.

In late 1985, conflict with the United States over Japan's $50 billion annual trade surplus intensified. Under heavy American pressure, Prime Minister Nakasone formed the Maekawa Committee to study medium- and long-term policy measures to deal with Japan's economic and social structure in a changing international environment. One of the mandates of this high-profile advisory committee was to expand domestic demand and to consider the social or "nontariff barriers" to foreign investment, including the closed nature of local governments in Japan. As this was the turf of the Ministry of Home Affairs, a number of its officials, including Nosé, were brought into the process, and the race was on to piece together a package of reforms that would appease the American negotiating team at the upcoming summit between Nakasone and Reagan in 1986. Nosé recalls:

> During the year of the trade conflict between Japan and the United States—and I didn't get a vacation at all that summer—I was thinking about how to deal with the demands that we buy more things such as computers and cars. I realized that trade friction was not going to be solved by manipulating material things, and besides, I wanted to demonstrate the fact that not all Japanese are economic animals who gobble up real estate. There was no one in Japan who intentionally planned all this economic conflict, especially out in the countryside. I wanted to show things like that, simple truths in Japan.
>
> In order to do all this, I decided local governments must open their doors and let people come and see the truth directly—not just any people, but those with a college degree and under the age of thirty-five, since people start to lose flexibility after that age. I thought this would be a much better way of solving the trade conflict than using money or manipulating goods. I thought that seeing how Japanese live and think in all their variety, seeing Japan the way it really is, would improve the communication between younger generations in Japan and America.[7]

The upcoming summit provided a perfect opportunity for the Ministry of Home Affairs to revisit the plan for an English teaching program involving public schools. The JET Program was particularly attractive because it would provide a solid nucleus around which to fashion other efforts to enhance the ministry's international reach. Now that the trade conflict had been recast in terms of opening up local governments, it could count on the support of both the Ministry of Foreign Affairs and the Prime Minister's Office for a major initiative. Nosé and others in the secretariat quickly hatched a plan for a large program to be jointly sponsored by three ministries.

Getting the Yen for Change

Many a proposal that looks good on paper has fallen under the budget ax, and the first problem that Ministry of Home Affairs officials faced in realizing the JET Program was locating a viable source of funding. Though the initial price tag of approximately $120 million was relatively insignificant during the heyday of the bubble economy, the annual JET Program budget is now more than four times that amount. Clearly, packaging and selling the JET Program to the Finance Ministry was no easy matter.

In pursuing this task, Home Affairs officials were in their element. Playing to their primary strength as managers of local taxes, they devised an ingenious plan for financing the program through the local allocation tax (kōfuzei). The allocation tax is a form of general revenue sharing that provides about one-fifth of local government revenues. Basically, the Ministry of Home Affairs calculates the demand for services that local governments provide, subtracts the annual revenue of the local government, and then supplies the difference up to a certain ceiling.[8] By allowing JET participants to sign their employment contracts with the prefecture or municipality in which they were hired, the ministry enabled those localities to include expenses for the JET Program in the list of services they provided. In turn, calculations of the allocation tax benefit for each local government entity would include a sum to cover salary, transportation, and conferences for JET Program participants. In effect, Home Affairs created a program at the national level but presented it to the Finance Ministry as a local initiative.

Yet we are still left wondering why the Finance Ministry would agree to use taxpayer money to fund what looked like a multimillion-dollar giveaway to foreign college graduates. The answer is that a strong argument could be made for the JET Program as an investment in the Japanese economy. The program would provide additional revenues for Japan Airlines (on whose flights many of the JET participants are booked), Daiichi Kangyo Bank (which is entrusted with the operating budget for the program), and Kintetsu Travel Agency (which arranges travel for the JET participants and accommodations at the Tokyo orientation and other conferences). In addition, roughly 80 percent of the JET participants' salaries ultimately stays in Japan and is recycled into the local economy. Thus the JET Program is not only a generous gift to the youth of participating countries but also a massive public works program.[9]

Moreover, Ministry of Home Affairs officials had an inside track in appropriating funding. Unlike the Ministries of Foreign Affairs and Education, it had dozens of "old boys" in the Diet. And as we will see, Home Affairs had the blessing of the Nakasone administration on this proposal. Virtually without effort, it was able to acquire funding for the program.

Once the major hurdle of funding JET participants' salaries was cleared, the next problem was to finance the program's administration. While small grants have been obtained from the Japan Lottery Association and from the Motor Car Racing Association, the bulk of the funding has come from the Sasakawa Peace Foundation (SPF), which agreed to assist with funding for the Tokyo orientation, the midyear and renewers' conferences, and the production of training manuals and teaching resources. The SPF's financial support in fiscal year 1990 stood at roughly $1.27 million dollars.[10] Support from the SPF has certainly raised some eyebrows, as its founder, Sasakawa Ryoichi, is renowned in Japan for both his philanthropy and his alleged links to underworld crime. Scheduled to be hanged for war crimes in 1948, Sasakawa received a last-minute pardon, and he has gone on to become one of Japan's most generous and visible private promoters of cultural exchange and peacemaking activities. Nevertheless, his conduct during the war years, his sympathy for right-wing causes, and his rumored earlier connections with the underworld continue to shadow his foundation. Though officials in the Council of Local Authorities for International Relations were often reluctant in public to discuss the background of Sasakawa, I found no indication that the SPF influenced program policy. According to one Home Affairs official, "They're a real pain about making sure we publicly acknowledge their assistance, but they've never interfered in decision making about program content."

CULTURAL EXCHANGE AS DIPLOMATIC STRATEGY:
THE MINISTRY OF FOREIGN AFFAIRS

Once a viable plan for financing the program had been formulated, the next step was to secure the cooperation of the Ministry of Foreign Affairs in recruiting JET participants through its overseas consulates. Nosé recalls:

> After my proposal was adopted by our ministry we took it to Foreign Affairs. That was the year when the Maekawa Report was written due to the severe economic conflict between Japan and the United States. My counterpart there was Mr. Sato. I believe he was director of general affairs at the time. Anyway, I remember that he was the person who actually acted on the idea. He approved the idea as soon as he heard about it and asked me if it would be all right to present the plan at the Reagan-Nakasone summit. . . . I believe Nakasone ended up telling Reagan about it directly.[11]

As the agency charged with promoting Japan's image overseas, it is not surprising that the Ministry of Foreign Affairs would give the proposal its enthusiastic endorsement. Indeed, the timing could not have appeared more opportune. American pressure was intensifying and the Reagan-Nakasone summit was just around the corner. In addition, a number of foreign consulates had already approached the ministry about being included in one of the smaller English teaching programs then being administered by the Ministry of Education. Officials immediately grasped the diplomatic potential of the proposed program, particularly if the number of participating countries could be expanded. And the JET Program would also contribute to several other long-term goals crucial to the Ministry of Foreign Affairs. By improving the oral dimension of foreign language education in Japan, it would help to cultivate a new generation of diplomats who were comfortable in English and who could begin to chip away at the "3-S" stereotype of Japanese diplomats abroad—silent, sleeping, and smiling. In addition, the proposed program would serve as a visible symbol of Japan's goodwill among participating countries, and it would make a small but significant dent in the "education gap" by giving more individuals from Western countries access to Japan's educational institutions.

Most important, if implemented smoothly, it would enhance foreign understanding of Japan, particularly among young people who were likely to rise to positions of power in their respective countries. In fact, the Ministry of Foreign Affairs had already adopted a more general policy of utilizing cultural exchange programs as an international diplomatic strategy.[12] While this motive was viewed cynically by some I interviewed—one person from the Ministry of Education scoffed, "All they're trying to do is create a pro-Japan faction (*shinnichiha*) in participating countries"—most Foreign Affairs officials seemed to genuinely subscribe to the idea of the JET Program as an antidote for a "misunderstood Japan." Jibiki Yoshihiro, the senior ministry official assigned to the JET Program, waxed eloquent about this dimension with particular frequency. Noting that Sarajevo had hosted the 1982 Winter Olympics, he would often point out how quickly the world can change. This is what the JET Program is all about, he would say—people from many backgrounds coming together and, like threads, tying the rest of the world to Japan.

Officials in the Ministry of Foreign Affairs saw the JET Program as falling into the category of attempts to build cooperative relationships outside areas of binational conflict. John Campbell is cautious in his assessment of this approach: "The widely held hope is that enough friendly ties will eliminate conflict or that feelings of gratitude will outweigh resentment; perhaps a more realistic expectation is that a few positive actions will balance the constant flow of negative news to some extent."[13] Ministry officials themselves, however, were quite optimistic. Unless the JET Program was a complete disaster, they felt it could not help but be good public relations.

THE PRIME MINISTER'S OFFICE:
PREPARING FOR GLOBAL LEADERSHIP

After gaining the Ministry of Foreign Affair's approval, the proposal was taken to the Prime Minister's Office and immediately was favorably received by the prime minister at the time, Nakasone Yasuhiro. Unlike most Japanese prime ministers, Nakasone found in foreign affairs a source of political strength and public popularity. Yet when he first took office, he was widely seen as a puppet of Tanaka Kakuei, the kingpin of postwar politics, whose career was ultimately derailed by the Lockheed scandal. Tanaka's quip when asked who he would support as the next prime minister—"Tanakasone"—was much quoted and captured a general attitude. As Nathaniel Thayer notes, "Nakasone needed to get Tanaka off his back. . . . He needed a strategy; he needed new allies. The strategy was to bring Japan into active participation in world affairs. His new allies were to be, initially, the Foreign Ministry and, eventually, Ronald Reagan and the summits."[14]

The plan for the JET Program was a natural extension of Nakasone's policies, beliefs, and style of leadership. Nakasone was unusually at ease interacting with foreign dignitaries and took every opportunity—such as speaking English before the press—to create an image of himself as competent to handle Japan's international relations. He preached that a major power like Japan was responsible for promoting "internationalization"—indeed, such an endeavor should be undertaken proudly by a nation that sees "its glorious place in the global community of nations."[15] The JET Program thus fit in extraordinarily well with Nakasone's grand design. In accord with the broader neoconservative agenda, making Japan into an international state entailed reforming national institutions to bring them more in line with international expectations. Japan had recently staked its claims to a larger role in international policy-making bodies, a role befitting its economic muscle, and the JET Program would further demonstrate Japan's readiness to assume a position of global leadership.

To the Prime Minister's Office, the JET Program was rich in symbolic capital. The proposal would be taken by the American negotiating team at the summit as a gesture of goodwill and, while not directly related to opening up Japan's economy, it would nevertheless provide a concrete example of Japan's determination to change how it relates to the outside world. The proposal was ultimately presented as a "gift" to the American side and thus represented a prime example of what Aurelia George has called "package diplomacy," a process by which Japanese negotiators present a plan that may be tangential at best to American demands but that nevertheless demonstrates their good intentions.[16]

The JET Program also meshed with Nakasone's policy goals in another area—the field of education. In the mid-1980s the sense of crisis over Japanese schooling seemed to climax as the news media ran daily stories of bullying, teen suicides, and students attacking teachers. In response, Nakasone formed a blue-ribbon commission to make recommendations on sweeping changes for public education. This council, according to Leonard Schoppa, was "originally conceived by the Prime Minister as a means of breaking Mombushō's conservative hold on the education system and radically transforming Japanese education."[17] Schoppa goes on to argue that the council will ultimately be remembered for behind-the-scenes struggles and its failure to deliver significant reform proposals. The ad hoc committee was sharply divided between members chosen by Nakasone, who favored liberalization but were fiscal conservatives, and representatives from the Ministry of Education, including Liberal Democratic Party Diet members with a special interest in education (*bunkyōzoku*). Major changes such as deregulating textbooks, restructuring the 6–3–3–4 system, and building more flexibility into the entrance exams were largely tabled or were blocked by the Ministry of Education during the implementation process.

Viewed from a long-term perspective, however, the impact of Nakasone's educational reform appears to be more substantial than Schoppa allows, particularly in areas such as international education.[18] The JET Program represented a chance to implement Nakasone's will in a small but symbolically important manner. By leapfrogging the reluctant ministry's decision-making apparatus, the administration could administer shock therapy to English language education. Better yet, it could be covered by the excuse of foreign pressure.

THE MINISTRY OF EDUCATION PUTS ON THE BRAKES

Under the proposed plan, over 90 percent of JET participants would be placed in public schools. Technically, this was the turf of the Ministry of Education, and to work effectively the proposal needed its support. This was the final, and most difficult, hurdle for Ministry of Home Affairs officials—securing the cooperation of their counterparts just down the street in the Kasumigaseki section of Tokyo. In marked contrast to the reaction of the Ministry of Foreign Affairs and the Prime Minister's Office, the initial response was decidedly negative. The issue was not so much that the Ministry of Education was opposed to internationalization in principle; it had endorsed most of the general proposals offered in this area by Nakasone's ad hoc council. Rather, its reluctance centered on the twin issues of control and scope of change.

The "New, Improved" JET Program

Though the fanfare surrounding the arrival of the first wave of JET participants in 1987 would seem to testify to its novelty, the Ministry of Education saw the JET Program as simply the "new, improved" version of a long history of attempts to reform English education. In fact, ever since the grammar and translation method had established hegemony in the late Meiji period, there had been periodic attempts to move the public school system back toward a more communication-oriented focus. The JET Program had a number of postwar antecedents.

In the early 1950s a small group of American reformers had formed the English Language Exploratory Committee (ELEC); sponsored by John D. Rockefeller III, they had enthusiastically launched a campaign to promote the oral approach of Charles Fries in Japan. ELEC, however, refused to establish formal ties with any Japanese groups, and after ten years of heavy expense and intense effort, even Rockefeller's staff recognized that "ELEC had failed to achieve its main objective. . . . ELEC was not able to change the grand strategy of English-language teaching in Japan or to bring overall improvement in teaching methods."[19]

The next effort was a joint enterprise in the late 1960s between the Japan Association of College English Teachers (JACET) and the Japan-United States Educational Commission (JUSEC) of the Fulbright Program. Their collaborative effort to bring over from the United States specialists trained in English as a second language (ESL) also failed miserably. The intense conflict that erupted when ESL specialists, wedded to their particular techniques and goals, were placed in the public school system forced speedy abandonment of the idea of recruiting foreign specialists. Japanese public school teachers simply felt too threatened by Americans who thought they knew all about language teaching.

This failure set the stage for the first direct precursor of the JET Program. American college graduates with no special training in ESL theory and pedagogy were hired by the Fulbright Commission and then placed in prefectural boards of education by the Ministry of Education. In 1969 the first four assistant teachers' consultants (ATCs) arrived in Tokyo for orientation. Richard Rubinger was among them, and his recollections provide a sense of the time:

When we first came, this program was explained to us as the continuation of years of attempts by the Fulbright Commission to improve English teaching in Japan. They had already tried many other things; they had hired academics to give courses at teacher training colleges, and they were giving lectures on linguistics and direct method, that kind of stuff. In those days, direct method, practice drills, that was the thing, exactly what everyone is trying to get away from now.... Anyway this had gone on for some time and they had failed in everything. So now the idea was to hire people as assistants to the *shidōshuji* (English teachers' consultants) who would actually get into the public schools on a regular basis. They had never done that before. The point is, behind this program was a conscious, articulated effort to revolutionize English teaching in Japan. That was clearly the goal and that was the term they used, "revolutionize the teaching of English in Japan."

[DM: "But you never team-taught with a Japanese teacher?"] No, never. We would be invited as guests for the day to a certain school, and we would actually walk into the classroom and the class would be handed over to us. And I would teach the lesson for the day, using the textbook, using the direct method, with no recourse to grammatical explanation at all. And the Japanese teachers would sit in the back of the class and there would be a seminar afterwards where we would explain what we had done, and the idea was that the teachers would run home immediately and adopt this, but of course this never happened. And we were under some pressure to write monthly reports to the Fulbright Commission to convince them that things were changing, that we were useful. And this always involved some chicanery on our part. It soon became quite obvious that the Japanese weren't interested in revolutionizing anything.[20]

Nevertheless, by 1976 the number of ATCs had risen to fifteen, and the Fulbright Commission had contracted with the New York–based Council on International Education Exchange (CIEE) to handle recruiting. But that year the Fulbright Commission informed the Ministry of Education that because of budgetary constraints, it could no longer support the program. Caroline Yang, the executive director of the Fulbright Commission at the time, explained that "it was a very difficult decision to give up the program, but we simply couldn't afford its cost. We approached Mombushō, which canvassed prefectures, and there was enough interest that they decided to take over the program. Mombushō agreed to provide a subsidy from 1977 on and to require participating prefectures to cover the remainder of the cost."[21] Thus was born the Mombushō English Fellows (MEF) Program for American college graduates to teach English in Japan. CIEE was kept on to recruit in the United States and to coordinate orientation and counseling in Japan.

At the same time that the Fulbright Commission had been working to bring American youth to teach English in Japan, the British Council had been actively promoting the same idea in Britain. A few years after the startup of the MEF Program, the British English Teaching (BET) scheme was initiated. The latter, unlike the MEF Program, was administered by the Ministry of Education in cooperation with the Ministry of Foreign Affairs; it also had somewhat broader goals, including the promotion of foreign understanding of Japan. In any event, by 1986, the last year of both, over two hundred British and American youth were teaching English in Japan. This precedent has particular importance because that year virtually every one of Japan's forty-seven prefectural boards of education employed at least one or two American or British teachers. The JET Program thus involved not starting totally fresh but largely reorganizing and expanding two existing programs. Yet Ministry of Education officials continued to drag their feet.

First of all, they were upset at the prospect of losing control of these smaller English teaching programs that they administered. Relations with the Prime Minister's Office were already strained, and now it seemed as if larger, more powerful ministries, with Nakasone's backing, were attempting to go over their heads to radically change English education. In addition, the trained pedagogues and educators employed in the Upper Secondary School Division of the ministry worried that they would be forced to implement decisions made by politicians and bureaucrats who were untrained in educational matters. "The bureaucrats in the Ministry of Home Affairs don't have the power to judge educational ideas," one curriculum specialist noted. "They like to have festivals and go out in flowery parades and be in the newspapers." Second, in the context of the Ministry of Home Affairs' initial target of 3,000 JET participants, the MEF and BET programs suddenly seemed insignificant. Efforts to teach English conversation had always been peripheral to exam-oriented English instruction, and Ministry of Education officials were understandably worried that there would be considerable resistance among Japanese teachers if the numbers of foreign participants increased dramatically. The proposal forced the ministry to confront the result of decades of relative inflexibility in foreign language education policy and the complete lack of major reforms in the system since the 1950s.[22]

At the same time, there were several arguments to be made in favor of the proposal. The Ministry of Education had already committed itself in principle to internationalization. In the report of Nakasone's ad hoc committee on educational reform, it had endorsed the call for education compatible with a new era of closer international relations. Having caught up with other advanced industrialized nations technologically, the report argued, Japan could not survive in cultural and educational isolation but would have to interact in those spheres as well. Among the report's concrete proposals were calls for more exchanges of educational personnel, greater acceptance of Japanese students returning from abroad, and more emphasis on Japanese students mastering English as a tool for communication. In addition, growing local demand for native speakers in the public schools was coupled with the prospect of no more than incremental increases in the budgets for the MEF and BET programs. If the Ministry of Education could keep the numbers of JET participants from increasing too rapidly, some argued, this was an opportunity to continue a fundamentally sound program without having to foot the bill. A further complication was the feeling on the part of ministry officials that by the time the proposal had been brought to them, it was a virtual fait accompli. If they refused to cooperate, the Ministry of Home Affairs would in all likelihood go ahead with the plan with the backing of the Ministry of Foreign Affairs and the Prime Minister's Office. Even at the local level, superintendents of education are political appointees: given the leverage of Home Affairs with governors and mayors, it was not inconceivable that officials could implement the program without Ministry of Education support.

The ministry's point man at this time was Wada Minoru, a senior curriculum specialist in the high school education section (*kōtōgakkōkyōiku ka*). Fluent in English and holding a master's degree in teaching English as a foreign language (TEFL), he had served as the Ministry of Education's coordinator for the MEF Program. Shortly after Wada retired from the ministry in 1993, I was able to talk with him about the behind-the-scenes negotiations when the program was being formed:

> I remember the new idea was discussed by a very limited number of Ministry of Education officials—fewer than five. The *kachō* (section chief) of the section in charge of MEF, a few other persons in the section, and myself. At the early stage of the discussion we didn't like the idea because we were afraid that the Ministry of Home Affairs would take control of the program and the educational purpose would be lost. If we participated in the new program, we thought it would be impossible to keep our influence in the field of teaching English. But we knew that it would be impossible to increase the budget, and local prefectures and cities and towns wanted to have more native speakers of English. The Ministry of Education couldn't support them financially. So we were in a dilemma.[23]

While Wada and others in the high school education section were cool to the JET proposal, in the end their superiors agreed to the new plan under which the Ministry of Education would supervise the team-teaching dimensions of the program. I asked Wada whether outside pressure was involved in this decision, and he replied:

> We discussed the idea for about three months—is it good to join the new project or is it better to stay with the old? During that time, there was no pressure openly from any other ministries or sources of power. But the final decision in our ministry was made by higher-ranking officials at the *kyoku* (division) level. I'm not sure, but I guess there was very strong pressure on high-ranking officials of our ministry from the prime minister or from the Ministry of Home Affairs. There were some political and economic reasons that motivated Home Affairs. The prime minister at that time was Mr. Nakasone, and he was very eager to show that he took an interest in relations between Japan and foreign countries. The *kyokuchō* (division chief) must have felt some pressure from Nakasone's office in a very subtle way.

Whether there was direct pressure or not, Education officials clearly perceived that their choices were constrained, and they conveyed this sentiment to local educational administrators. One educational administrator in Osaka recalled: "When the decision was made to go ahead with the JET Program, we [English curriculum specialists at the prefectural level] were called to Tokyo by the Ministry of Education for an urgent meeting. They told us that the ministry had not been adequately consulted about the plan and would never have increased the numbers of participants so rapidly. The Ministry of Education was very upset and felt that their program had been taken away from them (*torarete shimatta*)."

The ministry did set one condition for its support, however. It would go along with the program only if it was made clear that the foreign participants served as *assistants* to the regular Japanese language teacher: thus Japanese teachers would not feel that their own jobs were either legally or symbolically threatened by the influx of native speakers. The resulting compromise gave rise to what has become one of the most talked about and controversial aspects of the program: team teaching. Wada explained, "I myself thought a lot about that [the issue of Japanese teachers worrying about losing their jobs]. I didn't want Japanese teachers of English to think that I didn't pay attention to that aspect. The idea of team teaching has something to do with that issue. When you look at the situation at private schools, they don't do team teaching because the owners of private schools don't want to spend money on both a native speaker and a Japanese teacher. They think they don't need two teachers."[24] It is worth noting that the title initially given to the JET participants—"assistant English teachers" (AETs) and later "assistant language teachers" (ALTs)—symbolized an important lowering of status from "English fellows," the name used throughout most of the MEF Program.[25]

It was also striking that the Ministry of Education's approval of the JET Program did not lead to any formal resistance from the Japan Teacher's Union, which has systematically opposed virtually every postwar initiative offered by the ministry. Although some union members did attack the program, the overall response was quite muted. Wada clarified the apparent contradiction: "What is very interesting is that union leaders are against the JET Program on the surface. If they are asked whether they support government efforts to invite JET participants, they say no . . . but union teachers like to work with ALTs. So they cannot oppose the JET Program in the same way they oppose other policies promoted by government. Union teachers have been pushing for communication-oriented English and for internationalization for a long time."[26]

Thus, although the Ministry of Education finally acceded to the JET proposal, it is fair to say that those officials who would actually have a hands-on role were at best lukewarm to the idea. Moreover, a surprisingly small number of people were actually involved in the decision. At no time were discussions held with the textbook oversight committees or other groups that shaped the larger structure of English education in Japan. Instead, the JET Program would simply be added on to existing policies, with all the glaring contradictions that would inevitably follow.

SETTING INITIAL PROGRAM POLICY

Once a tenuous alliance between the three sponsoring ministries had been forged, it remained for a planning committee consisting of representatives from each to set initial program policy. What were the decisions about program structure that were explicitly debated, and how were they resolved? What were the "nonissues"—that is, on what aspects of program policy did broad agreement already exist?

The most immediate problem arising from the diverse sponsorship of the new program was to articulate the "official" statement of program goals for the press release on 8 October 1986. The intersectoral nature of the policy meant that program goals had to be worded so as to please all three sponsoring ministries—the diplomatic goals of Foreign Affairs, the local development goals of Home Affairs, and the foreign language–teaching goals of Education. Insofar as the JET Program was a response to American pressure, the statement of purpose also had to be couched in terms that satisfied the critique of Japan as a closed society. What emerged after much deliberation was an exceedingly broad statement designed to satisfy each of the above constituencies:

> The Japan Exchange and Teaching Program seeks to promote mutual understanding between Japan and other countries including the U.S., the U.K., Australia, and N.Z. and foster international perspectives in Japan by promoting international exchange at local levels as well as intensifying foreign language education in Japan.[27]

Another major decision regarding program policy was how to structure intergovernmental linkages. Who would be responsible for which aspects? I was quite surprised to find Japanese ministry officials referring to JET as a "grassroots" exchange program, calling up images of ideas and actions bubbling up organically from volunteer networks in local communities. It would seem to be the direct antithesis of government-sponsored programs.

But Japanese sensibilities gave a different flavor and meaning to the term. For the national-level bureaucrats, there was never any question that "grassroots internationalization" needed both impetus and management from the top. National-level ministries, in spite of being highly compartmentalized, all view the policy process similarly. Put simply, ministry officials subscribe to a theory of top-down change that sees the national government providing training of, encouragement to, guidelines for, and subtle pressure on prefectural governments, who in turn leverage the next level of the system; this process continues downward until satisfactory policy outcomes are achieved. The theory is that enough muscle applied at each level will eventually bring compliance.[28]

The formal administrative structure of the JET Program that resulted from this approach is shown in figure 1. Local initiative was to be encouraged, and employment contracts were to be signed with the local host institution (prefecture or municipality), which could request the number and kind of JET participants desired each year. That local institutions, not a national-level body, were designated as the "official employers" goes a long way toward explaining the variation in working conditions experienced by JET participants (see chapter 4). Nonetheless, local autonomy played out within a framework set largely at the national level. The sponsoring ministries would make key decisions about programwide policies and the annual number of participants; they would provide the services of selection and placement in host institutions; and

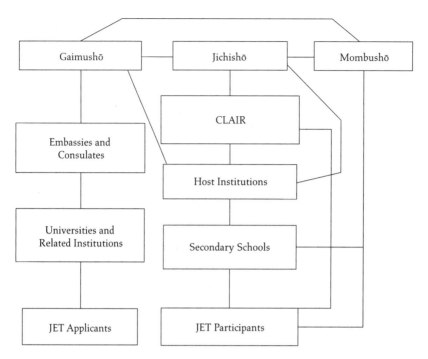

Figure 1. Formal administrative structure of the JET Program. Source: Advertising brochure, *The JET Programme, 1995–96* (Tokyo: Council of Local Authorities for International Relations, 1995), n.p.

they would coordinate the Tokyo orientation, midyear block conferences, and other support services.

CLAIR: A Cultural and Structural Broker

At the center of JET Program administration stands the Council of Local Authorities for International Relations (Jichitai Kokusaika Kyōkai), more commonly known by the acronym CLAIR. With its own staff and building, this nonprofit, quasi-governmental agency is responsible for the day-to-day management of the program at the national level.[29] Like most Japanese organizations, CLAIR consists of an entirely symbolic advisory council; it was initially chaired by Shunichi Suzuki, the former mayor of Tokyo. Significantly, it also serves as a "retirement post" (*amakudari*) for one former bureaucrat from each of the three sponsoring ministries. In theory, these individuals are to serve as liaisons with their respective ministries, but in fact they are quite marginal to the day-to-day operations of CLAIR.

Appointments to CLAIR are made by the Ministry of Home Affairs, local governments, and private companies in fairly regular patterns. As one corporate representative noted, "There was a strong feeling that the JET Program could never be made to work solely by the power of the hard heads of bureaucrats." There are representatives from Kintetsu Travel Agency and Daiichi Kangyo Bank, as well as lower-level staff from selected prefectural and municipal offices. These staff members usually serve one year in CLAIR's Tokyo office and then a second year in one of the growing number of overseas offices (they serve as windows on the world for the Ministry of Home Affairs).

But in spite of the presence of these representatives, CLAIR is beyond question an administrative arm of the Ministry of Home Affairs. The top three CLAIR officials in terms of day-to-day decision making—the secretary-general, the deputy secretary-general, and the General Affairs section chief—always come from Home Affairs; and since these upper-level staff must return to that ministry after their appointment in CLAIR, they have little incentive to exercise independent judgment or initiative. Other than the *amakudari*, the Ministries of Foreign Affairs and Education are not represented in CLAIR, and the only person with educational experience is the chief of the Counseling and Guidance Section (*shidōka*). The result is a government-business alliance in which educational specialists are marginalized.

Most intriguing is the employment in CLAIR of a handful of JET Program alumni as liaisons between the Japanese staff and the mass of JET participants. Sometimes called "gaijin handlers" because they coordinate large numbers of foreigners, their primary responsibility is to manage the flow of information to and from the JET participants and to assist in those aspects of program implementation that require the linguistic and interactional skills of a native speaker. In the same way that Japanese officials at CLAIR act as brokers between national ministries and local host institutions, the program coordinators, by their own admission, serve as buffers. One, rather uncharitable in his depiction of the Japanese staff, put it this way: "There's no question we're used as buffers. All information to ALTs goes through the program coordinators. We always have to break the bad news because if they [the Japanese staff at CLAIR] do it, they come across as bureaucratic sods. The less contact they have, the better." In theory, assuming good coordination within the CLAIR office, there would be no need for the Japanese staff at CLAIR to become directly involved with JET participants, nor for the program coordinators to negotiate with local Japanese officials. But on numerous occasions (regional block meetings, crisis intervention, etc.) both Japanese and foreign staff at CLAIR have entered into direct negotiations with JET participants and local Japanese officials.

As an administrative office, CLAIR is in a very delicate position. It must negotiate with a whole host of ministries and agencies at the national level, with local governments throughout the country, and with the thousands of JET participants themselves. Though CLAIR has little input on major policy decisions, the Japanese staff and the program coordinators have considerable power when it comes to shaping program content.

Participating Countries

Having embarked on an ambitious plan to enhance Japan's valuing of diversity, the next decision government leaders faced was selecting those who qualified for inclusion. Four countries were invited to join the JET Program in its inaugural year: the United States, Britain, Australia, and New Zealand. Canada and Ireland were added in 1988, and France and Germany joined in 1989 (see chapter 3), for a total of eight countries participating in the ALT component of the program. Table 1 shows the breakdown of ALT participants by country for JET's first five years.

The already functioning MEF and BET programs made the choice of the United States and Britain obvious. In fact, participants were given the option of renewing their contracts and staying on in Japan under the JET Program.[30] The addition of Australia and New Zealand was engineered primarily by the Ministry of Foreign Affairs. Now that the English program was loosened somewhat from the viselike grip of the Ministry of Education, diplomatic considerations could be entertained. Japanese language study was booming in those countries, and both had been knocking on the door for admission to the MEF and BET programs for some time. Significantly, their participation would not greatly increase the overall number of applicants.

Indeed, the numbers indicate a strong American bias. During the first year of the program, 70 percent of the foreign participants hailed from the United States; even after two more participating countries were added in 1988, the figure was just over 60 percent. This overrepresentation is due not only to the larger pool of potential applicants in the United States but also to the close relationship that Japan has developed with the United States in the postwar era. One Ministry of Home Affairs official told me bluntly: "The first thing you should know about the background of the JET Program is that Japan likes the United States." The origins of the program

Table 1. Assistant Language Teachers by Home Country, 1987–91

Country	1987	1988	1989	1990	1991
U.S.	570	832	1,034	1,159	1,440
U.K.	149	247	364	389	483
Australia	72	131	134	132	128
New Zealand	22	33	42	67	124
Canada	—	121	276	350	470
Ireland	—	20	36	41	43
France	—	—	5	4	6
Germany	—	—	3	4	5
Total	813	1,384	1,894	2,146	2,699

SOURCE: Adapted from *The JET Program(me): Five Years and Beyond*
(Tokyo: Council of Local Authorities for International Relations, 1992), 24.

in U.S.-Japan trade friction also provided some impetus to recruit heavily in the United States. Finally, since prefectures were allowed to put in a request for certain nationalities, both the Ministry of Home Affairs and the Ministry of Education expected that local governments would primarily request Americans in the first year of the program. They did not wish to disappoint local officials.

The initial list of participating countries also reveals that in Japan internationalization is primarily perceived as linking with Western countries. No native English speakers from India or Singapore, for instance, were invited. This attitude stems at least in part from the striking differences in Japan's historical relationship with Western and with Asian countries. Asia has been colonized by Japan for much of the last 150 years and until recently has been regarded largely with contempt; but the technological, military, and economic superiority of Europe and the United States during most of the twentieth century has led Japanese to view Westerners with a mixture of fear and awe.[31] To achieve greater international status, the Japanese feel they must concentrate on their relations with Western countries.

SALARY AND WORKING CONDITIONS

Another noteworthy structural feature of the JET Program was the generous package of benefits offered to the foreign participants. Their salaries were set at 3,600,000 yen per year. This came to about $25,700 in 1987, but with the stronger yen it has averaged about $31,000. Not only is this package more generous than most college graduates in the humanities could hope to earn in an entry-level position in their own countries, it is also slightly higher than most beginning Japanese teachers make.

Why such a high salary? According to ministry officials whom I interviewed, members of the original planning committee were extremely nervous about their ability to attract enough qualified applicants. This uncertainty as to whether JET would crash or fly was captured by the qualifier printed at the bottom of advertisements for the JET Program in 1987: "This program will be reviewed on an annual basis." Given the concern over the image of Japan that had given rise to the program in the first place, the prospect of failure held added terror. They were therefore inclined to bend over backward to provide the teachers with a good impression of Japan. The planning committee consulted the pay schedule for foreigners teaching at public universities in Japan before arriving at the figure chosen.

The workweek for the JET participants was set at five days in accordance with common practice in Western countries, even though Japanese schools at the time operated for a half day on Saturday as well (the Ministry of Education has since endorsed a plan for all Saturdays to be holidays, though its implementation is gradual). The six-day workweek had been the focus of many complaints from the foreign participants in the MEF and BET programs, and officials worried that such a large number of foreigners new to Japanese customs would be unable to physically tolerate the demands of the longer workweek.[32]

With these policies in place, the only other initial task was to secure visas for the JET participants. Consultations with the Justice Ministry enabled both ALTs and CIRs to be accorded special visas under the discretion of the justice minister. This simplified, faster process would also alleviate the need for official sponsorship from the prefectural governments. According to one member of the planning committee, "In the beginning there was no problem with the Justice Ministry. We simply explained that the JET participants are not delinquents (*furyō*), and they agreed to admit them because they are positive participants who are going to contribute to local internationalization and progress."[33] Under the agreement, JET participants were given a ninety-day grace period to return to their respective countries after they had completed the JET Program.

RECRUITMENT OF JET PARTICIPANTS ABROAD

Once the basic administrative structures of the program as well as its key framework policies were in place, the Japanese turned to the problem of attracting a large pool of high-quality applicants. This was the purview of the Ministry of Foreign Affairs, and in the United States it fell to the Embassy of Japan in Washington, D.C., to coordinate the selection process among its fifteen consulates.

The ministry did not hire any additional Japanese staff at its consulates abroad to handle the considerable demands of JET Program recruitment. As a result, some lower-level attachés, though personally quite sympathetic to the program, felt tremendously burdened. From advertising the program to reviewing applications, forming a selection committee, conducting surveys of participants, and planning a predeparture orientation, the administrative time required was considerable. Moreover, the cycle had to be repeated annually for an ever-increasing number of applicants.

Nor did the ministry hire any former MEF participants or other individuals knowledgeable about Japanese education to assist administratively. In fact, in keeping with the critical role of the personal introduction in personnel decisions in Japan, the embassy in Washington took just the opposite approach.[34] Carrie, a Wittenberg graduate, recalls the day she was hired to serve as administrative coordinator of the JET Program in the embassy's Press and Information Section:

> I sent off a résumé on a Wednesday. They called me Friday and said, "Can you come interview on Monday?" So I drove down there and it was the most bizarre interview of my life because I sat on a couch across from three Japanese diplomats, and only the guy in the middle talked. And he explained the entire job to me, everything it would entail, and then he said, "So do you want it?" I said "Yes, and here's why," and I started giving him all the reasons I could think of for why I should get the job. But he stopped me and said, "No, I mean when can you start?" You know, I thought they were playing a joke on me because I had absolutely no knowledge of Japanese culture or language. It turned out a friend of mine was working there and had pulled my résumé from the stack and said, "Oh, I know her. She's a good person." So that's how I got it. The decision wasn't based on my qualifications to manage an intercultural exchange program, it wasn't based on my Japanese skills. It was the power of introduction. It was hysterical.

The ten months between the official announcement of the program and the arrival of the first wave of JET participants was a time of extreme administrative confusion. For one thing, ministerial negotiations over the precise number of new JET participants dragged on and on. The Ministry of Education was intent on keeping it as low as possible; for its part, the Ministry of Foreign Affairs waved the flag of internationalization and replied that a hefty increase was necessary. A compromise was finally reached—715; but the infighting delayed the advertising brochures, which in turn delayed the application process. As a result, only three weeks separated the announcement and the deadline. Late January had been set as the cutoff for submissions, but applications arrived at the consulates abroad only in late December. Carrie remembers sending 75-pound boxes of applications to Hawaii and Guam by Federal Express. Responses to an evaluation form sent to all applicants who had been accepted into the program but had declined to participate underscored this chaos: "most would-be JETs' reasons for not entering the Program stemmed from a lack of confidence in the Program and delays in the recruitment process."[35]

Once applications were received, however, the selection process itself was based almost entirely on local input. To handle the initial screening, the Japanese embassy in Washington chose the prestigious Meridian International Center. A Washington-based nonprofit organization that administers the International Visitor Program of the U.S. Information Agency, this agency is famous for its training of international diplomats. A Japanese official in the Boston consulate explained to me that the Meridian Institute was chosen primarily on the basis of its high status: the Ministry of Foreign Affairs was determined that such an important program should have nothing but the best. Curiously, though, for many years there were no Japan specialists on the Meridian committee that reviewed the initial applications.[36]

The composition of the interview committees at each consulate was also determined by local input. Committees consist of three or four "local persons" from academia or Japan outreach programs, such as the Japan Society. The invitation to be an interviewer—which includes a stipend of $400 per day—is hard to turn down. Only one Japanese representative sits on each committee. While the Ministry of Foreign Affairs retains the right to overturn the recommendation of the selection committee in making the final decision, this authority is rarely exercised.

The JET Formula: Social Fit and Social Type

The specific criteria used by the Meridian Institute to screen the initial applications are confidential, but a numerical score is assigned to each application based on academic performance, letters of reference, and the personal essay. Moreover, there is anecdotal evidence that Japanese language ability and the prestige of the applicant's college are factors considered. I discovered quite by accident that too much fluency in Japanese could actually work against one's chances of being accepted. At the time, I was on the selection committee for a separate program, the Ohio-Saitama English Teaching (OSET) Program, to which an Oberlin graduate had applied. This young man had a very strong academic record, a cogent personal statement, and outstanding recommendations. What set him apart from the pack, however, was his extraordinary language skill. He was a unanimous top choice of the OSET selection committee. But when he submitted the very same application to the JET Program, he was rejected in the initial screening by the Meridian International Center. Apparently, ALT applicants with outstanding Japanese ability are seen as working against two major purposes of the program: the teaching of English and the introduction of Japanese language and culture to a new generation of foreign youth.

The prestige of one's alma mater clearly figures into the equation, as graduates of high-status universities are particularly desirable. In Britain, graduates from Oxford and Cambridge were especially sought after. In the American case, Carrie recalls,

> Gaimushō really wanted the Harvards and Yales. It's never in writing, but you know that. There's a lot of tension between D.C. and Boston, with our office putting pressure on them. Gaimushō would sometimes get directly involved. I remember the second or third year the JET applications from Harvard were misplaced in a file drawer by the Harvard liaison and by the time she discovered them and sent them in to us, the deadline was way past. There was a huge fight between the educational attaché here in D.C. and Gaimushō in Tokyo because we had already been through the interviews. We felt it just wouldn't be fair to let them in, but Gaimushō said, "We must have these people." In the end, they didn't get in. It was just too late. But it was not a happy scene.

Approximately two-thirds of American applicants make it through the initial screening and move on to the interview stage.[37] In 1992 I had the opportunity to serve on the interview committee at the Boston consulate and thus experienced the selection process firsthand. After coffee and introductions, we were divided into three teams of four members and given a brief refresher course on scoring procedures and criteria. A list of sample questions was handed out, as was a summary of past cases in which the interview committee had clearly erred by endorsing an applicant who later encountered serious difficulties in Japan. Over the course of three days, each interview team conducted approximately twenty interviews, each lasting twenty minutes. At the end of the day we pooled our scoresheets and divided interviewees into three categories: definitely recommended, recommended with reservations, and not recommended.

If an applicant makes it to the interview stage, personal qualities become the dominant criteria for selection. The packet of information we were given instructed us as follows: "To be considered for recommendation, applicants must meet certain basic conditions. They must be outgoing, well-mannered and have a sunny disposition. A nervous temperament is not desirable." The evaluation form was then divided into six categories for a full score of 120 points as follows:

a. *Personality* (40 points—same in both CIR and ALT)
   Consider flexibility, strength of personality, ability to adapt to foreign cultures, etc.
b. *Ability* (20 points—same in both CIR and ALT)
   Consider self-expression, creativity, general knowledge.
c. *Motivation* (CIR—20 points, ALT—25 points)
   Consider desire to participate in JET Program, sense of purpose, interest in Japan.
d. *English ability* (10 points—same in both CIR and ALT)
   Clear pronunciation, proper word use, etc.
e. *Japanese ability* (CIR—10 points, ALT—5 points)
   Applicants for the CIR position must have a functional ability in Japanese, an ability not only to speak and understand well but ideally to read and write as well. For applicants for the ALT position, evaluate conversation and reading ability.
f. *Overall impression* (20 points—same in both CIR and ALT)
   Please recommend those applicants who seem sociable, stable and can adjust well to new situations.

While the JET Program as a whole has been well received in the United States by Japan scholars in all disciplines (after all, it provides a wonderful opportunity for one's own students to live and work in Japan), the tendency to emphasize youth and personality in the selection of participants has not gone uncriticized. What struck me about the way the interviews were set up was not only the preoccupation with social fit and social type but also the relatively short time we were given to make difficult assessments about character—integrity, adaptability, openness to learning, genuine interest in children.[38] One professor on the selection committee at the University of Washington told me that she was fed up with the whole process: "All they do is choose people who are cute and cheery instead of those with teaching experience or sustained interest in Japan." Cliff Clarke, who coordinated the selection of participants for CIEE under the old MEF Program, was especially critical of how the Ministry of Foreign Affairs handled the selection process after taking over from CIEE:

In the early years of the MEF Program, they only wanted single males under the age of twenty-six, and no one but Caucasians. We fought all of these one at a time because of lawsuits against CIEE. Also, there was no predeparture training at first, and they didn't want people to come knowing the Japanese language. The Japanese side was hoping for complete novices. But after a 5 to 6 percent failure rate, we convinced them that we needed a more thorough selection and orientation process. By 1986 we had the selection process so fine-tuned that we could spot the right American for the program in 30 seconds. Now [with the start-up of JET] they've gone right back to square one. Gaimushō has refused help from Mombushō, and they've created an application form that asks for age, race, sex, marital status, the whole works.[39]

WHO ARE THE JET PARTICIPANTS?

In spite of the initial administrative delays and the criticism of some selection committee members, the JET Program in its inaugural year attracted considerable interest in all four participating countries. As table 2 shows, for ALTs the percentage of successful applicants in 1987 was below 30 percent in both the United States and the United Kingdom, and below 10 percent in Australia. In 1988 the percentage of successful applicants rose considerably in the United States, the United Kingdom, Australia, and New Zealand, in part because of the increase in the numbers of new participants; but it was still low for the two newcomers, Canada and Ireland.

A closer examination of the characteristics of participants chosen in 1987 reveals a number of interesting points. The large majority (93 percent) were single, and there was a slightly higher percentage of females (56.5 percent) than males (43.5 percent). The age of participants during the first year of the program ranged from twenty-two to forty-three, with an average age of twenty-five. Among ALTs, 35.6 percent of JET participants indicated they had formal teaching experience, but it is hard to know what this means since "teaching experience" was not defined. While 46.8 percent indicated they had some Japanese language skills, this initial information was quite misleading because JET participants were only given two options from which to choose ("some skills" or "no skills"). Yet even with this crude distinction, striking differences between countries emerged. While 60 to 80 percent of Australian and New Zealand participants indicated they had some Japanese language ability, only 15 percent of British participants did, a reflection of the relative lack of Japanese language programs in British high schools and universities.[40]

Later a more sophisticated attempt was made to categorize the characteristics of JET participants (see table 3). A five-tiered scale of language ability was introduced, and the results indicate that on the whole, the JET

Table 2. Percentage of Successful JET Program Applicants, 1987 and 1988

Country	1987			1988		
	Applicants	New Participants	Percent	Applicants	New Participants	Percent
U.S.	2,075	570	27.5	1,492	598	40.1
U.K.	620	149	24.0	649	182	28.0
Australia	773	72	9.3	293	90	31
New Zealand	81	22	27.2	47	23	48.9
Canada	—	—	—	590	121	20.5
Ireland	—	—	—	151	20	13.2

SOURCE: Adapted from *The Jet Program(me): Five Years and Beyond* (Tokyo: Council of Local Authorities for International Relations, 1992), 162–63.

Table 3. Characteristics of Assistant Language Teachers, 1991

Country	Sex		Marital Status			TEFL certification		Japanese Proficiency[a]				
	Male	Female	Single	Engaged	Married	Yes	No	A	B	C	D	E
U.S.	427	497	841	40	43	73	851	22	58	141	254	449
U.K.	126	204	315	10	5	38	292	0	1	9	21	299
Australia	26	47	58	4	11	17	56	0	1	13	18	41
New Zealand	38	51	76	8	5	9	80	0	0	4	13	72
Canada	141	167	269	12	27	61	247	0	3	12	49	244
Ireland	7	20	27	0	0	7	20	0	0	1	7	19
France	0	4	4	0	0	0	4	2	1	1	0	0
Germany	0	2	2	0	0	1	1	0	1	0	1	0
Total	765	992	1,592	74	91	206	1,551	24	65	181	363	1,124
Total (%)	43.5	56.5	90.6	4.2	5.2	11.7	88.3	1.4	3.7	10.3	20.7	64.0

[a] Standard for evaluating Japanese proficiency: A: Can read and speak Japanese well enough to manage his/her duty; B: Can speak Japanese well enough to manage his/her duty; C: Has no trouble with casual conversation; D: Has trouble with conversation; E: Has no Japanese

SOURCE: Adapted from *The JET Program(me): Five Years and Beyond* (Tokyo: Council of Local Authorities for International Relations, 1992), 58.

participants are not very conversant in Japanese prior to arriving in Japan. Thus in 1991 fully 85 percent of new ALTs indicated that they could speak no Japanese whatsoever or that they had trouble with daily conversation. Only 1.3 percent said they could speak Japanese well enough to manage their work duties.[41] The same survey also revealed that 93.8 percent of ALTs came to Japan with a bachelor's degree, while 6.1 percent came with a master's. Just under 12 percent of ALTs had received some kind of TEFL (teaching English as a foreign language) certification.

Ministry officials told me that they kept no statistics on the ethnic and racial background of JET participants, and thus their observations are speculative. They noted that requiring a B.A. or B.S. degree for participation in the program was bound to skew the demographics of participants, as low-income and nonwhite youth are underrepresented in the population of college graduates in each of the participating countries. The 1987–88 *JET Participant Directory* (which includes both names and pictures) revealed that JETs of African descent comprised roughly 1.5 percent (10 of 683) of the participants pictured.[42] Judging from surnames, JETs of Japanese descent comprised 5 percent (45 of 848) of JET participants. It would seem that the former tended to be underrepresented, while the latter fared very well. There were few Hispanic participants, and no participants from indigenous groups such as Native Americans, Maori, or Australian Aborigines.

Motivation: Japan Meets Generation X

The motivations of current JET participants differ qualitatively from those of the young people, including myself, who came to Japan in the 1970s. Then we were more often than not lured by the image of the "exotic"—the tea ceremony, Zen, martial arts, and Kabuki. The yen for Japan among today's JET participants, however, is more likely to involve the other kind of yen. Amply aware of Japan's economic success, some hope to cash in on their Japan experience by working in international business. Almost all participants (especially those who are saddled with student loans) find the JET Program salary attractive.

Although JET participants represent a fairly narrow social slice, they have a wide range of motivations for entering the program. Approximately 25 percent of those whom I interviewed did draw some connection between Japan's economic rise, their participation in the JET Program, and a future payoff. In some cases they were quite specific. For instance, one twenty-two-year-old American noted, "I really want to go to business school and work in international business, and if this is the case, my study of Japanese and government should be useful." Others had only a vague notion that exposure to the Japanese economic miracle would pay off in the future. The comments of a twenty-four-year-old British participant demonstrate just how powerful Japan's economic position was perceived to be in the late 1980s: "I wanted to travel east after finals, and I caught sight of this at the career programs office. It seemed prestigious since it was run by the Japanese government. I thought if I could learn Japanese it would be beneficial to my career since Japan will lead the world in the next century."

Roughly 20 percent of the participants I interviewed mentioned some personal or family connection as the key force behind their interest in the JET Program. This was overwhelmingly true for Japanese Americans. A second-generation Japanese American recalled: "My father brought his chef skills to the States where he is self-employed, and my mother imparted my love of Japanese language and culture to me." By contrast, a fourth-generation Japanese American confessed that there was not much of Japan left in her household other than her mother cooking rice with hamburgers, but she still wanted to seek an understanding of Japanese culture in a way a tourist would not. Other participants had personal connections as well, ranging from a formative childhood experience such as studying the violin under the Suzuki method to the curiosity aroused by having a neighbor who was Japanese.

Another 15 percent expressed an academic interest in Japan. Many in this group had studied Japanese language, culture, or history in college, perhaps even venturing to Japan on an undergraduate exchange program. Thirteen percent of the participants I interviewed had a deep interest in teaching and ESL or had some experience in these fields. A roughly equal number said their motivation to travel to Japan was simply a desire to see a different part of the world. As one participant noted, "I had lived in Russia and the explorer side of me wanted to see a new place and experience a different lifestyle." In the same vein, another explained: "Japan was always a country I wanted to visit because of its combination of Eastern and Western influences. I was intrigued by diversity in the human race and wanted knowledge of a setting different from home." Finally, 9 percent of my interviewees mentioned their fascination with traditional Japanese culture. For many in this group, the martial arts, particularly membership in university aikido clubs, proved to be the impetus.[43]

At one end of the continuum, then, are those who come with what their Japanese hosts disparagingly referred to as a superficial interest (*karui kimochi*). Possessing a tourist mentality, they are perfectly content to operate in English for the duration of their stay and tend to become very cynical about the JET Program and Japanese education. At the other end are those who practically reject their own cultural background in the rush to embrace Japanese culture. Intent on going native, they may eschew interaction with other foreigners, preferring instead to cultivate an all-Japanese social network. Usually their initial idealism becomes tempered over time, but they still retain a critical stance toward their compatriots. The majority of JET participants fall somewhere in the middle between these two extremes. They view the JET Program as a chance to see the world and perhaps to take time off from school before making decisions about career plans, all the while harboring a vague expectation that the experience may prove valuable later down the line.

THE JET PROGRAM AS A "MEGAPOLICY"

Several themes are worth highlighting in the story of the origins of the JET Program, for they continue to influence its implementation. First, there were important antecedents for the idea itself. The Ministry of Home Affairs was embarking on a serious attempt to improve its overseas connections, prompted by the pace at which independent ties at local levels were proliferating; the Ministry of Foreign Affairs was committed to cultural exchange as a foreign policy strategy for providing a human face to counter the negative stereotypes of Japan circulating abroad; and the Ministry of Education, which already was administering two smaller English education programs, had committed itself (at least in principle) to improving foreign language education and intercultural educational exchanges. Holding these diverse threads together was a public discourse surrounding internationalization that stressed the need for Japan to emerge from cultural isolation and assimilate a new set of values. The JET Program thus was not just window dressing, as some critics have charged, but an attempt to integrate a relatively insular and homogeneous population with a global society made increasingly important to Japan by its own economic progress.

There is a sense, however, in which the JET Program can best be categorized as a "reactive" policy. Without Nakasone's deep interest in foreign affairs and the catalysts of U.S.-Japan trade friction and the Maekawa Report, it is doubtful that the JET Program would have ever materialized in its present form. It was generated largely by pressure from the outside: its goal was to demonstrate Japan's commonality with other countries in order to protect what Nakasone himself described as Japan's "vulnerable security system and international economic encirclement."[44] Consequently, there were people in each of the sponsoring ministries who were not thrilled by its announcement, and I was continually struck by how frequently the passive voice and the phrases "have to" and "must" (*shinakereba naranai koto*) were used when Ministry of Home Affairs and local officials explained the origins of the program.[45]

It is also important to stress that the JET Program involves three government ministries, identifying and targeting a problem that cannot be solved through ordinary sectoral policies. Insofar as the program transcends sectoral boundaries, creates new institutional structures and patterns of interaction, and requires new forms of behavior, it can be categorized with those innovative approaches that have been termed "megapolicies."[46] Yet intersectoral policies cannot just supersede existing policies. They must always be adapted to conflicting sectoral policy goals.

In addition, the three sponsoring ministries were not equal partners. The Ministry of Home Affairs took firm control of the budget and overall coordination of the program. Because diplomatic relations and strengthening Japan's role and image in the world often receive high priority in policy formation at the national level, the voice of the Ministry of Foreign Affairs was also strong. Indeed, it was the growing realization that preparation for world citizenship as conceived by the Ministry of Education did not accommodate Japan's new global needs that provided much of the initial impetus for the JET Program—and that ministry was clearly placed on the defensive by its adoption.

In spite of conflict and compartmentalization, the refusal of any ministry ultimately to undermine the policy speaks to the power of the concept of internationalization itself. For the politicians and bureaucrats concerned, pressured as they were by outside forces, proclaiming the existence of the JET Program was at least as important as the details of the policy's execution—not because they were hypocritical but because they realized the substantial symbolic significance of political actions. Wada Minoru himself confessed, "Since we have proclaimed the high ideals of internationalization, at the very least we must go through the motions of accommodating those ideals. But," he added, "and I'm sure I'll be criticized for saying this, I don't think Japan will change that much. We're not going to become like other countries."[47]

3   The Start-Up Years

The "Crash Program" Nearly Crashes

Dozens of flights converged on Narita Airport on 31 July 1987 carrying hundreds of Japan Exchange and Teaching Program participants, many of whom had flown business class.[1] Private buses whisked the new arrivals to the luxurious Keio Plaza Inter-Continental Hotel, where they were greeted, in the glare of the media spotlight, by the ministers of foreign affairs, education, and home affairs and the governor of Hyogo Prefecture.[2] Following the official introductions, all the JET participants, as well as a host of current and former Japanese officials connected with the program, were treated to a gourmet dinner reception. The beer flowed nonstop, and an elegant buffet was served by kimono-clad hostesses.

The Japanese speakers, by and large, expressed their expectation that the participants were to be "cultural ambassadors," indeed reformers of Japanese society. One noted, "It is my honest wish that through mixing with local people you will play your part as a stone in protecting the castle of peace." Another told the group, "You are participating in this great experiment. The process of internationalization is here to stay, and that is why you will be welcomed all over the country. . . . The understanding you can bring is so vitally needed in this turbulent world of today." Over the next four days of workshops on the nuts and bolts of teaching a foreign language or working in government offices, the theme of change was constantly in the air and a spirit of goodwill dominated.

But by the end of August, when the JET participants had finally settled in local schools and communities, the positive atmosphere had begun to dissipate. For assistant language teachers (ALTs), life in Japanese secondary schools seemed focused on preparing for entrance exams to the neglect of spoken English. Some coordinators for international relations (CIRs) arrived in prefectural offices to find that the "coordinator" part of their title was something of a misnomer: their employers had little clue as to what they might do other than translate documents and teach English to prefectural employees. Prefectural conditions of employment varied greatly, and school visitation schedules seemed to promote superficiality. Negative reports about the JET Program began to surface in the national media, and questions were raised about the commitment of CLAIR and of the Ministry of Education to racial and gender equality and about the capacity of bureaucrats to provide the human touch. The first few years of the program were thus marked by numerous problems and misunderstandings as the reform-minded participants, most of whom spoke no Japanese and had little understanding of Japanese culture, vented their frustrations to anyone who would listen.

These program-related complaints were directed primarily at the small cadre of Japanese officials and alumni of the Mombushō English Fellows Program and British English Teaching Scheme at CLAIR who had been assembled to administer the program. This chapter examines the administrative and cultural problems that arose during the first three years of the program from the vantage point of national-level officials. What issues were raised by JET participants and their brokers at CLAIR, the program coordinators? What were the major concerns on the part of Japanese officials at the Ministry of Education and at CLAIR? Most important, through what process were conflicts actually defused, and with what effect on each of the parties concerned?

It is important to remember that the initial CLAIR staff numbered fewer than twenty and was anything but the stereotypical Japanese organization—a cohesive, tight-knit group. While the influence of the Ministry of Home Affairs was great, only three of the five ranking Japanese officials (*yakuin*) hailed from that ministry. As a group, the *yakuin* had only minimal experience with internationalization and were simply anxious to get through the start-up year without major problems. Most did not consider being posted to CLAIR as a step up in their career ambitions; instead, they usually viewed it as a lateral move, or even as removal from the career ladder entirely. In addition, there were eight staff members (*uneiiin*) representing local governments from as far away as Kumamoto Prefecture and as near as the Tokyo Metropolitan office. Though they were ostensibly appointed to CLAIR to acquire know-how for internationalization, these local government officials saw their stay primarily as a chance to develop ties with the central authorities that could later benefit their locality.

Finally, there were three foreigners chosen as program coordinators for the pilot year: Philip, a soft-spoken American who had spent three years teaching in Saga Prefecture in the MEF Program and had married a Japanese woman; Caroline, an outspoken American who had spent two years in Chiba Prefecture in the MEF Program after graduating with a major in Japanese studies from a small midwestern liberal arts college; and Ben, a native of Britain and an alumnus of the BET Scheme. They would be responsible for designing all English-language materials for the program and handling most of the direct interaction with JET participants. Having worked hard to promote English language reform and cosmopolitan attitudes in their respective prefectures, they were excited about the great changes that the JET Program would make possible.

The composition of CLAIR was thus even more complex than that of the agencies John Campbell has described as "pseudo-uchi"—agencies that cross ministerial jurisdictions in order to deal with recurring or permanent problems.[3] There was no natural community of interest among the initial staff at CLAIR; on the contrary, the potential for fragmentation was tremendous. Yet this group with diverse interests quickly became focused on the shared task of managing an extremely complex and unwieldy program.

THE RISE OF AJET AS A PRESSURE GROUP

The very first development unanticipated by Japanese officials was the establishment by JET participants of a quasi-union/support group at the 1987 Tokyo Orientation. While similar organizations had existed earlier, no one guessed that MEF and BET participants who stayed on under the JET Program would be so successful in mobilizing incoming JET participants to their cause. With the stated purpose of providing support and assisting CLAIR and the Ministry of Education in responding effectively to a variety of program-related problems, the Association of Japan Exchange and Teaching (AJET) convinced over 80 percent of JET participants to pay the $100 dues required to join during their first year. Prefectural, regional, and national representatives were elected, and AJET immediately began publishing a monthly newsletter. By 1988 this publication had become a "magazine" that provided "a forum for sharing teaching ideas, travel tips, complaints, triumphs, humor and even recipes." The August 1988 issue began with a letter from the group's chair describing the rationale and purpose of AJET:

> The program is simply too large to be carried out effectively given the present government's administrative provisions. Another body is necessary, one which addresses the needs of program *participants*. In fact,

such an association exists. AJET is an independent, self-financed support organization which exists to represent the interests of participating ALTs and CIRs.

AJET is a network which addresses the personal and professional needs of its members through a three-tiered hierarchy of representatives. There are seven Block Representatives and 47 Prefectural Representatives serving in addition to the four National Officers (a Chairperson, a Vice-chairperson, a Treasurer and a Secretary). These representatives seek solutions to problems on the program participants' behalf and attempt to preempt those which threaten to disturb our well-being. . . . AJET is *independent* and self-governing, it need not concern itself so extensively with the spectre of censorship which looms at official levels.

It should be mentioned here that AJET is not a labor union. No wage bargaining will ever be attempted, no wild-cat strikes called, no buttons issued, no love-ins or walk-outs sponsored; foreign unions are by law forbidden in this country. If we were ever to appear to conduct ourselves as such, one can be certain that we would be directed to pack our *omiyage* [souvenirs] and take our respective brands of native English elsewhere.[4]

Though AJET's elected leaders assiduously avoided the label "union," arguing that the group was necessary simply to coordinate and facilitate smooth implementation of the program, it was never entirely clear to Japanese officials whether this was to be a support group or a pressure group. Privately, several of the Japanese officials I interviewed confessed that initially they perceived AJET as a vote of no confidence on the ability of Japanese officials to handle the program. It is clear from even a cursory look at AJET's activities during the first few years that the organization began pressing CLAIR and the Ministry of Education for change on a host of controversial issues. AJET not only took up the problems of taxes, insurance, and pensions but also established special interest groups for minority JETs and for female JETs, as well as a peer support network to fill the perceived gap in counseling services.

Private opinions aside, the issue for CLAIR and ministry officials quickly became how to manage AJET. How much formal recognition and support should be accorded? How much leverage should AJET representatives be allowed over program policies? How should AJET be explained to prefectural and municipal officials? AJET's struggle for a formal and legitimate role in program administration was a recurring theme during the early years of the program.

There was by no means unanimity in the Japanese camp on how to handle this development. Initially, Wada Minoru at the Ministry of Education was quite unsympathetic to AJET requests for a greater role in determining speakers and the content of sessions at the Tokyo orientation, the midyear block seminars, and the renewers' conference. The first secretary-general at CLAIR also adopted a wait-and-see attitude toward AJET, and even forbade program coordinators at CLAIR from contacting AJET representatives directly without first going through the relevant Japanese prefectural official. Finally, at AJET's request, CLAIR did send out official notification to each prefecture explaining the association and asking for cooperation in facilitating meetings of prefectural and district AJET representatives. Yet prefectural receptivity to and understanding of the purpose of AJET varied tremendously.

In 1988, however, under a particularly sympathetic secretary-general, CLAIR's strategy began to change. In effect, Japanese officials at CLAIR decided that it would be counterproductive to take an overly confrontational stance toward AJET; rather, they would monitor AJET activities and cooperate when possible. CLAIR even granted AJET a small budget and agreed to host three "evaluation meetings" each year that brought a small group of JET participants to Tokyo to provide feedback on the program. These meetings, which are attended by all top-ranking officials at CLAIR, are now an important source of input from the JET participants. Moreover, AJET was granted an additional day at the renewers' conference, with hotel rooms subsidized by CLAIR, during which they could schedule their own speakers, hold meetings of their interest groups, and elect officers.[5] By 1989 the question "What's AJET's stance on this?" was asked automatically of almost any proposed change in program policy. While CLAIR and Ministry of Education officials were often far from willing to capitulate to AJET demands, AJET had at least established its legitimacy as a conduit through which concerns of program participants could reach the ears of Japanese officials.

ADMINISTRATIVE SNAFUS AND INTERMINISTERIAL RIVALRIES

In her case study of intercultural friction in a U.S-Japan joint venture company, Tomoko Hamada provides a fascinating account of a disagreement over how to calculate for tax purposes the depreciation of newly purchased equipment. She describes how Japanese officials preferred the method of their parent company, which spread the depreciation over a number of years. The American side, however, was under considerable pressure to show short-term profit to the company's stockholders and thus preferred an accounting method that allowed for the largest possible tax deduction immediately. In the end, a seemingly trivial distinction in calculating taxes led to a series of misunderstandings that proved highly significant in shaping mutual perceptions. The JET Program, too, was full of seemingly "neutral" administrative procedures that led to much questioning of intentions and motives.

The Australian Tax Controversy

The first mini-administrative crisis involved a controversy over the tax status of Australian participants during the first year of the program.[6] According to Japanese law the JET participants could be exempt from Japanese income tax for their first two years of employment, and the government had advertised the year in Japan as tax-free income. In the haste of the start-up, however, they had overlooked the fact that Japan had no bilateral agreement on taxes with the Australian government. Moreover, Australian tax laws made it clear that nationals residing outside the country were required to pay taxes either at home or abroad. Any change in this policy would require nothing less than an act of Parliament.

By the time Australian participants arrived in Tokyo in August 1987, the rumor mill had begun to whirl. Up to 40 percent of their JET income would have to be forked over to the government on their return home! Even if they paid Japanese taxes, they would be held responsible for the difference, since the Australian tax burden was higher! Calls to the Australian embassy or to CLAIR asking for clarification seemed to lead nowhere. All this created a panic among Australian participants, some of whom had already signed a form exempting them from Japanese taxes. They began to confront CLAIR officials as well as local board of education personnel and school principals. AJET got involved, petitions were signed, letters of protest were written, and an Associated Press reporter was brought into the fray. Several Australian participants threatened to resign unless the issue was resolved by a specific date. Miriam was one:

> We had all kinds of meetings at orientation about the tax problem and for six months afterwards as well. It was a horrible way to start what should have been a wonderful experience. We'd been told when we applied that we were all tax-free, but they obviously didn't do their homework. CLAIR kept saying, "Don't worry, as far as we're concerned you won't have to pay taxes," but they wouldn't give us any evidence. Finally I told my boss, "Look, you're not going to be there when I have

to pay my tax. Get me something in writing by the end of this month, or I'm going home in January." That got his attention. It seems the only time they respond to us is when we give them ultimatums.

Pressured both by the Australian embassy and by educational administrators in the prefectures to do something about the tax problem, CLAIR officials contacted the Australian Taxation Department (via the Ministry of Foreign Affairs via the Japanese consulate in Canberra) to ask if an exception to the tax laws could be made for the JET Program. After all, the Japanese government was doing Australia a favor by including their citizens in it. The reply from Canberra was clear: this was Japan's problem, and the burden of accommodation rested on the Japanese government. But Australian officials did suggest that if JET participants were to pay taxes in Japan, they would be exempt from taxation in Australia. The only difficulty came with the relatively large percentage of Australian participants who were public school teachers. As civil servants, they could not be exempted from Australian tax unless they were "consultants" to a foreign government.

After months of deliberation, correspondence, and visits among all the relevant agencies, including the Finance Ministry, Home Affairs officials and the secretary-general of CLAIR decided on their course of action. They would raise the actual salary of the Australians by the amount required to pay Japanese taxes. This would ensure that after Japanese taxes were deducted, their salaries would remain the same as those of other JET participants. The solution to the predicament of those who were teachers in Australia involved a more substantial dose of administrative sleight of hand. CLAIR advised local governments to change the official status of Australian ALTs to CIRs on all tax forms, thereby qualifying them as "consultants to a foreign government."

Yet the fallout from the Australian tax problem was heavy. During the months that CLAIR had been negotiating their tax status, the Australian participants themselves had been in limbo, receiving little in the way of consistent or reliable information. Frustrated by the bureaucratic inertia and by the teaching conditions at local levels, their reports back home were far from glowing. While more than 1,100 applications had been received from Australians in 1987, the number fell to barely 250 the following year. There was also a significant decrease in requests for Australians by prefectural offices of education fearing unpleasant confrontations and extra administrative work. This placed the Ministry of Foreign Affairs in a very difficult position. Eighty-three Australians had been hired to participate in the program in 1987, and it would hardly do if in 1988 the number were to decrease. An Osaka board of education official recalls, "After the Australian tax problem many prefectures didn't want Australians but Foreign Affairs called us and said, 'Please take one or two because if you don't it will look bad for Japan.' It was a real difficult situation because of the diplomatic considerations (*gaikō ga aru kara muzukashii*). So we ended up requesting a few Australians even though they weren't our first choice." In the end, 143 Australian participants were admitted to the JET Program in 1988, but the percentage of Australian participants relative to the total JET population later fell steadily, from 9.79 percent in 1987 to 4.9 percent in 1991.[7]

Health Insurance and Pensions

A second controversial question involved health insurance and pension payments for the foreign teachers. During the first year of the program the amount that JET participants were required to pay for health insurance varied greatly among prefectures, ranging from as little as $30 to nearly $200 per month. JET participants began complaining to CLAIR immediately after their arrival: individuals asked why they should have three or four times as much taken from their salary for health insurance as friends in the neighboring prefecture.

The discrepancy arose because prefectural offices and municipalities were choosing between two insurance plans, the "Kenpo" (Seifu Kansho Hoken) plan and the "Kokuho" (Kokumin Kenkō Hoken) plan. The former is the government-operated insurance plan designed for nonregular employees (regardless of nationality) who are employed for more than two months in the public or private sector. The latter applies to anyone employed for less than two months or to those who are self-employed. According to Japanese law, the Kenpo plan is compulsory for any public or private organization employing personnel for a period of more than two months. In reality, though, many prefectures and municipalities were enrolling all their nonregular employees (not only JET participants) in the Kokuho plan because it was cheaper.

In 1987 the Social Insurance Agency (Shakai Hoken Cho) notified local governments that they must comply with the law, and the National Audit Board began investigating health insurance procedures in host institutions. Prefectures and municipalities that had been using the Kokuho plan saw the audit coming and switched to the more expensive policy. This solved

the problem of discrepancies between prefectures, but some JET participants were outraged by their new high premiums. Moreover, those premiums were automatically deducted from every employee's salary. When
several prefectures switched the health insurance of their renewing JET
participants without notice, renewers charged that they had not been accu-
rately informed of the terms of their new contracts.

The switch also created an entirely new and even more intractable problem: the Kenpo plan required JET participants to pay into a pension fund
even though they would receive no pension. Indeed, that contribution is
what makes the Kenpo plan considerably more expensive than the Kokuho
plan. The "pension issue" became a perennial sore point during the early
years of the program. The *CLAIR Newsletter* and the *AJET Magazine* ran
regular updates on developments in the debate. In a 1989 letter to the *JET
Journal*, one CIR summed up the indignation felt by many JET participants:

> While I am sure none of us totally reject the idea of paying for an in-
> surance policy, I believe many of us find almost criminal the fact that
> half of the actual insurance premium we pay each month is for the pur-
> pose of a pension fund payed [sic] to retired individuals. It is simply the
> principal [sic] involved. Why should we be required to pay for a pen-
> sion fund which we will never benefit from? Unless we have aspiring
> Kent Gilberts among us (Kent is the quintessential *gaijin*-turned-
> Nihongo star to be watched almost nightly on TV), we are in Japan on a
> temporary basis and will certainly not be here when we retire.[8]

Japanese officials at CLAIR were completely stymied by this problem.
Most agreed that there was a logical inconsistency in the policy, and one
secretary-general even told me that he ranked it the major unresolved
issue of his tenure at CLAIR. Yet the outspoken, even self-righteous, manner in which some JET participants pressed their claims seemed to catch
CLAIR officials off guard. From their point of view, the JET participants
were guests in Japan, and fairly well-paid ones at that: to press monetary
demands in this way seemed highly inappropriate. Japanese officials were
also quick to point out that the same situation existed in many other countries.

Nevertheless, by May 1988 CLAIR had already approached the Social
Insurance Agency to request that it reconsider the pension requirement.
But CLAIR was clearly at the mercy of more powerful external agencies.
Because the pension payment was prescribed by Japanese law, any changes

would require the introduction of new legislation in the Diet, and in the late 1980s the Social Insurance Agency seemed to be in no mood to consider such action. For the time being, JET participants were forced to swallow the bitter pill of paying over a hundred dollars per month into a fund from which they would never benefit.

The Prime Minister's Office Rediscovers JET

At the same time that the tax, insurance, and pension issues were being negotiated, interministerial rivalries resurfaced in dramatic fashion. By 1988 the office of prime minister had been taken over by Takeshita Noboru, a former English teacher who, unlike Nakasone, had only limited experience with foreign affairs. Yet in a speech given while visiting Europe in 1988, Takeshita suddenly promised to include French and German participants in the JET Program the following year. I happened to visit CLAIR the day after his announcement, and I found that it had come as a complete surprise to officials there and in the Ministry of Education.

It later became known that his speech had been written by the Ministry of Foreign Affairs: the diversification of participating countries was part of the ministry's larger strategy to move beyond bilateral ties with the United States and to reposition Japan in relation to the European market. One CLAIR official put it this way: "One of the ideas of the Ministry of Foreign Affairs and the Prime Minister's Office was that while the ties between the Japan and the United States were strong, the ties between Japan and Europe were less so. In trying to think of various approaches for strengthening ties with Europe, it was decided that the JET Program was one way to go about it."

In any event, it was Ministry of Education officials who were put on the spot by the announcement, and they quickly charged that in emphasizing the contribution of the JET program to Japan's diplomatic relations the Ministry of Foreign Affairs was ignoring domestic realities. While a number of Japanese private secondary schools offer French and German, English so dominates foreign language instruction in public schools that finding places for the French and German participants was virtually impossible. In fact, fewer than a dozen French and German participants were invited in 1989; much to their chagrin, most of this token number ended up teaching English in addition to a few classes in their native language. One assistant French teacher reports that he was told by the Japanese consulate in Paris that none of the French JET participants would need to teach English, but he ended up teaching sixteen hours per week of English, and virtually no French, for the entire year. In addition, the application forms were all in English, as were the employment contracts they had to sign. Not surprisingly, French and German participants—who, as a rule, were very highly qualified—began applying in much greater numbers for the CIR portion of the program, in which they could assist prefectures or municipalities that had French and German sister cities.[9]

The invitation to include France and Germany had another ironic complication as well, as the Canadian embassy had requested that French Canadian participants be allowed into the program. Now that France had been admitted, the Japanese government felt that the few slots available for French teachers had to be reserved for participants from France; predictably, the Canadians were not pleased.

NEGATIVE PUBLICITY AND THE STRUGGLE TO CONTROL THE MEDIA

The sensitivity to foreign pressure that characterizes politics at the national level raises the stakes riding on the success of the JET Program. Favorable publicity is an important means of achieving the program's political goals; on a practical level, it also helps guarantee a large number of high-quality applicants. Having invested considerable resources in the JET Program, Tokyo bureaucrats certainly hoped for positive coverage.

Yet media assessments both within Japan and abroad were very mixed during the early years of the program. The English-language newspapers in Japan—especially the *Japan Times*, the *Mainichi*, and the *Daily Yomiuri*—became sites for a vigorous debate on its pros and cons.

The Wakabayashi Controversy

Just over a month after the program began, Professor Wakabayashi Shunsuke of the Tokyo University of Foreign Studies wrote an article voicing the fear of the teachers' union that Japanese jobs might ultimately be threatened by the JET Program. Blasting the government for perpetuating an "ugly system that allows amateurs to teach," Wakabayashi argued in the *Japan Times* that "all teachers should be licensed for any subject they teach." He lamented that since Japanese teachers are very polite toward foreigners, they "will be forced to busy themselves taking care of the young people" to the detriment of their own classes. He pointed out the folly of assuming that students can learn English with only three classes a week and went on to argue for a position long held by the teachers' union: "it is more urgent that the government send as many Japanese English teachers as possible to other countries."[10]

Reaction to his attack came swiftly and from several quarters. Numerous ALTs wrote letters taking issue with various points. Kimberly Kennedy in Nagasaki questioned Wakabayashi's reference to JET participants as "boys and girls," noting that the men and women on JET were subjected to a careful screening process and included people with master's degrees and years of teaching experience. Michelle Long in Toyama took a different tack, pointing out that "Amateurs teaching English in public schools is a problem that is more a result rather than a cause of the sorry state of English education in Japan." Andrew Barnes wrote in from Fujioka, Gunma, that Wakabayashi's view "undermines the cultural and educational importance of the JET Program."[11]

On the Japanese side, Iizuka Shigehiko, an independent researcher in English language education, published a rejoinder to Wakabayashi titled "We Welcome JET Teachers." Iizuka noted that although quite a few Japanese teachers of English oppose JET, the majority are eager to study their own subject and want to be proficient in speaking English. He criticized Wakabayashi for suggesting that the government should invite only professionals while knowing full well that specialists in English as a second language (ESL) are scarce even in English-speaking countries. Iizuka continued: "Is [Wakabayashi] afraid that Japanese teachers of English will lose their jobs if the influx of JET teachers continues as the government is reported planning? If so, he is very right in saying, 'the people are far from being internationalized,' and he is typically one of them."[12]

All of this squabbling finally led the secretary-general of CLAIR to write to the *Japan Times*. Noting that "there is considerable misunderstanding regarding the JET Program and its purpose," he proceeded to downplay the Ministry of Education's view of the program. "The JET Program's objectives encompass much more than English education," he asserted, and he was "confident that all 848 JET participants . . . upon returning home will contribute much to improving the understanding of Japan abroad."[13] One ALT addressed the last claim in a letter published the following month: "My response is, Don't be so sure. Greater understanding of Japan does not necessarily mean greater empathy. . . . I don't accept any postcontractual obligations for public relations work on Japan's behalf."[14]

Wakabayashi's article highlighted several issues that became widely debated. It called attention to the program's failure to actively recruit candidates with teaching credentials or to particularly encourage those with ESL degrees to apply (though, to be sure, holders of such credentials were not actively discouraged from applying). On this issue, the views of Ministry of Education officials shaped policy. They felt that experienced teachers were too set in their own teaching strategies to adapt effectively to Japanese schools.

Wakabayashi's reference to the JET participants as "boys and girls" also threw into relief the government's tendency to see the program as primarily geared toward people not yet fully mature. Obviously, this tended to annoy many of the participants themselves, just out of college and feeling ready to take on the world. Yet JET participants' perception of themselves as "adults" notwithstanding, I found Wakabayashi's view to be widely shared among Japanese administrators and teachers.[15] In fact, although the term "Jetto" (JET) is sometimes used in Japanese renditions of the name of the program, the official title in most ministry documents is Gaikoku Seinen Shōchi Jigyō (literally, "a program to invite youth from abroad"). Similarly, "AJET" for many years was translated into Japanese as Gaikokujin Seinen No Kai (the Association of Foreign Youth), a rendition that AJET fought vigorously; they eventually succeeded in changing it to Jetto Puroguramu Sankasha No Kai (JET Program Participants' Organization). In a society in which age and experience still go a long way in determining the level of respect one is accorded, the JET participants were widely seen as greenhorns. Many had not experienced life as *shakaijin* (persons living on their own and holding down a job) prior to their employment in the JET Program. Moreover, as Merry White has shown, Japanese have high expectations for individuals in this age range and are unlikely to see any testing of ideas and social experimentation in a favorable light.[16] I often heard the Japanese criticizing JET participants' behavior as youthful self-centeredness.

Yet in spite of their difficulties in dealing with the "youth factor," the Japanese broadly agreed that younger persons were more desirable. One senior curriculum specialist in the Ministry of Education explained, "If the JET participants are too old, Japanese teachers feel threatened. Also, people just out of college are more flexible and can adapt easier to Japanese schools." This sentiment was strikingly demonstrated by CLAIR's 1988 decision to set an upper age limit of thirty-five for participation in the JET Program. Although the rule had been in effect in the early years of the MEF Program, it was struck down by a lawsuit against the New York–based Council for International Educational Exchange. Now that the Japanese government was in charge of the selection process, lawsuits in U.S. courts were less of a threat.

We should note, however, that the Ministries of Foreign Affairs and of Education supported the age limit for very different reasons. To the extent that Foreign Affairs officials saw the program as a vehicle for increasing foreign understanding of Japan, it was desirable to catch applicants at a formative stage in their lives—preferably young people who might later take up leadership positions in their respective countries. But Education officials wished to select the kind of participant most acceptable to Japanese teachers and educational administrators. In both cases, youth best met their concerns; in spite of complaints from various quarters, the age limit remained generally in effect.[17]

The Mie Incident

While Wakabayashi was harangued for his opinions about the JET Program, no one accused him of intentionally misrepresenting it. In two subsequent cases, however, reports on the JET Program proved to be extremely misleading and one-sided. On 5 November 1988, the views of the teachers' union on the JET Program received another airing in a *Yomiuri Shimbun* article titled "Verbal Abuse of American Teacher Leads to Student Expulsion, Controversy." According to the article, a Japanese student was expelled from a Mie prefectural high school for shouting "Speak Japanese!" (*Nihongo de shabere!*) and other insults at an ALT identified as "B-san." The author blamed the incident, which "has once again brought into relief the problems connected with ALTs," on the ALT's favoring those students who were motivated in English and ignoring or treating with "American-style discipline" those students who couldn't follow the lesson.[18]

The article itself, however, supplies virtually no details; in fact, it is simply a summary of critical reports given about ALTs at the annual meeting of the Mie Prefectural Teachers' Union. The author concludes, "Most ALTs have received a high-class education and come to Japan with enthusiasm, but suddenly come up against exam English, some teachers who have a 'gaijin complex,' and a society that lets low achievers get by—none of which they can understand. While the situation in Mie is not as extreme as that in Nagasaki Prefecture, in which three-fifths of the ALTs returned home early in despair, trouble spots arising from the different views of education seem to be everywhere."

After the article appeared, CLAIR officials visited the site and talked at length with the ALT, the principal, and the board of education. As it turned out, the student was expelled because of a cumulative history of poor class work, disruptive behavior, excessive absences, tardiness, and verbally abusive language toward many of the teachers. The ALT in question had never been interviewed by the *Yomiuri Shimbun* reporter, and the student had stopped attending her class more than two months prior to being expelled. She had had two unpleasant interactions with him, however. During the first term she had taken the student down to the teachers' room, because he was thirty minutes late to class with no written excuse. The second confrontation took place in the nurse's room: "I walked into the nurse's room to meet with another teacher and 'A-kun' was there. He yelled *#!gaijin@Y! at me, I gave him a disgusted look, walked by him and the nurse told him to be quiet. A-kun left and I met with my teacher."[19] While the ALT's actions in the first instance could be seen as problematic by other teachers, neither of these interactions had anything to do with the student's expulsion.

The ALT herself wrote an open letter to JET participants: "I am the same 'B-san' that has been asked to give countless speeches on 'The Internationalization of Mie-ken,' and yet was a victim of a worst-case scenario of just how 'uninternationalized' people really are. In effect, the mass media got away with an article that bordered on nationalism and racism."[20] CLAIR officials also sent a plea to JET participants in the *CLAIR Newsletter*:

> As many of you may already have heard or read, an ALT in Mie Prefecture was described (by Yomiuri Shimbun) as being responsible for a 1st year student being asked to withdraw from his high school. Such, however, was not the case. The ALT was regrettably mentioned by the principal as *also having had trouble* with the student and was drawn into the center of the fray to suit the interests of the mass media. . . . While everyone directly involved knows that the ALT has become a scapegoat, CLAIR asks for your help in setting the record straight when questioned about the matter by teachers, supervisors or the press.[21]

The Tokyo Journal *Controversy: A Case of Missing Identity*

Later in the same year, under the title of "Teacher Torture" an article in the *Tokyo Journal* began:

> Patricia Smith was a JET. She thought Japanese were diligent, obedient people with a high regard for education. But to her, Japan was like a bad dream. . . . Every class was supervised by a Japanese teacher. Soon Patricia felt like a living tape recorder. "Here, read this part," the teacher would command. . . . She went to the principal to discuss the situation and was immediately given a sermon: "You dress too colorfully. Please wear more conservative clothes. . . ."
> One day five students came to her and said they had some questions. She brightened for a moment, thinking "progress at last." Then she found out what they wanted to know—the meaning of a list of words: F——, S——, D——, C——, B——. "The students giggled as they watched my face while I read that list," Patricia said. "I have never seen more hateful expressions than were on those students' faces. Even though I feel I can take a lot, a month later I decided to go back to

America. Now, when I tell people what kind of experiences I had in Japan, no one will believe me."[22]

Alarmed by such an extremist perspective, CLAIR officials decided to look into the matter. They discovered that the article, though not so identified, was a composite of interviews with several JET teachers. To compound problems, the author had inadvertently chosen as a pseudonym a name that in fact belonged to a former participant in the program. Indeed, that Patricia Smith had had a very different experience. CLAIR officials and the program coordinators decided to go on the offensive. They persuaded the real Patricia to write a letter in defense of the program, and they pressured the editor of the *Tokyo Journal* (using the threat of a lawsuit) to publish it with an apology. "JET Brag" appeared in June 1989:

> This is in response to the article which appeared in the March '89 issue of the Tokyo Journal as an excerpt from the monthly, *Shincho 45.* . . . [It] tells of a gaijin nightmare-existence as a JET and reads like anti-Japanese propaganda. It is, however, anti-JET propaganda. There was only one Patricia Smith in the JET Program in 1987. I am she, and I did *not* write that article. I loved my year in Japan and have the utmost respect for the JET Program. It is suspected that the article is in fact by a Japanese writer working for *Shincho 45* who was in hopes of stirring up resentment toward the JET Program. . . . This attempt to manipulate public opinion through subterfuge can only be viewed as malicious and cowardly.
>
> In addition, *The Tokyo Journal* is equally culpable in this subterfuge because of its failure to verify the authenticity of the article. . . . The damage done to my reputation and to the trust I worked so hard to build in the community in which I lived is permanent; however, I expect the editors of *The Tokyo Journal* and *Shincho 45* to do something to redress this wrong.
>
> *We hope that by running this letter from the real Patricia Smith that we can put this matter to rest for all parties involved. We feel, as Patricia points out, that this unfortunate case could have been avoided by a more extensive checking on all levels, including the translation stage—Ed., Tokyo Journal.*[23]

Racial Insensitivity?

A much more serious blow to the credibility of the JET Program came in April 1989, when Karen Hill Anton, who was subsequently featured in Reggie Life's documentary *Struggle and Success: The African-American Experience in Japan,* devoted her weekly column in the *Japan Times* to the JET Program. Anton had written an earlier article praising the JET Program; now, in "Japan Pulls in Welcome Mat with Racial Insensitivity," she described the experience of a pseudonymous African American ALT, Sandra Evans, with impeccable academic credentials and considerable international experience:

> Evans remembers well her first meeting with the head of the English department[;] . . . he greeted her not with Hello or Konnichiwa, but "Hey, you're big!" His first two questions were: "How many black ALTs are there?" and "Will you teach the black dialect?" Later she would regularly hear, "Can you speak standard English?" . . .
>
> Evans says it was clear from the beginning her school felt they were being "punished" by being assigned a black person. It was obvious they were let down; the administration acted as though they'd been cheated; had been given a defective *gaijin.*
>
> Evans is both sad and confounded when she says "the Japanese don't realize how ugly their behavior is." Clearly, it's impossible to reconcile the image of Japanese politeness with the crude, unconscionable behavior she's been subjected to; difficult to draw parallels between Japan's well-educated populace and the narrow, ignorant racially insensitive people she's encountered.[24]

Anton was not the first to voice the issue of race. The "white bias" in program structure was also criticized by the AJET vice-chair in an article widely circulated among JET participants:

> More to the point, the JETs from all six countries represent a very narrow and carefully selected segment of their respective nations. Apart from Asian-Americans, very few of us fall under headings other than WASP. . . . Color, variety and pattern have been screened out of the controlled sample brought here for this experiment. . . . What about native English speakers from India? Why haven't the Philippines been added to the list of participating countries?
>
> Through the JET Programme, the Japanese government has stated very clearly its position on racial and social equality. The JETs working here show in black and white, mostly white, that the concept of "internationalization" has been grossly distorted. . . . Japan is alone in its reluctance to promote racial equality, and this exposes the hypocrisy that it calls "internationalization." Japan is connected with the rest of the world; it can't ignore what the rest of the world thinks.

While the above article was circulated only among AJET members, Anton's feature story reached much of the foreign community in Japan; obviously, it raised quite a stir at CLAIR and the sponsoring ministries. One African American participant teaching in the same prefecture as "Sandra Evans" recalled: "You can imagine what happened when this story hit the press. I had Mr. Wada call, I had CLAIR call, I had everybody calling, asking 'Was it me?' I said, 'Well, she [Anton] interviewed me, but it was not me who was written up in the paper.' Then they kept warning me about how I have to be careful with the press."

My conversations with several persons acquainted with the situation verified the accuracy of Anton's account. Shortly after the story broke, I also had the opportunity to attend a meeting of the Minority Support Group at the 1989 Tokyo Orientation.[25] The comments by several renewing JET participants of color confirmed the ways in which the social perception of skin color in Japan constrained their experiences.

> You're gonna have to deal with stereotypes. The first day I walked into class and on every desk there were Little Black Sambo pencil cases and bags. I nearly hit the roof, but then I thought, "OK, it's just my first day," so I asked them why they bought them, and they said, "Oh, they're cute—*kawaii*." I said, "No, they make me wanna cry."
>
> If I had a dollar for every time someone says, "Oh, I bet you can run fast!"
>
> Here's what I do, I get on my soapbox. I use blue chalk and yellow hair and I say, "On TV you see this, but guess what? This is not the sum total of America." We need to let them know the U.S. and the world has different people and different languages.
>
> Media come and they don't want to interview me; they don't want my picture, just the blond hair and blue eyes.

Yet my interviews with African American JET participants also revealed the dangers in pigeonholing any group. The experiences of minority JET participants showed considerable diversity, and many had very positive assessments. One program coordinator put it this way: "Most of the schools would say, 'We're amazed, we've got this black and she speaks fantastic English; she's so enthusiastic and the kids love her.' So there was this one place that hit the newspapers and that was unfortunate. There were other black participants who were doing a great job but you never heard about them." Anton herself eventually came to see the JET Program as a positive force, and she became a very popular keynote speaker at JET Program conferences in the early to mid-1990s.

Nevertheless, her article raises a very pertinent policy question, drawing our attention to how CLAIR negotiated between its sincere desire to foster understanding of diversity and the reality of widespread preference for whites at the local level. It is important to note, first of all, that from the beginning CLAIR has stated that prefectures are not allowed to make requests about the race of the foreign participants (though they could specify preferences for nationality, sex, teaching credentials, Japanese language competence, and sister-city locations). But some prefectures and municipalities let their desire for whites be known in other ways. Philip articulated the problem to me:

> Philip: Naturally one of the things we never considered asking prefectures was whether they wanted someone who was black or white or Asian or whatever. But not surprisingly some prefectures on their request sheet wrote in they didn't want someone of a particular race.
> DM: How many?
> Philip: Very few. Two prefectures out of forty-seven. But still two too many. Luckily, the other two people in my department and the *kacho* (section chief), the four of us absolutely opposed even considering that sort of request. And we told the prefectures involved, this is impossible. At the same time, you're faced with an interesting dilemma. That is, you already know that X prefecture doesn't want someone of a particular race. So what do you do? What if someone of that race goes there? Is it fair for the person going because he or she isn't going to know that, at least initially. But there's a chance they'll find out the prefecture made a particular request, or else they'll sense it. Ethically, it's a difficult question because you refuse to accept that type of request, but at the same time once you know that sort of situation exists, you can't really ignore it and throw that person to the wolves, so to speak. So that was awkward, but perhaps because the number of nonwhites in the first year of the program was so small, it didn't become a problem.

In the early years of the JET Program, CLAIR's solution was to use *hairyō*, which literally means "special care" or consideration. One former secretary-general of CLAIR described it this way: "We do give those applications special consideration in placement (*hairyō wa shimasuyo*). But it's for their own benefit." What *hairyō* meant in practice was that nonwhites were rarely placed in rural municipalities that had been assigned only one JET participant, as everyone from the mayor down to the parents and students was probably counting on a white face. Instead, most were sent to prefectural or large city boards of education, where often there was a history of receiving minorities; sometimes they were placed in high schools, where students were assumed to be more mature, or in the prefectural education center, where they interacted primarily with teachers. In addition, the supervisor at the local level was consulted beforehand.[26]

This practice of singling out African American and other nonwhite applicants in the placement process deeply disturbed some of the program co-

ordinators. Because it involved separating groups by race, it was often perceived as yet another example of discrimination. Caroline recalls: "What I
found is that the foreign ministry is still very prejudiced. Those applications will come from the foreign ministry with tags on them for CLAIR.
. . . And John was furious, especially when he went back there and found
two Korean Americans applications and one for a black guy that was married to a Korean. 'If you can't place them, please tell them that they can't
come' type of thing."

The practice of *hairyō*, then, illustrates a problem endemic to cross-
cultural interaction. The checkered history of Japan's relations with nonwhites and the visible presence of subordinated groups in Japanese society lead many JET participants, including some program coordinators, to
be suspicious of the intentions of CLAIR and ministry staff. Yet Japanese
officials in the late 1980s and early 1990s steadfastly refused this interpretation. For them, it was precisely the knowledge that sentiment in
some local areas was still "backward" that necessitated their approach to
intervene, moving very cautiously to deal with each potentially volatile
situation. In the very act of working to create an ideal of a cross-cultural
learning in which race becomes irrelevant, Japanese officials felt it necessary, at least initially, to call attention to race as an issue in the placement
process.

Contradictions in English Education

While the articles discussed above generated the most vigorous responses
from CLAIR and the Ministry of Education, most newspaper and magazine
treatments of the JET Program between 1987 and 1989 examined the difficulties created by introducing native speakers into a school system dominated by government-controlled textbooks and entrance exams. Some of
these articles were quite positive in their assessment of the program, reading almost like a series of mission statements from CLAIR.[27] Also upbeat
were the dozens of features that began appearing in local newspapers
throughout Japan, introducing the new foreigners in town and profiling
their activities. Pieces in the *San Francisco Examiner* ("Foreign Teachers
Find Fame") and the *Christian Science Monitor* ("How to Make English
More Fun for Japanese High School Students") stressed the potential for
cross-cultural learning inherent in the JET Program.[28] In June 1988, Gerald LeTendre in Fukui-ken wrote a series of three feature articles for the
Daily Yomiuri that chronicled his work at Takefu Higashi High School and

suggested positive steps ALTs could take to integrate themselves into the school community and to engage their students in conversational English.[29]

Other feature stories seemed to sit on the fence. The *Japan Times* ran an article after the first year of the JET Program titled "English Teaching Project Feeling Growing Pains," which cited the one-shot school visitation system as a major disappointment of the program scheme and the reduction of gaijin phobia as a significant achievement. A more positive view was offered the following year: in "English-Teaching Program a Success After Overcoming First-Year Trouble," the practice of basing more ALTs directly in schools and improved communication with participants and host institutions were said to have lowered the percentage of participants who left prematurely, breaking their contracts.[30]

Most disturbing to CLAIR and Ministry of Education officials was the persistent regularity with which reports sharply critical of the JET Program surfaced throughout the inaugural years. The first year that Canadian participants joined the JET program, the *Toronto Globe and Mail* published an article on the frustrations of Canadian teachers in Japan: "They [JET participants] arrived in Japan last August to discover that, for the most part, their role was to replace tape recordings of English dialogue. Not only that, but many of them faced hostile attitudes on the part of local teachers who feared the outsiders would derail the process of preparing students for the 'examination hell.'"[31] The author went on to note that the Japanese government apparently finds it easier to foot the bill for the imported language teachers than to create a substantive role for them. In a similar vein, in 1988 the *San Jose Mercury News* ran a scathing front-page article on the "tough lessons" of the JET Program, claiming that it had exposed the insularity of Japanese culture. It related stories of JET women being sexually harassed, JET men being called "AIDS" as they walked down the street, JET minorities being grossly misunderstood, and Japanese teachers of English displaying fierce resentment. The pull-quote for the article cited an anonymous Japanese official: "People just aren't ready to listen to foreigners tell them what to do, to be perfectly blatant. The most unfortunate fact is that the Japanese government is spending millions of yen to create potential enemies, people who don't like each other, and that's exactly contrary to what they intended to do."[32]

Nor were the critical articles confined to overseas or to English-language newspapers. In the third year of the program, the *Daily Yomiuri* took aim at the Japanese government, particularly the Ministry of Education, in "Apathy Prevails in English Classrooms." The reporter sat in on a team-taught class of forty-eight boys at an exam-oriented school in Saitama-ken and observed students who gave only a faint reply to roll call, mumbled through the song "Puff the Magic Dragon," and struggled to give simple answers to simple questions asked by the ALT. Claiming that English education has not changed as much as JET participants expected, the author concludes that the Japanese government "should take the blame, as it introduced ALTs into Japanese middle and high school English classes without changing anything else in the English educational environment."[33]

The *Mainichi Daily News* carried an article in which Japanese teachers took issue with the high salaries and favorable working conditions of JET participants. The reporter also cited a student survey done by a Japanese teacher in which 28 percent of fifteen-year-olds called conversational skills useless on the exams.[34] A *Yomiuri Shimbun* summary of presentations at a prefectural teachers' union meeting had this to say:

> What stood out in the reports is the favorable reception of students (80 percent in one survey said they enjoyed team-taught classes). But this becomes the seed of a new worry for Japanese teachers (*atarashii nayami no tane*). . . . Whether Japanese teachers like it or not, it is their fate to have been assigned the task of making strong test takers out of all students. To do well on the exams, what is important is grammar, translation, and essay-writing skills. . . . The kind of classes the ALTs conduct is another species entirely, and among most ALTs exam English has a terrible reputation. Yet Japanese teachers feel that the students must live in an exam-governed society and at a time when the number of English classes per week is down, they can't afford to spend time on conversation.[35]

Articles about the JET Program in Japanese language papers typically picked up on this theme of the tradeoffs in emphasizing conversational English. The *Kyoto Shimbun*, for instance, ran an article titled "Is Live English Useful on Exams? Foreign Teachers Have Been Invited, But." Even more revealing was the subcaption, "Students' Reactions Are Feeble; Some Teachers Have Returned Home Early in Despair."[36] It also featured a cartoon (see figure 2) in which a stereotypical ALT (big nose, polka dot tie, blond hair), surrounded by Japanese students, is taken aback as they ask him all manner of personal questions (Are you married? Are you single? How old are you?). Meanwhile, the JTL, suddenly ignored, is shown standing behind the podium with a textbook in hand, tapping his foot angrily. As the cartoon suggests, puzzlement and anger over being asked numerous

Figure 2. Students in a classroom. Illustration by Suzuki Yasumasa.

personal questions by Japanese students and teachers were not uncommon among ALTs, yet from the Japanese point of view such questions were usually just intended to gather information that would allow them to be helpful and to place the foreigner meaningfully in the larger framework of social relationships. Questions that were seen by ALTs as "meddlesome" and as an invasion of privacy were often sincere attempts to gain a better basis for communication with the foreigner. Such efforts to size up a new member of the group are ubiquitous in Japan. The age and marital status of one's conversational partner, for instance, can be crucial determinants of the language and demeanor used during face-to-face interaction.

That media accounts of the JET Program in the early years tended to play up the negative aspects of the JET Program, to pigeonhole Japanese responses, and to sensationalize JET participants' complaints caused great consternation among Ministry of Education and CLAIR officials. Even by the fall of 1988, the secretary-general of CLAIR thought the matter important enough to raise at the midyear block seminars:

One matter which has been of concern to those of us at CLAIR is that several articles have appeared in the press about JET. Some are constructive but some are negative, and most of the negative articles seem to be based on misunderstanding or intentional distortion. For instance, *Orient*, a leading English newspaper, interviewed an Australian JET who said he had no interest in teaching and came to Japan mostly for the money. I'm sure this idea does not reflect the majority. I think we must make efforts to defend the program from unfair coverage. Please raise your voice for the protection of the program against unfair attacks.[37]

Many JET participants were already puzzled about their role in Japanese schools and communities; this plea only strengthened their suspicion that the government was trying to keep them in the dark and even played into their stereotypes of an authoritarian Japanese state. After the secretary-general finished speaking, an ALT next to me turned with an exasperated look: "I really thought he was going to ban us from talking to the media, period."

THE LIMITS OF "INTERNATIONALIZATION": HOMOSEXUALITY

One issue that caused a considerable amount of friction between CLAIR and AJET but never made it into the media was CLAIR's response to gay JET participants. I first learned of this "problem" when I attended the orientation for new participants at the Keio Plaza Inter-Continental Hotel in Tokyo in 1989. Mingling with JET participants on the first day I soon caught snippets of a rumor that was making the rounds. "We tried to start a support group and CLAIR freaked out. You can guess what it was about!" commented one ALT. "The head of AJET said CLAIR really played hardball," noted another. Finally, I was able to interview Garth, a gay JET participant, who was at the center of much of the controversy and who filled in the pieces for me:

When I first got to Japan I went up to one of the program coordinators and said, "Is there any information at all for gay JETs?" And she's like suddenly pulling me aside, "Oh, you better come over here, let's not talk about this in the open." And she said there was nothing. No possibility of any formal support network. After about four months of struggling along on my own, even though I was in a very good prefecture, I finally met another gay JET at the midyear conference. I finally had someone to talk to about issues that were important to gay JETs— you know, when you come into a society with very different concepts of sexuality and body language, it can be very disorienting. And there's always the questions, "Who do I tell? How much do I tell?" Keeping it a secret is a very difficult thing, a very stressful thing.

Finally I talked to the chair of AJET and told him I wanted to form a gay support group. Well, we started, we had some meetings, and then the people in AJET wanted me to write an article for the Tokyo orientation issue of the AJET newsletter to (a) let gay JETs know that support was available, (b) tell them that things are different in Japan—you can't use the same assumptions as in your own country, and (c) tell them to be discreet—don't come out! At the time that was my basic message. You have no idea what's going to happen—don't come out!

Well, for some reason, CLAIR saw a copy of that before it came out and basically threw a litter. The situation was made more difficult because the vice-chair of AJET at the time was gay. CLAIR was doing all sorts of things. They were threatening to close down AJET, they were threatening to stop the newsletter altogether, they said the future of the JET Program would be in jeopardy. And ultimately what happened is that they printed the page blank in the newsletter because it was too late to pull it out altogether. Even so, AJET let all prefectural representatives know that they could have the page sent to them if they wanted. And we went around to all the prefectural meetings at the orientation, basically to say "I'm here, there'll be a meeting at a certain time, support is available—if you're gay, don't freak out." We did that anyway.

When I asked CLAIR and Ministry of Education officials about this incident, the responses were virtually identical. All stressed that homosexuality was still highly stigmatized in Japan, particularly for those in public office. One CLAIR official ventured: "Because JET participants are government employees, we have to hold them to very high standards. There's no way we can tolerate a public discussion of homosexuality in connection with the JET Program. Anyway, the JET participants themselves are very much divided on this issue. There are lots of JETs who don't feel comfortable with the idea of homosexuality." So fearful were Japanese officials that the possibility of requiring AIDS testing of all JET participants was seriously discussed (but rejected) at a meeting between program coordinators and Ministry of Foreign Affairs officials during the first year of the program.

Although AJET gave in to CLAIR's demand over including information on the gay support group in their monthly magazine, the issue of how CLAIR should respond to gay JET participants did not disappear. And in one of the JET Program's great ironies, Japanese officials at CLAIR actually hired Garth to be a program coordinator two years later, unaware that he was gay. The offer of employment came shortly after the Japanese management at CLAIR had done away with the practice of allowing program coordinators to choose their own successors. Because they had consolidated the decision-making apparatus entirely in their own hands, they had to rely primarily on reports from prefectural officials and a short interview.

Garth himself realized that he would most likely not have been hired had input from current program coordinators been sought: "The program coordinators that preceded me, with one exception, were against hiring me because they all knew I was the 'gay troublemaker.'" Even a subsequent secretary-general of CLAIR admitted that hiring Garth came to be viewed as a mistake: "Eventually everyone found out that Garth was gay, but if they had known for sure at the time, they never would've hired him."

In any event, Garth took up his assignment at CLAIR only to find it full of personal difficulties:

> My first promotional trip abroad happened to be with the secretary-general of CLAIR and I remember we were in the Midwest—I think it was in Kansas City—and we were having breakfast, and one of the articles in the paper was on Governor Wilson in California vetoing a gay rights law. The secretary-general suddenly turned to me and said, "Is there any way we can screen out gay participants from the program?" I was completely taken aback and managed to say, "I think it's more trouble than it's worth. It'll open a can of worms that we don't want to deal with." But it was galling to be put in this position by someone who could make my life really difficult. Later when things came to a head, we started talking about issues gay people face and he said, "These people are choosing their lifestyle. We don't have to give them any support whatsoever," and I'm like "Excuse me, why would you choose a lifestyle that involves alienation?" So I went out and got all the information about how this is hereditary and he said, "Hmm, I'll have to think about this," and he went to his son who was a psychiatrist who corroborated everything I'd said.

Things "came to a head" because of the increasing dissatisfaction on the part of gay JET participants with having to stay completely closeted, even at conferences. In the question box at one renewers' conference, for instance, a gay participant had scribbled, "Why is CLAIR ignoring the gays?" Garth recalls: "My job was to collect all the questions and write official answers. Well, that meeting with the Japanese staff went on for about three hours. There was one program coordinator who was getting very vocal and emotional about human rights issues, but the Japanese staff basically responded, 'What gay issue?' For the secretary-general it was the first time he'd heard about it, institutional memory being what it is. The official response we settled on was 'CLAIR is open to discussion on this.'"

Unable to press their concerns for fear of being outed, eventually the support group settled on a name that would tell other gays and lesbians people exactly what they were about but that, according to Garth, "was sufficiently vague to keep the Japanese off the secret." For his part, Garth became involved in numerous other JET Program projects, some of which were quite successful; he nevertheless left CLAIR feeling quite bitter at what he termed "the rampant whitewashing and blatant disregard for truth endemic to Japanese bureaucracy."

DRUNK DRIVING, DRUGS, AND SUICIDES

The first wave of JET participants represented nearly a 400 percent increase over the MEF and BET programs. This dramatic escalation in numbers only magnified the cultural gulf between JET participants and their hosts and encouraged numerous misunderstandings and incidents that required national-level intervention. Indeed, during the first year of the program, CLAIR alone counseled 164 JET participants encountering various difficulties in adjusting to their life in Japan. In the overwhelming majority of these cases, the JET participants approached one of the program coordinators directly. CLAIR officials broke the problems down into four categories: relationship with host institution, including disputes over housing, vacation time, and other work regulations (64 cases); daily life in Japan, including taxes, privacy, and medical care (43 cases); secondary employment and returning early to the participant's home country (33 cases); and other causes, such as sexual harassment (24 cases).[38] Since local officials were often at the center of these complaints, typical cases are described in depth in chapter 4.

In the third year of the program, however, events unfolded that would shake the foundations of the program and highlight cultural contrasts in approaches to morality and counseling. In the fall of 1989, JET participants were involved in two well-publicized incidents of drunk driving. First, in early October a JET's accident led to serious property damage, embarrassment, and ultimately his resignation from the program. Complicating the situation was this JET participant's extreme popularity in the small town in which he was working; indeed, town officials lobbied for him to stay. But to drink and drive is a serious moral transgression in Japan, especially for teachers: CLAIR made the difficult decision that for the sake of the program as a whole and to atone for his poor judgment, he should be terminated from the program.

In December, a much more serious accident occurred. While driving under the influence, a male JET ran a red light and was hit by a 4-ton truck. He was not alone—a Japanese friend was in the car. It took about a half hour to extract them: both unconscious, they were rushed by ambulance to the hospital. The JET arrived at the hospital in very serious condition with chest injuries and cerebral hemorrhaging. After surgery and several months' rehabilitation, he recovered. His Japanese friend, although initially not expected to live, came out of a coma after about a week and began her slow recovery.

These incidents brought JET participants under the authority of a law enforcement system that treats alcohol-related offenses much more strictly than do most of their home countries. Because the JET participant was drunk, Japanese insurance did not cover the accident: he was ordered to work in Japan until he repaid the debt in full. The *CLAIR Newsletter* published a strongly worded cautionary note after the incident:

> We cannot emphasize enough the far-reaching effects of such actions.
> . . . Insurance will not cover alcohol-related accidents, and there is the
> probability that criminal charges and fines will be brought against you.
> And, according to Japanese law, friends that drink with you prior to an
> alcohol-related incident may be held responsible as well.
>
> Please remember: in Japan, the moral standards for teachers are
> strict. Teachers are held in especially high regard. This extends to ALTs
> as well. . . . Don't abuse that respect. What you do has the potential to
> affect not only your reputation, but may also damage the respectability
> of future JETs in your area.[39]

Unfortunately, drunk driving was not the only serious problem confronting CLAIR officials. Many of the JET participants travel to other Asian countries during their summer or winter break, and the temptation to bring back illegal substances into Japan can be great. When two JET participants were arrested in the mid-1990s for possession of minute amounts of marijuana, the incident proved traumatic for all parties concerned. The host schools and students were shocked, and the prefectural board of education called an emergency meeting of all JET participants. As the arrest was widely reported in both English and Japanese media, nationally and locally, it caused extreme embarrassment to the governor, who had supported the JET Program's growth.

After the incident had run its course, CLAIR persuaded one of the convicted participants to write an open letter to all future JET participants warning them of the consequences of using drugs in Japan. This is now published in the general information handbook provided to all JET participants each year:

> It's not just I who was affected by all of this. My neighbors had their
> flowers trampled as the camera crews came to peep through the windows of my mansion [i.e., Japanese apartment]. My fiancee's mother
> (68 years old) had to pedal her bicycle about four miles to the police
> station to be interrogated. People I've worked with or knew, including
> [program participants], were subject to the same treatment or worse.

The hardest thing about this all is that there is no way to be forgiven, to repay the respect and kindness I once received. . . .

From arrest to indictment took in my case 22 days. During this period you stay at a police station. When not in your cell you are handcuffed and led around the station like a dog on a rope. I was questioned an average of nine hours a day (one hour for lunch in my cell) for the first 17 days . . . I spent my first five days in custody in a six-mat room with a glass-enclosed toilet, no way to wash your hands or get a drink. I shared it with a *yakuza* [gang] member and an old man fresh from a garbage can with some skin disease. Constantly scratching, we slept six inches apart. Eventually, I was put in isolation. And all the time, 24-hour daylight conditions with guards moving in the shadows. . . .

Besides the emotional suffering and breakdown (imagine seeing your fiancee's eyes when you are handcuffed to a chair, thinking you'll never be able to marry her let alone see her again—and she knows nothing about dope!!), the financial loss for me is mind-boggling.[40]

The writer then itemizes the roughly $21,000 in expenses he incurred. In the interest of deterrence, the handbook does exaggerate the potential fallout from such an infraction ("It is quite fortunate for everyone that the Diet—the Japanese national assembly—was preoccupied with other, more pressing issues at the time"), but this section on illegal substances is by far the most toughly worded part of the orientation manual.

Perhaps most traumatic were the three suicides that occurred within eighteen months of each other. On 9 September 1989, at 12:43 in the afternoon, a Canadian woman, Sherill Anderson, was struck by an express Odakyu train passing through Tamagawa Gakuenmae station: according to the driver and two other eyewitnesses, she jumped. Local newspapers drew on the negative publicity that had surrounded the first two years of the JET Program as they began speculating that she was unhappy with her situation in Kanagawa Prefecture. But an investigation revealed no problems relating to her living and working conditions. It appeared that she had arrived in Kanagawa a month earlier with unrelated personal issues. In an open letter sent to all JET participants, the secretary-general gave a brief factual account of the suicide and then noted: "Although the reason may never be made clear, rumors have a tendency to develop when clearcut answers cannot be given. Therefore, without making assumptions as to the root cause of the incident, it is CLAIR's opinion, contrary to some newspaper reports, that her working and living conditions were both of a very satisfactory standard. In addition, she did not, to our knowledge, discuss her intentions with anyone connected with the Program." The greatest fallout from this incident came from irate and thoroughly embarrassed Kanagawa prefectural officials who held CLAIR and Ministry of Foreign Affairs officials responsible for the inadequate screening of applicants.

Less than four months later a second suicide occurred—this time an American in her second year in the program. An immensely likable, engaging woman, Jamin had been placed in Kyoto Prefecture's premier "international school." Her outgoing personality made her extremely popular among the students, and she was one of the favorites of prefectural administrators as well. Yet on a rainy New Year's Eve in Nara, Jamin, too, stepped in front of an express train and ended her life. Immediately following her death, the press descended on the prefectural board of education and the speculation began. Had her base school been remiss in failing to notice the warning signs? Should the prefecture have made certain that she had plans during the holidays instead of leaving her alone? Since her parents were in the process of getting a divorce, were there personal factors involved? In Japan, one who commits suicide traditionally leaves a note that includes a statement of self-accusation and an apology for causing trouble; here, the lack of any note made her actions even harder for the Japanese to understand. The *Kyoto Shimbun* ran an article with an apt title: "A Sudden Death: She Loved Her Work and Her Students . . . Why?"[41]

In the end, no clear-cut motives emerged, but there is no question that this second suicide in four months came as a tremendous shock to CLAIR officials. Two representatives were immediately dispatched to Kyoto to assess the situation. This time, before Japanese officials at CLAIR sent out a letter notifying JET participants, they asked the program coordinators to rewrite the first draft because it sounded too cold.

The third suicide came on 28 February 1991 when Lisa Isobe, a Hawaiian-born JET participant, jumped in front of a train in Kyoto. Lisa spoke Japanese quite well, as she had been an ALT for two years before switching to become a CIR in her third year. She was well-liked and seemed on the verge of a promising career, having been accepted at Harvard. As with Jamin's death, it proved difficult to make sense of a motive; Lisa too left no note.

THE PROFESSIONAL COUNSELING DEBATE

The back-to-back-to-back suicides highlighted a long-standing demand by the program coordinators and embassy representatives for a carefully thought-out system of crisis management. Arguing that the Japanese approach was reactive rather than proactive, they pointed to the complete absence of any kind of professional counseling services for JET participants.

To be sure, on paper the counseling system looked impressive; a "Special Committee on Counseling and Training" included representatives from the three sponsoring ministries and the embassies of the participants' home countries. But the name was misleading: the committee's main function was to report program developments to representatives from the foreign embassies and get their feedback. Minutes of its meetings reveal that they tended to be quite formal, with few questions and little discussion of the details of particular cases.

As the JET liaisons in the respective embassies began to be contacted directly by JET participants with various concerns, embassy officials began to press CLAIR for a more responsive system. Indeed, the program coordinators and one American embassy liaison conspired to raise this question at meetings of the committee on counseling and training. Caroline told me:

> The American embassy representative especially, every meeting, really brought up the fact that there should be a psychologist connected to the program. I'd say he brought it up at four different meetings. Actually, he was really good because we could feed him information, because the Japanese of course took the embassies' requests very seriously, as opposed to ours [laughter]. We learned that lesson very quickly. Anyway, [the JET liaison in the American embassy], because he was an American, I was an American, he let us feed him information and if he agreed, he'd bring it up at the meeting. And as a result of that the secretary-general actually agreed to have somebody on call if there was a serious problem. We had someone to call when we felt like it was over our heads and also to give program coordinators training, serious counseling training.

In addition to hiring a professional counselor, CLAIR also instructed prefectures to set up a counseling system for JET participants. Ironically, though, it was not initially stipulated that these "advisors" had to be fluent English speakers, and some prefectural offices of education chose older Japanese educators who had had some overseas experience but were certainly not prepared to be the confidants of foreign youth.

Still, a rudimentary system of crisis management was not implemented until nearly three years after the program had begun, and only after a number of unfortunate incidents. Such slowness to perceive a need for this service and then to provide it may seem surprising, but the ministry officials tended to believe that JET participants' need for serious counseling lay in personal dysfunction or family problems. One Ministry of Education official put it this way: "We can't mix up personality and culture. Traffic accidents and suicide are personal acts and shouldn't be confused with culture. If it was because of the system (*ukeire seido*), that would be a serious matter."

This response is rooted in cultural definitions of morality—more specifically, in the ways in which Japanese are socialized to see subjugating individual desires in the service of one's social relationships as virtuous behavior. Indeed, the Japanese tend to view the very nature of the self as bound up in relations with others.[42] The implications of this view of personhood for counseling are profound. Rather than helping people change their circumstances, counseling in Japan more often involves helping them improve their capacity for *gaman*, for putting up with the situation and making the best of it. Takie Sugiyama Lebra calls one form of therapy in Japan, *naikan* (literally, "inner observation"), "conformance through reformation." Through a process of intense, guided self-reflection, "resentment and self-pity are expected to be replaced by the realization of one's egocentric social insensitivity, an insurmountable sense of debt and gratitude to others, and a deep empathetic guilt toward those who have suffered because of one's heartless, ungrateful conduct."[43] Instead of discovering one's burning desires and passions, and formulating a plan to achieve them, its goal is to better appreciate one's interconnectedness with and dependency on others.

Given this cultural logic, it is easy to see why Japanese officials would be skeptical of Western-style counseling that might only fuel JET participants' demands for change. Privately, CLAIR and Ministry of Education officials were quite unsympathetic to those participants who exhibited an irresistible urge to reconcile the ideal and the real and a tendency to view Japanese culture as in need of "development." Japanese bureaucracies generally define virtuous behavior as conformity to the demands of social roles. In addition, a premium is placed on knowing one's "proper station," to use Ruth Benedict's term—and according to the rules of hierarchy in Japanese organizations, the JET participants ought to take their places as willing learners at the bottom of the totem pole. Wada Minoru was characteristically blunt on this point: "When Japanese go to another country," he asserted, "we try to adjust to the expectations there, but ALTs don't do that. They're always criticizing Japan and acting according to their own commonsense rules." He continued:

ALTs are much too sensitive (*binkan sugiru*) and they interpret things we do innocently or out of kindness in a negative light. Their responses are countereducational (*hikyōikuteki*). Many ALTs complain that Japan is a closed society but I don't think ALTs are very open-minded either. I think they are too demanding. I can understand that to a point, because they don't understand Japanese culture, but if they react too strongly, then Japanese react negatively. One local administrator told me her prefecture is thinking of stopping the yearly increase in ALTs because if the numbers get too high, the demands are too great.

Wada's use of the term *hikyōikuteki* (countereducational) is especially revealing, as it points to competing visions of the educational enterprise. By exercising their critical judgment and attempting to stamp out inequities, JET participants were enacting in various ways an individualism that demands action. But the forcefulness with which some JET participants asserted "unfairness" during the early years of the program, together with their tendency to leapfrog the normal chain of command (*atamagoshi*) by taking their complaints directly to the top, was viewed with suspicion in a culture that values avoiding conflict in interpersonal relations and refraining from action that might embarrass one's immediate superior. One CLAIR official, the section chief of counseling, surprised me with his answer to a question about what he had learned about foreigners in his two years with the JET Program. After discoursing at length about the self-expression of JET participants as opposed to the modesty of Japanese, he suddenly added, "And one other thing is that ALTs tell lies without having a second thought (*uso wa heiki de iu*). Japanese don't tell lies like that. Whenever a call comes into the counseling section of CLAIR from an ALT, the first thing you should know is that we never believe his story outright. We always contact his superior to find out the real circumstances." In light of Lebra's claim that one of the highest moral values in Japan is "trustworthiness" (*shinyō*), this is a very serious charge indeed, though it must be qualified. First, his view was undoubtedly skewed by his position: he dealt primarily with the problems of a minority of ALTs. Second, program coordinators were also unlikely to accept at face value the facts as presented by a JET participant seeking counseling. Such cases inevitably took CLAIR staff into that nebulous arena between fact and fiction, and the most effective counselors were those who adopted a *Rashomon*-like technique of employing multiple perspectives to approach the "truth." Finally, the section chief's comparison may strike Westerners as particularly odd because in Japanese society it is common to perpetuate half-truths both to maintain the *tatemae*, or official, version of events and to preserve harmony and save face. But perhaps he was referring not to lying per se but to a deeper virtue—reliability or dependability; his criticism seems to have been directed at ALTs who would distort reality to enhance their own position rather than that of their superior.

Complicating the privately held view that JET participants were overly judgmental, however, was what Japanese officials referred to quite self-critically and self-consciously as their "gaijin complex"—the strong cultural tendency to view Westerners with a mixture of awe and fear, and to give in to foreign pressure. Added to this was the tremendous constraint felt by national-level officials to make internationalization work, which to some extent meant ensuring that JET participants were happy and gained a favorable impression of Japan. The result was a constant mental struggle over where to draw the line on counseling cases and how to say "no" as delicately as possible. Consider, for instance, the predicament of one Ministry of Education official: "One time a British woman of German descent called me directly from her educational office and demanded to know why the women had to serve tea to men. I listened politely, but then she asked me to tell them to stop. So I told her I would call her superiors, and I called them all right, but rather than asking them to stop, I simply told them that she had called me. I don't think ALTs have the right to make such barbaric demands (*yaban no kōi wo iu kenri wa nai to omoimasu*)."

By contrast, the program coordinators tended to see the Japanese attempt to construe the suicides as entirely personal acts as representing an enormous "empathy gulf." Meredith was outspoken in this assessment: "They [CLAIR officials] put almost everything into to the category of 'personal issues.' They'll do anything to avoid responsibility." Other concerned outsiders tended to agree. William Horsley, a BBC correspondent and the token foreign member of the Advisory Council for the JET Program, criticized the impersonal approach to program implementation: "As a member of the advisory panel to CLAIR I have been rather taken aback at the coldness and solemnity of the deliberations. The JET scheme should be a voyage of discovery, not some kind of laboratory experiment. Reading through the official papers about the scheme, including detailed figures on the academic backgrounds of the participants, and their various problems in settling down to Japan, I look in vain for the 'human touch,' or the sense of adventure."[44] Even Caroline Yang, executive director of the Fulbright Commission during the early years of the program, expressed her puzzlement over the lack of a viable support network and crisis management system, speculating that "the suicides might not have occurred if they hadn't been in Japan."[45] Philip recalled his own frustration in negotiating the issue:

> I had a very heated discussion at one point with one of the upper administrators in CLAIR about their concern for the participants' health, particularly mental health. It came, I think, after the third suicide, because it so happened that that person had been in touch with CLAIR for some type of counseling some months prior to the suicide. Of course, when I say "counseling" it's not the type of psychological counseling that's expected in the U.S., but that person had contacted the program coordinators with some problems. But they were not the kind of problems that had any real relevance to what finally happened. In fact, it had nothing to do with the program.

But the first and second suicides, they were people who had never been in touch with CLAIR whatsoever. So my impression is that it was much easier for CLAIR to sort of say that we were absolutely not involved with it. But it was after the third person died that CLAIR actually arranged some sort of professional counselor and provided some counseling training to the program coordinators. So my thought was that the motivation to finally do something was that CLAIR couldn't say their hands were absolutely clean. . . . That was an incident I felt sort of exemplified that CLAIR was a bureaucracy that was very adept in planning things and preparing papers but not at all experienced in taking care of peoples' lives.

And that became a recurring topic, you know. They're taking a risk coming here and joining this program, and I think you have to consider more seriously that what you're inviting them to do is affecting their lives; it's not only providing a service for Japan. And that's a very difficult, probably impossible, thing for most bureaucrats to understand.

One final point of contention between the program coordinators and the Japanese staff at CLAIR pertained to privacy. Typically, a call would be received from a JET participant involving a private matter: sexual harassment, emotional instability, a threatened suicide, or a medical problem of a personal nature. After hearing the report from the program coordinator, the Japanese staff member would instinctively reach for the phone to call the host institution. Since such problems usually meant missed work, the Japanese staff felt that local officials ought to be fully appraised of the situation. Yet if the JET participant had wanted officials at the host institution to know about the problem, he or she would have told them first. As a result, before the call would go out, a debate would ensue about whom to call, what details could and could not be told, and what solution to insist on. The program coordinators were usually uncomfortable with the amount of private information that was leaked to local officials, and feelings of mistrust on both sides increased.

QUALITY CONTROL: ELIMINATING THE BAD APPLES

While CLAIR officials were moving cautiously toward providing in-house professional counseling, they were moving aggressively to address what they felt to be a more fundamental problem: poor screening at the selection stage. CLAIR officials perceived a conflict between quality and quantity: how could they achieve a high-profile program, which depended on raising the numbers quickly, and yet still get quality people? One CLAIR official reflected, "When we started the JET Program we hoped only good ALTs and CIRs would come. Now we realize there are good and bad foreigners." Much of the energy of Japanese officials during the first few years of the program was invested in various approaches to screen out the bad apples. For instance, applicants were required to provide graduation certificates as well as transcripts of all college courses. They were asked if they had ever been convicted of any crime other than a minor traffic offense; if so, they were asked to sign a form authorizing the release to the embassy of Japan of any documents or records pertaining to the offense. Finally, applicants were required to fill out a self-assessment medical form that asked about personal history of hospitalization, psychological or psychiatric treatment, prescription medication, and dietary restrictions.

In the wake of the first suicide and increased pressure from local governments to send "healthy" JET participants, another idea discussed was the psychological testing of all JET participants. Philip recalled:

> After there had been a suicide, they were trying to think of a way to incorporate some sort of psychological testing into the interviews. At which point the program coordinators said, "Who's going to administer these test questions?" I mean, right now you have the consulate people doing the selection, and most of them don't know anything about teaching English in Japan. Now you're going to have them pretend to be physicians? Besides, there's the practical problem of asking people who have no psychological background or training to evaluate people's psychological stability. We said, "That's not fair." Because you have people who may have all kinds of problems in their home country, but once they get away from the society that made them uncomfortable, they'll have no problem whatsoever. And the exact opposite is also very possible. It's ridiculous. But there was this feeling that because of this incident, something had to be done to reassure prefectures.

Though the idea of psychological testing was rejected, CLAIR officials decided to increase their efforts to get the Ministry of Foreign Affairs to improve the selection process and lower the percentage of those selected. They began by inviting representatives of selection committees from the United States, Canada, Great Britain, and Australia on a two-week study tour of Japanese schools to familiarize them with the actual working conditions of ALTs and CIRs. They also asked the ministry to circulate among selection committee members a list of problem cases that had developed. In addition, directly as a result of the serious incidents that occurred in 1989 and 1990, a cautionary statement appeared in 1991 at the top of the rating sheet given to members of the screening committees at Japanese consulates abroad: "If the applicant appears to be overly sensitive/emotionally fragile, not sociable, cheerful or polite, or does not appear to like children, DO NOT RECOMMEND their acceptance to the program." CLAIR officials traveled overseas in pairs (one *yakuin* and one program coordinator) to talk with consulate officials and to give presentations on the JET Program at colleges and universities abroad.

These actions were taken because CLAIR officials felt strongly that the Ministry of Foreign Affairs (i.e., the Japanese consulates abroad) needed to portray JET participants' jobs more realistically. Indeed, the ministry was in a difficult position: it had to promote a positive image of the program abroad in the face of criticism from the foreign media. Realizing that most potential applicants were not primarily interested in English instruction, ministry officials tended to downplay the teaching component of JET, instead presenting the program as a chance for foreigners to experience Japanese language and culture. Predictably, the result was confusion; during the first few years of the program a handful of ALTs reported that they didn't realize they would be involved in team teaching until they arrived in Tokyo for their orientation.

Tightening Visa Regulations

At the same time that CLAIR officials were discussing with the Ministry of Foreign Affairs how to improve selection procedures, they were also talking with Justice Ministry officials about how to tighten the visa regulations. Japanese officials saw two problems in this area. First, a small minority of JET participants whose hearts were not in public school teaching were resigning from the JET Program in favor of other employment in Japan. Private English conversation schools, for instance, offer roughly the same salaries for only four hours of work per night; though some of these are fly-by-night operations, in some cases JET participants were willing to take their chances. A few even won jobs in Japanese corporations or at English-language newspapers and left the JET Program early in order to take up their new posts in April, according to Japanese custom. While CLAIR had little standing to protest if the JET participant had a Japanese sponsor, officials did ask the Justice Ministry to intervene in such cases. In addition, CLAIR added a stipulation that return airfare would be withheld if it was discovered that a JET participant signed another contract for employment in Japan while in the program.

Second, an increasing number of JET participants were staying on to work in Japan after their term of service was up. This problem was of growing concern to the Justice Ministry, the agency concerned with regulating the flow of personnel across Japan's borders. One secretary-general of CLAIR explained:

> The Justice Ministry doesn't welcome the idea of ALTs changing jobs and staying on in Japan, and makes it difficult for them to do so. It's all right if they stay on to study, but JET is a simplified screening process, so if they use this as a route to get working visas, that's not good. I agree with this, and have personally instructed the Justice Ministry to make it difficult for ALTs to secure working visas. It's true, there's a sense in which this constitutes poor treatment of ALTs (*ijiwaru to iu men mo arimasu*), but as a principle I think it's preferable if ALTs return home when they finish here.

In addition, to discourage JET participants from using the program as a stepping-stone to get working visas the grace period for leaving Japan on completion of the program was changed from ninety days to thirty days.

This determination that JET participants should quickly return home is curious, particularly in light of the demands to open up Japanese society that gave rise to the program. One could argue that the desire of a high percentage of JET participants to stay on and work in Japan is a striking indicator of the success of the program, and should be encouraged. Yet the Japanese caution is fully consistent with studies that have shown a preoccupation with protecting a pure and homogenous society from foreign pollution. Jackson Bailey's characterization of the underlying mind-set seems apt here:

> The thrust and structure of Japanese rules and regulations regarding the entry into Japan of people or things whether they are part of commercial or of cultural exchange demand that proof be offered that the person or item should be allowed to enter. The implicit assumption is that persons or things should not be allowed in until there is clear and explicit evidence that they should be. This assumption underlies all transactions whether they involve a small matter such as a video cassette of a television program from the United States, a set of photo negatives for a cultural exchange poster, or the appointment of a foreign professor to a regular faculty position in a university. In each and all of these cases the implicit parameters of the situation *assume* that the answer is "no" until incontrovertible proof is supplied, normally in writing, that the item or person is eligible to come in.[46]

According to this logic, although the entry of JET participants into Japan had already been negotiated, a continued stay must be renegotiated from scratch. It is worth noting, however, that with the help of a legitimate Japanese sponsor, JET participants do not find it too difficult to subvert the general principle and keep working in Japan. In fact, there are numerous JET alumni currently living and working throughout Japan, and neither tightening the visa process nor imposing a three-year limit (discussed below) was enough to thwart their determined efforts to stay on.

Cautions to Renewers and the Three-Year Limit

Realizing that several serious incidents involved renewers who presumably had become complacent and whose reasons for staying were not job-related, in 1989 CLAIR sent out a list of the pros and cons of renewing to discourage ALTs and CIRs from extending their contracts for the "wrong" reasons.[47] CLAIR also encouraged local governments to exercise their option of rejecting applications for renewal from "problem JETs." To that end, the wording on application forms was strengthened: "Contracts are for one year[,] . . . renewable in certain circumstances by mutual consent between the host institution and the JET participant." In reality, prefectures are loathe to refuse a request for renewal. One prefectural official confessed to me, "This year there was one person we didn't want to renew, but because CLAIR didn't give us the forty we had requested (only thirty-three) we had to renew him. If they gave us all we wanted, there would have been room to refuse renewers." The cultural aversion to face-to-face confrontation was also a factor. Their fears were not unfounded. Chiba Prefecture refused to allow an American woman to renew, pointing out that she did not have good relations with her schools and that she had been ill for some months without a clear diagnosis; she became incensed, contacting CLAIR as well as the American embassy to demand their intervention. When they did not act, she contacted lawyers to see about legal recourse. Ultimately, she left the program, but the possibility of this kind of reaction makes local governments reluctant to take a tough stance.

Because renewals are so common, an incoming prefectural teacher's consultant, with limited English skills and little knowledge of the JET Program, may find him- or herself dealing with JET participants who have three or more years of experience working in the program. These veterans both know internal precedents and, as a result of visiting a number of schools in the prefecture, they are often more in touch with teachers and school-level realities than the teacher's consultant is. Though most long-term ALTs and CIRs are dedicated to their jobs, others manage to minimize their exertions while cultivating other interests or even augmenting their already-generous income by offering lucrative classes in private conversation on the side. In other words, they have learned how to milk the system to great advantage.

To remedy this problem, a handful of local government officials approached CLAIR and asked for a new national policy stipulating that JET participants renew no more than two times. This would make it easier for local officials, who jokingly referred to themselves as "the Japanese who can't say 'no,'" to get rid of problematic ALTs and CIRs: they could say that the three-year limit was set by higher authorities and therefore out of their hands. For a while, CLAIR wavered on this issue and even conducted a survey of local governments, which showed mixed sentiments. But the suicides and serious accidents led to a reconsideration; beginning in 1991–92, those serving in or beyond their third year were not allowed to renew.[48] Not coincidentally, this policy was vigorously supported by Ministry of Foreign Affairs officials. They thought the renewal rate, which had averaged 44 percent for the first four years of the program, was too high for a cultural exchange program and limited the number of new participants.[49]

Indeed, the official explanation for the three-year limit was that since JET is a youth program, it is important to let as many youth as possible participate. This did not satisfy long-term JET wanna-bes, and voices were raised in protest, as this excerpt from the minutes of the first evaluation meeting for the 1989–90 JET Program reveals:

> Putting limitations on the application criteria is acceptable, but once a JET has been on the Program demonstrating his/her ability, how can the host institution disregard the efforts made and say, "Go back to your home country?" Could it be that Japan doesn't want foreigners to stay so long that they learn/understand too much? Gaining too much insight into the system represents a threat? For JETs who have done their best and contributed a lot, it is a slap in the face to suddenly be told that they are no longer wanted. Very distressing. It is a very arbitrary decision reflecting very badly on CLAIR.[50]

To be sure, some incompetent JET participants have stayed on primarily to collect their salaries, and CLAIR's wish to deter them is quite understandable. CLAIR officials even noted that should a JET participant really become indispensable to a host institution, local authorities could hire that person directly for the fourth year and beyond. There is no question, however, that by setting the three-year limit, Japanese officials were explicitly acknowledging that the ALT and CIR slots would forever be positions for temporary outsiders.

WHEN TRUST BREAKS DOWN: BETWEEN PROGRAM
COORDINATORS AND CLAIR OFFICIALS

The first few years of the program suggest that a bureaucracy known the world over for its organizational efficiency had suddenly run aground. Many participants themselves, disillusioned by the gap between rhetoric and reality, adopted conspiracy theories. In addition, ministry infighting proved to be as strong as ever. The Ministries of Foreign Affairs and Home Affairs berated Education and the conservative public school system for sapping the enthusiasm of the JET participants. The Ministry of Education responded that Home Affairs officials were interested only in "symbolic internationalization." Both the Ministries of Education and Home Affairs criticized Foreign Affairs for lack of rigor in the selection process and for putting Japan's diplomatic priorities above internal needs. In retrospect, we can see that in addressing one set of concerns at the national level—the trade crisis and Japan's image in the world—JET created a whole host of new problems, which continued to snowball.

In the face of this administrative confusion, the striking contrast between the informal evaluations offered by the program coordinators and those offered by Japanese ministry officials is particularly significant. On the whole, the program coordinators in CLAIR were severe in their assessments of the Japanese policy response during the early years of the program. Philip described the first year as a "disaster" but pointed to steady, if incremental, improvement after that. Tellingly, though, he attributed successes largely to the efforts of the program coordinators in overcoming the barriers erected by the Japanese ministries:

> The program coordinators were certainly closer to the JET participants and most of us felt that the bureaucracy made it very difficult to provide the kind of care and support the JET participants deserved. But I don't think the lack of personal touch on the Japanese side really undermined the program because we had a lot of dedicated program coordinators. And of course the result was that the program coordinators were very stressed out most of the time. We received no overtime compensation and yet we had emergency phone calls at all times of the night and on the weekends. But we felt it was our job, so we did it. It was a very awkward position to be part of the Japanese administration

and at the same time having to represent the interests of the foreign participants on the program.

Meredith had much harsher words for the CLAIR staff:

> As program coordinators, our primary job is to push. Most of the time I'm sure we're looked at as difficult. As international as they say CLAIR is, they're treating the program as an internal Japanese group would. People should walk in here and feel it's different. To be perfectly honest, they're clueless. This is an office of mediocrity. They allow themselves to be mediocre, to cut corners, to be less than honest, to out-and-out deceive. When you have integrity become a nonentity in international affairs, it's scary. The staff here are good people, but they're not willing to push and the few that are get shoved out.

Perhaps the most frustrated of all was Caroline, whose volatile outbursts at Japanese staff and tendency to bang her computer when frustrated fueled gossip even among JET participants. It was widely rumored that the CLAIR staff eventually stopped listening to her opinions and finally asked her to re- sign. In any event, she found another job and left in despair. "The reason I quit," she confessed to me, "was because basically nobody at CLAIR cares."

"Uncaring," "clueless," and "prone to deception": the reasons for these strong negative appraisals are worth exploring in some detail because they reveal a set of evaluative criteria sharply diverging from those used by the Japanese hosts. First, the program coordinators tended to judge the success of the program, and of CLAIR in particular, both by its transformative out- comes and by the decisiveness with which Japanese officials anticipated, confronted, and resolved problems. Their basic assumptions were that Jap- anese culture was in need of "development"; that the desired changes en- tailed moving toward a Western model, variously defined; and that the JET Program was the vehicle by which theory and practice were to be joined. By these standards, the responses of Japanese ministry officials simply did not measure up. They did not anticipate problems well, they reacted too slowly when problems did arise, and they seemed to lack the gumption to tackle the really tough issues. It wasn't long before the phrase "it's glacial," referring to the cautious reaction that seemed inevitable when any specific change was proposed, had entered the vocabulary of program coordinators as a running joke.

In short, the program coordinators felt that Japanese officials were not treating CLAIR as different from any of the other hundreds of bureau- cratic offices in Tokyo, arguing that several policies at CLAIR illustrated an attitude of business-as-usual instead of a commitment to substantive change. They lent credence to William Horsley's caution that "Japanese officials who run the scheme should guard against the power of their country's culture to transform outside influences into another version of Japan's own value system."[51]

Personnel Procedures

The program coordinators' first complaint, concerning personnel policies, cut three ways. First, the program coordinators saw the high turnover rate among secretaries-general as evidence of a lack of concern for continuity in program policy. Meredith noted: "The Japanese staff is transient. We worked so hard to get the embassy liaison meetings to involve some real give-and-take and then [the new secretary-general] came in and went right back to the formal style of meetings." "Institutional memory" tended to be fairly poor and worked to the disadvantage of long-term change, according to Philip. Caroline agreed: "CLAIR has been through four directors in just over two years, and if you know anything about Japanese organizations, that says a lot."

It is certainly true that at times the brief tenures of CLAIR's directors have suggested a game of musical chairs, but the meaning of this rotation may not be obvious. It is widely known that *jinji idō* (personnel rotation) is a common practice among the ministries to offset the powerful tendency toward sectionalism. But critics are less likely to note that in the Ministry of Home Affairs such rotation is particularly common, because of its close relations with local governments. In fact, CLAIR and ministry officials see nothing significant in the frequency of shifts. "There's nothing special about CLAIR. We're always shifting personnel on the spot to make room for people coming and going to local governments," said one ministry official.

Second, program coordinators were deeply skeptical of the criteria used by the Ministry of Home Affairs in choosing the secretary-general. If the government were really serious about reforming Japanese society and education, their reasoning went, then it logically should choose the most "international" person to head up that effort. Yet the Japanese staff at CLAIR proved to vary considerably in their command of English and their willingness to support the program coordinators' requests. This variability led program coordinators to cast the Japanese staff starkly as heroes and villains. Those who supported their causes were good people, and those who played by the rules of Japanese bureaucracies were either obstructionists or cowards.

For instance, in the second year of the program, the reins of secretary-general were handed over to Nakamura Hajime, a generous man, warm by almost any standards. He genuinely enjoyed dialogues with the program coordinators. He would stay up late at night memorizing his speeches in English and was very responsive to the concerns of program coordinators. Reaching out to AJET members as well, he worked with them to further program objectives. His reassignment after one year was widely regarded by the program coordinators as retaliation for the reputation he had achieved as a "gaijin lover."[52] Nakamura's successor, by contrast, promptly moved his desk to the far end of the room, where he was much less accessible; suspended regular meetings with the program coordinators, claiming that he was "too busy"; and thus quickly acquired the label of obstructionist.

The third and final personnel complaint concerned the issue of overlap. Meredith explained: "They have every single program coordinator quitting in August and the secretary-general is oblivious. He had never thought of the fact that we needed to overlap." Here again, however, different cultural models seem to be operating. Under the personnel rotation system, it is considered extremely rude for the outgoing person to offer unsolicited advice to the newcomer. The basic philosophy is to start with a new spirit, not influenced by the jaded perceptions of the incumbent. This nondidactic approach to learning on the job, which requires of the newcomer an acute sensitivity to job expectations, can be seen in numerous other contexts as well. G. Victor Soogen Hori, for example, has labeled this approach "teaching without teaching" in his description of the training of Zen monks.[53]

Us-Them Mentality

The second major factor underlying the disillusionment of program coordinators was their perception that they were not treated as equals and were "excluded" in various ways by the Japanese staff at CLAIR. On the one hand, this involved being shut out from the little things that are a crucial sign of group membership in Japan. According to Meredith,

> We're still outsiders and they're insiders. We're foreign and treated differently. We're not told things that concern us. Even if we work late, they forget to ask us if we want an *obentō* (box dinner). They forget to say *otsukaresamadeshita* or *osaki ni* (see you tomorrow) to us when they leave the office. . . . One time someone came over and wanted to ask where [A-san] was. I was the only one there at the time so he went back to his seat and waited till a Japanese came back. They treat us the same as them when it's convenient for them and when it's not, they don't.

On the other hand, program coordinators also felt they were gradually closed out of the decision-making process. Initially, the program coordinators had been consulted about virtually every aspect of program policy; they held primary responsibility for publishing all guidebooks, writing the *CLAIR Newsletter* and *JET Journal,* handling all counseling calls from JET participants, planning conferences, and interacting face-to-face with the JET participants at the orientation and midyear conferences. As a result, they quickly came to feel that the success of the program rested largely on their shoulders. Over time, however, as program policies and procedures became more routinized, the program coordinators began to feel excluded. Meredith noted, "We often feel we're not a part of CLAIR and have to fight for a place. Caroline's in charge of Tokyo orientation, and she wasn't even invited to a meeting yesterday with Kinki Tourist to organize the airport greeting." Sarah pointed out that "Whenever money is involved, we're not consulted." Even Philip, widely respected as the "most Japanese" of the program coordinators because of his thoughtful and restrained demeanor, spoke somewhat bitterly about CLAIR's refusal to draw on his experience during his third year:

> For me personally, being in CLAIR the longest, it became extremely difficult because I had been there longer than any of the Japanese. And maybe I was just so stressed that I was imagining more than there actually was. I felt a sense of, not so much animosity, but almost a sense of fear that there was a non-Japanese in this government-affiliated office who knew more about what the office had done up until now than any of the Japanese there. So there was, for me, what seemed an active effort on the Japanese part to keep me in place. "You may have been involved in the administration up till now, but it's not necessary any more. We know how to run the program." Certainly those of us who were there from the beginning felt that our opinions were welcomed and valued and in many cases heeded and put into practice, but once CLAIR had successfully run the program a year or two, well, the amount of innovation and modification became less. So I think CLAIR probably felt that "if we have to, we can do without the program coordinators."

Contributing to strained relations between the program coordinators and the Japanese staff was a sudden change in how new program coordinators were hired. For the first few years the program coordinators had more or less handpicked their successors. The Japanese staff had asked the departing program coordinator to recommend someone and then had interviewed that person. But in 1990, the program coordinators were informed that they would not have an official voice in the selection process. Meredith recalled the soap opera–like events that followed:

> Meredith: But we wouldn't let them. . . . They had extended my contract, but there were seven points I had added to my contract before I would extend it, and one of those stipulations was being able to choose my successor. I already had the person picked out, so for that one slot anyway, it was already guaranteed that I could select it. Then we got wind of some of the other people they were considering. It was such a secret thing. They kept lists away from us, and my manager wouldn't let me look at them. We actually stayed late one night so we could go through his drawer because we knew he had the list of people they were considering. And they were holding the interviews on days where they wouldn't even tell us these people were coming in, and they told the candidates they couldn't contact us. We felt like we were working at the CIA or something, it was so ridiculous. And it was all very much the way [the secretary-general] operated. It was all coming down from him, and he said he didn't want us involved in that kind of thing. So it really caused a lot of hurt feelings, hard feelings. There were at least three people on that list that we were appalled they were even considering.
>
> DM: How did they come up with the lists, do you have any idea?
>
> Meredith: It was from letters, from people who had been brownnosing the secretary-general. So then we called the people that we wanted them to choose and said, "Look, he's taking these letters people are sending him seriously! Send him a letter! Have someone from your office call him and tell him you would be a good program coordinator." So we went through the back door. And we had a Japanese guy helping us because he understood that the secretary-general didn't know what kind of person would make a good program coordinator.

In fact, the rationale for the Japanese decision was not as sinister as Meredith made it out to be. By the third year of the program, the number of program coordinators had to be increased to four (and in the fifth year, as the program continued to grow, to five), and more and more JET participants were asking how to apply for the position. Indeed, some had begun accusing CLAIR of unfair hiring practices because the method was entirely subjective. CLAIR officials thus felt pressure to switch to a more formal process.

Yet excluding the program coordinators from any direct voice in the selection was clearly a political move. Having had their fill of embarrassing confrontations with overly "aggressive" program coordinators, CLAIR officials reasoned that the problem would continue as long as they let those currently in the position pick their successors. By controlling the selection process and relying heavily on recommendations from local officials, they could guarantee that those chosen spoke better Japanese and were more in tune with Japanese bureaucratic norms. While this decision did not sit well with most of the program coordinators, it spoke volumes about the growing confidence of the Japanese. As one deputy secretary-general put it, "We began to feel that since this was a program run by the Japanese government, it made sense that we ought to be in charge of all personnel decisions."

Within this climate of mutual skepticism about motives and goals, program management often turned into a game of opposing strategies. For instance, in order to fend off their demands, CLAIR officials attempted to ascertain whether there was serious disagreement among program coordinators. Such conflict was then used as support for the official position—for example, on rescinding the age limit ("Britain and the United States disagree") or on censoring the advertisement placed by the gay support group ("many JET participants themselves are uncomfortable with homosexuality"). For their part, faced with what they believed to be an unresponsive bureaucracy, the program coordinators made great efforts to present a unified front. Sarah told me, "One of the things the program coordinators tried to do was stay united, like if three of us agreed and one didn't, then that person would have to bend because we're trying to get some kind of unity going. If we don't present a solid front, the secretary-general will play us off each other. [X] was really good at that."

Of course, presenting a unified front meant informal censoring of behaviors of other program coordinators that were deemed too "Japanese." Consider Sarah's recollection of what happened when the secretary-general proposed that JET participants pay for their own lunch at the Kobe renewers' conference. A controversy arose after Japanese officials realized their calculations for the budget were off and asked Don, the program coordinator in charge of the conference, for his opinion:

> Don, whom we had a lot of trouble with, to be honest, decided to be Japanese and agreed to that plan without consulting us, and he also contacted AJET, and they had a fit. Like, it's a business meeting and you're telling them it's mandatory, and then you're telling them they have to buy their own lunch? Well, Don went ahead and approved it without all of us, and so Meredith and I called over the secretary-general and the section chief of implementation and in the middle of the office we had a good yelling match—well, we were yelling a lot at Don, too. They usually let me do the yelling because I've been there longer, and after a while, the Japanese will usually say, "Oh, we agree."

But this time it came down to a lack of communication, and again it came down to cultural differences. The secretary-general couldn't see anything wrong with making them pay for their own lunches and being back in an hour. And we're saying, "It's not going to happen." That was a sore point, but ultimately, after he'd heard everyone's side, the secretary-general ended up paying for lunch, and they just shifted the budget around.

Worth noting here is not only how the charge of being "too Japanese" is leveled against a compatriot, but also how routinely the strategy of foreign pressure ("they usually let me do the yelling") is used to achieve their objectives—successfully, in this case.

While the comments and behavior of some of the program coordinators could easily be seen as exemplifying what Donna Haraway calls the cannibalistic logic that readily construes other cultural possibilities only in terms of resources for Western goals and actions, I believe such an interpretation falls short.[54] First, there were strong and weak versions of this reformist approach, even among the program coordinators. Philip and Caroline, for instance, while sharing the underlying goal of change, differed dramatically in their willingness to use confrontational strategies to achieve their ends. Second, youth and idealism undoubtedly played a role in this stance. Their relative lack of job experience may have led program coordinators to blame "Japanese bureaucracy" for problems common to bureaucratic organizations more generally. Third, the program coordinators were a unique subset of the pool of JET participants. Members of the initial group were selected because they had become known in their local areas for championing reform while at the same time acknowledging the importance of Japanese approaches. They tended to be idealists, viewing the goal of the JET Program as transforming not only English education but also Japanese society more generally. In addition, as spokespersons for and representatives of the JET participants they were under some pressure to achieve results, and the gap between program rhetoric and reality was especially acute during the early years.

Finally, their disparaging stance toward Japanese bureaucracy can be seen as a kind of cultural performance: they take on the role of "foreigners trying to show Japanese how to do internationalization." With the best of intentions, and intensely desiring to help bring positive change to a culture in which they found many attractive features, they set themselves up for frustration. At times their exuberance overruled their common sense. It is also worth noting that a similar attitude toward Japanese culture can be observed among the "hired foreigners" (*oyatoi gaikokujin*) of the Meiji period and the educational consultants brought in during the Allied Occupation.[55] In many cases these individuals saw Japan as fertile ground for experimentation; as they tried out ideas whose implementation in the United States had been quite problematic, they developed sudden amnesia about those earlier difficulties.

The Japanese Response

The contrast between the generally negative evaluations of the program coordinators and the positive assessments of Japanese officials could not be starker. While Ministry of Education officials remained lukewarm about the program—after the rash of accidents and suicides, one official noted with a hint of smugness, "They must be really worried over at CLAIR right now. I do wonder about the future of the program"—the other two sponsoring ministries had no such doubts. At the midway point of the first year of the JET Program, a report by the Second Cultural Affairs Division of the Ministry of Foreign Affairs stated,

> Though it may be a bit premature to evaluate the program since it is only six months old, judging from the voluminous reports, the impressions of participants, and the fact that only a small handful of people have gone home early (most for personal reasons), this ministry can say with certainty that the program is making a tremendous contribution to the promotion of our country's internationalization both in terms of bringing about historical reform in English language education and fostering international exchange and mutual understanding and goodwill.[56]

The expansion of participating countries itself testified to the program's success in achieving the goals of this ministry. Home Affairs Ministry reports were very upbeat as well and cited the overwhelmingly enthusiastic response of local governments throughout Japan.[57] They also noted that the percentage of JET participants who returned home early had decreased from a high of 3.1 percent (26 out of 848) in 1987–88 to less than 2 percent by 1990–91. This percentage, which compares very favorably to the rates of premature departure in other youth exchange programs, has continued to fall (see table 4).[58]

My first impulse was to dismiss these reports as just more examples of bureaucratic whitewashing. Yet when I posed this question in 1990 to a

Table 4. Numbers of JET Participants Who Resigned, 1987–92

Academic Year	Total Participants	Number Who Resigned	Percentage Who Resigned
1987–88	848	26	3.1
1988–89	1,443	37	2.6
1989–90	1,987	44	2.2
1990–91	2,284	37	1.6
1991–92	2,874	12	0.4

SOURCE: Adapted from *The JET Program(me): Five Years and Beyond* (Tokyo: Council of Local Authorities for International Relations, 1992), 80.

former secretary-general of CLAIR, he confirmed the positive evaluation: "Actually, we expected much more serious problems than we've had so far—AIDS, rape, illegitimate children. The JET Program is going much better than anyone thought it would." The roots of these favorable assessments lie in the very different model of internationalization that Japanese officials brought to the program. My first clue to that difference came when I bumped into the secretary-general of CLAIR at a reception in 1989. I asked him how things were going and, somewhat inebriated, he replied enthusiastically, "Experience is everything! Experience is everything!" His comment seemed straightforward enough, even simplistic; and yet the more I thought about it, the clearer it became to me that he was voicing the philosophy of "learning by doing" (*karade de oboeru*) that has been shown to be a cornerstone of Japanese approaches to learning in a variety of contexts.[59]

What I believe the secretary-general was saying was this: We can talk about internationalization all we want, but the best way to learn is to jump right in and rub shoulders with each other. To an anthropologist who is accustomed to lecturing on the virtues of cross-cultural orientation and the need to learn more about one another before working together, this advice seemed counterintuitive. Diversity is not an end in itself. Without nurturance and careful instruction, placing diverse peoples together may just as easily result in intolerance, misunderstanding, and the confirmation of preexisting stereotypes. It also ran contrary to the sensibilities of the program coordinators, who had long pressed CLAIR officials to provide Japanese officials involved in the program with a more substantive orientation on cultural differences.

But for the Japanese involved, internationalization never implied erasing national boundaries or coming to know others as "autonomous individuals." Instead, it was seen as a process of improving understanding between groups who, it was assumed, would always be fundamentally different. Most ministry officials saw the JET Program not as dramatically changing Japanese society but as providing the experience that they felt was a precondition for true learning to take place. On the one hand, foreign youth would increase their understanding of Japanese society. On the other hand, a whole cadre of Japanese officials, national level and local, would be trained in Western styles of negotiation and interaction. One CLAIR official noted, "We're getting our own internationalization just by being here in CLAIR and interacting with the program coordinators. You know, Japanese can't just 'do' *kokusaika* (internationalization). We have to 'touch it' first."

Given this framework, one could easily have predicted serious problems in the program's infancy, as expectations were adjusted on all sides. In spite of these problems in implementation, however, what impressed me most is that Japanese officials at CLAIR and at the sponsoring ministries did not give up. One by one, they took on virtually every difficulty raised by the JET participants and wrestled with it: sometimes holding their ground, sometimes capitulating entirely, but more often than not reaching some kind of compromise. Before examining in more detail the learning curve at the national level (see chapter 6), we need to journey downward through the administrative system to examine the diverse and contradictory ways in which the JET Program was translated into practice in local prefectures and cities, schools and classrooms.

4 Managing Diversity

The View from a Prefectural
Board of Education

National-level bureaucrats in Japan by and large subscribe to a theory of administrative guidance according to which they pressure prefectural officials, who pressure local school officials until the desired policy outcomes are achieved. But how are national-level directives and guidance received and interpreted at the prefectural level? What administrative niche does the JET Program occupy within local boards of education? The key figures in this process are the teachers' consultants, who constitute a relatively unstudied yet key educational conduit between the national and local levels. Who are these people, and what is the nature of the environment in which they work? What are their experiences with the assistant language teachers, and how do they evaluate these experiences? This chapter explores the intersection of internationalization and the bureaucratic model at the prefectural level, largely through the eyes of two prefectural administrators assigned to coordinate the JET Program from 1987 to 1990.[1]

Almost five months after my arrival in Japan, I first met Tanabe-san and Sato-sensei. My Japanese mentor at the local university had graciously agreed to provide an introduction to prefectural officials overseeing the JET Program, and our taxi glided up to the prefectural office at about ten minutes to the hour. Too early. Though a light rain was falling, we stood outside for a few moments so that we might enter the education wing at exactly 9:00 A.M. Satoshi Sakai, the division chief for school guidance (*shidōbuchō*), rose from his desk at the head of a cluttered but cozy office holding a dozen individuals. He quickly motioned to his assistant, Tanabe-san, who led us to a private guest room. We exchanged business cards and pleasantries, and Sakai explained that Sato-sensei, the English teachers' consultant (ETC), would not be able to join us as he was visiting a school that morning.

The meeting itself took less than a half hour, and my mentor did virtually all the talking. After explaining my affiliation with the university, and my general aim of exploring the prefectural system for receiving JET participants, he asked me to present the résumé and statement of purpose that I had carefully prepared in Japanese. This, and the fact that I spoke some Japanese, seemed to relieve both officials considerably.[2] I immediately liked Tanabe-san, sensing a genuineness and earnestness in his manner. When he asked me what specific help I would need, I replied that if I could visit some host schools for ALTs and observe a few seminars for JET participants, I would be most grateful. The meeting ended abruptly, and we were ushered gracefully to the door with assurances that Tanabe-san would be in touch. It was only later that I realized how crucial this introduction would be in allowing me to see behind the curtain that prefectural officials intentionally draw around most of their activities.[3]

Within a matter of days Tanabe-san called to let me know he had arranged visits to a half dozen schools and district boards of education in the prefecture and to ask if I could meet him and Sato-sensei for dinner. I was excited at the opportunity to finally meet an ETC, for this was the person who technically served as the ALTs' boss. Though there are prefectural school boards in Japan whose members are appointed by the governor, their influence is exercised through the administrative office of the boards of education (*kyōikuiinkai*). These boards of education are the center for recruiting and training an elite group of educational administrators known as teachers' consultants (*shidōshuji*). Coming directly from the ranks of teachers, they are vital liaisons between boards of education and the schools; teachers' consultants typically spend much of their time advising school-based personnel on prefectural and national policy regarding their subject area. Most become vice-principals or principals shortly after they return to schools. Thomas Rohlen succinctly describes this position:

> Offices of education are staffed by people who come from the ranks of teachers. After serving in the administration, they return to positions in the schools. The responsibility to implement policy and almost all of the contact with schools is thus in the hands of teachers temporarily detailed to administrative jobs. All are seasoned teachers, but few are on the edge of retirement. They earn appointments by excellence as teachers and loyal service. . . . Respected, hardworking, and aligned with the administrative goal of maintaining efficient schooling, these staffers are also politically savvy. They tend to be firm pragmatists who can navigate the tricky waters of education politics.[4]

Significantly, though the ETCs were English teachers before moving to the board of education, they were usually not chosen on the basis of their conversational English or international experience. If anything, they represented the more conservative English teachers, predisposed to toe the administrative line; and they sometimes found the prospect of sustained face-to-face interaction with foreigners terrifying.

That first evening, Sato-sensei matched Rohlen's description. As he came off the train, I noticed that unlike most school-based teachers, he was impeccably dressed in a three-piece suit and was punctilious in demeanor. Joined by Tanabe-san and Ueda-sensei, an English teacher at a nearby high school, Sato-sensei quickly took charge and directed us to a small drinking establishment. Once seated in a semiprivate tatami room, he immediately brought out a critical article on the JET Program that had just appeared in the international edition of *Time* magazine. With two eager listeners, hot snacks, and mugs of cold beer, both Sato-sensei and Tanabe-san quickly warmed to the task of sharing recollections of their first year coordinating the program.

> Sato-sensei: The first trying moment (*taihen na koto*) was when we had the reception and signing of contracts for the new ALTs in the prefecture and the superintendent had to make a speech. Of course, he asked me, the person below him, to write the whole thing—one hundred percent. So I wrote it in Japanese and took it to him and he said, "Fine." But then when he gave the speech and I had to interpret for him, he went and said something entirely different. I was sweating up a storm and my heart was beating so fast all I could think was, "I hope he's going to end quickly."
> DM: Why would he do something like that?
> Sato-sensei: You know, he'd been abroad on a Fulbright grant for a year. But actually the main reason he could do this was because [the ALTs] were so far below him in status that he could deal with them lightly. On serious occasions, like when he's talking to the assembly (*kyōiku iinkai*), he never deviates from his planned speech—he reads everything word for word! . . . Anyway after the second time I learned that I didn't have to translate all of it exactly—so I'd only translate about half of what he said.
> Tanabe-san: At least you know enough to improvise. My worst fear is when the phone rings and you aren't in the office. If it's an ALT, my mind immediately focuses on all the other people in the office who are listening to me. After "How are you?" it's useless. I can't say anything else.

During the course of the evening the talk turned to the placement system for ALTs, critical incidents in the prefectural administration of the JET

Program, and the pros and cons of team teaching. Tanabe-san even brought up Emperor Hirohito's death:

> When I was listening to reports from Britain and other countries on re-actions to the emperor's death, it really struck home that even though Japan was a leading economic nation, we weren't admitted into the so-cial group (*nakama*) of the world. A big red flag went up in my mind. Why is that the case, when other nations have had wars just like us? I'll bet when Queen Elizabeth dies, she'll be revered without any of the criticism our emperor received. This is why we must work harder on internationalization through programs like JET, to teach people from other countries about Japan.

I was immediately struck by how clearly Tanabe-san's words resonated with the notion of a "misunderstood Japan" that I had already encountered at the national level. As the night wore on, the theme recurred: the imper-ative of internationalization was juxtaposed to stories of the difficulties of working with foreigners who didn't follow the cultural standards of behav-ior in Japanese schools and society.

I also discovered more about their respective backgrounds. A native of Mie Prefecture, Sato-sensei had graduated from Sophia University, where he had been active in the English Speaking Society (ESS) and debating clubs. He had taught for ten years at several area schools and had chaired the High School English Teachers Study Group in the prefecture before taking the supplementary courses in educational administration that would allow him to qualify for an administrative position. He had been ap-pointed to the board of education in April 1988 from his position as an En-glish teacher at one of the premier academic high schools in the prefecture. His overseas experience was limited to a short "educational tour" to the United States, though he had team-taught with several participants in the Mombushō English Fellows (MEF) Program at his earlier schools. Later I would learn that his English skills were quite good at a textbook level; his understanding of colloquial expressions was more limited.

Tanabe-san's background was quite different. He had no special training in educational matters and his English skills were negligible. He had joined the prefectural office as a career civil servant on graduating from a local four-year college. Because he had just been transferred to the board of ed-ucation from the personnel division, he had very good contacts in other parts of the prefectural office. His main job was to handle the budgetary and administrative aspects of high school education, including the JET Pro-gram. Sato-sensei later confided that Tanabe-san was on the track to becoming a section chief. Extremely dedicated to his job, he faced a daily two-hour commute from the neighboring prefecture and rarely returned home before 10:00 P.M.

Like the majority of those assigned to coordinate the JET Program in their respective locales, neither Tanabe-san nor Sato-sensei had much prior personal contact with foreigners. I learned that administering the JET Program made up only about one-third of their job; they also supervised "returnee children" and the other educational exchanges in the prefecture. Yet judging from the dinner conversation, they seemed quite willing to share their perceptions of the JET experiment with me. Returning home on the late train that evening, I determined that I would do my best to let them be my eyes and ears in understanding Japanese prefectural responses to the JET Program.

PREFECTURAL AND MUNICIPAL RECEPTIVITY

The widespread image of Japan as an insular society might lead us to guess that there would be considerable resistance among local governments to hiring large numbers of ALTs. But just the opposite seems to be the case. Judged strictly by the numbers of JET participants officially requested by local governments, the receptivity has been astounding. Even in the first year of the program, every one of Japan's forty-seven prefectures and eleven designated cities (i.e., large cities with populations over one million) requested ALTs. Moreover, not a single prefecture has reduced their number in subsequent years; by the program's twelfth anniversary in 1999, over half of Japan's forty-seven prefectures employed at least one hundred JET participants. Cities and prefectures that had previously hired foreigners with their own funds began to replace them with those supplied through the JET Program, in some cases severing or weakening ties that had been developed over the years with universities or cities abroad. In fact, local government requests for JET participants have been so high that CLAIR quickly found itself in the unexpected position of being unable to grant the entire number of JET participants requested.

The most common explanation I encountered for the desirability of JET participants was that the program represented a chance for mayors and governors across the country to gain political brownie points. Tanabe-san noted, "When it comes down to the numbers of ALTs, the bottom line is whether it could help the governor at election time. All they're really interested in is creating an appearance." Indeed, each year there are complaints from assistant language teachers and coordinators for international relations who arrive in municipalities only to find no viable plan for how to use them.

But a very strong grain of pragmatism was involved as well. In the short term, it was hard to turn down an attractive offer from Tokyo that was "low cost" (because of the way it was funded) and "low maintenance" (in that selection was handled at the national level). Also, many mayors and governors, genuinely concerned about the future of their locality in an increasingly global economy, felt that their schools had done a poor job of preparing young people to play a productive role in a global society. In addition to being good public relations, the JET Program thus offered an opportunity both for the next generation of leaders to chip away at the language barrier and even for current officials to improve their communication skills.

Japan's long history of local receptivity to top-down government initiatives undoubtedly was a factor in the enthusiastic response of local leaders as well. To some extent, this reflects a power differential; Jackson Bailey, for instance, has argued that "the combined fiscal power of the three ministries responsible for [the JET Program] is so great that local boards of education can do little to resist when this power is applied to them."[5] Yet while Nosé Kuniyuki, who drafted the original proposal for the new program, himself called every governor in Japan to urge their participation, I found little in the way of overt coercion on the part of the Ministry of Home Affairs. Rather, prefectural officials seemed anxious that they might be left out of a major government initiative.

Finally, the importance of precedents—the MEF Program and British English Teaching (BET) Scheme—cannot be underestimated. By 1986 virtually every prefecture in Japan employed at least a handful of foreign teaching assistants: the basic mechanism for implementation was thus already in place.[6] Had most boards of education not already been participating in these programs, it is doubtful that the politicians could have so easily persuaded superintendents of education (who are political appointees) to participate.

To this overall picture of local enthusiasm for the JET Program, however, several qualifications must be added. First, and most important, the ETCs are rarely as enthusiastic about raising the numbers of JET participants as are governors and mayors, who find the JET Program attractive precisely because it allows them to be "international" without having to worry about face-to-face interactions. Second, there were significant differences among the prefectures. For instance, in 1987 Fukui-ken ranked third in number of ALTs invited but forty-ninth in number of public secondary schools; conversely, Aichi-ken ranked forty-fourth in the number of ALTs but fourth in public secondary schools. This variation was caused by a broad combination of factors: the history of English reform efforts, experiences with the MEF and BET programs, the strength of the teachers' union, and especially the attitude of the governor and the superintendent of education. All of this means that the responses of prefectures have changed from year to year, reflecting new leadership and new priorities (see table 5). For example, in 1987 Hokkaido had the greatest number of public schools but was well back in the middle of the pack in numbers of ALTs; by 1998, however, as a result of an aggressive attempt to place ALTs in all municipalities, it had leapfrogged to sixth place with 163 ALTs, putting it behind Saitama-ken (324), Hyogo-ken (234), Chiba-ken (179), Nagano-ken (167), and Shizuoka-ken (164).

Many of the above themes can be traced in the experiences of Sato-sensei and Tanabe-san. As luck would have it, their governor happened to be a former Ministry of Home Affairs official; as Sato-sensei noted rue-fully, the ministry therefore saw their prefecture as "easy to ask favors of." The governor felt strongly that the prefecture ought to do its part in supporting the program. But it would not be easy to raise the number of participants dramatically from the nine MEFers employed in 1986. The prefecture was campaigning intensely to make their public high schools students more competitive on the university entrance exams. English test scores had been targeted for major improvement, and there was concern that too much emphasis on conversational English would undermine this effort. In addition, the prefecture's strong history of unionism caused some worry about how receptive certain high schools would be to hosting an ALT. After consulting with the superintendent of education, the governor agreed to settle for a modest initial request of sixteen ALTs.

The responsibility for seeking subsequent increases fell largely to the superintendent of education, who relied on Sato-sensei and Tanabe-san's recommendation. Each year before suggesting a number to the superintendent, Sato-sensei called all the neighboring prefectures; "We want to make sure that our prefecture isn't out of step," he said. Sato-sensei told me that his predecessor had hoped to stay at sixteen because even that low number was such hard work for him. But the superintendent decided that there should be twenty-two in 1988. Tanabe-san recalled that for the following year, "We proposed a relatively small increase in numbers in order to keep our workload down, but the superintendent asked us, 'Are you sure that's enough?' So we had no choice but to increase the numbers. We ended up with twenty-seven in 1989." In 1990 the superintendent recommended

Table 5. The Number of Assistant Language Teachers by Prefecture and Designated City, 1987–91, 1996, and 1998

Prefecture/City (North to South)	1987	1988	1989	1990	1991	1996	1998
Hokkaido	11	26	40	53	90	145	154
Aomori-ken	8	19	34	41	48	65	71
Iwate-ken	16	31	40	46	53	84	100
Miyagi-ken	12	31	39	43	56	99	123
Akita-ken	7	20	30	35	41	65	73
Yamagata-ken	11	18	25	27	31	53	60
Fukushima-ken	19	37	47	52	73	89	98
Ibaraki-ken	27	42	54	57	69	95	103
Tochigi-ken	23	25	38	40	49	84	94
Gunma-ken	23	41	53	60	75	119	125
Saitama-ken	33	61	80	84	110	265	313
Chiba-ken	49	69	86	89	101	166	175
Tokyo-to	28	30	31	31	33	37	25
Kanagawa-ken	10	19	30	38	43	59	55
Niigata-ken	10	27	49	54	72	119	137
Toyama-ken	18	37	51	56	64	105	114
Ishikawa-ken	15	25	39	42	50	77	83
Fukui-ken	36	44	49	53	62	88	96
Yamanashi-ken	8	30	39	44	51	67	69
Nagano-ken	15	32	42	46	62	123	132
Gifu-ken	21	24	35	39	54	92	124
Shizuoka-ken	30	52	65	71	85	145	161
Aichi-ken	7	11	23	33	50	82	92
Mie-ken	15	23	33	38	46	73	89
Shiga-ken	10	26	32	38	47	76	87
Kyoto-fu	16	23	32	36	44	66	75
Osaka-fu	19	37	53	63	79	113	112
Hyogo-ken	44	70	88	89	102	186	227
Nara-ken	5	17	25	29	37	61	68
Wakayama-ken	3	13	18	29	33	64	73
Tottori-ken	6	9	17	22	39	60	61
Shimane-ken	10	15	24	28	33	58	65
Okayama-ken	15	28	46	47	63	89	94

Table 5 *(continued)*

Prefecture/City (North to South)	1987	1988	1989	1990	1991	1996	1998
Hiroshima-ken	11	17	25	34	52	91	105
Yamaguchi-ken	10	22	32	39	48	55	60
Tokushima-ken	5	11	18	23	33	56	63
Kagawa-ken	6	12	20	22	29	45	50
Ehime-ken	12	12	14	16	22	65	82
Kochi-ken	12	16	17	21	23	39	58
Fukuoka-ken	17	25	32	40	56	124	128
Saga-ken	11	23	35	41	51	80	85
Nagasaki-ken	5	12	16	23	39	113	131
Kumamoto-ken	31	47	59	66	79	135	146
Oita-ken	11	18	30	33	38	83	85
Miyazaki-ken	11	19	24	28	40	61	68
Kagoshima-ken	25	32	44	50	62	107	114
Okinawa-ken	15	27	33	35	40	51	67
Prefectural Subtotal	759	1,300	1,780	2,012	2,542	4,274	4,770
Sapporo-shi	3	3	4	4	4	11	20
Sendai-shi	0	0	2	3	4	48	56
Chiba-shi	3	5	5	5	5	14	16
Yokohama-shi	11	23	27	30	30	45	45
Kawasaki-shi	2	2	2	3	3	6	8
Nagoya-shi	5	9	15	19	24	32	32
Kyoto-shi	2	2	4	6	6	16	16
Osaka-shi	12	17	23	25	27	48	50
Kobe-shi	2	2	5	8	17	26	26
Hiroshima-shi	6	10	10	10	10	16	18
Kitakyushu-shi	6	7	11	14	17	21	22
Fukuoka-shi	2	4	6	7	10	17	17
Subtotal	54	84	114	134	157	290	326
Total	813	1,384	1,894	2,146	2,699	4,574	5,096

SOURCES: *The JET Program(me): Five Years and Beyond* (Tokyo: Council of Local Authorities for International Relations, 1992), 169–278; *JET Programme: Ten Years and Beyond* (Tokyo: Council of Local Authorities for International Relations, 1997), 360; advertising brochure, *The Japan Exchange and Teaching Programme, 1998–1999* (Tokyo: Council of Local Authorities for International Relations, 1998), p. 3.

thirty-four ALTs, but to the board of education's dismay the governor announced to the general assembly the hiring of that number well before CLAIR had approved the prefecture's request. Sato-sensei made a special trip to Tokyo to ask CLAIR officials to meet their request, but he returned home with the news that local governments sought 2,400 ALTs and CLAIR could only guarantee a total of 1,900. In the end, only thirty-one were approved. To match the number already officially announced, Sato-sensei spent a considerable amount of time using his own connections to find three additional ALTs who were hired privately. Tanabe-san reflected, "CLAIR is always telling us to get tough with renewers, but we can't tell someone to go home as long as CLAIR doesn't give us the number we request."

Prefectural and municipal receptivity to the JET Program was perhaps most striking in its mirroring of patterns on the national level. Just as Ministry of Home Affairs officials forged ahead with plans for the JET Program despite foot-dragging by Ministry of Education officials, so too at the local level did politicians and their political appointees largely set the tone for requests of JET participants regardless of the desires of local educational administrators. Those administrators privately expressed reservations about the rate of increase and complained frequently about the stress of dealing with the ALTs, all the while striving to fulfill the expectations of their superiors and to maintain the public image of the program.

DOWNWARD LINKAGES: SCHOOL VISITATION SYSTEMS

In talking about their dealings with the JET Program, prefectural officials frequently compared the process of hosting ALTs to an arranged marriage. "The first time I went to meet the new ALTs in Tokyo," confessed Sato-sensei, "it was like going to meet my prospective wife at the *omiai* (arranged meeting of possible marriage partners)." The metaphor is particularly apt because it captures the standard reactions: competing emotions of excitement and anticipation, on the one hand, and fear of the unknown and the unpredictable, on the other. One perceptive ALT marveled, "They're more nervous about us coming than I could have ever imagined!" On the whole, however, JET participants failed to appreciate the level of anxiety and the extent of prearrival preparations caused by their visits. Between the time CLAIR notified prefectures of placements in April and the face-to-face meeting with the ALTs at the Tokyo orientation in early August, Sato-sensei and Tanabe-san were constantly scrambling to get ready.

At the outset, their most challenging task was arranging and coordinating the school visitation system. With 45 public high schools and 104 public junior high schools under one prefecture's jurisdiction, there would seem to be ample room to absorb several dozen ALTs. Yet according to Sato-sensei, the path to smooth placement was filled with potential pitfalls. An examination of the process by which the ALTs are assigned to schools thus reveals much about the management of diversity at the prefectural level.

Spreading the Wealth: The One-Shot System

The most prominent, and ultimately the most controversial, school visitation pattern in the first year of the JET Program was what came to be known as the "one-shot" system. ALTs were given a desk in a district board of education, and from this administrative office, they were sent out to area junior high schools for irregular visits. The duration of these visits varied—a day, a week, or a month—but even when they went back repeatedly, the ALT rarely taught the same group of students twice. The school could be a five-minute walk from the ALT's office or a two-hour boat trip to a secluded school.

In 1987 Sato-sensei and Tanabe-san placed about 70 percent of their prefectural ALTs (11 out of 16) in this manner, with each of the seven district boards of education prefecture receiving one or two; this pattern was typical of the first year of the program. For instance, Laura was assigned to a district board of education with jurisdiction over twenty-one junior high schools. In 1987 she made 151 visits to thirteen different schools, rarely visiting a single school for more than three consecutive days. Typically, the JTL (Japanese teacher of language) assigned to teach with her would send a tentative lesson plan to Laura at the board of education before her school visit. It indicated the grade, period, and atmosphere of the class, as well as a breakdown of how the fifty-minute team-teaching period would be spent. The JTL usually saw such a class as a special event and thus reserved a substantial part of the allotted time for the ALT's self-introduction and for conversation practice.

Unfortunately, the emphasis on bureaucratic efficiency underlying this method ran directly contrary to the ALTs' expectations of a deep and meaningful encounter with students and teachers, and they wasted no time in conveying to Sato-sensei their utter disdain for the one-shot system. Because there was no continuity over time, they argued, the school visit became far more effective as entertainment than as pedagogy.[7] It thus perpetuated the notion of the foreign teacher as a curiosity, a "living globe" wheeled out on special occasions. Moreover, the grueling travel schedule and the necessity of constantly repeating the same lesson made burnout extremely likely. One ALT compared himself to a tea bag, dipped in cup after cup of tea. "And that," he concluded, "makes for one weak cup of tea!" Another complained to me, "One-shots are the desert of human relationships. Smile. Smile. Smile. I think they're dehumanizing and totally humiliating. It's basically utter strangers asking me rude and insensitive questions. I don't give a damn about my one-shot schools. But the fault is with the system not the Japanese people. It would be better to expose us to a few people that we could get to know warmly." Still another elaborated: "For me, the JET Program fails because I have to change schools frequently. Although I only have six schools, I feel I'm here for a '*gaijin*' show—not for teaching. I feel no challenge in my work and very little reward."[8]

Nor were such criticisms restricted to isolated prefectures or municipalities. After the start-up of the JET Program, it was only a matter of months before the Association of JET Participants (AJET) and the program coordinators at CLAIR took up the cause. In response, the JET Program orientation manual regularly includes a cautionary note designed to temper unrealistic expectations: "The one-shot's duties can produce more culture shock and demands than those facing many world travelers and may result in isolation if the ALT doesn't seek out a network of support and friendship. The rush of autograph signing, hand-shaking and drinking parties on some days can seem as unreal as behind-the-hand giggling and terror-stricken teachers seem on others!"[9] Japanese critics of the government were also quick to echo the complaints of the ALTs. In a 1988 newsletter of the left-leaning Institute for Research on Language Teaching (IRLT, also known as Goken), a university professor commented:

> The ALTs look for satisfaction and meaning (*ikigai*) in their jobs. In the classroom they want to be treated like people, not machines, and they want to interact with students with some continuity. But what repeats itself every month is . . . a "show-your-face" entertainment industry. The ALTs who came with the desire to reform the educational environment realize that the realities of Japan will not change so easily. As a result, they begin to think, "only a few more months till my contract expires . . . ," and they go through the remaining school visits with indigestion. An ALT I met told me this: "If we can find some meaning in our work, then it's easy to renew our contracts. But most of us don't and so we leave quietly after a year. The biggest reason is that we can't find any significance in our work." Is this acceptable? To put it another way, doesn't this amount to throwing away the foreigners? . . . The reality of English education in Japan is that we are creating people who

more or less lack a sense of purpose and meaning in life (*shitsubōshita ningen*).[10]

Such criticisms make the question of why the one-shot system was initially so appealing to board of education officials even more pressing. Sato-sensei and other prefectural ETCs I interviewed offered two rationales. First, posting ALTs to district offices of education made it possible to ensure that the participation of schools in team teaching would be voluntary. We must remember that teachers and principals were never consulted about the start-up of the JET Program despite being the ones most directly affected by it. Each district board of education would typically have fifteen to twenty-five junior high schools under its jurisdiction, so the likelihood of finding schools enthusiastic about an ALT's visit was quite high. When one district office notified fifteen junior high school principals under its jurisdiction that it was accepting requests to host an ALT for three months, six of the fifteen applied. The matter was decided by lottery, and the winning principal returned to his school boasting that he was responsible for getting the foreigner. In this way, the integrity of those schools that did not wish to participate could also be preserved. Among the nine who refused to participate was a small rural junior high school; one of its middle-aged JTLs recalled:

> The board of education asked the Principal's Association who wanted an ALT this year. Then the principal asked me because I'm the head English teacher. I asked the other two English teachers, but they are very nervous because their English is not good and they're afraid students might notice their lack of English ability. One is a real introvert and doesn't want to get in touch with foreigners. Anyway, they told me, "Of course," but I knew it was only because they were deferring to me as their superior. I have to be considerate to them. So when I said, "Let's not have an ALT this year," I could see the relief in their faces.

Second, defenders of the one-shot system argued that because the ALTs were a valuable asset, they should be spread as broadly and as equitably as possible. Indeed, Tanabe-san noted that he had felt subtle pressure from the budget section of the prefectural office, aware that taxpayers' money was funding the program. The board of education did not want to be accused of favoritism; by posting ALTs to each of the district boards of education, they were in theory making the ALT available to every junior high school in the prefecture.

Some disillusioned ALTs had a less benign interpretation of the motives of prefectural administrators: they saw the initial placement system as a means of spatial segregation and of diluting the impact of a required but threatening commodity. The one-shot system allows schools to "do internationalization" and to participate in the campaign to promote conversational English without seriously disrupting exam preparation and without putting the burden of prolonged face-to-face contact with foreigners on a small set of schools. In this view, the dehumanizing quality of the one-shot visit is evidence of the prefectural officials' lack of empathy. Indeed, the entire structure of the one-shot visitation system is predicated on the notion of foreigners as oddities.

To be sure, prefectural officials were clearly concerned about the impact ALTs would have on schools; but interpreting the one-shot system as the inevitable outcome of a deep-seated cultural desire to keep foreigners at arm's length oversimplifies matters considerably. For one thing, the system was hardly universal. In 1987 roughly a third of Japan's prefectures sent the large majority of their ALTs to district offices of education, from which they were dispatched to junior high schools; another third sent the majority of ALTs to prefectural high schools; and the remaining third split their ALTs fairly evenly between district offices and senior high schools.[11] Furthermore, in many prefectures the models of school visitation evolved over time. Beginning in 1988, for instance, Sato-sensei and Tanabe-san began placing most of their new ALTs in senior high schools; by 1991 the bulk of prefectural ALTs were based there rather than in district boards of education.

An added complication is that in many prefectures the most curious pattern in the school visitation system was the absence not of base schools but of *junior high* base schools. Pedagogically, it would appear to make sense to concentrate the efforts of ALTs in seventh and eighth grade classes. Formal study of English begins in the seventh grade, and ALTs and JTLs agree almost unanimously that students just beginning English classes are more eager and uninhibited than their older counterparts. When entrance exams are still three years away, the opportunities for cultivating conversational skills seem most promising. Yet even though public junior high schools (12,000-plus) greatly outnumber senior high schools (4,000-plus), in 1987 only about 60 percent of ALTs were posted to junior high schools—and virtually all were rotated among a number of schools under the one-shot system.[12]

According to Sato-sensei and other ETCs with whom I talked, this pattern was explained primarily by the greater English proficiency of high school JTLs and high school ETCs. Sato-sensei put it this way: "Since high school teachers have a better command of English, they are the ones who take control. Junior high school teachers, because of their poorer conversational skills, just aren't ready to accept ALTs to the extent that high school teachers are. It's more threatening to them to host an ALT for a long period of time."

Junior high schools teachers are also intimately involved in fostering the social and moral development of their students. Ninth grade marks the end of compulsory education in Japan, and prior to this cutoff point teachers spend enormous amounts of time engaged in informal counseling and advising in addition to their academic responsibilities. Rebecca Erwin Fukuzawa's study of student guidance, for instance, reveals that although nurturance and experiential learning in the elementary grades shift to more lecture- and text-centered methodologies in junior high schools, a personal approach to discipline remains a key constant.[13] In this context, the presence of a foreigner is likely to be viewed as a burden. As one teacher explained, the preoccupation with nonacademic concerns in junior high leaves less lee-way to accommodate the ALT. But by tenth grade, compulsory education is finished; though approximately 94 percent of students continue their education, they have been sorted into different types of high schools based on their entrance exam scores. Concern for student behavior remains, but there is more emphasis on academic and career guidance at the high school level.

Yet some cultural dimension may be present in the one-shot patterning. In numerous interviews, I heard Japanese administrators and teachers complain that the students had come to take the ALT too much for granted. This seemed like a curious comment, and when I asked for clarification, they explained that if the students become too accustomed to the ALT, then the power of the foreigner to motivate the students is lost. The term that Japanese teachers use in describing this phenomenon is *tarento kōka*, or "talent benefits," thus equating the ALTs with the television personalities and pop stars known in Japan as "talent."[14] A difference in cultural sensi-bilities led the Japanese to disparage the very process that the foreign teachers idealize: breaking down the barriers and cultural distance between themselves and the students. Assumptions about the ability of native speakers of English (particularly whites) to motivate, not well-thought-out pedagogy, underlies the one-shot system.

The JET Program is now approaching 6,000 ALTs annually; and with more municipalities applying to host an ALT directly, junior high schools are increasingly being asked by municipal boards of education to host an ALT. The pool of possible schools to visit is thus shrinking dramatically as municipalities stake a claim to "their" schools for "their" ALTs. Thus, while the number of ALTs posted to senior high schools has gradually increased over the first ten years of the program, postings to district offices of education have actually decreased since the third year of the program—and a few prefectures have dropped the practice altogether. As greater numbers of municipalities get aboard the JET Program it will be interesting to see whether they take up the base school approach at the junior high level or continue to circulate ALTs around to a number of schools.

The Struggle to Find Base Schools

So widespread was the criticism about the one-shot system that the Ministry of Education finally issued a directive to local governments urging them to assign all ALTs to a "base school" if at all possible. The concept of the base school was quite straightforward; instead of reporting to a desk at the district board of education when not visiting schools or during school vacations, an ALT would be based in a particular school. While the ALT might continue to travel to other "visit" schools, perhaps one or two days a week, most time would be spent at the base school. Once the ALT was more or less integrated into school activities like any other teacher, he or she therefore would be able to develop meaningful relationships with students and teachers.

Though the goal was very attractive, there was, of course, also a rub. Those at the base school—particularly the Japanese teachers of English—suddenly were forced to assume a tremendous burden. Not only did base schools have to arrange housing and help ALTs settle in, but they were also responsible for the ALTs' healthy adjustment to Japanese society, ensuring that their stay in Japan was rewarding and that they gained a favorable impression of Japan.

The ministry's directive, coupled with complaints from the ALTs themselves, prompted Sato-sensei and Tanabe-san to emphasize expanding the number of base schools at the high school level after 1987. Because he had participated in the prefectural High School English Teachers' Association and had traveled extensively to schools around the prefecture for consultations and seminars, Sato-sensei was keenly aware of the atmosphere, needs, and problems of each school as well as the personalities of the principals and the English teachers. Several prefectural high schools were natural choices for hosting ALTs because they already had an international component to their curriculum. For example, the primarily female Northwestern High School offered a special course in conversational English, and many of its graduates went on to study foreign language at local universities. Two ALTs were placed there as early as 1987. In addition, the prefecture boasted a commercial high school with a special course in international business; two ALTs were posted there in 1987 as well. Finally, one ALT was placed in the prefectural high school that was a "designated school for returnee children" and was actively engaged in a variety of international exchange activities. In all three cases, school officials boasted loudly about the arrival of the ALTs, for their schools were competing in the prefecture with private high schools that had long hired foreign teachers.[15]

Beyond these five placements, however, Sato-sensei and Tanabe-san were forced to make hard decisions that involved multiple tradeoffs. One of the board of education's most obvious strategies was to avoid asking schools with strong ties to the teachers' union to serve as base schools. Although the union's influence both nationally and in the prefecture was at an all-time low in the late 1980s, at least a half dozen schools in the prefecture were still considered to be union strongholds. I visited several of these schools and discovered that to protest Ministry of Education policy, students were not required to wear uniforms and teachers would often show up at school just in time for their first class rather than attending the "mandatory" morning meeting. Sato-sensei had harsh words for what he called the "self-centered" attitude of these teachers, whom he claimed thought only of their own salaries and working conditions rather than of their students, who suffered for it. He found particularly galling the refusal of some "union" schools to participate in the grading of the "practice entrance exams" that were used to gauge students' chances of admission to a university. Because of their antagonistic relationship with the board of education, Sato-sensei rarely considered any of the union schools as serious candidates for base schools.

No love was lost on the other side either, as union-dominated schools rarely showed enthusiasm for the JET Program. Their resistance was far more rooted in politics than in philosophy. Acceptance of an ALT implied acceptance of the authority of the prefectural board of education and, by extension, of the Ministry of Education. Sato-sensei encountered union resistance in a number of forms. Shortly before a team-teaching seminar for prefectural English teachers was to be held in 1989, he received word that one school would not be sending representatives after all. In a heated meeting, the English teachers had ultimately decided to boycott the seminar because such administration-sponsored seminars were seen to be platforms for the dissemination of politically conservative ideas. The ALT thus became an inadvertent participant in the ongoing struggle over schools attempting to define their own educational goals and methods, ones that de-emphasized competition and entrance exams. Ironically, many ALTs share these beliefs, and many union teachers are active supporters of communication-oriented English teaching.

This ideological affinity has led to curious policy twists. One ALT posted to a strong union school, for example, found that her JTL absolutely refused to use ministry-approved textbooks. While she enjoyed her unusual freedom to teach conversational English, she had strong reservations about this practice because Sato-sensei had repeatedly told prefectural

ALTs that they were required to use the approved texts. When she raised the issue with Sato-sensei, he advised her to refrain from pushing the issue. Another interesting case involved a prefectural high school with a moderately high level of union support whose English teachers actually approached Sato-sensei and the board of education to request an ALT. Ito-sensei, a twenty-eight-year-old JTL, described what happened: "The board of education chose [the neighboring school], even though it was an exam-oriented school and the teachers didn't take care of the ALT, simply because that school was more attractive (*kawaii*) to the board of education. It's a shame that this is the case, but schools are circumvented simply on the basis of whether they are strongly influenced by the union or not (*kumiai no iro ga tsuyoi ka dōka*)." Because the percentage of teachers who are union members varies considerably among prefectures, in some union resistance is a relatively large obstacle to implementing the JET Program while in others it may have little effect.

Another huge difficulty for Sato-sensei was that while his contacts were strongest in the more academically rigorous high schools, it was precisely these schools that were most reluctant to accept a JET participant. Not only was there likely to be great resistance from the teachers, who saw teaching conversational English as a distraction from exam preparation, but parents who had high aspirations for their children and who often felt that conversation could be learned at college might weigh in as well. If such schools did accept an ALT, he or she would probably be relegated to the role of "walking dictionary"—that is, simply consulted about the proper usage of key grammatical phrases that appeared on the entrance exams. Such treatment, in turn, could frustrate the ALT and lead to other problems for the board of education. In one prefecture I visited, the board of education had attempted to alleviate the problem by advising schools not to use the ALT in ninth- and twelfth-grade classes since these students were preoccupied with studying for entrance exams. To some extent, Sato-sensei sympathized with this approach; while he issued no such directive, he was keenly aware of the burden he was placing on schools: "To tell you the truth," he admitted, "it's a lot easier on the English teachers if you're not a base school."

At the other end of the spectrum, schools with major discipline problems were less likely to be chosen as base schools, for several reasons. Teachers at these schools said that they were too busy with disciplinary issues to properly attend to a foreign guest. One middle-aged female JTL put it this way: "If you invite an ALT to a school with problems, usually nothing good comes of it. In between periods the teachers are always patrolling the school. There's no time to give to ALTs. Some of my kids can't even find their way to the subway station after school. And you talk about internationalization! We need to take care of the basics in this society first!" A further complication is that ALTs are perceived by classroom teachers as representatives of the board of education, and thus there is often a strong desire to prevent them from knowing actual school conditions. In general, Japanese schools with discipline problems are extremely concerned with keeping internal problems out of the view of the public; this sentiment is only strengthened when that public is identified with the international community.[16] One male JTL, twenty-eight, told me, "My first year at this school, the head English teacher didn't want an ALT. When I asked him if we could have an ALT that year, he said, 'Oh, I already told the principal we didn't want one.' I said, 'Why?' He said, 'Because of the condition of the students.' And he did that without even discussing it with other teachers." Thus the schools that were average were the most likely to be initially considered as base schools.

Finally, two other tendencies are worth noting. Urban high schools were more likely to be chosen as base schools than were isolated high schools in remote areas, largely as a result of the strong preference of most ALTs for living in or near a large city. Tanabe-san commented, "If an ALT asks to be placed in a rural area, it's automatic for us because there are so few who want to go there." Vocational schools were also unlikely to serve as base schools unless they had a special course of study with an international dimension; schools for students interested in fisheries or agriculture, for instance, tended to be underrepresented. Prefecture officials generally felt that students in these schools would have little interest in an "academic" subject such as English. Yet such schools also offered some striking success stories: if discipline problems were not too serious, the ALT often had more flexibility in teaching conversational English since university entrance exam pressures were not so pervasive.

Given these various types of school-level constraints, Sato-sensei and Tanabe-san were extraordinarily successful in placing ALTs in base schools. Though some district boards of education in the prefecture still allow schools control over requesting a foreign teacher, the rapid increase in numbers of JET participants has meant that in most cases ALTs are placed in schools where the large majority of Japanese teachers of English are quite ambivalent about their presence. One ETC's comments captured the prevailing sentiment about the evolution of the school visitation system: "If we said, 'Do you want to have (*Okurimashōka*) an ALT?' very few schools would sign up. So we tell them, 'Here we come!' The whole program is forced down (*oshitsukete iru*) from the top to a considerable degree." Still, both Sato-sensei and Tanabe-san had a very clear notion of where polite but persistent prodding crossed over to become aggressive pushing. By the fourth year of the JET Program, Sato-sensei noted: "After we get up to thirty-four, we're not going to be able to accommodate many more ALTs at the high school level. It would be pushing it too much. We'll have to expand at the junior high level if we want to increase the numbers." In fact, this is precisely what has happened. In the eight-year period (1991–99) following Sato-sensei and Tanabe-san's tenure, their successors increased the number of prefectural ALTs only slightly; the rest of the growth occurred as municipalities began to hire ALTs independently of the prefectural office, usually placing them in junior high schools.

Hierarchies of Foreigners: ETCs as Matchmakers

After the application forms of ALTs assigned to their prefecture are received from CLAIR, individual applicants must be matched with specific schools or boards of education. Each year, Sato-sensei and Tanabe-san spent a marathon weekend session in the board of education, laying out all the applications and attempting to make suitable pairings. When I asked Sato-sensei what it was like to play matchmaker, he replied: "It's really difficult to tell from an application what a person will be like. We do our best to match each person with an appropriate school but it rarely works out as we planned. Three (out of twenty-seven) this year are doing well, but all the rest have had trouble of one kind or another."

Although the two men did not tell me the precise criteria used to match ALTs with particular schools, over the course of fieldwork period they made a number of revealing informal comments:

> We really made a mistake by putting Aki in the education center. We thought that because he was Japanese American, he would be disappointed by the reaction of teachers and students if we sent him out to schools on a regular basis. We thought he would do better in a setting where he could organize seminars for teachers. But now that we know how outgoing he is, we realize we should've sent him out.

> Sending Jennifer and Rick to [the international high school] was definitely our best move. Rick had a master's degree in English and teaching experience before coming to Japan so we wanted to make sure that he was in a challenging situation, and those are our best English teachers out there. And Jennifer gets along fabulously with the students. She has them writing diaries and even spends her own time writing replies on the weekends.

> Remember how we agonized over whether to send Patrick [age thirty-five] to the rural area or not? He was quite a bit older than the

other ALTs so we really worried about how he would adjust and how the teachers would react to him. But it's worked out quite well.

I thought Ueda-sensei would want a British woman because he's the serious type. But I think the English teachers will have a hard time at first until they adjust to British English.

I found that skin color, sex, nationality, age, English accent, teaching experience, educational level, and major field of study were all taken into account at various times in the placement process, and informal hierarchies clearly existed. ALTs with lighter skin color were more desirable than those with darker skin color because their motivational effect on teachers and students was perceived to be higher; younger ALTs were more desirable than older ones because they were seen as more flexible and therefore less threatening to Japanese teachers; males were more desirable than females because they were thought to be better able to withstand the hardships of life in another culture.

The hierarchy of foreigners was particularly rigid with respect to accent. Participants who spoke American and Canadian English were seen as more desirable than those who spoke other versions, as one Australian ALT noted: "In my experience, foreigners in Japan are constantly assumed to be American. At first meetings, there is a very good chance that one will be asked, 'Are you American?' or 'Where do you come from in America?' It seems that the word 'Australia' simply does not register in the minds of some Japanese. Many times I have been asked what language is spoken in Australia. Many times too I have heard, 'Please say something in Australian,' 'You speak English quite well,' or 'You speak English with a British accent.'"[17] One Australian ALT in the prefecture even reported having been told by Japanese teachers not to use his Australian accent while teaching, and to use only American English.[18] Perhaps most telling was that in this prefecture only American ALTs were selected to tape-record listening exercises in English; Sato-sensei was responsible for clandestinely producing these "practice exams" (*mogi shiken*) for prefectural high schools.

A final criterion used by Sato-sensei and Tanabe-san in the placement process was personal appearance, judged by a photograph of the ALT. Photos required for visa purposes were widely used in the selection and placement process at the prefectural level. Sato-sensei noted, "It's hard to tell good ALTs from the application so in this sense the picture is important." Various messages were read from the photo. Obviously, the picture allowed ALTs to be placed into social categories—such as white (*hakujin*) or black (*kokujin*), Japanese descent (*nikkeijin*), and so on—that were useful in determining school placement. Also apparent was whether a female ALT fell into the category of *bijin*, or "beautiful girl," particularly one with stereotypical blond hair and blue eyes. More generally, neatness in appearance could be judged from the photo. In one instance I observed Tanabe-san apologize to teachers from a base school for the informal picture of the ALT, who was shown in a T-shirt. "This is not an accurate reflection of what this ALT is like," he said. Here prefectural officials were working on a well-documented cultural assumption that outward appearance and comportment mirror one's inward state. Many ALTs, however, found this concern with appearance offensive, preferring instead to subscribe to the theory that looking like one's passport picture is the worst possible indicator of one's fitness to travel—and says even less about one's character.

This preoccupation with the photo as an indicator of social type was not limited to prefectural administrators. In the first year of the program, the Ministry of Foreign Affairs required photos of all *applicants* to the JET Program; though no evidence of misuse of the photos ever surfaced, there were protests, even from selection committee members, that this practice raised the possibility of discrimination based on skin color or other physical features. As a result, photos are now required only of those applicants who make it to the interview stage. At the opposite end of the process, I discovered that pictures of ALTs were often circulated throughout the teacher's room and were even shown to students on occasion, providing fodder for much speculation and good-natured teasing. Having grown up in a society in which such use and exchange of photos is ubiquitous, most Japanese administrators and teachers did not think twice about their actions.

ALTs were rarely privy to this backstage deployment of photographs, but when it did come to their attention, they reacted warily. Their cautious reaction seemed to rest on a discomfort at being turned into an object at which Japanese *looked,* and on a corresponding suspicion that it was precisely their foreignness that simultaneously defined them as noteworthy and kept them distant. The concerns of these ALTs mirrored Michel Foucault's analysis of the relation between photography and power; he argues that the "normalizing gaze" of the photo is in fact a kind of surveillance that establishes a visibility through which people are differentiated and judged.[19]

In sum, matching individual ALTs with schools was a far cry from rocket science; it was conducted in a haphazard manner described by one program coordinator as "akin to throwing bones on the ground to divine the future." Though the matchmaking almost never turned out as Sato-sensei hoped it would, the method used clearly left open the possibility of favoritism. ETCs could reward certain teachers and schools with certain kinds of ALTs. Sato-sensei commented to me on a colleague in a district board of education, "Ehara-sensei has had some rough years with his ALTs, so this year I really want to give him someone good." In rare cases it was even possible for teachers to use their personal relationships with the principal or the ETC to influence placement decisions. Consider the story of this head English teacher, age thirty-five, at an Osaka City junior high school:

> I decided I wanted to have an ALT for one semester, but when I asked the other three English teachers at my school, they said, "Fine, but it's none of our business. You have to handle everything." Before the ALT came, though, the board of education asked our school to host a team-teaching demonstration class and seminar for the whole city. This would take months of preparation, and it would be necessary for all four of us to work with the ALT. The problem was I knew that Ishida-sensei didn't want to work with ALTs any more. That's why we needed to have Marian. She had taught here for a short while the year before and she was so in tune with Japanese culture. You know, I have to re-spect the older teachers—Ishida-sensei is fifty-seven—and I knew the only way the seminar could be successful is if we got Marian. So I called the ETC and requested Marian, but he refused, saying that all schools must have the same opportunity. Then I asked the vice-principal to contact him, but he refused. So finally I went to the principal and explained the situation. The principal, who happens to be the ETC's superior, called the board of education with the request. The very next day I was called to the teacher's room and the ETC was waiting there for me. He bowed his head and apologized to me in person for his behavior. It was unbelievable. So we got Marian after all.

Tanabe-san also recounted several instances of principals stopping by his desk on their way out of the board of education to request an ALT of a certain nationality (usually American) or sex. Such requests, he noted, were especially difficult to ignore because the principals were senior to both him and Sato-sensei; fortunately, they did not occur very often.

HEADACHES IN THE PREFECTURAL BOARD OF EDUCATION:
THE ALTS ARRIVE

When the preparations were finally complete, the time came to travel to Tokyo to meet the new ALTs and escort them back to the prefecture. I accompanied Sato-sensei and Tanabe-san on this trip in 1989, and after we arrived Sato-sensei confessed that while on his first trip to Tokyo in 1988 he was filled with eager anticipation, his heart was heavy this time. Through the grapevine, he knew this was true for other ETCs as well. An ETC in the neighboring prefecture, he said, had been shocked by the loud and boisterous behavior of the ALTs she was escorting on the bullet train back to her prefecture. "She said it was just like traveling with a group of elementary school students; it gave her a terrible headache." Nevertheless, I was struck by the amount of time Sato-sensei had spent trying to memorize faces and names beforehand. He was clearly intent on making a good impression on the ALTs, and during the first few days of interaction, feelings of goodwill and mutual enthusiasm were high enough to offset any potential misunderstandings.

After returning to the prefecture, all ALTs participated in a contract-signing ceremony. Following the ceremony, a daylong orientation was held to give the ALTs a much more specific idea of the terms of their contract and the state of team teaching in their prefecture. The last order of business was the rendezvous between the ALTs and their host teacher or supervisor, who escorted them to their apartment, assisted them in the process of moving in, and introduced them to neighbors and colleagues at school. In the first few weeks, then, the ALTs were exposed to a whirlwind of information and people; many of them described their first month in Japan as a blur.

The demands of extensive periods of English conversation at the Tokyo orientation and in the prefecture took their toll on Sato-sensei and Tanabe-san as well. Both sighed with relief when the ALTs were taken away by school and district representatives. Their work for the remainder of the year would be twofold: promoting team teaching and internationalization in the prefecture and dealing with the myriad requests, demands, and ultimatums levied by the ALTs. The ETCs are often directly confronted by ALTs or asked to defuse conflicts between ALTs and school personnel; as the number of ALTs grows, the probability of problems skyrockets. These conflicts between ALTs and the board of education can be generally divided into two types: irritating disagreements that heighten mutual suspicion but do not lead to a serious breach and confrontations that lead to a permanent rupture, resulting either in an emotional divorce or a physical separation. We will consider typical smaller conflicts first.

Prefectural versus Municipal ALTs

Alison, twenty-two, a graduate of a small liberal arts college in the midwestern part of the United States, was one of the first ALTs in the prefecture to be hired by a municipality, a small town that had become quite wealthy because of its local steel company. Having had a very positive experience at the Tokyo orientation and having already made friends with several other ALTs in her prefecture, she was eager to go through the prefectural orientation. Though Sato-sensei had told her that she was employed by a city rather than the prefecture, her unfamiliarity with the structure of local government in Japan prevented her from appreciating the full import of his remarks.

The morning of the contract-signing ceremony, however, Alison was pulled aside by Sato-sensei and introduced to the man who had come to pick her up. Since Alison would be signing her contract with the town, Sato-sensei said, she would not be participating in the prefectural orientation for other ALTs. This differential treatment confused and angered her because she felt she had lost a chance to gain much useful information about team teaching. Moreover, she had been looking forward to cementing friendships with other ALTs before they met their liaisons and were officially dispersed. From her point of view, she was working in the prefecture just like everyone else, and it did not make sense to exclude her from prefectural activities. Alison was so annoyed that she complained to her boss at the board of education immediately on arriving in her host town; on the next day Sato-sensei received a call from an irate superintendent of education demanding to know why Alison had been excluded from the orientation.

Alison's was not an isolated case. As late as 1990, the minutes of a meeting between AJET representatives and CLAIR officials contained the following complaint from an unnamed ALT: "The segregation of 'prefectural' and 'other' JETs began at the airport. City, town and village JETs were grabbed and taken away while prefectural JETs had an orientation. The division bothers JETs very much; forming relationships/friendships is very important at the early stages of arrival."[20] Understanding what happened requires a quick review of the complicated horizontal and vertical linkages that constitute the JET Program's administrative chain of command.

Below the national level, the most important distinction for Japanese officials is whether the JET participant is employed by one of the 47 prefectures (*kenhaichi*), by one of 12 "designated cities" (*shitei toshi haichi*), or by one of the 3,245 municipalities (*shichoson haichi*) further divided into cities, towns, and villages. Although jurisdictions overlap to some degree, all of these are administratively distinct entities with independent hiring and firing powers. The problem is further compounded because the Ministry of Home Affairs (through CLAIR) and the Ministry of Education have separate administrative windows (*madoguchi*) at each of these levels.

Ironically, even though over 90 percent of JET participants are assigned to boards of education and schools, the official administrative window for the JET Program at the prefectural level is not the board of education at all but rather the international relations division (*kokusai koryūka*). All information about the overall operation of the program from CLAIR goes first to the contact person in the prefectural international relations office, who in theory relays the information to the board of education. At the same time, however, all information and advice about the team-teaching component of the program travels directly from the Ministry of Education to the prefectural boards of education, and the ministry calls the prefectural ETCs to Tokyo at least once a year to instruct them in educational and counseling matters relevant to the JET participants (CLAIR relies on a similar series of regional meetings to impart guidelines to representatives of international relations offices in local governments). It is the duty of prefectural boards of education to forward relevant information to district boards of education, who in turn send it to municipal boards of education. While district boards of education are relatively fixed within the prefectural orbit, the municipal boards of education are more difficult to control.

In effect, then, two vertical chains of command exist side by side. Mirroring the uneasy relationship between the two ministries at the national level, no love is lost at the prefectural level between the international relations division and the board of education. Instead, competition and compartmentalization flourish, and skirmishes over money and educational policy occur with great regularity. Concern for the damage that such strained relationships might cause the JET Program even led one progressive governor in Kumamoto Prefecture to appoint a JET liaison between the two offices.

In Alison's case, her municipality had sent its request for an ALT directly to the international relations division of the prefectural office. While this was the proper official channel, Sato-sensei was somewhat upset; he felt that the request had been approved simply because it came from a powerful mayor, not because it had any educational merit. In fact, he argued that since there was only one junior high school in the entire village, Alison would not have enough to do: to him this was proof that the mayor had absolutely no plan for employing the ALT effectively. His exclusion of Alison from the orientation was thus a function of the logic of bureaucratic compartmentalization, according to which the personal responsibility taken for an action is inversely related to the degree to which one is consulted beforehand. Because Alison "belonged" to a different administrative unit, and because Sato-sensei had not been consulted about her placement or her job responsibilities, his response was to keep his hands off. Put positively, he was respecting the jurisdiction of Alison's municipality. Put negatively, administrative rivalry lead him to refrain from offering to include Alison in the orientation. Either way, the result was a practice that made no absolutely no sense to JET participants.

The interplay between municipality and prefectural control has had two other unfortunate outcomes. First, there is disagreement over the extent to which ALTs can be asked or required to participate in community-based and informal educational activities (*shakai kyōiku*). To the mayor and citizens of a small municipality, it seems a terrible waste to have the ALT spend all his or her hours in one or two secondary schools. As a result, ALTs appointed to small towns or villages frequently are asked to teach elementary school or kindergarten classes, to hold seminars for adults in the community, and to participate in a variety of festivals and other activities. Yet at a meeting for municipal and school representatives Sato-sensei forcefully echoed the Ministry of Education position:

> The main focus of the program should be on junior and senior high schools. I think since we hired them for English teaching, we should just use them for that purpose (*eigo kyōiku ni senmen shitai kimochi desu*). On the other hand, the difficult point is in the connection between municipalities and schools. We can't say that you should absolutely refrain from using them in community events. You have to use your own judgment based on your experience with the ALT. If it's only a few times it's probably all right, and we're not going to place a limit on the number of times you can use an ALT in community activities, but our thinking and the Ministry of Education's thinking is that classroom teaching is their job and anything else is not desirable.

Nevertheless, many ALTs report becoming involved in all manner of community projects that have little to do with conversational English in a narrow sense.

Second, jealousy and resentment sometimes arise between prefecture-based and municipality-based ALTs concerning "preferential treatment" in living and working conditions. On the one hand, some prefectural ALTs claimed that municipalities generally provided better living conditions than did prefectures. Since municipalities hired only a small number of ALTs (usually one or two), it was argued, they were more apt to provide allowances of various kinds. On the other hand, some municipal ALTs claimed that prefectural ALTs were more likely to be given extra vacation time during August instead of being expected to report to work every day like a civil servant. My own informal assessment of living and working conditions revealed a substantial lack of uniformity at the local levels (dis-cussed below), but I found the variation *within* the pool of participating municipalities to be at least as great as the variation *between* municipalities and prefectures.

Local Variation in Living Conditions

Though taxes and insurance proved to be the biggest administrative prob-lems at the national level, disputes over housing arrangements caused major headaches for Sato-sensei and Tanabe-san. The stereotype of Japan as a homogeneous society with a centralized system of government led many JET participants to expect that conditions of employment at the local level would be roughly the same for everyone. Insofar as JET was adver-tised as a "Japanese government program," there was no information of-fered to prospective participants during the first years of recruiting to sug-gest that local discrepancies might exist.

Yet JET participants arrived to find considerable differences in their con-ditions of employment. Apart from monthly salary, the five-day work-week, and required participation in orientation and midyear conferences, virtually every aspect seemed to be up to the discretion of individual pre-fectures or municipalities. For instance, a 1989 "living conditions survey" conducted by CLAIR showed great variation in how much JET participants paid for rent each month; 12 percent paid less than $50 per month, 17 per-cent paid between $50 and $100, 30 percent paid between $100 and $300, 29 percent paid between $300 and $500, 7 percent paid between $500 and $700, and 5 percent paid over $700 per month. All told, 63 percent of JET participants had their rent partially subsidized. In addition, while 67 per-cent of JET participants did not have to pay the "key money" (equal to one to two months' rent) required to rent an apartment in Japan, the remain-der were responsible for covering part (11 percent) or all (20 percent) of the costs (2 percent "didn't know" if they had paid key money or not). In addi-tion, a few prefectures and municipalities set aside a study allowance to as-sist ALTs in their travels to various parts of Japan.

During the first few years of the program the living conditions of ALTs placed in Tokyo drew the most attention. Unlike many prefectures, the Tokyo Metropolitan government refused to subsidize rent for JET partici-pants; as a result, rent for Tokyo-based ALTs was two to three times higher than that of other ALTs, consuming nearly a third of their salary. In addi-tion, Tokyo-based ALTs were required to pay the deposit and key money out of their own salaries. In late August 1987, the seventeen JET participants working in Tokyo's public high schools sent a letter of complaint to the Tokyo Metropolitan Board of Education. Ministry of Home Affairs officials found themselves caught in the middle. As their ministry was in charge of preserving and encouraging local autonomy, they did not want to appear heavy-handed; neither, however, did they want the Tokyo rent problem to continue and possibly undermine the program. CLAIR officials visited the Tokyo city office to ask local government officials to work on a solution. But the Tokyo government showed little interest in changing their policy, even though the mayor was the symbolic chair of CLAIR at the time. The CLAIR official who visited the Tokyo Metropolitan Office explained: "In small municipalities the mayor can click his fingers and bureaucrats will jump to do whatever he says. Not so in large, compartmentalized seats of government. The bureaucrats are extremely smart and powerful. They know the detailed rules and regulations and whether something is violating the law or not." Several years later the ALTs in Tokyo even threatened to leave the program unless conditions improved. But CLAIR's hands were tied; and as the ALTs in Tokyo numbered only a few dozen (many of Tokyo's wards hire foreign teaching assistants through other means), they were never able to mount a programwide campaign. In subsequent years, CLAIR simply made greater efforts to inform those ALTs placed in Tokyo of the rent situation in the hopes that they would adjust their expectations accordingly.

The conditions of employment in Sato-sensei's prefecture were average in many respects. No study allowance was offered, but key money was covered by the prefecture and apartment rental ran in the $300–$500 range. The prefecture also provided five crucial appliances for all ALTs' apartments: refrigerator, washing machine, gas range, telephone, and television.[21] The average size of the apartment was small compared to what most ALTs were accustomed to back home—it usually consisted of two six-mat tatami rooms plus a small kitchen, bath, and toilet—but this was true of housing throughout Japan. And though one ALT in a small village near the Japan Sea complained publicly about being forced to live in a house with a pit toilet (much to the embarrassment of the host institution, who saw it as an indictment of "backwardness"), that was the exception rather than the rule.

Each year a handful of ALTs were not satisfied with their accommodations and requested new ones. The motivations ranged from proximity to the workplace to the cost of rent to fears for safety, but rarely were they compelling from the perspective of Japanese officials. Kim, a twenty-three-year-old Australian ALT, asked her district board of education if she could move because she had noticed men following her home on two occasions, but her boss told her to consider three options: carrying a beeper, having someone from school walk home with her, and being home by 9:00 P.M. "Can you believe it?" she asked me in exasperation: "It's just like Big Brother. They want to treat me like a child, like I'm not even a human being. Finally, I told them I'm going to move even if I have to pay the extra money, and they said, 'Wait, give us a week.' And just like that they worked it out. I think it was partly the key money and partly because they were afraid it would set a precedent." In another case Laura, a twenty-two-year-old American ALT, was posted to a district board of education in a rural part of the prefecture. Though her apartment was close to the board of education and was well-furnished, it was nearly an hour's commute by train and bus from most of the schools she visited. After several months, Laura decided it was too inconvenient. She spoke with her supervisor; but when he refused to budge, she took the initiative (with the help of a friend) to find a cheaper apartment, one closer to her schools. Laura's supervisor, Haruo Nishimoto, reacted this way: "We were very angry when she decided to move. She just did it on her own, even though we'd spent all that time buying furniture, refrigerator, dishes, everything. It's true that it was about a forty- to fifty-minute commute from that apartment to most of her schools, so we can understand her reasoning, but from our point of view she has a responsibility (*giri ga aru*) to stay in the place we arranged."

This feeling that ALTs who moved were somehow lacking in their sense of obligation and their willpower to hang tough in the face of slight inconveniences was widespread among Japanese officials. As one twenty-eight-year-old JTL explained,

> Many schools have trouble finding housing because they must get a guarantor, so we had an agreement to rent an apartment for five years and had paid the key money and deposit. Then the ALT wanted to move. They just don't understand. At first the school said, "OK, if you do that, you'll have to pay with your own money." But eventually they backed down. I told the vice-principal and principal, "Why don't you make a contract?" but they said, "It's not a good way to treat the ALT," and so they helped her out. I think some ALTs are spoiled and make unreasonable and immature demands.

While there is no question that some ALTs took advantage of their "foreign" status to press unreasonable demands, in many cases they felt justified precisely because prefectural variations in employment seemed so unfair. As one AJET vice-chair put it, "all people hired for the same job should get the same duties and terms!" Adding to the injustice was that JET participants had little say over where they ended up. Whether one paid $500 per month in rent or had one's rent subsidized, for example, pretty much depended on the luck of the draw. Ironically, JET participants were pushing for more standardization in a country that has long been taken to task by some Western countries for its top-heavy regulatory system.

The disparities raise another issue as well. Because funding for the program is based on the local allocation tax (see chapter 2), each host institution receives approximately 5.5 million yen per participant to pay for salary, airfare, conferences, and other related expenses. That some host institutions pay less for housing and other allowances means that these institutions pocket more of the money allocated to them by the government than do others.[22]

Sudden Departures

Much more serious than apartment switching, however, was vacating the apartment for good. While every prefecture in Japan had a handful of early departures during the first years of the program, Sato-sensei and Tanabe-san were hit particularly hard. The first case occurred less than two months into the program when an American woman became depressed over the strain of a long-distance relationship and decided to return home suddenly. Anxious to avoid embarrassment to the school, Sato-sensei negotiated with CLAIR officials to have an alternate fill the spot. But when Sato-sensei went to Tokyo to meet the new ALT at the airport, he was informed that the alternate had changed his mind at the last minute and had not boarded the plane in Chicago!

At Christmas yet another sudden resignation occurred. In this case, a British ALT had returned home for a brief vacation over the holidays. Sato-sensei and Tanabe-san never spoke with him again. He called CLAIR in early January to say that because a friend had been killed in a plane crash, he had developed a fear of flying and would not be coming back to Japan. Both officials were clearly baffled by this story, which they said was "inconceivable from the Japanese point of view" (*nihonjin no kankaku de arienai koto*), but they had no way to verify the account. In both cases, the departures left an apartment to be cleaned, unpaid bills, and numerous other loose ends that took days to wrap up.

The Sexual Harassment "Accident"

Later in the spring a more serious incident occurred, one that changed one ALT's "Japan experience" irrevocably and left a profound impression on

Sato-sensei and Tanabe-san as well. The incident itself lasted less than ten seconds. Lisa, a California native posted to a base high school in a major city in the prefecture, came out of the bath in her first-floor apartment one evening to find a man standing inside her living room, pants open, hand at his fly. Before she could even scream, he turned and was gone, as quietly as he had entered. Shaken and in tears, she immediately notified the board of education and called her parents.

Sato-sensei was not available at the time, but the section chief, Ikuo Tsurukawa, went immediately to Lisa's apartment, bringing along an Australian ALT, Clara, to translate. They found themselves dealing not only with a distraught young woman but also with her extremely irate parents on the phone. Panicked at the thought of an assault attempt on their daughter thousands of miles across the ocean, they demanded to know why no one had warned their daughter of the danger of rape. From everything they had heard, Japan was a peaceful society with admirably low crime rates. How could the prefecture have let this happen? At the very least, the prefecture should compensate them for round-trip airfare to travel to Japan to be with their daughter. Clara tried to interpret the logic of their request as best as she could, and at first Tsurukawa hesitated at what he clearly considered to be an overreaction. But it soon became clear that Lisa's parents would not be easily appeased. Were round-trip airfare not forthcoming, they would take the case directly to the American embassy in Japan. In the heat of the moment, and under the considerable weight of this foreign pressure, against his better judgment he verbally acquiesced. At the very least, he thought, this gesture of goodwill would be enough to convince Lisa to stay in Japan for the remainder of her contract.

But Tsurukawa had miscalculated, and his offer to fly Lisa's parents to Japan to see their daughter raised a storm of protest within the prefectural government. The budget section and the general affairs section chiefs balked openly at the request, arguing that Tsurukawa had overstepped the boundaries of his authority. Apologetic, he offered to pay for the trip out of his private bank account, but this was rejected as inappropriate, and a meeting between representatives of the board of education, the budget office, and the general affairs division was called to weigh the pros and cons of the matter. Tanabe-san, who participated in the subsequent negotiations, recalled:

> That meeting lasted for three hours! Most of us felt the response of Lisa and her parents was out of proportion to the magnitude of the incident and that Mr. Tsurukawa had erred in making the offer. But we also felt that since it had already been extended, the prefecture proba-

bly ought to go through with it. Frankly, we were afraid that this could turn into an international incident if we mishandled it, particularly since Lisa's parents were doctors. We simply couldn't risk the chance that our handling of it would backfire. But the thing was, the general affairs section chief (*sōmu bucho*), who had been sent here from the Ministry of Home Affairs, was dead set against paying. Finally, he phoned a colleague in Home Affairs' Tokyo office to get some advice. I happened to be right there in his office during the whole conversation. He kept yelling, "Why do we have to pay? Why do we have to pay?" It was quite a scene!

Much to the section chief's dismay, the ministry advised him to authorize payment for the flight. Ultimately he relented, and Lisa's parents were reimbursed for their airfare.

In the meantime, the circumstances surrounding the incident, and the starkly contrasting interpretations of them, had become clearer. The intrusion had occurred shortly after Lisa had returned from jogging alone in shorts and a tank top, something she did on a regular basis and usually along the same course. Moreover, she had not locked her front door while she was in the bath. These two facts alone were enough to convince Sato-sensei, who visited her apartment the following morning, that Lisa was largely responsible for what had happened: "It was her mistake. She was quite attractive, you know, and had a propensity for jogging in shorts and sleeveless shirts; and for some reason she didn't lock her door. Someone probably followed her home that night, and being curious and most probably drunk, entered her house. I doubt he intended to harm Lisa."

Lisa and Clara perceived the same events quite differently: they saw a criminal offense and a gross violation of Lisa's basic human rights and they expected the Japanese to respond accordingly. Though Tsurukawa's initial reaction had seemed sympathetic, the general tone shifted the next morning. The head English teacher at Lisa's base school called to express dismay that she wouldn't be coming to school to participate in the humorous skit they had practiced the day before for English class; later, he chided her for not acting as a Japanese woman would have. When Sato-sensei arrived at her apartment, he consulted the contract and after some deliberation decided that the only way Lisa could be excused from school without being docked in pay was if she filed a police report, which she did. Lisa then asked if she could move to a second-floor apartment, but Sato-sensei said that the prefecture was bound by their agreement with the landlord. If she moved, she would have to make all the new arrangements herself, including payment of key money (roughly $3,000). When she asked if the prefecture would pay for her return trip should she decide to go home, Sato-sensei read her the section in her contract about the penalties she would incur for leaving early.

The stalemate continued for a day, and Lisa was still undecided about what action to take when her parents arrived. Sato and Tsurukawa expressed their deep regret for the incident and their intention to put it behind them. They stressed the changes that Lisa could make in her behavior—wearing more conservative clothes when she jogged, changing routes, and locking the apartment door afterward. But Lisa's parents were quite adamant that the prefecture take some action to ensure that such an intrusion would not happen again. When Sato-sensei resisted, they demanded that CLAIR officials be contacted; under pressure from CLAIR, he finally agreed to search for a second-floor apartment. By this time, however, Lisa and her parents had become thoroughly disillusioned by the apparent reluctance of the prefecture to deal effectively with the problem, and they decided to return home together.

In the end, the incident left all parties with a bitter taste in their mouth. Most of the other prefectural ALTs who learned of the incident from Clara saw the prefectural response as confirming their preconceptions about bureaucratic insensitivity. Chad recalled, "I heard Sato-sensei called the attack incident an 'accident.' That phrasing was more than a little humorous to all of us. The women involved were very upset because it was clearly an assault, and the term 'accident' removes responsibility. By cautioning them on how to dress, they felt like they were being told not to act out of line, and that Lisa had somehow caused the problem." John suggested that blame lay mainly with national and prefectural officials who had failed to provide enough information at orientation. Lisa apparently was never told that her jogging wear might be interpreted as suggestive, nor was she cautioned about locking her door.

Nevertheless, the few ALTs who knew Lisa personally felt that she and her parents had overreacted. Pat, a Japanese American ALT in a neighboring school, commented that Lisa had not been particularly happy in her school placement because the head English teacher, Ikuno-sensei, was an overbearing man who treated her more like a pet than a human being. All the other teachers were afraid to talk to her because Ikuno-sensei was sure to show up to embarrass them. To make matters worse, her high school was one of the top academic schools in the prefecture; its disciplinary policy was extremely strict and entrance exam preparation ruled the day. Pat concluded, "So, I don't know, she may have used the incident as a chance to get out of a difficult situation. I don't think she had many friends among the rest of us ALTs either. She struck me as very naive and immature; it was almost like she fit the 'valley girl' stereotype perfectly." Even Clara, who was quite critical of the way that prefectural administrators handled the incident, found some fault with the behavior of Lisa and her parents.

But Lisa's inadequate sensitivity to customs in Japan hardly excuses the "blame-the-victim" mind-set of the male board of education officials. Though Tsurukawa was never officially reprimanded for offering to reimburse Lisa's parents for airfare, he was informally censored within the prefectural office for overstepping the bounds of his authority. For their part, Sato-sensei and Tanabe-san were completely nonplussed by the reaction of Lisa and her parents and by their demands for plane fare. "I can't believe a doctor would be that worried about money," Tanabe-san recalled with bafflement. Sato-sensei added, "We can't imagine a Japanese woman reacting the way Lisa did. And you know," he continued, "Lisa never even apologized to us for leaving the door unlocked or for causing such an inconvenience to her school and the board of education."

A broader moral to be drawn from Lisa's story is that while the experience of some form of discrimination and harassment at the hands of males may be universal for women, there are culturally specific repertoires of responses. In spite of the considerable gains made in the legal and economic position of women in Japanese society after World War II, attitudinal and behavioral changes have lagged far behind statutory reforms.[23] The brave talk about a new generation of Japanese women is occurring against the reality that economic and political power is still largely in the hands of men; thus, female resistance to harassment in the workplace still largely takes the form of subtle manipulations (not serving tea in a timely manner, etc.) rather than outright confrontation or lawsuits, though the latter approach is becoming more frequent. It is not uncommon to see Japanese women who have been the object of offensive talk or groping at a party find non-confrontational means of coping, perhaps even sending the drunken offender off in a taxi with a flurry of bows.

Lisa's was not the first case of the ill-treatment of women to come to CLAIR's attention. AJET had formed a Women's Support Network during the very first year of the program to assist female JET participants in making the transition to a society with a higher degree of gender inequality than their own. Unlike Lisa's case, most of the complaints addressed inappropriate conduct on the part of ETCs or JTLs themselves, such as that described in this anonymous letter to the *JET Journal*:

As a woman I do not feel safe at *enkais* [parties] because people casually joke about *sawari* [groping] and there are men at my office who are well known for *sawari*. I have never been physically molested but nonetheless, I feel threatened by the possibility that I may be subject to abuse.

Initially, I trusted my supervisor as we had briefly discussed sexual harassment and he reassured me that he had read the CLAIR handbook and was aware of the problem. . . . However, at my *Kangeikai* [welcome party] my supervisor got drunk and he verbally sexually harassed a woman I work with. At one point he turned his attention to me. He looked at me lecherously and began to tell me I was attractive, but I quickly shrugged him off. He then continued to bother the other woman as he tried to make her dance with him, but she escaped by making an excuse to go home.

As a result of that incident I no longer trust my supervisor and even find it hard to respect him. I finally discussed this incident with him last week. I tried to be tactful by explaining that sexual harassment is not just physical but verbal as well. He assumed I was referring to someone else. . . . I finally had to tell him it was he that offended me. He listened to me politely but it was clear that he did not understand my point when he responded that sexual harassment is a matter of cultural interpretation.[24]

The most prominent public case of sexual harassment occurred in 1993, when a village assembly in Nagano-ken voted to remove a deputy mayor from his post ostensibly for pawing an ALT at a village party.[25] But the ALT involved argued that the action taken by the village assembly was disproportionate to the seriousness of the event, leading to speculation that "sexual harassment" may have been used as an excuse for an internal political move; I was unable to determine the validity of this account.

Japanese officials at the national level were quick to line up for the fight against sexual harassment. At the annual information meetings held for prefectural administrators, CLAIR and Ministry of Education officials regularly allowed the program coordinators to give short lectures on "the meaning of sexual harassment," though Tanabe-san, who attended one of these meetings, recalled that most of what program coordinators warned against was considered normal behavior for men in Japan. In 1989 CLAIR directed all prefectures to ensure that single women not be housed in first-floor apartments, regardless of their preferences. And CLAIR officials even agreed to conduct a survey of JET participants about sexual harassment; these questions were eventually included in the annual living conditions survey. At first glance, the results were striking; nearly 40 percent of respondents in 1989 indicated that they had been harassed verbally (19 percent), physically (5 percent), or both (15 percent).[26] It is difficult to assess the significance of these replies, however, since "sexual harassment" was not defined in the questionnaire.

To my mind, what is most revealing here is the extent to which Japanese policymakers conceptualized sexual harassment as a "foreign problem." By Tanabe-san's own admission, it was the fear that the situation might turn into an "international incident" that ultimately determined how the prefecture treated Lisa. At the national level, too, CLAIR officials wholeheartedly supported the program coordinators' lectures to prefectural administrators on sexual harassment even though no comparable training was conducted regarding the harassment of Japanese women and even though the program coordinators' well-intentioned efforts to raise awareness at times crossed the line into "the West knows best" sermons.

The Pension Confrontation

Only a few months separated Lisa's departure and what Sato-sensei described as another of his most disagreeable memories (*iyana omoide*): a heated confrontation with an Australian ALT over the requirement that JET participants pay into a pension fund from which they would receive no benefits (see chapter 3). The actual clash took place in May 1988, in a district board of education to which two ALTs had been posted—Toby, a thirty-two-year-old former schoolmaster from Australia, and Trisha, a twenty-two-year-old American woman. Both felt strongly about the injustice of the pension policy and decided to fight it. Toby laid out their case: "Our argument was that we would accept it if there was some potential benefit to us, but without that, it seemed unjust to say the least. So we each wrote a letter to Sato-sensei explaining our position, and he actually came out to [our district board of education] to explain the policy. He basically said that every group which employed twenty or more people was required by law to do this." This explanation did not appease Toby and Trisha, however, and they firmly told Sato-sensei that they were not satisfied with his response. They also informed him that they were planning to write to the local newspaper about the matter and to consult with other ALTs in the prefecture to decide on a course of action.

Sato-sensei was quite upset by these threats, particularly because his relationship with Toby was already stormy. He had contacted Toby several times prior to his departure from Australia to ask him to bring textbooks and encyclopedias that could be used to design reading comprehension tests in the prefecture. After being invited by Sato-sensei to meet him for dinner one night to receive the books, Toby had returned to his board of education and listed the trip and dinner as a business expense. This led his ETC there to call Sato-sensei, who angered Toby by labeling the trip and dinner a personal expense. Having gone to some trouble to find and transport the books, Toby expected to be reimbursed. In addition, Toby was close in age to Sato-sensei and was not at all inclined to play what he called the "subordination game."

After consulting with the board of education section chief, Sato-sensei decided on a course of action. He traveled to Toby's office on Saturday morning, called him in from his house, and proceeded to read him the article in the JET contract on political activity. In doing so, he was warning Toby that if he wrote a letter to the newspaper or contacted other ALTs about this, a fine would be deducted from his salary and he would be barred from renewing his stay for an additional year. But Sato-sensei was totally unprepared for Toby's reaction. In the middle of the office, Toby suddenly raised his voice and began yelling that threats would not work and that he couldn't be responsible for the actions of other ALTs. Flustered and visibly embarrassed, Sato-sensei tried to recover his poise and hold his ground, but as Toby later described it, "he began twitching all over—he's really a very nervous person." That night Toby rounded up seven other ALTs for an emergency meeting at a local pub that catered to foreigners, and numerous letters were written to CLAIR. Beyond that, however, Toby backed off his threat to write to the newspaper and Sato-sensei took no further action. At our next meeting over coffee, Sato-sensei and Tanabe-san engaged in a lively appraisal of the run-in and discussed how they would handle similar incidents in the future. Sato-sensei warned, "We can't forget that that kind of person is among us. I suspected right from the start that he had other reasons for coming here, like making money. Why else would he quit his job as a principal? In his case, there's no effort put into team teaching and nothing changes. His district office has had a terrible time, so I really want to put some good people there this year." Tanabe-san half-jokingly came up with a plan for future action: he would sacrifice himself on the front lines should a similar problem arise. "Since I don't understand English very well," he pointed out, "it won't bother me so much if the ALT gets upset."

That Sato-sensei would find this kind of face-to-face conflict extremely unpleasant is hardly surprising, but I was completely taken aback by a subsequent development. Because of his age, nationality, and, ironically, his involvement in protesting against the pension payments, Toby received a phone call the next month from a British program coordinator at CLAIR asking him to come to Tokyo for an interview for that position. Because he had already been handpicked for the job (CLAIR needed an Australian program coordinator at the time), the interview was perfunctory, and CLAIR recommended that he be hired on condition that his current supervisors agreed on his suitability for the position. And when the documents asking for Sato-sensei's comments arrived, he declined to fight Toby's nomination. "I just wrote that I had no reservations," he recalled. "It's not worth creating a fuss over it." Though he had been given the opportunity to sabotage Toby's nomination, Sato-sensei chose the path of least resistance. In this case, his potential exercise of power was deflected by an even more powerful cultural preoccupation with avoiding direct confrontation.[27]

School Switching

One of the more common headaches for Sato-sensei and Tanabe-san was caused by the desire of renewing ALTs to switch schools. But in 1989 they instituted a policy that an ALT must spend two years at a school before the board of education would entertain any such request. "We're just not going to listen to their ultimatums any more," Sato-sensei told me. "From now on, if they want to renew, they have to stay where they are for two years."

It was only a matter of months before the new policy was tested. Chad was a twenty-three-year-old American; though based at Kitano High School, he also made irregular visits to six other high schools, including several dominated by union teachers. Chad thoroughly enjoyed his newfound celebrity status at his base school; although he was not particularly attuned to Japanese culture, his outgoing personality made him well-liked by students and teachers. At the midpoint of his stay, he had indicated to Sato-sensei that he planned to renew for the following year. Only a few weeks later, at a team-teaching workshop, Sato-sensei had told him that he would remain at Kitano as his base school and that he would visit only Sano and Yamaguni; a new ALT would take over the other three schools. Chad was excited about the idea of making fewer visits while still being able to keep Yamaguni, which had by far the most active group of JTLs and students.

But sometime thereafter, Sato-sensei decided to reshuffle the visit schools for the new ALT to include Yamaguni, precisely because the teachers there were such an enthusiastic group. It was exchanged with a strong union school that had expressed little interest in team teaching, where

Sato-sensei felt it was dangerous to send a new ALT. Unfortunately, Sato-sensei forgot to directly notify Chad, who felt betrayed when he received word from a JTL at Yamaguni that Sato-sensei had changed his mind. The prospect of staying for an additional year seemed much less appealing to Chad if he would be traveling to schools that were lukewarm about team teaching and the ESS club. He immediately called Sato-sensei, who apologized for the misunderstanding but stood firm, saying that the decision had already been made.

After some thought, Chad decided to press his cause. He met with several of his favorite teachers at Yamaguni and explained how much he liked the school and that he wanted to stay on the following year. Chad then developed a three-pronged argument: first, it was unconscionable that he was not consulted before his visit school was rearranged; second, it was unfair to put the new ALT into a teaching situation that would demand so much work; and third, the teachers at Yamaguni did not want him to leave. All of this Chad put into writing in a lengthy letter that closed with a veiled threat: he was not happy with the way his situation for the following year was shaping up, and he hoped to be able to come back to Japan and start afresh with a good attitude after his short trip home during summer vacation. Chad then took the extraordinary step of calling Yoshiro Tagai, the section chief and Sato-sensei's boss, at 10:00 P.M. on a Sunday night to explain his difficulty. Tagai, a former principal at one of Chad's visit schools, listened carefully to Chad's explanation and promised to see what he could do, though he stressed that the matter was Sato-sensei's responsibility.

The following day Chad hand-delivered his letter to the board of education. Though he had planned to just drop off the letter and leave, he happened to encounter Sato-sensei, who, without reading the letter, began to reiterate that his decision was determined by structural arrangements. At this point Tagai intervened and called Sato-sensei and Chad over to his desk, where he explained to Chad that in a sense, his argument was valid, but the decision had actually been made by a superior. Chad replied that he should have been consulted before a decision was made, and he was asking the board of education to reconsider its decision in light of the arguments in his letter.

Three days later, Sato-sensei called Chad to inform him that he had been allowed to keep Yamaguni. When I asked Tanabe-san what had happened to change his mind, he replied: "That was a really difficult case. We called the principal of Yamaguni, and it turned out that Chad was very well liked by teachers and students there. We also didn't want another ALT to leave the prefecture since we had had such bad luck up to that point. But Sato-sensei felt strongly that we had set a policy and ought to abide by it. He didn't think we should cave in to ALTs' demands. We went back and forth a long time, but ultimately Mr. Tagai and I persuaded Sato-sensei to give in." Tanabe-san also noted that even though Chad had ignored the usual protocol by leapfrogging Sato-sensei and issuing an ultimatum, he had acted with some restraint. Moreover, both Tagai and Tanabe-san liked Chad as a person and thought he was doing a good job in his school visits.

Chad's case offers several important lessons for understanding the response of Japanese bureaucracies to conflict. Especially interesting was how Tagai handled his encounter with Chad, ensuring that Sato-sensei would not lose face. In reality, there was no other "superior" involved in the decision, but it was crucial for him to support Sato-sensei at that moment. In addition, in dealing with Chad as in dealing with Lisa, the principal decision makers at the board of education differed markedly on how to reconcile conflicting factors. While all three of the administrators involved felt Chad was out of place in making his demands, that agreement by no means led to a natural consensus on what action to take. Finally, the case illustrates yet again the susceptibility of Japanese officials to foreign pressure and the persistent concern with how "international conflict" might harm the prefecture's image.

More Problems

Over the next few months, there was no letup in problems. First, an Irish ALT, Pete, was arrested for drunkenly kicking a police car on the main thoroughfare of the prefecture's capital city, and it was up to Sato-sensei and Tanaka-san to vouch for his character, apologize to school personnel, and ultimately bail him out after a two-day stint in jail. Tanabe-san explained that Pete had antagonistic feelings toward police in general as a result of growing up in Northern Ireland.

Some months later, Wendy appeared at the board of education with her letter of resignation. She had been placed at Subame High School—the oldest, most traditional, and most academic high school in the prefecture—and from the start it had been a bad match. She did not get along with most of her teachers, and there was very little room in the curriculum for conversational English. With little training in Japanese language and culture and little patience for difference, she had quickly soured on Japanese education and society. Recently, she had become pregnant and her husband had found a job elsewhere, so she had decided to call it quits. But she had two financial demands. First, according to the contract, if she quit in midmonth she would have to pay back some of that month's salary, which she had already received. This infuriated her, and Sato-sensei generously offered a compromise, realizing the futility of trying to recover money already disbursed. Second, Wendy insisted that the prefecture pay her airfare home even though her contract stated clearly that she would forfeit it if she left early. She argued that she knew of cases in other prefectures in which the rules had been bent. On this point, however, Sato-sensei held his ground.

Shortly after Wendy's departure, Brent, an ALT who had been based in the prefectural education center for two years, was notified by the board of education that he was to travel by bus once a week to teach in Wendy's place. He replied that he was not interested in doing that, as it was not part of his job description. In no mood to bargain, the head of the compulsory education section told him that he was not asking for an opinion but telling Brent to do it. Reluctantly, Brent agreed. The next morning, however, his boss at the education center secretly went to the bus station and hid nearby, reading a newspaper, to see whether Brent actually showed up. When he did not arrive, his boss called the board of education; after the confrontation that ensued, Brent quit. Then, having sent home thousands of dollars in savings, he told Sato-sensei and Tanabe-san he did not have enough money to cover his financial obligations (outstanding bills for rent, phone, utilities, etc.) before leaving. These two cases only confirmed for Tanabe-san and Sato-sensei what they had already surmised: some ALTs could be downright cheap. A Japanese person, they said, even if he only made a third of the ALTs' salary, would never consider lodging such complaints and demands. After recounting the stories later, Tanabe-san fumed, "Sometimes I think money is all the ALTs worry about!"[28]

BUREAUCRATIC INFORMALITY AND RESPONSES TO CONFLICT

Moments of crisis often expose taken-for-granted assumptions embedded in structures of power, and the prefecture's handling of the incidents described is quite revealing. Most notably, Sato-sensei and Tanabe-san would go to extremes to prevent ALTs from leaving prematurely. Their sensitivity to outsiders' perceptions and desire to shield signs of conflict from the public eye were typical of prefectural responses more generally.

Yet their readiness to appease by no means suggests that they saw the ALTs' demands as justified. Both Sato-sensei and Tanabe-san tended to blame their misfortunes on the selection of "bad" (*shitsu ga yokunai*) foreigners by the Ministry of Foreign Affairs. Tanabe-san, for instance, informed me shortly after my arrival that there were basically three kinds of ALTs: those who came to teach, those who came to vacation and sightsee, and those who came to further their business careers. The latter two types, he explained, generally approached their work in schools with a less-than-serious demeanor and therefore were unacceptable to the board of education. Noting that the quality of ALTs seemed to be declining with each year of the program, he added: "The main thing we try to avoid is ALTs leaving early. So far we haven't been very successful at that, but our colleagues understand that it's because of problems with the foreign assistants, not us. If someone left because of conditions at his school, that would really be an embarrassment for us." This separation of (structural) conditions of employment and personal responses of ALTs into mutually exclusive categories has little explanatory value, for it ignores the complex interaction between the two that occurs in international exchanges; it does, however, usefully shift fault away from the prefectural school system.

One way to improve the quality of their participants was to game the selection process to their advantage. After the second year of the program, Sato-sensei and Tanabe-san decided that since they had had considerable trouble with Americans and Australians, they would request only British and Canadian participants the following year. When that made no difference, they then requested only men, on the grounds that women had a harder time adjusting to Japanese society. This second request was not granted by CLAIR, yet the sentiment behind it—the belief that women were more likely to suffer from adjustment problems—was one I encountered frequently among educational administrators. Data only slightly support this notion; as of 1991, women accounted for 57 percent of all JET participants and 65 percent of those who resigned prematurely.[29]

Hiring a Human Shield

At the same time that they were trying to tweak the selection process to their advantage, Sato-sensei and Tanabe-san were taking several other decisive steps to ward off future problems and to reduce the chances of more face-to-face conflict in a foreign language. The most dramatic of these measures was the decision to hire a veteran ALT to work as liaison in the prefectural board of education itself. In the summer of 1989 Kevin, a clean-cut, likable American with a master's degree in English literature, was reassigned from the commercial high school to full-time duty in the board of education. Sato-sensei had become acquainted with Kevin in a very unorthodox manner: Kevin's Japanese girlfriend had become pregnant, and the two had hastily decided to get married. In spite of the awkwardness of their encounter, Sato-sensei was impressed with Kevin's sense of responsibility and his sensitivity to Japanese cultural nuances. He also had two other traits that were indispensable for the job: he enjoyed after-hours drinking, and he had a very effective and charismatic classroom presence.

Bringing Kevin into the prefectural office had several benefits. First, he could act as a human shield. Not only was Kevin expected to help mediate crises, but he was also asked to work proactively, calling all ALTs soon after the school year began to learn how they were adjusting and to offer advice when possible. Eventually, he was dispatched to every single base school hosting an ALT to consult with each about team teaching and how to improve relations with the school.[30] In addition, Kevin provided important administrative help. Only months earlier Tanabe-san had requested that the prefectural office establish a new position to help coordinate the ALT project, but the budget office had denied his request. Assigning an ALT to work in the prefectural board of education was an alternative strategy for gaining assistance at minimal extra cost to the prefecture.

A final benefit to hiring Kevin was the role he could play in deflecting AJET's demands. Sato-sensei was adamantly against AJET, and he felt that CLAIR had gone overboard in acceding to the group's wishes. For example, when CLAIR asked prefectural boards of education to classify the meetings of AJET prefectural representatives as an "official business trip" (*shucchōatsukai*), thus allowing them to miss their school classes without taking vacation time or losing pay, Sato-sensei complained, "We really ought not to allow them to do that." He continued:

> Sometimes at [Tokyo] orientation when I hear AJET people criticize the textbooks, I feel like telling them, "If you don't like them, go home!" Today at the Ministry of Education meetings for ETCs, Mr. Wada said that ideally they would just follow the ministry's plan for orientation, but that we have to let AJET play a role or they won't cooperate with us. In some ways I think they're just like the teachers' union because the AJET representatives spend so much time working on their own projects that they don't spend time trying to improve relations with Japanese teachers at their school. So we don't want our prefectural ALTs to get involved with AJET.

So eager was Sato-sensei not to have to deal separately with AJET's prefectural representative that when Kevin went to the renewers' conference in the spring, he urged him to run for the position of prefectural representative. But Kevin lost, and the following year saw much tension between the board of education and AJET's prefectural representative, who felt that Sato-sensei's tendency to consult with Kevin about ALT policy left him out of the loop. "It would be so much easier," lamented Sato-sensei, "if the board of education could choose the AJET representative."

Apparently, Sato-sensei and Tanabe-san were not alone in recognizing that some buffer was needed in the board of education. In 1991 CLAIR formally instituted a position of "prefectural liaison" in response to the decline in AJET membership and to the growing realization that AJET prefectural representatives did not always share the views of the majority of ALTs in their prefecture. By 1995 roughly 70 percent of prefectures and designated cities employed a veteran ALT in the board of education for at least a day or two a week.[31] While ALTs in this position had limited influence over decisions made by the board of education, their mere presence in these offices forced prefectural administrators to come to grips with diversity on a daily basis.

When Trust Breaks Down: The Role of Employment Contracts

Yet another strategy devised by Sato-sensei and Tanabe-san for dealing with their numerous problems was to create an increasingly detailed and airtight employment contract. Each year, they would revise the contracts, adding new articles or rewording old ones, in light of the previous year's events. By 1990 the contract had become a small booklet that elaborated in excruciating detail every conceivable expectation and contingency. Its twenty-eight "articles" covered resignation, dismissal, reduction of salary, traveling expenses, holidays, paid leave, special holidays, special holidays for female ALTs, absence, prosecution leave, prohibition from outside work, procedure for taking sick leave, supervisors' orders, diligence, conduct restrictions, confidentiality, restrictions against involvement in profit-making enterprises, religious activities and related matters, restrictions on operating motor vehicles, disciplinary action, and more.

The use of detailed employment contracts runs contrary to Japanese custom. Typically, contracts are short, symbolic documents used to signify the cementing of a long-term relationship of trust and mutual cooperation. Tacit understanding and an implied sense of trust are preferred to a formal, written delineation of job responsibilities, rules, and regulations. It is assumed that unforeseen problems will be worked out through mutual goodwill and cooperation, and the entire system takes for granted that individual and institutional goals are not by definition in conflict. In contrast, the legal formulations of employment in the JET participants' home countries grow out of a very different notion of justice, as Frank Upham has pointed out: "If society is built on individualism and competition and the only acknowledged common ground is enlightened self-interest, social life becomes a desperate contest and community nothing more than a temporary equilibrium among fundamentally unconnected and potentially antagonistic actors. Because mutual trust and personal relationships are contingent and make unreliable guides for resolving conflict, the rules of the contest and the mode of their application become all important."[32] This legal-rational model emphasizes explicit, context-free standardization of rules and procedures and the importance of public contracts that delineate, item by item, specific rules and responsibilities.

In most Japanese organizations, however, expressive exchange relationships of a general, long-term nature coexist with more instrumental and contractual ones. Within the formal bureaucratic structure, we find one-to-one relationships between superiors and subordinates that are based on mutual trust, confidence, and loyalty and that involve a variety of expressive exchanges even outside the workplace. In effect, there are two social orders operating in Japanese bureaucracy. One is the formal level of universal principle, which in Japan is referred to as *tatemae*. The other is the informal level, or *honne*, influenced by the realities of particular situations and relationships.[33]

During the MEF Program only a two-page contract was used, but Japanese officials quickly realized that adherence to this custom would prove disastrous as the numbers of participants who were unfamiliar with Japanese cultural expectations increased exponentially. For prefectural administrators, the crucial problem was how to control and manage ALTs given that informal mechanisms of social control did not seem to work. They could not count on the ALTs' having internalized Japanese norms of proper behavior, valuing the nonverbal conveyance of information, or striving to understand what was expected of them without being told.

Rather than attempting to socialize ALTs to the expectations of Japanese work groups, Japanese administrators took the opposite approach and tried to meet the JET participants on their own terms. This tendency was encouraged at the national level. In 1987 CLAIR sent a model contract to all prefectures, with instructions that it could be modified in accordance with local expectations, and included in its orientation manual for local governments a strongly worded directive:

> If your explanations of the terms of the contract, rules of conduct, and other important matters are ambiguous, trouble will most likely result,

especially with regard to working conditions and prohibited activities. The foreign assistants, having been raised in a contractual society, are used to listening to such explanations, even when they are very strict. It is necessary to refrain from ambiguous treatment and to give firm and persistent explanations, making sure at all times that the foreign assistants understand.[34]

Caricatures such as these may partially explain why Japanese prefectural officials not only used an employment contract but embraced it with a fervor that seems puzzling in light of their own preference for informal modes of conflict resolution. Ironically, Sato-sensei's inclination to rely primarily on the contract to resolve disputes earned him a reputation among prefectural ALTs as cold and calculating. Both Lisa and Toby, for instance, interpreted his verbatim reading from the contract as exemplifying perfectly the lack of a human touch that was the problem with Japan's internationalization. Even Kevin, who was viewed as more of an insider by Sato-sensei and Tanabe-san, sometimes objected to the extent to which appeal to the contract became Japanese officials' knee-jerk response: "It seems like whenever I bring up things involving ALT requests—like someone wants extra vacation time or if they can't be at a required meeting—it's like a wall goes up and they just say, 'No' and go straight to the contract." Adding to the suspicion of ALTs were several misunderstandings that resulted from discrepancies between the Japanese version of the contract and the English version that they received. To the ALTs such discrepancies seemed irresponsible at best and downright dishonest at worst.

Cultures differ in their assumptions about motivation and human nature, as well as in their repertoires of techniques for interpersonal influence. Moreover, different historical experiences generate and perpetuate distinctive myths about how specific groups of people behave and how they ought to be managed.[35] In this case, prefectural officials had little faith that the ALTs would respond to appeals directed at internalized norms. The ALTs tended to focus on particular issues and immediate circumstances, in part because they knew that their stay in Japan was limited. In addition, Sato-sensei and Tanabe-san had to worry about precedents. The bureaucratic impulse is to standardize procedures in order to ensure smooth and efficient operation, and they did not like exceptions or disruptions. The failure of their preferred, symbolic means of control thus led Sato-sensei and Tanabe-san to embrace the contract with a fervor that at times seemed to border on desperation. But although they could certainly operate under this Weberian model in which rewards and punishments were explicitly spelled out, I sensed that they were never entirely comfortable with it. The clear-cut dualism of good and bad, right and wrong, that is characteristic of the "contractual model" did not fit well with their sense of morality.

It is crucial to note, however, that the day-to-day behavior of ALTs was never tightly supervised and controlled. Stanley Heginbotham has suggested that there are three compliance mechanisms available to maintain indirect control over the behavior of physically inaccessible field agents— material incentive control, feedback control, and preprogrammed control[36]— and his model seems to apply well here. Material incentive control was clearly evident in the arrangement of the overall employment package, for it was in the ALTs' best interest to fulfill the requirements of the job. Preprogrammed control, which is achieved by persuading the individual worker to accept the goals of the program, was manifest in the orientation, midyear conferences, and newsletters organized by CLAIR, as well as in a variety of team-teaching seminars and publications at the prefectural level. These attempts to get ALTs to buy into the goal of team teaching were nevertheless constantly in danger of being undermined by actual conditions in the schools.

Feedback control, which involves some monitoring of the ALTs' job and regular reports, was rarely implemented. In fact, one of the frequent complaints from ALTs regarded the *lack* of feedback from their superiors (particularly ETCs) about how they were performing their jobs. This lack of feedback is quite understandable, however, given the difficulty of objectively assessing much of the ALTs' work, the uneven nature of the ETCs' own expertise in team teaching, and their strong preference for avoiding confrontation with a foreigner. Feedback control would make explicit the limitations of trust and confidence in the ALT and could easily undermine the hosts' fragile commitment to team teaching, on which the entire program depended.

THE FRONT LINES OF INTERNATIONALIZATION

At the prefectural level, JET participants are pulled into a complex, heavily bureaucratic institution with ongoing programs, priorities, and operating procedures. Board of education bureaucrats must respond to a bewildering array of objectives and pressures—from school officials and teachers, district administrators, the ALTs, and national-level ministry bureaucrats. When the formation of coalitions at the national level is aided by leaving policy goals somewhat ambiguous, then lower levels must take on the task—and the unpleasantness—of removing ambiguities. Sato-sensei and Tanabe-san inherited a whole host of problems that had been left unresolved, including the pension issue, Japanese language training for ALTs, and the relative emphasis to be given to conversational and exam English.

Numerous other small factors—conflicting commitments, dependence on those who may not fully support the program, procedural requirements—accumulate to affect how prefectures implement the JET Program. Other difficulties arise because the local bureaucrats charged with implementation may not have the necessary proficiency in English. Finally, as the actors frequently change, their attention (on both sides) shifts: prefectural officials rotate every few years, and the turnover among ALTs is constant. Indeed, nearly 40 percent of ETCs report that they are working with foreigners for the first time. Under these circumstances, it is little wonder that Sato-sensei and Tanabe-san most frequently described their JET-related job responsibilities to me as "burdensome" (*futan*).[37]

The teachers' consultants thus employ a variety of methods to protect established routines and existing institutional priorities. They exhibit a tendency toward what Harry Wolcott has referred to as "variety-reducing behavior."[38] That is, the ETCs respond to the ALTs with inherent conservatism because they are anxious to keep things manageable and to minimize the program's burden to themselves and others. Changes in policy are avoided because new initiatives usually arouse more controversy than leaving things as they are—even if the status quo includes contradictions and jurisdictional overlaps. In many ways the picture that emerges confirms what is already known about Japanese strategies for resolving conflicts when making and implementing policy. It very closely approximates what Michael Blaker has described as "coping": that is, "carefully assessing the international situation, methodically weighing each alternative, sorting out various options to see what is really serious, waiting for the dust to settle on some contentious issue, piecing together a consensus view about the situation faced, and then performing the minimum adjustments needed to neutralize or overcome criticism and adapt to the existing situation with the fewest risks."[39] While coping in foreign policy is usually seen as spineless or immoral, it could also be viewed as a pragmatic and realistic response.

In spite of the difficulties in conflict management and the extra work the JET Program created for them, Sato-sensei and Tanabe-san did not once consider forsaking their responsibilities. Eager to remain true to the spirit of the program, and feeling very acutely the high expectations of the superintendent and the governor that they make internationalization a

"success," both of them worked mightily not only to defuse potential conflicts but also to create support and momentum for team-teaching activities. Under their guidance the prefecture sponsored a series of team-
teaching workshops and seminars, and in the final year of their tenure it
published a sourcebook of ideas for the communication-oriented English
language classroom. Most ETCs strongly believe that the JET Program is
in the national interest. Prefectural officials remain receptive both to pressure from the ALTs themselves and to top-down guidance from national
ministry officials.

The ETCs did not have their hands entirely tied by environmental constraints or cultural preoccupations: like most people, they are self-
interested actors and, as we have seen, they wield considerable power in
shaping program content. Indeed, their power lies precisely in the ambigu-
ity of their role. Bureaucrats can interpret policy directives in ways that
align their own desires and those of policymakers or they can ignore directives altogether. Each course of action has costs and tradeoffs, and the
choices are real. The prefectural board of education is thus the focus of
pressures from all sides, and the teachers' consultants are the fulcrum
around which the system moves. Influenced by outside guidance and authority, they nonetheless shape program structure and content in ways
that protect local meanings and institutions.

In the summer of 1995 I had the opportunity to revisit Sato-sensei and
Tanabe-san and to swap stories again over beer and karaoke. After four
years working for the board of education, Sato-sensei had been appointed
head of curriculum at a prestigious prefectural high school, where he was
biding his time before being appointed vice-principal. Tanabe-san first had
been sent to a district board of education, and then was promoted to assistant section chief (*kacho hosa*) in the personnel department of the prefectural office. He had a much more distinguished look about him, enhanced
by the addition of some gray hairs, and Sato-sensei joked at how quickly he
was ascending the prefectural career ladder. Neither had had any significant contact with subsequent administrators of the JET Program. "It would
be rude and inappropriate to offer unsolicited advice," Sato-sensei told me.

With a bit of prodding they began to reminisce about their time together in the board of education. Tanabe-san commented that he missed
those days because he now had less variety in his job. By contrast, Sato-
sensei was much more relieved to be out of the line of fire, even though he
still taught English regularly with an ALT. "We just gave up being a base
school," he noted, "and to tell you the truth, it's a lot easier that way." But

he did not regret having worked with the ALTs. "I'm thankful for taking that position because I've learned I should just say what I think. If ALTs can express their opinions freely, then we have to be able to do the same." We talked late into the night, and I was particularly impressed by Tanabe-san's long-term perspective on internationalization:

> You know, everyone talks about *kokusaika*, but it's a lot harder than it looks! It takes a lot of time, and there's a lot of disappointment along the way. Ten years from now we'll probably be saying, "Look at that stupid stuff we were doing back then." The first few years are the hard-est part—getting everyone used to foreigners. But our sensibility is to put up with the bad part of hosting ALTs so as to reap the benefits of the good part. That's why we keep inviting more and more ALTs. And this is definitely the trend. There's no turning back now.

5 Beyond the Stereotypes
The JET Program in Local Schools

Prefectural officials, of course, must turn the assistant language teachers over to school-based personnel, and it is at the school level where the symbolic agreement, so easy to maintain when the concept of "internationalization" is fairly abstract, really begins to break down. Japanese schools, like their counterparts elsewhere, often elude the administrative reach of national and prefectural policies. They are also quite different in many ways from secondary schools in the ALTs' home countries. Most Japanese secondary schools display close daily cooperation and interaction between teachers centering on twin goals: preparing for entrance exams and socializing students toward norms of group process. By the standards of this environment, the ALTs often behave very poorly, because their cultural assumptions lead them to view the goals of education in general, and the meaning of internationalization in particular, somewhat differently. Consequently, their presence in schools requires a delicate balancing act on the part of Japanese teachers who are eager to ensure that the ALTs have a pleasant stay but also need to shield themselves and their students from the undesirable effects of the ALTs' presence. In the early years it was not uncommon to hear JTLs half jokingly refer to the JET Program as "the second coming of the black ships" (*kurofune raishū*), drawing a parallel with Commodore William Perry's uninvited "opening" of Japan to Western trade in 1854.

Yet despite the shared administrative and normative framework for public secondary education, individual schools vary considerably in atmosphere. One of the most remarkable features of the JET Program is its capacity for transporting participants past the stereotypes of Japanese education; if there is one refrain that is sung by every ALT, it is "no two JET experiences are alike." In chapter 4, we considered how such differences between small mountain village and city, between academic and commercial school, can lead to complaints by participants; but they can also underscore the richness of the system. This variation within public secondary education is all the more significant because it is routinely ignored by the Western media.

This chapter examines both the cultural patterning of and the diversity in school-level responses to the ALTs. In many ways, an ALT arriving at a local school can be likened to a stranger being brought into a preexisting culture. What are the cultural rules governing this process, and what are the possible social dramas that can unfold? How do persons with radically different cognitive frameworks interact when they are asked to work together on a short-term project? I begin with several vignettes: while they by no means cover the range of JET experiences, they start to address the challenging question of how ALTs can have such radically different "Japan experiences" in a culture that has long been portrayed as homogeneous.

NISHIKAWA: AN ACADEMIC HIGH SCHOOL

Early in 1989 the principal of Nishikawa High School received word from Sato-sensei that his school would be asked to serve as a base school for an ALT beginning in August. Up to that point, Nishikawa had only been visited one day a week, but the numbers of JET participants had expanded. Would the principal bring this matter to the attention of the head English teacher and secure the approval of the entire English teaching staff? The principal called in Hayano-sensei, an energetic and savvy teacher who served as head of both career guidance and the English department, and the two of them discussed the problem.

Founded in 1982 and accommodating roughly 1,500 students annually, Nishikawa was one of the newest and most rigorous academic schools in the prefecture. Nestled amid rice fields in a suburban community approximately fifteen miles from the capital city, it was the flagship of the prefectural project to improve performance on university entrance exams; the public schools were competing fiercely with the private high schools in the prefecture. This determination to fashion an academic reputation was manifest in a number of ways. Each year the school held an open house for prospective students and their parents; nearly 1,000 people attended in 1989. The annual Culture Festival (Bunkasai), an important schoolwide activity showcasing students' artistic and musical talents to parents and guests, had been renamed "Cultural Event" (Bunkateki Gyōji) in the hopes that students would view it as a serious learning experience rather than simply a carnival; preparations began weeks in advance. Similarly, the annual school trip eschewed popular destinations such as Tokyo Disneyland or ski resorts in favor of more intellectually stimulating venues. The school allowed nearly a quarter of its students to leave for after-school classes (*juku*) immediately after sixth period, missing homeroom, cleaning, and club activities. Hayano-sensei even told me that shortly after the Ministry of Education decreed that public schools would close for the first and third Saturday of each month, Nishikawa's twelfth graders began coming to school on Sundays for special review sessions. "We have to keep the curtains pulled," Hayano-sensei confessed, "because the media will have a field day if they find out about this."[1]

The presence of an ALT would take away valuable time from entrance exam study as well as constantly threaten to embarrass the majority of the Japanese teachers of language, whose spoken English skills were limited. Thus, when Hayano-sensei presented the board of education's request, he was not surprised that the English teachers fell completely silent. But isolationism was not an option: the long-term viability of Nishikawa depended on acquiring base school know-how. The principal and head of curriculum lobbied to consent to hosting an ALT and Hayano-sensei returned to the English faculty with the verdict: "In the present climate of internationalization," he declared, "this is a must (*masuto*)."[2]

Out of a staff of twelve full-time and three part-time English faculty, only Ueda-sensei was genuinely enthusiastic at the prospect. Hayano-sensei knew he could count on three others—Kawakami-sensei, Kuwano-sensei, and Ikuno-sensei—for varying degrees of support, but that left seven of the full-time faculty dragging their heels. But the decision to be a base school had been made, and Hayano-sensei stressed the importance of all English faculty being "in step" (*ashinami wo sorou*) as they implemented it. He appointed Ueda-sensei to be overall coordinator of the ALT's visit (*ALT tantō*). This proved to be a masterful move. An experienced and dedicated teacher possessing a rare combination of wisdom, perspective, and empathy, Ueda-sensei was deeply respected by both students and faculty. Moreover, even though he was extremely busy as head of the health section and constantly involved in counseling students who were suffering from academic and social stress, he was truly excited about hosting an ALT.

Under the watchful eye of Hayano-sensei and the pragmatic, down-to-earth leadership of Ueda-sensei, the English faculty began preparing for hosting the ALT. No fewer than six informal positions were created for overseeing various dimensions of the ALT's visit: head of orientation and

settling in, counselor, coordinator of the team-teaching schedule, administrative liaison with the board of education, chair of the welcome party and
other special events, and coordinator of a once-a-month discussion group
(*kenshūkai*) for the English teaching staff. Three teachers visited another
high school in the prefecture with a long history of international involvement and attended an informational meeting held by the prefectural board
of education, in both cases receiving valuable pointers on how to be an effective base school. This pertained both to practical administrative tips on
finding housing and helping the foreigner to adjust and to more subjective
matters—in particular, advice on the importance of integrating the ALT
into school routines, on keeping tabs on the ALT's emotional and mental
state, and on making sure that the ALT was well aware of his or her specific
role (*ichizuke*) within the overall academic and social curriculum.

Finally, in July, the vital information about Nishikawa's ALT arrived
from Sato-sensei. They would host a twenty-two-year-old British woman,
Karen Chambers, who had taken a degree in English literature and German
at the University of St. Andrews in Scotland. According to Karen's application, which was circulated around the teacher's room along with her photo,
her coming to Japan stemmed primarily from a desire to travel and to experience different cultures. Her Japanese language skills were negligible.
Over the next few weeks, the two hottest topics among the English teachers were Karen's nationality and gender.

Karen's actual arrival was somewhat anticlimactic; because it coincided
with a four-week summer vacation, the teacher's room was largely vacant
during her first few weeks. Though some ALTs have complained bitterly
about the boredom of the first few weeks, Karen was relieved to have a chance
to settle in before her teaching responsibilities began. In a farewell letter two
years later, Karen recalled: "I remember Sato-sensei saying to me at the prefectural orientation, 'That's your supervisor, Ueda-sensei, over there.' I
turned around and faced about thirty Japanese men—I had no idea who he
was talking about and I was very nervous! After that, August is a blur of new
experiences. My apartment ('How small!' I thought); eating *sōmen* [noodles]
in the office while everyone watched me using chopsticks; a hot teacher's
room; cycling to work through rice fields; and lots of official forms." Karen's
apartment was small but adequate: two six-mat tatami rooms, a small dining
room, bath, and flush toilet. Perched on the edge of a small rice paddy, it was
a convenient five-minute bike ride to the school or to the train station.

Karen was especially appreciative of the warmth and kindness exhibited
by the faculty at Nishikawa. Shortly after the school year began, the English faculty threw her a welcome party at an expensive restaurant. Her

picture and self-introduction appeared in the school newspaper. "I'm so lucky to have come to such a great school," she kept exclaiming during the first few months. Karen was also assigned to visit the neighboring school, Yamagi High School, on Mondays and Thursdays, and happily discovered that Yamagi teachers were much more laid back than Nishikawa's. She soon settled into a weekly routine. Even her first experiences team teaching were positive, and she quickly overcame her fear of being unqualified. "This job certainly doesn't take much brains," she told me two months into her stay. "[All I have to do is] talk about myself. 'I have a brother . . .'"

The one thing that caused Karen concern early on was the lack of privacy. Shortly into her stay, she complained, "Last week I went into the city with another ALT, and one of the students saw us and must've told one of the teachers at my visit school. She asked me if I was with my boyfriend. What I do in private is none of their business. It's like, if I cough in the teacher's room, everyone knows it." Karen's interpretation of this treatment was that she was singled out because she was a foreigner, and she began warning teachers and students against using the label "gaijin." Yet Karen also fairly forcefully espoused respect for all cultures. "I think if we can realize that at heart we are all the same, no matter where we come from or what race we are, then we will have taken a great step towards true understanding," she once told me. Though perhaps somewhat naive, this view did lead her to downplay what she saw as negative in Japanese culture and accentuate the positive. She began studying the Japanese language and was a regular participant in the evening Japanese classes taught by Sato-sensei and Tanabe-san. She enjoyed experimenting with all kinds of Japanese foods, and she took calligraphy classes for a good part of her stay. She used her vacation time to visit famous historical spots in Japan (and even Korea), and on her return she wrote summaries for her English classes of her impressions of such places as the Hiroshima Peace Park. In many ways, then, Karen epitomized the type of young person national-level officials envisioned as an ideal JET participant.

Integration into School Routines

Japanese schools have been praised for what they accomplish not only academically but socially. At the heart of every high school in Japan is a simple set of activities, all supervised by faculty: classes, special events, and after-school programs. Like most Japanese schools Nishikawa was organized with the teachers' room as its hub, a central station from which teachers ventured out to the classrooms for their specific lessons. Indeed, the overall architecture had been designed with student guidance in mind. The school looked like a hollowed-out, three-story cube with a garden in the middle, but the teacher's room was perched right by the window on the second floor, affording an unobstructed view of hallways throughout the school. Desks in the teachers' room, too, were arranged to facilitate student guidance and school management; the homeroom teachers of each grade all sat in their own clusters and in another grouping sat teachers who had positions in the "school affairs" division (*gyōmubu*). Nishikawa also had a half dozen part-time teachers who shared several desks at the end of one cluster, and it was here that Karen sat. Her desk placement thus carried both a symbolic and pragmatic value: placing her with the part-time teachers symbolized her marginality in terms of the overall administration of the school, but it also ensured that none of the Japanese staff would have to shoulder the burden of sitting by Karen and speaking English to her regularly.

While the atmosphere in the teachers' room varies tremendously from school to school, Nishikawa's large size, academic prestige, and leaders dedicated to protocol made for a very formal and businesslike place.[3] Students here, unlike in many junior high schools, rarely entered the teachers' room, and any conversation among faculty occurred in full view of others—most particularly that of the stern vice-principal, whose desk, tucked in a corner, overlooked the entire room. The lack of privacy made the JTLs rather self-conscious about speaking English with Karen. In part, they were worried about being misunderstood or, conversely, not understanding what Karen said. But they also feared being poked fun at, on the one hand, or being accused of showing off their English, on the other. Even Ueda-sensei admitted, "I'm careful not to speak too much English when other teachers are around, but if it's just the two of us I enjoy speaking English a lot." JTLs rationalized their reluctance in other ways as well. Akamatsu-sensei confessed one of the reasons it was so hard to approach Karen was the fear that they would have nothing to talk about (*wadai ga tsukunai*): "We always worry about that when talking with foreigners." Kawakami-sensei told me that Karen became so engrossed in preparing class materials at her desk that the other teachers worried they would be bothering her if they interrupted.

Karen was largely unaware of this behind-the-scenes hand-wringing, however; and with twelve English teachers on the staff, usually enough people mustered up the courage to speak with her to keep her from ever feeling ostracized. In addition, a mathematics teacher who spoke English better than most JTLs had absolutely no compunctions about engaging her in conversation. But Karen did chafe a bit under what she perceived as the oppressive atmosphere of the teachers' room, and for this reason she eagerly anticipated Wednesday afternoon faculty meetings, which emptied it out. "I love Wednesday afternoons," Karen admitted, "because I can do anything I want."

Nevertheless, from the outset Hayano-sensei and Ueda-sensei were concerned about Karen's emotional well-being. "To be honest," Hayano-sensei told me, "we worry a lot about Karen because she's a single woman." Ueda-sensei, too, confessed that he worried that when everyone else in the teachers' room was talking, Karen must be lonely. They had observed that while Karen was extremely sincere and likable, she was not particularly outgoing and would rarely initiate conversation with students or teachers. At one point Hayano-sensei even approached me to see whether I thought Karen was depressed. Though I replied negatively, it was only a short while later that he asked all teachers to make an effort to talk with Karen as much as possible. In addition, Ueda-sensei began briefing Karen each day on what was said at the morning meeting.

The thorniest issue to resolve was Karen's team-teaching schedule, and understanding how it played out at Nishikawa requires a knowledge not only of the distinct personalities among the JTLs (and how these individuals related to one another) but also of the place of English classes within the larger organizational and curricular structure of the school. Ability grouping is usually said to be anathema to the strictly egalitarian mind-set of Japanese educators; although this characterization holds for public schools at the elementary and lower secondary level, exam-oriented high schools such as Nishikawa have begun experimenting with tracking. At Nishikawa each grade comprised eleven classes (with approximately forty students per class), and the classes were divided into three groups with slightly different curricula. In each grade, the "third stream" (*sanrui*) contained one class of students concentrating in physical education; the "second stream" (*nirui*) held three advanced classes of students concentrating in either the natural sciences or the humanities; and the "first stream" (*ichirui*), for the average students, numbered seven classes.

This complex structure seemed to leave little room for team teaching. A memo distributed to all English faculty on 1 September outlined the plan of action for the first month of Karen's visit in great and revealing detail. First, it was assumed from the outset that Karen would not visit the same class more than once a week even though students were taught English class three times a week, as mandated by the Ministry of Education. Second, twelfth-grade students rarely benefited from team teaching. With university entrance exams looming on the horizon, the English faculty as a whole decided that these classes would be off-limits except for "irregular visits." This meant that Miyatani-sensei and Murakawa-sensei, veteran teachers in their fifties who held primary responsibility for preparing the twelfth graders for the exams, almost never team-taught with Karen. They had limited contact to get the "native speaker's point of view" on particularly tricky grammar points that cropped up on the "practice exams" (*mogi shiken*) every now and then. Finally, only six classes were scheduled for weekly sessions with Karen. Most Nishikawa students experienced team teaching only as a one-shot deal; moreover, the team-teaching load fell disproportionately on five JTLs.

The first decision of the English faculty, made by consensus, was to target the tenth- and eleventh-grade *advanced* classes. Ueda-sensei explained: "We were quite worried that, being British, Karen had a level of English that would be hard for our students to understand, so we decided to put her with our best students on a regular basis." In principle, the four JTLs who taught the advanced students were thus bound to team-teach with Karen. In practice, however, only three did so—and only Ueda-sensei did so with enthusiasm. The fourth, Omori-sensei, had so little interest in team teaching that he got himself exempted from the policy by pointing to an informal survey he had conducted: there was widespread student sentiment, he explained, that devoting one class a week to conversational English would detract from their exam performance.

The JTLs with whom Karen taught once a week were Kira-sensei, a young female JTL who had just returned from a summer trip to the United States; Kamada-sensei, a young male JTL who was interested in experimenting with team teaching; and Ueda-sensei, whose elective class in conversational English was directed at students who were concentrating in language and literature. This optional class, made up mainly of female students who hoped to study at one of the "foreign language" universities nearby, was held in the school's language laboratory. Smaller than most classes, it became one of Karen's favorites because in it she could use creative lesson plans. The remainder of the JTLs were asked to sign up for one of the regular or irregular visits from the ALT so as to experience team teaching at least once during the semester, and all but two complied.

Over the course of the year, then, Karen team-taught with thirteen different teachers, and she quickly discovered that they took radically different approaches to her role in the classroom. Ueda-sensei's classes were consistently the most cooperative, in both the planning and the teaching stages. But the classes Karen really threw her heart into were those she taught with Ikuno-sensei, who had been transferred to Nishikawa the same year that she arrived. Ikuno-sensei had a reputation among the other English faculty as being extremely antisocial. A staunch union supporter, he was critical of the school—the stifling atmosphere in the teachers' room, the proliferation of rules and regulations, and the overly serious focus on exams. He refused to use the official form sent by the board of education for the lesson plans used in team teaching, preferring instead to type out his own lengthy plans as well as a personal evaluation of each class. For this class Karen even made a mailbox, which she placed on her desk. She had Ikuno-sensei's students write letters to her, and then she wrote replies.

Karen was particularly enthusiastic about the political message embedded in many of these classes. For instance, the two addressed world hunger in one lesson by playing the hit song "We Are the World" and asking students, working in small groups, to translate it. Then she and the JTL had the students write essays on poverty, which they sent off to a development agency. Ikuno-sensei even spent a whole period telling students about differences between "developed" and "developing" countries, though he admitted that the principal did not know about this. So excited was Karen to discover a teacher who tried to help students think critically that she began to spend as much time preparing for Ikuno-sensei's classes as all the others combined.

I was completely surprised, therefore, when I discovered that Ikuno-sensei did not volunteer to team-teach; in fact, he was far from satisfied with the team-teaching arrangement:

> I've had a hard time with her British accent and her being female. Ideally, I should be able to tell her, "'Here's how I want you to interact with students, I want you to do this . . . ,'" but I can't bring myself to tell her. There must be a better way to do it. It seems like she's always a guest (*itsu made mo okyakusan*). Until today I planned everything. But actually I want her to direct the class more. That's my self-evaluation (*hansei*). She should teach more so that students can hear her English. I just don't have time for all this preparation. Before class is the hardest. I get this sinking feeling in my stomach and keep thinking to myself, "There must be a good idea for this class," but no good ideas ever come up. I want her to do interesting things, but not games—even songs are better than games.

Yet in spite of these reservations, he continued to prepare diligently for his classes with Karen, in part because of his poor relations with other teachers. The following year he asked to be transferred to another school.

Several teachers tended to forgo the textbook when team teaching with Karen. One was a part-time teacher, Tsuda-sensei, who volunteered to do several one-shot classes: "I decided I wanted to give it a try. The risk is high and it's more work, but I'd never done it before so I wanted to try it. The first few times we didn't use the text. The students have the mind-set that team-taught classes are fun because we don't use the textbook. I think the best part of team teaching is that it motivates students to take an interest in English. We can do exam preparation apart from team teaching. So to me, it's difficult to use the textbook for team teaching." Turning the activities over to Karen, however, had its pitfalls. In one class I observed, Karen had planned to show three pictures of pollution and ask students to write what they saw. But when they balked at writing an open-ended response, Tsuda-sensei immediately switched gears and asked Karen to use "yes-no" questions. As Karen walked by me in the back of the class she whispered, "Oh, Jesus Christ, this is not what we discussed at all. We had planned to let them use their brains a little." Afterward Tsuda-sensei confessed that he was depressed by the way class went. In addition to not being able to please Karen, he had been embarrassed when she had asked him a question that he had not understood. His response ("What?" [*Eh?*]) had sent students into peals of laughter. He consoled himself with the knowledge that "if students think, 'Even with that English they're communicating,' then I think I've been successful."

Most teachers at Nishikawa stayed fairly close to the textbook. According to Karen, Sasaki-sensei was "the worst." He always asked her to do conversation practice for the first ten minutes of class and then turned to grammar explanation, pattern practice, and new vocabulary words for the remainder of the period. One day he left a note on her desk in the teacher's room before she got there, explaining that he had things to do in class until 9:20 A.M.; Karen should come only for the last twenty minutes and do a game or whatever she wanted. The following week he canceled the team-taught class entirely, saying he needed to prepare students for the exam. Karen complained, "Sasaki-sensei always wants to do it separately. There's no team teaching with him."

Karen's reaction to being treated like a tape recorder was to concentrate on those team-taught classes in which she was given some leeway. She began to work very hard preparing materials for her "good" classes, and sometimes she would spend hours drawing pictures or composing questions. Although ideally team teaching is a sharing of responsibility for the class, Karen was not involved in students' English study beyond her guest appearances. For example, testing was central to life at Nishikawa, and during end-of-term exams her classes were often canceled; she was rarely involved in making out tests or grading assignments.[4] For the most part, Karen accepted this role without complaint.

On the whole, the students themselves were thrilled by the ALT's presence. One informal survey done by Kawakami-sensei showed that 90 percent of the students were enthusiastic about Karen's team-taught classes. Karen, too, was able to find some satisfaction in relationships established with students in the advanced classes as well as with a handful of the twelfth-grade girls who were taking an elective class in conversational English. The JTLs, however, by and large viewed team teaching as the bane of their existence. They struggled to find a comfortable teaching mode with Karen, and at an evaluation meeting after the first year, they unanimously agreed that team teaching was "stuck in a rut" (*mannerika*). Even Ueda-sensei admitted to some misgivings after a homeroom teacher in the eleventh-grade advanced track told him that none of his students achieved outstanding scores in English in the end-of-term exams. Ueda-sensei reflected, "He didn't say it was because of team teaching but I think it was implied in his comments, and I thought about stopping team teaching and just doing exam preparation. In the long term, though, I think team teaching is best so I've decided not to give it up."

Extracurricular Activities

The extracurricular activities and special events in Japan's secondary schools are as demanding as their better-publicized academics. Karen initially expressed interest in joining an after-school club, but her attempt to participate in track and field left her frustrated. With her limited Japanese skills, she felt uncomfortable in the relatively unstructured setting of club practices; and she discovered that high school age students, while more mature than junior high students, were also more inhibited. She quickly tired of their shy but polite demeanor toward her and informed Ueda-sensei that she would rather participate in the ESS (English Speaking Society) club.

Unfortunately, while sports clubs were very popular at Nishikawa, the culture clubs were not, in part because they were "required clubs" (*hisshūkurabu*). The ESS was made up almost exclusively of girls (fifty-five), not an insignificant number of whom, according to Kawakami-sensei (the faculty sponsor), had chosen it as a last resort. Karen did coordinate one cooking lesson (scones, English pancakes, and Swiss rolls), but the bulk of the sessions involved showing a movie or doing some kind of listening exercise. After going several times and feeling very awkward, she confessed, "I hate it when people join the ESS club who don't want to speak English. At 4:00 in the afternoon, I don't want to listen to Japanese." At one ESS meeting I attended, Kawakami-sensei was orchestrating a listening exercise followed by a quiz. She spoke in Japanese exclusively and interpreted every word that Karen said. "This is killing, isn't it?" she whispered to me. "A classic tape-recorder lesson."

Another relatively unsuccessful attempt to utilize Karen's expertise was the monthly "study session" instituted during the Wednesday morning meeting slot for the English teachers. Several times during the semester she gave short talks on various aspects of the United Kingdom, including "English Poetry" and "English Food and Drink." But these talks were sparsely attended, and several were canceled. On one occasion, according to Karen, "Kitano-sensei told me to go ask Sasaki-sensei to come because they said if they asked him he wouldn't come, but if I asked him, he would. So I did and sure enough, he showed up, but when he stuck his head in the room and saw that it was just me and four female teachers, he said he was too busy to make it that day."

About halfway through the year Karen became very interested in environmental issues in Japan, and she began weaving environmental themes into her team-taught classes. Eventually, she decided to begin an informal campaign against disposable wooden chopsticks on the grounds that their use was depleting the rain forests. She even got several teachers from Yamagi High School, the school she visited twice a week, to go to a local tourist venue to pass out leaflets about the perils of wooden chopsticks, and her efforts were written up in the local newspaper. But for the most part Nishikawa teachers kept a safe distance from this enterprise. They tolerated it politely, and even praised her for being true to her ideals—but those teachers to whom she had spoken on the subject told me they felt uncomfortable, as if they were being implicitly criticized, whenever she would bring out her plastic chopsticks to eat lunch at school. Hayano-sensei explained, "We admire her, but it's not the Japanese way."

Several conclusions can be drawn from Karen's overall experience at Nishikawa. First, there was certainly some slippage between the ideals and the actual implementation of the JET Program. Karen's potential to improve the English curriculum was effectively tapped by only one or two teachers, and JTLs saw little carryover effect on the English classes they taught by themselves. Only two of the JTLs said they had changed the way they taught; the majority noted that if anything they had to "make up" for the time lost to the team-taught class in the remaining two periods a week by focusing even more heavily on grammar. In addition, Karen's integration into the social routines of the high school was minimal, and the confusion and uncertainty over how to use her in class extended to extracurricular activities. Kawakami-sensei reflected:

> It seems like just yesterday when we visited a long-term base school to get advice on hosting an ALT. I remember nodding as they cautioned that the hard part is getting to the point where the ALT is living comfortably in Japan or the importance of treating them as one of the staff rather than as a guest. But the reality was different. I didn't know how to react to her most of the time. For example, even though we said we should treat her as one of us, I found myself struggling because there was no clear standard to indicate the extent to which she should participate in after-school clubs, special events, or the many kinds of meetings we hold during the year.

Murakawa-sensei concurred, "Even though she accommodates our way of doing things to a certain degree, it's still a real struggle."

Perhaps the larger story of Karen's visit, though, was that despite their initial reluctance, the JTLs succeeded in providing a positive experience for the ALT. Karen greatly appreciated the numerous kindnesses extended to her and the meaningful relationships that she formed with several JTLs. Both Kitano-sensei and a young, part-time JTL became her female confidantes, and Ueda-sensei became like a father, inviting Karen to his home and helping guide her through her entire stay. In a letter reflecting on the two years he mused, "Since August 1989 I have learned a great deal from Karen not just in English teaching but in life itself. By sharing various activities with her such as talking, teaching, eating, drinking, cycling, hiking together, I have come to feel Karen is one of my best friends. I've never felt any foreigner as close to me as Karen. When I am talking with Karen I find the similarity rather than the difference in her beyond the walls of nationality, race, age, and sex—she lives every minute in this world as I do." Karen found her experience so positive that she decided to renew for an additional year, and then returned to Japan the following year for a visit. Eventually, her JET experience ended up shaping her career: she went on teach English in a secondary school in Britain.

For the Nishikawa faculty, however, such success had a high cost: the mental and physical fatigue of the JTLs who were largely responsible for Karen's visit. In 1993 when I revisited Ueda-sensei and Hayano-sensei, I discovered that they had next requested a married ALT. Ueda-sensei explained: "Hosting Karen was a great chance to improve my English and learn more about foreign ideas, but it was an awful lot of work, not only in the summer with opening bank accounts and all the preparation for her visit, but also just looking after her during the year. We asked for a married couple because we felt that a young single woman was hard to manage. We guessed that a married ALT would be much more stable, and from an emotional standpoint, much easier. And to a certain extent we were right." This second ALT turned out to have a very different personality than Karen. Ueda-sensei continued:

> Tracy is very active and enthusiastic. She joined the judo club and she interacts with students a lot. She even has a group of students that she supervises during cleaning period. But that assertiveness has its difficult side too. She actually will bad-mouth other teachers right in the teacher's room while we're talking in English! Once Tracy told me that English education never changes in Japan, and that made me a little uncomfortable, but she has good relations with everyone so we don't take offense even though she's out of place (*katte ni*) criticizing us. After one open classroom, she got very excited at the discussion session and talked for a long time, exhorting us to study English and speak in English even during class. At the time I supported her and said we should all speak English more often, but not much has changed. We agree with her ideals, but we balance it with the knowledge that it's difficult.

In reflecting on Nishikawa's handling of Karen's visit, I was strongly reminded of Harumi Befu's classic description of a foreigner who is invited to a Japanese dinner party. Befu argues that the foreigner often goes into the situation without knowledge of crucial ground rules concerning reciprocity, modesty, and so forth and without the practice of improvising lines and behaviors in the way appropriate to the Japanese social scene. The result, he claims, resembles Fred Astaire trying to dance gracefully with a 200-pound woman who has never danced before. Because the Japanese hosts are too polite to tell their guests they are clumsy people, guests leave the scene believing they have played their part according to the script; but in reality, the hosts have strained themselves to make up for the guests' deficiencies by making their cues excessively obvious, covering up the mistakes made by the guests, and even trying to make mistakes look like charming improvisations on the correct script.[5]

NISHIKAWA IN COMPARATIVE PERSPECTIVE

Karen and the Japanese teachers and students at Nishikawa interacted in ways shaped by a variety of factors: school type, school size, composition of the school's faculty and administration, the level of enthusiasm of the JLTs, students' demeanor, and the motivations and personality of the ALT. Variation in any of these can produce strikingly different patterns of interaction, as the following examples make clear.

Minami: An "International" High School

Minami High School is a public "international" high school located in a new bedroom community just thirty minutes by train from the major metropolitan center in the prefecture. Only ten years old, it offers expanded selections in foreign language education, and many of its female students (roughly 70 percent of the total student body) go on to colleges specializing in foreign languages. Minami's teachers of English are the most competent in the prefecture; at the time of my fieldwork, even the vice-principal was a former English teacher. Many of the JTLs have lived or traveled abroad, and most are comfortable in speaking English. In addition to regularly hosting AFS (American Field Service) students and accommodating "returnee children," Minami also actively engages in other activities with an international focus over the course of a school year. Shortly before I visited Minami in the spring of 1988, for example, a UNESCO delegation had visited the school. Approached by the prefectural board of education in 1987, Minami's English faculty enthusiastically requested two full-time ALTs.

Because of the school's international theme, Sato-sensei took special care in assigning its two ALTs. Roger, a twenty-eight-year-old native of Rochester, New York, was chosen for his teaching experience and his degree in international studies. Tammy, twenty-three, a native of Chicago, was selected because of her cheerful disposition and love of children. According to Tanabe-san, the match was perfect. Six months into the assignment, Tammy concurred: "It's like a dream come true." In addition to holding a morning meeting *in English*, the JTLs actively solicited Roger's and Tammy's input about improving English classes in a variety of ways.

In part because of their own English skills and in part because of the generous time allotted to English classes (twice that required by the Ministry of Education), most JTLs were willing to experiment with new and innovative teaching strategies. English classes usually based on translation and memorization were filled instead with an assortment of skits, cooking lessons, and other communication-oriented activities that turned the teacher-centered model of learning on its head. Students even experimented with diaries and critical essays in English, on which they received feedback from their new teachers. For the annual English Recitation Contest, students wrote their own essays rather than reciting one from the textbook. Both ALTs complained that far from being underutilized, their main problem was meeting the many commitments they had made.

Extensive efforts were made to integrate Roger and Tammy into school life beyond their three team-taught classes each day. They took full part in the series of parties and workshops held by the English faculty throughout the school year, and their relationship with most JTLs was lighthearted and collegial. In addition, students were noticeably more comfortable with the ALTs at Minami than at other schools I visited, and this only served to encourage Roger and Tammy to get involved in school activities. Roger joined the judo club, while Tammy coordinated the ESS club. A music fan herself, she was thrilled to find that the ESS students loved to learn and sing the lyrics of popular American songs. Each was assigned to help a group of students during after-school cleaning, and each attended all school events even when they were held on Saturdays. Having forged meaningful relationships with both JTLs and students, both enthusiastically renewed for an additional year's assignment in the JET Program.

Kamo Junior High

Nishikawa and Minami seem like a paradise compared with Kamo Junior High School, located in the heart of a largely Korean working-class district in a major urban center. While many ALTs expect that all Japanese students are highly disciplined, schools with high concentrations of Korean students often reflect the economic, social, and political marginalization of Koreans within Japanese society as a whole. In 1989 the school of 700-plus had a reputation for some of the worst discipline problems in the city. On my first visit to the school to watch a baseball game I was shocked to hear firecrackers exploding at regular intervals from within the school building, and by the time the game was over the air had been let out of the tires of the car belonging to the head English teacher, Yamada-sensei. He explained that while he had succeeded in getting half of the "problem students" to join the baseball team, the other half were jealous that he was paying attention to those who had joined the team: the prank was one way of getting even.

Kamo had reached its low point with discipline problems shortly before my string of visits in 1989, and the principal asked the board of education to transfer several young male teachers to the school. Yamada-sensei was one: at age thirty-two, he would normally have been far too young to assume the position of ninth-grade head of student guidance, but difficult times called for drastic measures. When he arrived, he found that teachers were being routinely intimidated by a core group of students, who were divided into two main factions. These two gangs also regularly extorted money from other students. To make matters worse, the school's language lab had been taken over by one faction and converted into their hangout. At one point the situation became so desperate that in a complete reversal of societal conventions, the authorities opened the school up to parents to show the extent of the problems.

What impressed me the most about this school, though, was the utter dedication of its teachers, who refused to give up on their students. Viewing the students' misbehavior as a cry for love, they deliberately refrained from exerting authority and spent innumerable hours counseling students and trying to repair the social fabric without resorting to heavy-handed correction. Yamada-sensei established a close relationship with the father of one of the gang members in order to gain leverage. One teacher spent the night in the teachers' room every night of the week. Yamada-sensei explained, "Even if students are bad now, we believe they'll be good in the future. If we punish them too harshly, then students won't trust us. We usually give them lots of lectures so that they will realize their mistake."

Into this environment, the antithesis of the stereotype of orderly Japanese schools, entered the ALTs. Ordinarily a school with such severe discipline problems would not have invited an ALT, but Yamada-sensei was passionate about teaching English conversation and he was determined not to let the students' behavior sabotage his opportunity to bring in native speakers. The other two JTLs, however, were not interested in team teaching, forcing Yamada-sensei to take complete responsibility for the visits. He managed to arrange for twice-a-week visits from ALTs posted to a local board of education, though the specific ALT would change from one semester to another.

What was most instructive about this situation was how these ALTs reacted. Yamada-sensei recalled: "Our school had two ALTs, and they were completely different. Rebecca came barging in and wanted to change everything to her way of thinking. We all thought, 'Whoa, so this is what Americans are like.' But then Marian came, and we expected the same thing, but she was more Japanese than we were. All the other teachers and even the office staff and principal loved her. Myself, I can work with either type, but Marian was much more acceptable because she was sensitive, so they gave her lots of presents when she left." Yamada-sensei showed Marian's picture to his classes and had all his students write letters to her before she even arrived. By the time she appeared at the school, everyone was bubbling with anticipation. But neither Rebecca nor Marian were much involved with after-school activities, and though they loved working with Yamada-sensei they found the students to be extremely unruly in class.

It was with the third ALT to visit Kamo, an American named Richard, that disaster finally struck. Richard was quite irritated by the disruptive classroom behavior of some eighth-grade students who would hang out windows, talk with their neighbors, surreptitiously read comics or play handheld electronic games, or even move about in the back of the room. He found it virtually impossible to carry on the team-taught class. But Richard was even more nonplussed by Yamada-sensei's strategy for handling the disruptive students. Day after day he stood by helplessly as Yamada-sensei stopped class repeatedly to exhort the boys in the back of the room to pay attention. Sometimes he would ask one of the offenders to stand and would proceed to lecture him at length, completely disrupting the flow of the carefully devised lesson plan. Rarely did these approaches have much of an immediate effect, and in several instances Richard, against his better judgment, intervened. Once he lost his temper and screamed at the class at the top of his voice, "Shut up!" This worked like magic—once; by the next class period nothing had changed, and subsequently he found that raising his voice had only a minimal effect. On another occasion Richard actually walked to the back of the room, grabbed a boy by the shoulders, and pushed him firmly into his seat, but afterward it seemed that the class was even more unresponsive than they had been before.

One day, Richard decided he could take no more. He stalked out of the room in the middle of the lesson and went straight to the principal's office, where he complained that Yamada-sensei was unable to control the students. Because Yamada-sensei refused to resort to appropriate interventions such as physical punishment or suspension, Richard argued, there was no clear deterrent to the students' behavior. He also informed the principal that because teaching under such circumstances was useless, he would not return to Kamo until the situation had improved.

Yamada-sensei, however, was equally befuddled by Richard's insistence that he send the offending students to the principal, a strategy he believed to be simply a self-serving means of passing on the problem to someone else. For him, discipline began with a caring relationship, and effective control rested on warm interpersonal relations between himself and the offending students. Yamada-sensei knew that the class behavior of these students was a symptom of a much larger problem, and he was not about to sabotage his schoolwide attempts to mobilize peer and parental pressure to change these students' behavior by lashing out at them in anger or punishing them. Such a confrontational approach, he was convinced, would only lead these students to resent authority figures more deeply: it would do nothing to address the underlying cause of that resentment.

Yamada-sensei's disciplinary approach is consistent with Gerald LeTendre's and Rebecca Erwin Fukuzawa's descriptions of the philosophy underlying school guidance (shidō) at the junior high school level. LeTendre notes that the standard disciplinary techniques used by Japanese teachers—patient illustration of desired behavior, interviews with the offenders, reflection papers, formal apologies, after-school lectures, and informal counseling sessions—all rely on learner and teacher having an emotional tie based on a shared set of goals and values. An effective teacher-student relationship requires trust, and it assumes that the teacher is guide and the learner is follower.[6] Fukuzawa elaborates that discipline in this model is assumed to be largely psychological; that is, students reflect on their misdeeds until they "understand" (i.e., internalize the school norms and routines).[7] We should note that this normative model does not take into account the various attempts by Japanese teachers to come to terms with what they perceive as an increasingly unruly population of middle school students. More than a few ALTs have reported witnessing severe physical punishment, such as students being burned with a cigarette butt or slapped in the face, and Yamada-sensei himself contrasted the approach his school had taken with that in a neighboring school where teachers regularly used threats, intimidation, and physical punishment to keep students in line.[8]

To return to the case at hand, Richard's ideas about discipline fit neither with Yamada-sensei's educational values nor with the larger structure and rationale of middle school education in Japan. Because there is no tracking or ability grouping in most Japanese public junior high schools, disruptive students cannot be relegated to special classes or groups. Nor can students be removed from class or suspended from school at this age—teachers maintain that the constitutional guarantee of equal educational opportunity prohibits such action. Thus, as Fukuzawa reminds us, academic instruction and discipline are inseparable at this stage: "the quality and quantity of instruction for the most highly motivated students are directly related to the behavior of the most problematic students."[9] Yamada-sensei was not yet prepared to give up on the offending students in the interest of the academic progress of the rest of the class.

Moreover, Yamada-sensei saw Richard as contributing to the problem with the eighth-grade class at Kamo. First, he argued that students know that a JTL will not use severe punishment in a class with an ALT so they act up because it is a "class oriented toward the outside (*yosoyuki jugyō*)." Second, he took issue with Richard's attempts to become the disciplinarian himself, particularly when physical contact was involved: "It makes a huge difference who touches the student. For it to be accepted, it must be an in-group member—for example, a homeroom teacher with whom a relationship has been built up. If an outsider touches him, it's a loss of face for that student." Finally, he felt that in several instances Richard had not exhibited sensitivity toward "protecting" students who were weak in English, a sentiment with which other JTLs agreed:

> The ALTs don't know anything about students' situations—whether they're bad, violent, and so on. We are very careful in how we handle students because we don't want to make them feel ashamed, but ALTs can't know in what situations students feel ashamed. I remember once Richard taught many new words and then gave a test, but one student had low ability and a stammer, and he answered in a small voice. Then Richard raised his voice at him, "Why didn't you listen to me?" and the boy cringed. So I think ALTs don't worry enough about how students feel. We are very careful not to hurt the students' feelings (*kizu wo tsukenai yō ni*).

Yamada-sensei continues to be an active supporter of the JET Program, but his experience with Richard impressed on him the depths of some cultural gulfs between ALTs and JTLs. He concluded, "The problem is that most ALTs are too independent. We want them to depend on us, but they never ask our opinions in a serious way or say *sumimasen* (I'm sorry) and apologize for the inconveniences they create."

Kawaguchi Junior High School

Even the special treatment afforded Karen at Nishikawa paled next to Kristin's celebrity reception at a small, rural junior high school in the southwestern corner of the prefecture. A California native, Kristin was posted to a small district board of education where no one spoke any English at all. At first it seemed as if Kristin's year in Japan was headed for disaster. Before she left the United States, the board of education had written to ask if she wanted to rent furniture for the year. Kristin replied "yes"; but on arrival, she decided that it was all too expensive. She instructed the board of education to have all the furniture removed, informing them that she would instead buy the things she needed at a second-hand shop.

Komori-sensei, a JTL called in to serve as a liaison with the board of education, told me: "Well, it turns out that Kristin's predecessor wrote and said, 'Don't accept any expensive things because Japanese are soft toward foreigners (*gaijin ni yowai*) and will give you everything you need.' Sure enough, I ended up giving her my guest *futon* (sleeping mat)! Can you believe that? Even if it was expensive, if it was the board of education that had arranged it, we couldn't refuse it." She continued:

> Kristin had bad manners when she first arrived, too. Her nails were too long and her earrings too big and flashy. When I first met her, she was sitting in the board of education waving a fan, chewing gum, and wearing a T-shirt with no sleeves and a miniskirt. I was both depressed and shocked at the same time. The board of education officials asked me to advise her to cut her nails and not use so much makeup and big earrings, but when I brought it to her attention, she said, "Oh, don't worry about that. The Ministry of Education said that we're here to demonstrate American culture, not to become Japanese." I thought that answer was really self-serving. When I told the board of education officials what she said, they just decided to give up, saying she was too young to understand. But, you know, gradually she changed her behavior. I think it was experience more than my advice.

Kristin's board of education decided to dispatch her to three rural junior schools for one semester each. This, they speculated, would allow for a more concentrated and meaningful school experience. Her first school, Kawaguchi, with a student population of only 230, proved to be a perfect match for Kristin's temperament and outlook. The principal treated Kristin like his own daughter, and he even agreed to let the head English teacher temporarily forgo her duties as homeroom teacher in order to concentrate on team teaching. The JTLs as a group decided to completely suspend use of the textbook for team-taught classes during the three months Kristin was present.

When Kristen first visited her school, she was greeted by students staring, waving, and even venturing a bold, "Hello! Hello!" Her shoes were placed in the shoe box reserved for guests. There was a schoolwide assembly to introduce her to the student body. The English teachers held a welcome party for her and later gave her a present on her birthday (not a common practice in Japan). She was called on to give a speech to the PTA and to write an article for the local newspaper. One night she was interviewed on the local television news. She had a fan club among the boy students, and toward the end of her visit, many students approached her for an autograph or a handshake. Finally, there was a farewell party, which the Japanese teacher of English described to me:

For the students she was nothing less than a celebrity. All she had to do was say something and everyone would marvel at her beautiful pronunciation. For her farewell party the student council planned for weeks. They conducted a survey of all the students and then we made up a song to the tune of "You Are My Sunshine." Except we sang "You are my teacher, my wonderful teacher, please don't take my wonderful teacher away." They gave her paper cranes they had made, and there were speeches from student representatives and from Kristin. Then they gave her roses, and she paraded out of the gym to the music of "Let It Be." It was an incredibly touching occasion.

The only trying moment for the teachers was Kristen's reaction to the annual English recitation contest. She had helped students practice for it and was invited to come see the performances. One JTL remembered:

We had the kids do Martin Luther King's speech at the English Recitation Contest. The kids tried hard. We should have told them to do it in a more interesting way, but we had them memorize the speech. Anyway, we invited Kristin to the speech contest, but she suddenly got up and left without any explanation after a few minutes. We couldn't figure out what was wrong. One of the other teachers wondered if it might have something to do with the lack of emotion in the students' recitation. So later I called her at home and that was it—she was really upset because they seemed so insensitive to the real meaning of that historic speech. I never realized her feelings about blacks until she left the gym that day. You know, our students, they'll just scribble on pictures of blacks in their text without thinking. But because of this incident we've had a chance to reflect on the mistakes we're making, and next time we'll know to prevent this kind of thing from happening. Kristin understood that we should have done more to teach the students. Anyway, that was the biggest shock for me. Kristin always showed how she was feeling. We Japanese smile without showing our feelings.

In talking further with this teacher, I was struck that at least as strong as her desire to better understand African American history was a determination to learn the practical steps to take in order not to offend an ALT the next time.

DIVERSITY AMONG JTLS

If nothing else, the above vignettes all demonstrate beyond dispute the tremendous range in how JTLs and other school staff react to their encounter with the ALT. Such variety undermines the simplistic view that all Japanese respond to foreigners solely on the basis of a deep-seated cultural preference for keeping them at arm's length. No one better recognizes this diversity than the ALTs themselves, who, in the course of a year on the JET Program, will normally visit a handful of different schools and team-teach with dozens of JTLs. Though typologies—which tend to pigeonhole complex responses and to minimize change over time—have their limitations, they nevertheless are useful as a heuristic device to sketch out the varying stances taken by JTLs toward the ALTs.[10]

The Enthusiasts

Likening the JET participants to Commodore Perry's "black ships" opening a reluctant Japan to the Western world is not necessarily a negative metaphor; there are a small handful of teachers, quite competent in English conversation, who view the ALTs as much-needed medicine for what they consider to be the ailments of an outdated and insular system of education. These JTLs see the foreigners as providing a breath of fresh air—exactly what Japanese education and society need to bring the country into the twenty-first century. Historically, they point out, it is only through outside intervention and external pressure that Japan has been able to change. They must therefore rely on the ALTs to do what they themselves cannot, and thus they openly welcome the JET participants. Most larger schools can count on having one or two of these enthusiastic teachers, and not surprisingly the bulk of the supervision of the ALT falls on their shoulders. Of the fifty-four JLTs I interviewed, eleven shared this view of the ALTs.

Within this category there at least two subgroups. On the one hand are the "teachers turned social critics" who, as a result of their political views and more confrontational interpersonal styles, are already somewhat marginalized within the school. They may use the ALT as a sounding board for their critique of Japanese society, in many cases confirming the ALT's own superficial assessments of the "problems" with Japan. As we saw in the case of Ikuno-sensei at Nishikawa, the team-taught class becomes a fertile ground for developing not only oral communication skills but also a critical quality of mind about all manner of injustices in the contemporary world.

On the other hand are a group of "cautious enthusiasts," such as Ueda-sensei and Yamada-sensei, who embrace the ALTs but attempt to channel the positive energy of the visit in ways that are acceptable to the school culture. While by no means hiding their support for the program, they nevertheless recognize the imperative of maintaining goodwill with other teachers. As they are often expected to serve as the ALTs' liaison, they may face the challenging task of toning down ALTs' views or requests that challenge the status quo. In general, they bring imagination and creativity to the task of team teaching; they become true partners in planning and implementing lessons.

As a whole, the enthusiasts feel that the JET Program has been a great step forward, no matter what the current difficulties might be, because it has undeniably provided more Japanese teachers and students the opportunity to communicate with native speakers of English and, to a lesser extent, French, German, Korean, and Chinese. In addition, because Japanese teachers are rotated to a variety of schools over the course of their careers, ALTs are almost as likely to meet an avid supporter of team teaching in a remote mountain village as in a large metropolis. Even the enthusiasts, however, take the risk that team teaching will be blamed if their students' test scores should decline while they are embracing communication-oriented teaching techniques.

The Detractors

At the other end of the spectrum are a minority of teachers who view the ALTs with a great deal of skepticism and the JET Program as illustrating the problems created when Japanese leaders bow to foreign pressure. To these JTLs, the ALTs are a virus whose potential for harm must be controlled and contained as much as possible. They see Japanese education as in no way outdated but instead as a striking success precisely because of its emphasis on rigor, standardization, and homogenization. Not surprisingly, these JTLs talk at length about keeping ALTs in their proper place and have little tolerance for activities designed to liven up the English classroom. One female JTL, thirty-six, expressed her frustration with the JET Program in some detail:

> What I want to know is why the Ministry of Education hired so many people. I've heard it's because of the trade imbalance. But they can't even speak English in the ministry. What do they think they're doing? Which are they aiming for, ability (*nōryoku*) or individuality (*kosei*)? It's a terrible dilemma I face between choosing a fun class or raising students' abilities. Of course, I have to choose ability and exam preparation because that's what will help them more in the future, even though the questions on exams are ones that bright native speakers can't answer. . . .
>
> We don't know how to handle ALTs. We Japanese are all of one race and we understand each other. We disregard contracts. Maybe I'm a workaholic to Americans, but I don't care. Our prosperity is because of our hard work; it's because of education that we have today's standard.

If we educate like Americans, then our students will become lazy and idle. Nurturing students with individuality (*kosei yutakana seito*) really means producing overly frank and arrogant students (*jishin mochitsugi*). To understand the Japanese heart you have to understand a Noh play and the idea of modesty. This is a virtue in Japan. The merits of internationalization are that we'll learn to speak frankly and lose our inferiority complex. The demerits are that we risk losing the Japanese heart.

When we have ALTs at school, we fall behind in the textbook and then parents complain because many of them are *kyōiku mama* (mothers preoccupied with their children's education). When Katherine came to our school, she was very sensational and brought an international atmosphere, but nothing was gained in terms of ability. Her lesson was just an amusement. Of course, I didn't tell her, but inside I was thinking, "She's just a young girl, this is such a waste of time." So I'm against ALTs.

Though it is almost unheard of for Japanese teachers to speak in this way directly to the ALT, nine of the JLTs I interviewed expressed similar views to me.

Most JLTs in this category have little interest in interacting with foreigners in general and are likely to try to avoid team teaching. They usually have little skill in conversational English, and if forced to team-teach, they are likely to reduce the ALT to the status of a human tape recorder. Without question these teachers receive the harshest criticism from ALTs. One recalled:

> I had one teacher, a head teacher actually, who would only speak to me in Japanese and I'd ask him, a week ahead of time, "What are we going to do for class?" and he'd just smile and say, "Don't worry," and wander away. And so I'd keep trying to get information out of him but he'd either avoid me or profess ignorance all the way up to the lesson. He would send two students to bring me to class; he wouldn't even walk there with me! And all he ever did was follow the book. Completely book-centered, and the entire class was conducted in Japanese. After one class he'd tell the class monitor to mark page 17, and then the next class he'd check with the monitor and say, "We're picking up right here at the bottom of page 17." He'd put a big chair at the back for me, and I wouldn't have to do a thing, except read a few new vocabulary words. So I'd sit there in this chair while he taught and he'd do pair reading and choral reading and then ask them some true-false [questions], and then class was over.

The danger of such an approach, of course, is that the ALT may not accept it; thus the likelihood of conflict escalates. ALTs love to tell war stories when they get together socially, and an entire genre is dedicated to creative ways of sending a message to JTLs who, as one ALT put it, have their "heads in the sand." In addition to telling the JTL point-blank that "I don't do tape-recorder classes," these methods include taking out a novel to read in class or wadding up the lesson plan and depositing it in the trash in full view of the JTL and students.

The Ambivalent JTLs

Between these two attention-getting extremes lie the majority of JTLs, who are quite ambivalent about the JET Program and view the ALTs as a mixed blessing. These teachers acutely feel the difficulties created by the insertion of reform-minded native speakers into an exam-oriented school environment. They recognize both the limitations of their own training and the need to prepare students for an international age, yet by force of habit if not by conviction they are wedded to teaching English by the grammar translation method. Not only are they faced with losing precious class time to conversational activities and games, which they perceive as having little relevance to the entrance exams, but they feel at a severe disadvantage: because many of them were schooled via rote memorization with an emphasis on grammar, their own conversational skills are limited. As a result, many genuinely fear the prospect of interacting with an unpredictable ALT who may cause them to lose face (*kao wo tsubusu*) in front of colleagues or students by asking a question that they cannot answer. Indeed, the stress of working with an ALT can manifest itself in physical symptoms.[11]

Moreover, given the cultural imperative of treating the foreigner as a guest, the amount of extra work associated with hosting an ALT is considerable. One veteran high school teacher tried to put a positive spin on their situation, again using the black ship metaphor:

> "Black ship benefits" (*kurofune kōka*) accrue to teachers when the AE-Tea (only one cup keeps you up the entire night) awakens you from your peaceful slumber and causes acute anxiety. You begin to wonder whether you should have been using more classroom English and to worry whether the students will respond well to the team-taught class. In a dither, you hasten to make preparations but when the preparations take too much time or the paperwork becomes too much of a bother, you begin to resist and eventually fall into the "expel the foreigner" camp. On the other side, however, is the "open up Japan" camp, which seeks to usher in a new era and thus gives wholehearted approval to the appropriateness of the ALT system. Most teachers, myself included, are

probably somewhere in between these two extremes, fumbling along in a trial-and-error mode as we struggle to respond to this new system.

These teachers feel acutely that the JET Program has exacerbated tensions already present between those JTLs wedded to grammar translation and the study of literature in translation and those who see merit in cultivating the ability to communicate orally. If they weigh in too heavily on the side of conversation-oriented language activities, they run the risk of disappointing parents, the homeroom teacher, and the principal. If they opt to teach only in the traditional manner, they may incur the wrath of the ALT.

In their attempts to cope, several different strategies were discernible. Some JTLs attempted to script the entire visit, thereby making the team-taught classes as predictable as possible. On one-shot visits this meant marking the ALT's shoe box at the entranceway, arranging for the ALT's box lunch well in advance, and typing out a detailed lesson plan. One ALT described this type of JTL as "Mr. Serious" (Majime-Sensei): "He's very thorough, he types everything, it's like a movie script. You're to say, 'Hello everybody! Good morning!' Then the students must ask, 'How are you?' and you have to answer, 'Fine, thank you, and you?' If you say something different, he gets mad at you because you deviated from the script. Then he has you follow the traditional textbook pattern to a T. He doesn't want you wavering from it." JTLs in this category tended to be especially concerned about classroom management and often interpreted virtually everything the ALT said in English on the spot.

Another coping strategy was to view the ALT's visit in very narrow and instrumental terms. For example, he or she could be useful as a walking dictionary for solving complex grammatical problems that occurred on the entrance exams or as a practice partner for JTLs who wanted to improve their spoken or written English. In other instances the ALT could be used by JTLs to show off their competence in English. This could be taken to extremes, as one female ALT made clear: "One reason the other teachers never come over to my desk is because if they do Mr. Yano jumps right in and says, 'Why don't you try to make yourself understood in English?' until finally they slink away. One teacher told me he treats me like a pet, and no one wants to come near me." Sometimes the ALT served as a model of "typical" foreign behavior; in fact, a handful of JTLs told me they preferred ALTs who were stereotypically "American" (*Americappoi*) or "foreign" and thus more interesting for them and their students. Presumably, such ALTs also provided a clear standard against which these Japanese would define themselves. ALTs often resented such instrumental attitudes, particularly if they were working hard to learn Japanese and to fit into Japanese schools. One complained: "I've heard teachers say, 'We don't need that ALT because he can speak Japanese. We don't need anybody like that.' It just boils down to language. They don't even consider the idea that you might have a different way of looking at things or that you can just discuss things and have different viewpoints. It's completely alien. From their point of view, if you are not learning English from this person, then the ALT has no utility."

When I asked ALTs about the kind of JTL with whom they would most prefer to work, the enthusiasts won in a landslide. The characteristics they stressed as particularly desirable were a willingness to experiment with new pedagogical approaches and a willingness to make mistakes when speaking English.

DIVERSITY AMONG ALTS

ALTs are an extremely varied group, and their responses to the close-knit culture of Japanese schools differ considerably. Working in a system that speaks of a need for conversational English yet maintains a rigid examination structure, that advertises "internationalization" yet sometimes practices it only at arm's length, the JET participants sought strenuously to generate belief systems that made sense of their efforts. Such belief systems, which legitimize responses to a difficult situation, correspond to what Anthony Giddens has called "practical consciousness."[12] Much like the white teachers in Michelle Fine's study of a predominantly black urban high school in New York City, however, they often developed their belief systems defensively.[13] In addition, these defenses tended to calcify quickly and to shape the ALTs' further perceptions, preventing them from considering any evidence that might contradict their beliefs.

The Aloof

Nine of the sixty-five ALTs whom I interviewed expressed no real interest in learning Japanese language or culture. They were perfectly content to remain outside the reach of the "consensus model of social relations" that operates in Japanese schools and boards of education. Most of them saw their primary role in Japan as modeling foreign behavior and thus they generally ignored Japanese cultural expectations. "If they want someone to act Japanese, it's a bit of a waste of time hiring me!" commented one British ALT. Content to be tourists, these ALTs also have few qualms about

The Drill Instructor (*Homo sapiens scary*). Note: Difficult to spot outside of classroom; best observed while teaching. Distinctive call: "My students are so timid." This and the following caricatures are by Darin Price.

exploiting their foreign status to the hilt. "I dress casually all the time, even when I meet Japanese teachers," advised another ALT at the Tokyo orientation. "The rules will bend around you, so take advantage of this. Don't believe you have to conform one hundred percent." One Ministry of Education official recounted, with obvious mirth, how an ALT once visited him in the ministry building (located in the prestigious Kasumigaseki area of Tokyo) wearing a baseball cap, a T-shirt, and shorts!

The Cynics

A second group of ALTs (fifteen out of the sixty-five) made halfhearted attempts to learn Japanese language and culture but quickly became frustrated and disillusioned. Seeing little evidence at the local levels of Japanese commitment to reform, they tended to withdraw and establish a private counterculture. The perceived inadequacies in the Japanese school system

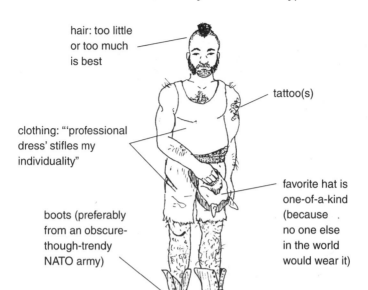

hair: too little or too much is best

tattoo(s)

clothing: "'professional dress' stifles my individuality"

favorite hat is one-of-a-kind (because no one else in the world would wear it)

boots (preferably from an obscure-though-trendy NATO army)

Mr. Gaijin (*Homo sapiens extreme*). Distinctive call: "These Japanese are so ——ing rude. All they do is stare."

and the JET Program led them to disengage emotionally from the job of teaching; their work obligations became a set of hoops through which they jumped in a perfunctory manner. A British woman, twenty-three, lamented: "I have one school where they just prepare for exams and they don't want to deal with me. I read books, write letters, prepare for my private classes, and do all kinds of things. It's easy work. Silly, but easy. I can easily take it for a year. If they want to pay me 30 *man* [$2,500] a month to come and do this, sure, I'll do it. But let's not have any illusions about changing the system. If they really want to do something, they should give JTLs a year's leave to study English, and guarantee their pay." These ALTs channeled their energy into other activities, such as tourism or making money through private classes on the side.

JTLs were quick to criticize what they perceived as an overly "salary-man-like" approach to the job. They might have used as evidence the exclamation of one ALT: "Stay till five o'clock? Are you kidding? Why stay around just so the kids can stare at us? If there's something special—like

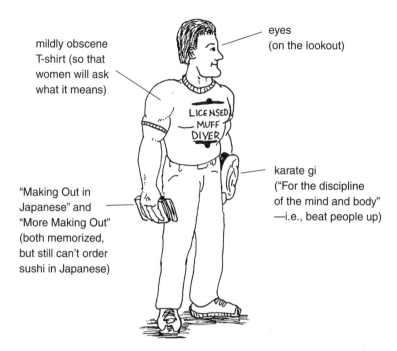

mildly obscene
T-shirt (so that
women will ask
what it means)

eyes
(on the lookout)

LICENSED
MUFF
DIVER

karate gi
("For the discipline
of the mind and body"
—i.e., beat people up)

"Making Out in
Japanese" and
"More Making Out"
(both memorized,
but still can't order
sushi in Japanese)

The Prowler (*Homo sapiens lusty*). Distinctive call: "Japanese women really turn me on."

the other day the teacher asked me to help the kids who were preparing for the English Recitation Contest—I'll stay, but otherwise I usually go home or back to the office. I'm not gonna hang around just so they can gawk at me." Such attitudes, of course, only fueled the resentment of JTLs, most of whom regularly stay at school until 6:00 P.M. or later. Other cynics lashed out at the system whenever given the chance. Two ALTs in one prefecture decided to switch schools for an entire day to make the point that they were being used as human tape recorders and thus were simply interchangeable parts.

Conspiracy theories thrive whenever social strains and stresses arise, and this group of ALTs wasted no time second-guessing Japanese intentions:

> In October of my first year I was so unhappy as an ALT that I started looking for another job. I wanted to teach English but I wasn't getting a chance to at my school. In classes I had no real role; when I was asked to do something it was trivial, reading word lists, holding posters for the Japanese teacher. No one was interested in how I thought English

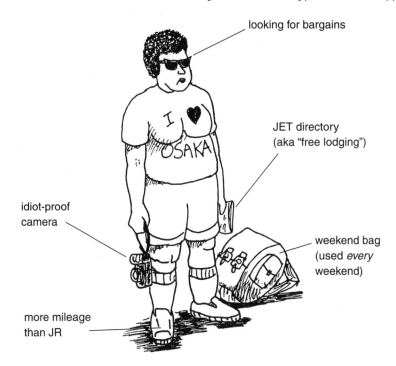

looking for bargains

JET directory
(aka "free lodging")

idiot-proof
camera

weekend bag
(used *every*
weekend)

more mileage
than JR

The Tourist (*Homo sapiens burdensome*). Distinctive call: "Hi! We met at Tokyo orientation, and I was just in the area, and I wonder . . ."

should be taught. I was so discouraged I preferred sitting in the staff room to going to class. Occasionally, I had to go. A teacher asked me to help him teach first-year students how to tell time. He gave me a cardboard watch, told me to set the hands and then ask the students what time was showing. This trivial use of my talents seemed the embodiment of everything I hated about my job. I held up the watch and asked "What is this?" I said it sarcastically and meant my job, the school, the town I was living in, the whole ALT experience. Several arms went up and I picked a girl sitting near the front. She stood, and smiling a smile as big as Asia said, "It's a crock, Mr. Hicks." I couldn't have agreed more.[14]

For the cynics, the gap between the public rhetoric of "internationalization" and the realities of public schooling was so huge that the JET Program could only be explained as a concession to foreign pressure. They became convinced that JET participants were invited to Japan strictly as "window dressing."

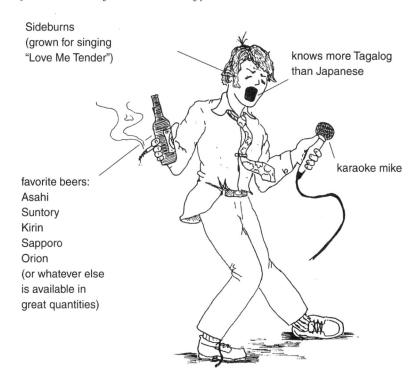

Sideburns
(grown for singing
"Love Me Tender")

knows more Tagalog
than Japanese

karaoke mike

favorite beers:
Asahi
Suntory
Kirin
Sapporo
Orion
(or whatever else
is available in
great quantities)

The Partier (*Homo sapiens collegian*). Distinctive call: "Thish country iza great playsh."

The Missionaries and the Sensitive Change Agents

The largest group of ALTs (twenty-two of the sixty-five) also perceived inflexibility in the dominant method of teaching English; but unlike the cynics, who tended to withdraw and establish a private culture, these ALTs embraced the larger task of transforming Japanese education and society. This group's belief system was summed up by an American ALT, age twenty-four: "We don't know what the hell we're here for. I haven't got a clue. Clearly, we're not here to teach English. So it must be to help them progress their culture. Recently, there have been two things that might keep Japan from entering the international community—its lack of defense and its own culture. We can't do anything about the first, but we can show them how to think critically. That's what it comes down to. There's no critical thinking. Just follow the pack, the way it's supposed to be done." They often tried to transform English classes into a forum to foster global education and awareness. Another ALT put it this way: "The JET Program

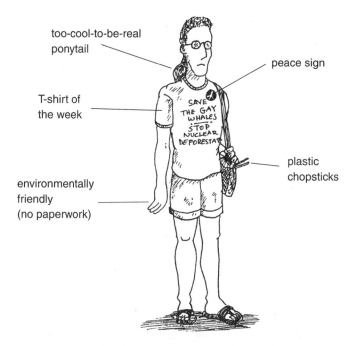

too-cool-to-be-real ponytail

peace sign

T-shirt of the week

SAVE THE GAY WHALES STOP NUCLEAR DEFORESTAT

plastic chopsticks

environmentally friendly (no paperwork)

The Activist (*Homo sapiens trendy*). Distinctive call: "My school is now a smoke-free and paper-free zone that observes the sanctity of Mother Earth. I teach a little English, too."

can be seen as revolutionary as ALTs attempt to rid the classroom of the stultifying atmosphere in which time is often wasted gathering consensus answers to rudimentary questions. The radical ideas of free speech and individual thought being encouraged in place of a non-critical, passive response to knowledge passed down from on high is a significant change."[15]

In some cases, ALTs actually instituted special "international understanding classes" (*kokusai rikai no jikan*) apart from the regular English curriculum; but for others, who encountered cooperative or cowed JTLs, the regular team-taught class provided their opportunity for experimentation. One Canadian ALT in a Tottori-ken high school, for instance, did a series of global education classes designed to point out gross economic inequities around the world. They included a simulation on the cacao trade to show how multinationals and foreign banks create poverty among small-scale farmers in Africa, as well as two classes on human rights. She explained, "I have the students fill in a questionnaire about human rights in Japan. I point out that Japan is the only non-communist country to have

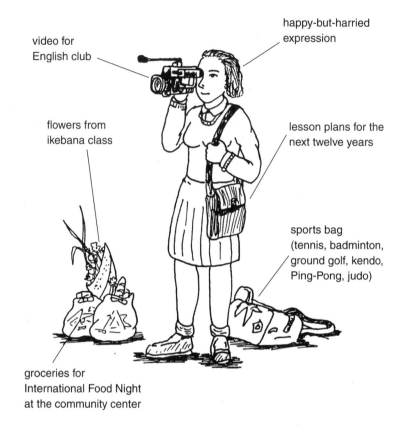

video for
English club

happy-but-harried
expression

flowers from
ikebana class

lesson plans for the
next twelve years

sports bag
(tennis, badminton,
ground golf, kendo,
Ping-Pong, judo)

groceries for
International Food Night
at the community center

The Overachiever (*Homo sapiens excessive*). Distinctive call: "Culture shock? Who has time for culture shock?"

ministry-authorized textbooks and I also show them my fingerprints on my Alien Registration Card (yes, according to this card I come from outer space . . .)."[16] The highlight of this class occurred when, in the middle of winter, she posted signs on the two doors of the classroom. Her door, which was near the kerosene heater in the back of the class, said, "Whites Only: No Japanese Allowed," while students entered through a door leading to the colder part of the classroom. That such classes were even permitted testifies to the extraordinary degree of discretion allowed to individual teachers and schools in spite of Ministry of Education guidelines. However, I did hear of several cases in which ALTs were told in no uncertain terms by the principal that classes with an overt political message were inappropriate.

To be sure, within this broad group ALTs displayed different levels of cultural sensitivity. At one extreme were those who embraced reform with a self-righteous zeal that was off-putting to all but the most radical JTLs; at the other extreme were "sensitive change agents," who worked within the structural limitations of their position. They were often able to find gratification and meaning in cultivating relationships with a select group of students and teachers, particularly those who were enthusiastic about foreign language learning and who seemed open to learning about the world. This latter approach was one that CLAIR and the Ministry of Education actively supported, and it is no surprise that in 1995 the winning essay of the Third Annual JET Programme Essay Competition took up this topic. In "More Than a Language Teacher," Jeffrey Strain found the lasting significance of the JET Program in ALTs' interactions with students *outside* the language classroom. He suggested a number of possible activities: joining after-school clubs, participating in other classes and in field excursions, creating other responsibilities at school, writing a monthly newsletter, working where students have access to one, and even wandering around the school asking questions. "Classroom time is now only a small fraction of the time I spend with the students, where in the past it had constituted the majority," he noted. "I currently try to spend a minimum of 50 percent of my time at school in contact with students outside the classroom."[17]

The Careerists

Among the ALTs, as among the JTLs, were some who saw the JET Program in narrowly instrumental terms. For them, it was primarily a vehicle for making connections and learning enough about Japanese society to further their own careers. Eleven of my sample fell into this category. While a few seemed preoccupied with finding a Japanese spouse as the first crucial step to his or her "international career," the majority were simply interested in acquiring enough linguistic and cultural competence to make them attractive candidates for jobs in the business sector. These ALTs quickly invested in business cards and were constantly on the lookout for résumé-building experiences and good personal contacts. In the early years of the JET Program, when the bubble economy was still growing, the program drew many career-minded college graduates. Some did in fact use their JET experience as a stepping-stone to Japan-related careers in journalism, tourism, government service, and so forth; in rare cases, an ALT would

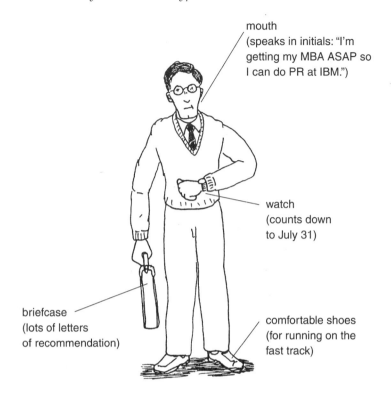

mouth
(speaks in initials: "I'm
getting my MBA ASAP so
I can do PR at IBM.")

watch
(counts down
to July 31)

briefcase
(lots of letters
of recommendation)

comfortable shoes
(for running on the
fast track)

The Yuppie (*Homo sapiens money*). Distinctive call: "I think that the JET Program(me) is the ideal stepping-stone for an upwardly mobile career."

jump ship in April if he or she found a suitable private-sector job. As more and more JET alumni flooded the job market, however, it became clear that the JET experience itself was not guaranteed miraculously to open doors. In the 1990s, as Japan has become mired in a recession, fewer participants single-mindedly depend on the JET experience to set them on their careers.

The Nipponophiles

Finally, the smallest number of ALTs interviewed (eight) approached the JET Program primarily as a learning experience and saw their time in Japanese schools as a golden opportunity to discover an alternative cultural worldview and to expand personal horizons. They took seriously the challenge of learning Japanese language and absorbing the culture, and they

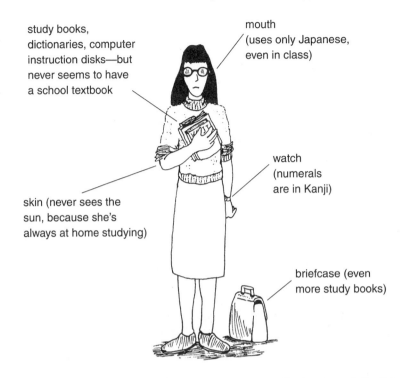

study books, dictionaries, computer instruction disks—but never seems to have a school textbook

mouth (uses only Japanese, even in class)

watch (numerals are in Kanji)

skin (never sees the sun, because she's always at home studying)

briefcase (even more study books)

The Linguist (*Homo sapiens grammarian*). Distinctive call: "Don't speak English. I need to practice my Japanese."

tended to be highly critical of the judgmental reactions of their peers. One article in the *JET Journal* captured the flavor of this approach:

> Vocal critics of Japan's seemingly slow internationalization process should maybe conduct a self-cross-examination. Is *Kokusaika* [internationalization] not a two-way street? I sometimes wonder if all JET participants are as internationalized as they pretend to be. Most of us feel internationalized because we are anglophones, presently living outside our home country dealing with people who lack fluency in English and who have limited experience in overseas travelling. We see the Japanese as the object of our presence in their own country. . . . However, how many of us can look at ourselves and sincerely assert that we are as internationalized as we want the Japanese to be?
>
> Many of us came to Japan without the faintest knowledge of this country, its customs, language, etc. Many of us only know the basics about our own country, and our knowledge about the outside world is

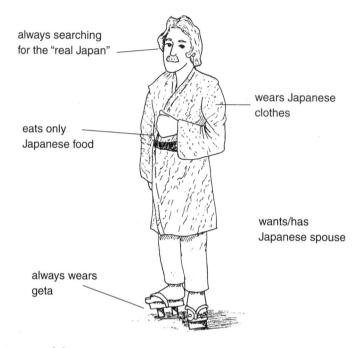

always searching
for the "real Japan"

wears Japanese
clothes

eats only
Japanese food

wants/has
Japanese spouse

always wears
geta

The Nipponophile (*Homo sapiens wanna-be*). Distinctive call: "I really feel at home here. The Japanese lifestyle is the best in the world."

just as scanty as that of the average Japanese. For many of us, landing a job in Japan and being the focus of so much attention instantly inflated our egos which in turn prevents us from remembering that we have been invited as guests—consultants—by this country. Voicing aggressively our opinions, frustrations, discontents and disapproval will only contribute to alienation rather than promote internationalization.[18]

Included in this group were those rare souls who practically rejected their own culture in the rush to embrace Japanese language and society. They would complain if their apartment was too close to those of other foreigners, and they avoided most ALT social gatherings. Ironically, they ran the risk of becoming too acculturated, opening themselves to criticism from Japanese that they had become a *henna gaijin* (literally, "strange foreigner")—someone who, in a sense, knew too much about Japan and behaved in a manner inconsistent with his or her upbringing.

These groupings roughly describe the range of JET participants. Darin Price, an ALT in Okinawa from 1990 to 1993, composed a remarkable set of

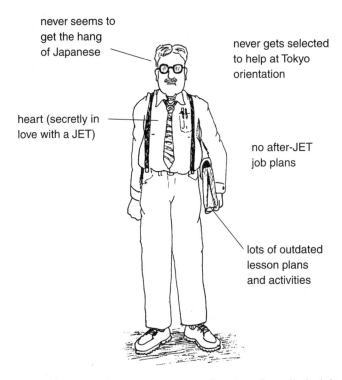

never seems to get the hang of Japanese

never gets selected to help at Tokyo orientation

heart (secretly in love with a JET)

no after-JET job plans

lots of outdated lesson plans and activities

The Loser (*Homo sapiens failure*). Distinctive call: "The only really bad thing about this job is the three-year limit."

drawings during his time in Japan that begins to capture some of the diversity of ALTs' reactions to Japanese culture and education in a humorous way; they have been scattered through this section.

INTERNATIONAL FESTIVALS

In the fall of 1989 I was invited to an "international cultural exchange festival" hosted by Higashiyama High School. Its objective, as stated in the program, was "to promote a true sense of international understanding among the young people who will be our leaders in the Twenty-first Century by inviting members of the foreign community . . . to exchange ideas concerning our different cultures and to promote friendship."

The fundamental plan was simple: to invite as many foreigners from as many different countries as the organizers could manage. Toward this end

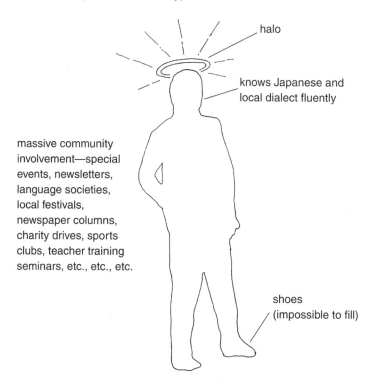

halo

knows Japanese and
local dialect fluently

massive community
involvement—special
events, newsletters,
language societies,
local festivals,
newspaper columns,
charity drives, sports
clubs, teacher training
seminars, etc., etc., etc.

shoes
(impossible to fill)

The Predecessor (*Homo sapiens saintly*). Distinctive call (about him or her): "X sensei was not as [pick one] fat/short/skinny/loud/sloppy/quiet/hard to understand/lazy as you are."

the chief organizer, a middle-aged teacher of Japanese language, both obtained permission from the board of education for JET Program participants in the area to attend and used the network of her husband (a university professor) to identify foreign students at local universities who might participate. The two ALTs based at this school were excluded from much of the planning process, though their names, pictures, and essays were displayed prominently on information disseminated about the event.

On the afternoon of the festival, most of the foreign guests were met at the train station by pairs of students, who accompanied them on the short walk to the school. Many of these students said that they had stayed up late the night before rehearsing short conversational phrases that might come in handy. On arriving at the school, all the guests were ushered into the guest room, where forty-five foreigners were briefed on the agenda of the afternoon. Though I had asked to sit in the background as an observer, it soon became clear that this would not do at all. The only place for foreigners here was on the stage or in designated seats—including the two AFS students at the school, in spite of their protests that they didn't want to be singled out from their classmates.

At the appropriate time all of the foreigners, myself included, were given flags of our respective countries and, with the flags displayed conspicuously in front of us, we were ushered into the gymnasium. There, in front of video cameras and to a standing ovation from the students, we marched down a carpeted aisle to the front of the gym, where some took seats under an impressive display of flags, banners, and ribbons hanging on the stage, while others sat in chairs set apart in the audience. On the stage, vases of flowers adorned tables with white cloths; the names and countries of origin of those seated behind them were displayed prominently on large cards.

The program had been meticulously planned down to the last minute, and a full rehearsal had taken place the day before. A young JTL with good conversational ability served as moderator. First, the principal gave an introduction in Japanese and in English, reading phonetically. (The speech had been written and translated by a JTL, and the principal had received coaching, I was told.) Then greetings were heard from a representative of the foreigners and from the student body president, who gave his short remarks in Japanese, English, French, and German. Next, the chief organizer of the event welcomed everyone and pointed out that there were over forty people representing twenty-three countries, making this the biggest such festival yet. As she went on to introduce everyone by name, students brought leis made of folded origami cranes, which they placed over each individual's neck. The moderator then noted that since there was not enough time to hear from all the foreigners, they would hear from just a few representatives. During the next twenty minutes, the students heard brief greetings and introductions about their countries from a Tanzanian, a Canadian, an Austrian, and a Korean. By my rough estimate, about a third of the students were dozing during this portion, another third were talking quietly among themselves, and the final third were quite attentive.

The next portion of the ceremony was titled "Question and Answer Session," and the moderator announced that the students would take charge of the program from here on out. The students designated as "question askers," all seated together, rose one by one and asked a question in English of someone on the stage. I was told later that deciding on what kinds of questions to ask was very difficult for the students, and that the organizer had told them to keep to noncontroversial subjects that would contribute to a light atmosphere. Indeed, the nine questions addressed topics such as fjords in Norway, clothing styles in Sweden, vacation time in Britain, foods in Singapore, seasons in New Zealand, festivals in Brazil, and so on. Immediately after this, two students grabbed the microphone and walked down the row of foreigners; all were asked their country's name and to say "*konnichiwa*" (hello) in their native language. Then the student body president did the same for the foreigners seated on the stage, but he made everyone laugh by telling the audience "Repeat after me!" after the words in languages such as Swahili that were not familiar. The final event had the two AFS students at the school come up and show their version of "rock, scissors, paper" (a popular way of making decisions among Japanese schoolchildren) in which the loser had to do whatever the winner asked. First, the boy lost and the girl asked him to do ten push-ups on the stage; then the girl lost and the boy asked her to kiss him on the cheek, which she did, pretending to be embarrassed. Everyone in the audience gasped. The two told me afterward that they had decided to do this at the last minute to "stir things up a little."

At this point, the ceremony was declared over and, to applause, the foreigners paraded out. Their departure marked the end of the required portion of the event for ninth graders, who were then dismissed to study for exams. Volunteers from the seventh and eighth grades were responsible for small "discussion forums" held in various classrooms. Most of this time was spent playing a language game and sharing snacks and tea. Depending on the mixture of students and the personalities of the foreigners, the atmosphere ranged from quite lively and fun to somewhat uncomfortable. At the end, the principal and the chief organizer suddenly burst into each room with a photographer, who snapped several poses of all of us (these pictures were later sent to all the foreign guests). The foreigners were then ushered back to the guest room, where we were given pottery bowls as a gift and bade farewell until the following year.

Less than a month after attending the high school festival I was invited to an "international understanding period" at a junior high school that the city board of education had designated a special school for returnee children. Each year this school conducted a schoolwide international event. According to a memo prepared by the planning committee,

> Last year, under the title "interacting with exchange students"
> (*ryūgakusei to no fureai no kai*) we tried to improve students' interest
> and understanding of intercultural differences by hearing from for-
> eigners currently living in Japan. This year we have planned a program

according to grade level under the general theme "the capacity for cross-cultural understanding" (*ibunka rikai nōryoku*). We want to impress on students that there are many people in the world who live and behave in ways that differ from their own lifestyles, and we want them to learn to respect these various moral frameworks. We also hope to encourage them to think about the question of how Japanese should conduct themselves in order to get along with people around the world.

As in the high school festival, there was an emphasis on form and careful attention to detail. A specific activity had been designed for each grade: seventh graders were to "learn about differences between Japan and foreign countries" by listening to three foreigners briefly describe life in their countries. The eighth graders were to participate in a symposium on "Japanese patterns of behavior." The ninth graders were to listen to two Japanese overseas volunteers tell of their experiences, the theme being "Japanese actively participating in the world community."

I attended the symposium, which involved a panel discussion with one foreign guest, one Japanese teacher, one moderator (also a teacher), and seven students (one representative from each homeroom), all of whom sat on the stage in the gymnasium. The remaining three hundred students sat in straight lines on the floor of the gym while the physical education teacher and several homeroom teachers roamed about, keeping strict order. The questions chosen for discussion were most revealing. There were twenty of them, all based on the pattern "Why do Japanese do such-and-such?" (*naze nihonjin wa . . . na no ka?*). These questions had been compiled by a social studies teacher in collaboration with a few of the returnee children at the school. For nearly forty-five minutes the panel discussed such questions as, Why are parking violations so frequent in Japan? Why don't Japanese buy groceries all at one time? Why has Japanese science not advanced relative to other countries? Why do so many Japanese wear glasses? Why do Japanese work too hard? The student representatives had all prepared written responses, and the moderator moved back and forth between the students, the foreign guest, and the Japanese teacher, calling for comments at random. Toward the end of the hour the moderator tried to elicit responses from some of the students in the audience, with limited success, by asking their opinions about a neighboring city's decision to require students to cut their hair a certain length.

These two festivals offer many insights into the cultural form and meaning of internationalization in Japan. We might observe first that the main event was compulsory for all students. In effect, the decision that it is important to be international was made for the students. One major consequence was that the entire event was standardized and ritualized. The Japanese attention to form, detail, and protocol in implementing this festival clashed with the sensibilities of many of the foreign participants, as the improvisation by the AFS students revealed. As Takie Lebra has pointed out, face is most vulnerable in unpredictable situations, and ritual—"the rigid, meticulous control of interaction behavior in a predetermined way so as to prevent embarrassing surprises"—is the most common means of preserving it.[19] Ritualization can thus be seen as a way to control foreigners, incorporating them while forestalling any challenge to local meanings.

At both events the distinctions between Japanese and non-Japanese were assumed and reinforced. The students who participated in "internationalization" by watching forty-five foreigners paraded in front of them learned firsthand that foreigners were to be treated differently from themselves. The second event is a bit more complicated to analyze, for my discussions with teachers afterward made clear that the entire affair was intended as an internal critique of Japanese behavior. Yet the critique itself began from a presupposition of Japan's cultural uniqueness, which was assumed to pervade even such things as how Japanese do their shopping. The potential for effective criticism was further weakened by the assumption that all Japanese are alike (are there no Japanese who do not work hard?), behaving in ways juxtaposed to an implied and equally monolithic set of "foreign" cultures.

THE CULTURE AND POLITICS OF TEAM TEACHING

Even more useful than school-based international festivals as a lens on the dynamics of intercultural encounters in the JET Program were the team-taught classes conducted daily by ALTs and JTLs. My first introduction to the controversy over team teaching came when I attended a fall 1988 meeting of a local chapter of Nihon Eigo Gakkai (the Japan English Association), a national organization for Japanese teachers of English. According to its chair, the main purpose of the meeting was to help JTLs who were having trouble (*kurō*) with team teaching, and three speakers talked at length about their personal experiences with ALTs. While the Ministry of Education's main speaker at the JET Program orientation had glowingly reported that 75 percent of JTLs were very positive about team teaching, this session painted a much bleaker picture. Even the moderator's introductory remarks about the JET Program were decidedly negative. Noting that the program began as a reaction to foreign pressure, he went on to argue that it had no clear educational rationale, that as a whole it was not going very well, and that numerous problems remained. Since most of the foreign youth were not licensed teachers, he concluded, the acronym ALT was itself a misnomer and should be replaced by ETA (English teaching assistant). This skepticism among JTLs was confirmed over the next few weeks at other conferences I attended. I even overheard one JTL refer to the "ALT problem" while talking with a local board of education official.

In my own observations of team-taught classes, I was repeatedly struck by how the Japanese teachers' strategies clustered around the two extremes. Either the entire class is turned over to the foreign teacher, or the foreign teacher becomes part of the furniture of the regular classes as a kind of human tape recorder. Often a single class was divided into conversation-oriented activities (which the ALT leads) and exam-related study (in which the ALT assumes a peripheral role). In both cases, the possibility of spontaneous interaction in the classroom is minimized. My observations were confirmed by a national survey conducted by the Institute for Research in Language Teaching in 1988. When asked how labor is divided in team-taught classrooms, 30 percent of senior high teachers reported that they let the foreign teacher take charge of the class, 25 percent responded that they themselves remained at the center of class instruction, and 36 percent said that they shared teaching responsibilities. As to whether Japanese teachers of English were satisfied with team teaching, half of the junior high school teachers and close to two-thirds of the senior high school teachers said they had reservations about the approach.[20]

The Teaching of English as a Foreign Language

Why was team teaching so threatening to JTLs? Certainly, deficiency in English conversational ability led many to fear loss of face in the classroom and in the teachers' room. While JTLs often claimed that they were too busy with other school affairs to spend time in preparing and evaluating team-taught classes, in fact language skills were the biggest roadblock. Truly cooperating on a lesson plan and its implementation requires a willingness to engage in the give-and-take of mutual criticism, and most JTLs found it difficult to convey what they really thought about the ALTs' ideas under these circumstances—particularly in light of the widespread tendency to refrain from criticizing foreigners.

The JTLs also resisted because team teaching required that they partially surrender their autonomy in the classroom. Reformers have been relatively unsuccessful in making team teaching integral to American public education for precisely this reason. And in Japan, the interaction was even more complex: each member of the "team" brought a different cultural model of what constitutes a "successful" classroom to the joint enterprise. The traditional method of teaching English in Japan fits with a cultural theory of learning and motivation that draws heavily on Confucian values. While recent studies of preschool and elementary classrooms in Japan have found, somewhat surprisingly, that play is central and students' contributions drive classroom learning, by junior high school a very different pedagogical model is in effect, one that is much more teacher-centered. According to Thomas Rohlen and Gerald LeTendre, "Secondary-level teaching employs a pedagogy almost entirely dependent on teacher-centered lectures to large classes of students engaged in note-taking for the purposes of passing exams. The use of small groups for instructional purposes is extremely rare, and student presentations are limited. Classroom proceedings center on the teacher, who elaborates at length on a fixed lesson."[21] The important elements in this approach are the idea of learning as a serious enterprise requiring hard work and sacrifice, the importance of repetition and memorization of a model, and the fixed roles of the major actors: the teacher as imparter of knowledge and the student as attentive but unquestioning learner. All of these features coincide nicely with accounts of Japanese patterns of learning outside the school, such as the apprenticeship model John Singleton describes in becoming a potter.[22] Academic study at the secondary school level in Japan is a sober business.

In observing English classes with the ALT absent, I found that they were taught primarily in Japanese, with English being used only when reading passages from the text or introducing new words. Third-year students often spent much time reviewing past exam questions and perfecting test-taking strategies. There was little variation in teaching methodology: teachers rarely strayed from the front of the room and students answered questions only when called on. An examination of students' English notebooks and homework also proved revealing. Many students spent a considerable amount of time studying English, but their time was spent on four primary tasks: copying the model dialogue into their notebooks word for word, translating this dialogue into English, memorizing and orally reciting the dialogue, and answering grammatical problems. Yoshie Aiga confirms that English classes today are still largely spent on reading, translation, and explanations of new words and grammar points in Japanese.[23]

The assumptions underlying the English as a foreign language (EFL) methodologies in which the foreign teachers are "trained" at the Tokyo and prefectural orientations run directly counter to those of the above model in many ways: they see as ideal the student as active learner; the teacher as facilitator; focus on content of language, not form; curriculum that is interesting and relevant to students; and classes that are marked by liveliness and spontaneity. ALTs generally believed that English classes in Japan are in need of livening up, and they therefore often tried to use games and other "fun" activities in their team teaching. From playing the guitar to turning the class into a dramatic scene to playing hangman and twenty questions, the ALTs seemed willing to try anything to energize the class, use "living English," and produce evidence, in the form of critical thinking and self-expression, that "real" learning was taking place.

The ALTs' approach also implied a specific theory of motivation. If students are viewed as naturally having a weak will, then it becomes the responsibility of the teacher to try to spark their interest and nurture it through incentives. At conferences and workshops for the ALTs in the late 1980s, for instance, the problem of how to motivate Japanese students was a central issue. ALTs were enormously frustrated by what they perceived as the lack of responsiveness or shyness of Japanese students, complaining that just to get a student to answer a question about his or her favorite food was like pulling teeth. The students, of course, viewed their hesitation not as a deficiency but as an accomplishment. Japanese students whom I interviewed repeatedly stressed the importance of not performing in such a way that would make them stand out. Both at home and at school, they learned that they must listen and that conformity demonstrated inner strength; it was difficult to ask them to set aside these values for one English conversation class per week.

Nevertheless, ALTs seem determined to do just that. At one conference held for renewing ALTs in 1989, a workshop on motivation attracted 130 ALTs; fewer than a dozen attended concurrent seminars on how to adapt existing textbooks to the team-taught class. One speaker at the workshop showed off a freewheeling English text not approved by the Ministry of Education and urged ALTs to buy copies, since "technically, we're only required to *have* Mombushō-approved textbooks at the school, not to use them." Another described his philosophy for motivating Japanese students: "I believe in rewards and punishments. Every time a student raises his hand and asks a question voluntarily I give them a $1,000 bill with my face superimposed on it and a lottery number on the back. Each month I have a small lottery and give out a pencil, but then I have a big lottery for a university T-shirt. Sometimes I read in a Donald Duck voice, though I have to warn the JTL beforehand. If a student mentions a singer, I'll start singing a song. I'm very spontaneous."

Though the philosophy of "education through play" may have warmed the hearts of a whole cadre of Western educators, beginning with John Dewey, it finds few adherents among secondary school teachers in Japan. They assume that students begin with a strong will, and their task is to strengthen that willpower by frustrating it and putting hurdles in front of it.[24] Even though Japanese teachers may give the ALTs great leeway in class, in private they usually described the sessions led by the ALTs as "classes without rigor" (*kejime no nai jugyō*), or as "just a playtime" (*tan no asobi ni natte shimau*). One JTL reported his first encounter with the motivational theories of the ALT: "I remember on the very first day of team teaching, the ALT asked me if I could find a volleyball to bring to class. I said, 'A WHAT?' It turned out he would throw it to students who he wanted to call on. That one really threw me for a loop!" Tellingly, JTLs will routinely mark the shift from conversation practice or a game led by the ALT to work in the textbook by saying, "Now it's time to get down to studying" (*soredewa benkyō ni hairimasu*).

Moreover, the lessons in conversational English so enthusiastically supported by the ALTs (and publicly endorsed both by the Ministry of Education and by prefectural ETCs) are viewed as largely irrelevant to preparing for entrance exams, which require the memorization and manipulation of discrete lexical items. Teachers that do focus on conversational English in team-taught classes note that they have to work extra hard in solo classes to compensate for time "lost" from studying the textbook.

The Reactions of Students

The wild card in this struggle of cultural mind-sets is the overwhelmingly positive reaction of Japanese students to the ALTs and to team teaching. For many, this program offers the first chance they have ever had to interact with a native speaker; though they express a great deal of nervousness about the encounter, they see the benefits to the team-taught class as far outweighing the drawbacks. Team-taught classes usually represent a break from the routine of teacher-centered instruction and thus are a welcome relief. Some team-taught classes seem more like entertainment than like study. There is the added plus that the ALTs usually do not give them grades. Though on occasion I did witness students taking the JTL's side and complaining, "Not games again," more often they begged the JTL to allow them to play a game during the ALT's class visit. Furthermore, students are thrilled to be able to hear native pronunciation; and for a generation whose prospects of traveling abroad at some point in their lives are high, it is reassuring to learn conversational styles that may actually be of use in the future.

Asked to write essays on their opinion about English education in Japan, one class of high school students in Kyoto almost unanimously described school English as exam-oriented and useless in real life and welcomed the ALT system. One student wrote, "It was wonderful to hear live English from the ALT and to be able to have a conversation in English. But, with such infrequent classes, we can't expect much effect, and it's hard on the ALTs too. I hope the program can be improved to its full potential so that we can learn from ALTs on a regular basis." In an Osaka school, 170 seventh-grade students were informally surveyed after they had experienced several team-taught classes: 87.6 percent of the students approved of the ALT coming to their school (the remaining 12.4 percent were indifferent), and fully 78.8 percent said that they preferred team-taught classes to those taught solely by the JTL (17.6 percent were indifferent). When asked about their impression of the ALT who had recently visited their school, 68 students used the term "interesting" (*omoshiroi*), 48 said she was "fun and easy to get to know" (*tanoshiku shitashimiyasui*), and roughly 10 students each described her as "good at English," "cheerful," "kind," and "big and tall." One student described her reaction to the ALT's visit as follows:

> When I heard the words, "An American teacher is coming!" I couldn't even imagine what she would be like. I was eager to find out if she would be a strict, scary teacher, an interesting teacher, or a kind teacher. When she arrived, I thought, "So this is the teacher from America," and I went to class eager to see what she was like. She was very animated and interesting. She let us hear real English pronunciation and taught us things that weren't in the textbook. When we played games, I couldn't understand her English sentences; it was real difficult. But I was happy that she could come to our school even for a short time. I want to hear real English again!

The positive response of Japanese students and the capacity on the part of some ALTs to forge meaningful relationships with them are a key source of the JET Program's transformative potential.

Team Teaching: The Mixed Results

Although most JTLs are not thrilled by the prospects of changing their approach in the classroom, in a fascinating contradiction they tended to see team teaching and internationalization as a cause. Again and again I was struck by the seriousness with which JTLs took to the task of learning how to team-teach. Workshops and books on the how-tos of team teaching burgeoned in the late 1980s and early 1990s, and English societies all across the country took up this theme in meetings and seminars. JTLs did not give up, and many talked frankly about the need to master team-teaching techniques. Workshops on team teaching were often very well attended. In one district I visited in which teachers were allowed on an in-service training day to choose between focusing on a traditional-style class and a team-teaching class, the seminar on team teaching attracted five times as many teachers as the other.

At the same time, it is possible to see the enormous number of seminars and publications devoted to the "how-tos" of team teaching since the start of the JET Program as signifying the desire of Japanese teachers for some "foolproof" method, an agreed-on form that will somehow render the unpredictable predictable. One book is particularly noteworthy in this respect. Just like the Ministry of Education–approved English textbooks, it gives a model dialogue, new words, and key phrases for a myriad of potentially embarrassing or conflict-laden situations, such as how to talk with an ALT on the phone, what to say if you bump into the ALT in the hall, how to introduce ALTs to students, and what to do if the ALT doesn't like the rainy season or complains that Japanese ask too many private questions.[25]

In spite of the continual efforts of JTLs, however, the transformation of English education remains limited by the extent to which the team-taught class is conceptualized as a distinct entity, something apart from their regular English classes. As of yet, there is little carryover between the two. Even at a school as enthusiastic about the program as Minami High School, by the admission of JTLs themselves, the teaching of basic classroom English was untouched by the ALTs' influence. Powerful notions about when it is appropriate for Japanese to use English are at work here: when I asked one JTL if he'd tried to use English in the classroom when the ALT was not present, he responded: "I tried using English in the classroom at our ALT's urging, but I gave up after a few tries. Most of the students couldn't follow me, and they would say things like, 'Sensei, you act just like a foreigner.' It felt really strange." Another JTL put it this way: "I think of the ALT as a motivator. For Japanese, it's very strange to speak only in English with each other. But if I have an ALT, it's much easier for me to speak in English." For these JTLs, solidarity with students who shared the same cultural heritage continued to be a far more powerful force than identification with the goals of the ALT.

On the one hand, the introduction of team teaching has led to great change in English education in Japan: one can go into any classroom and find the ALTs leading activities that never before seemed possible in the public school system. On the other hand, the degree to which Japanese teachers mark off these classes as distinct, both linguistically and conceptually, reveals that team teaching is best viewed as a type of situational accommodation rather than as marking a wholesale change in attitude.

CULTURAL CLASH AND CHANGE

Many ALTs work hard, in ways small as well as large, to remake Japanese culture into something closer to their own expectations of how things ought to be. Their daily behavior reflects deliberate choices and makes a clear symbolic statement. Male ALTs may make it a point to serve tea in the office. Others will protest against smoking etiquette or deliberately tell students of best friends who are minorities in order to test preconceptions. As an ALT recalled, "When I told them my best friend was Korean they nearly died. That's something they'll remember for the rest of their lives." Some JET participants also consciously strive *not* to exhibit any characteristics that would reinforce the stereotypes about their nationality, even lying on occasion. One ALT told me that when asked whether she'd had steak the night before, she said she'd had fish and rice—but she really had eaten hamburgers for dinner. And a couple decided to get married earlier than they had planned in response to those in their village who felt that their cohabitation was morally improper.

A critical stance toward Japanese culture even comes through in workshops designed by the ALTs to help improve the English of Japanese teachers. Consider the following questions, which were used to guide informal discussion at a "team-teaching workshop":

1. Why do Japanese give empty compliments (for example, when a foreigner can say a few words of Japanese: "*Ahh, jōzu desune!*" [You speak very well])?

2. Why are Japanese so surprised when a foreigner likes sushi or *natto* [fermented soybeans]?

3. Why do Japanese ask so many personal questions?

4. How do you feel when a *gaijin* sits next to you on the bus or train?

5. Why do the Japanese feel so unique as a nation when every other nation on earth is just as unique as Japan?

6. What meaning does the emperor of Japan have for you? Is the family of Korean descent?

7. With all their wealth, why don't Japanese families have necessary conveniences like dishwashers and clothesdryers (or is this a secret plan to keep Japanese women busy in the home)?

The clear message is that Japanese are too invested in their own culture for their own good. Speaking English requires the development of a critical frame of mind. In many of their criticisms, ALTs are implicitly demanding that the Japanese reconstitute themselves and their society in ways more compatible with Western norms and expectations.

Resistance

JTLs employed a variety of strategies to cushion the impact of the ALTs' visit and to lessen their potential for disruption. To be sure, powerful forces were marshaled on the side of change, and the term *kokusaika* contains a moral imperative. Moreover, most JTLs believe that they should be able to speak better English, conduct team-taught classes, and interact with ALTs. Yet the majority of JTLs—ambivalent or with private reservations about the JET Program—often found themselves being expected to change social routines and established behaviors. Though such uncomfortable transitions are a natural part of learning something new, considerable effort is needed to overcome the inertia of set patterns; and inevitably one feels compelled on occasion to reject the practical implication of an idea that sounded good in the abstract. JTLs who do not want to "be international" resist in subtle and not-so-subtle ways.

Simple avoidance is one common response. Some ALTs reported that they didn't find out certain Japanese staff were English teachers until months into their school visits. At one school's meeting to evaluate team teaching that I attended, the JTL who was most uncomfortable with the program arrived just as the meeting was ending, in gym clothes, explaining that he'd been tied up by club responsibilities. A twenty-eight-year-old JTL related a similar case at his school: "Once last semester all the English teachers decided to attend an ESS club activity together with the ALT. Everyone came except the head teacher, who took sick leave. He did it twice, actually. He was very worried because he doesn't speak English well at all. I understand his case, though. There's a big gap between teachers aged twenty to thirty and those over forty." Such avoidance can, of course, subject one to gossip and rumor among one's colleagues as well as the ALTs, but some JTLs clearly prefer that to confronting a potentially awkward situation.

Another approach is to reinterpret current practice so that it fits within the rubric of "internationalization." Japan has a long history of repackaging foreign ideas and objects to make them compatible with Japanese sensibilities. At one team-teaching workshop I heard a JTL eloquently defend direct translation as a teaching method (a method ALTs criticize mercilessly), arguing that it allows students to become familiar with foreign ways of thinking and thus contributes in its own way to internationalization. This glossing of existing behavior to match the demands of being a good global citizen is ubiquitous in the JET Program.

Perhaps the most common strategy is simply to capitulate to some extent to the demands of the ALT, ignoring the inconvenience as much as possible. In spite of widespread talk about the importance of letting the ALT know his or her proper place (*ichizuke*), many JTLs seem willing to go to extraordinary lengths to avoid direct confrontations. Perseverance (*gaman*) in the face of adversity is often celebrated as a virtue for Japanese students and teachers alike, and with the frequent rotation of ALTs, a JTL can rest content in the knowledge that a particular irritant won't last forever. I was told of an older JTL who was confronted by a young female ALT: she told him point-blank that his English class was terrible. The idea that this "child" would have the gall to tell him how to teach sent him into a rage, but he never once showed his anger to the ALT. When a younger colleague offered to talk to the ALT for him, the older JTL refused, saying, "It's only three more weeks. Let's just put up with it till she's gone."

Special Treatment

Most JET participants find themselves coping not only with subtle resistance but also with the special treatment extended to them. Nearly all must learn to deal with celebrity status and what some of them dubbed the "panda mentality," referring to the tendency of their Japanese hosts to fuss over them in the same way a zookeeper might give special care to one of his prized pandas. In conversation and in their writings, JET participants incessantly refer to the tendency of schoolchildren to stare, gawk, and, as one ALT put it, "view you like you just descended from another planet." Even Wada Minoru in the Ministry of Education recognized this dimension of local behavior: "When an ALT shows up at a school, the teachers and principal bow their heads and idolize them (*sūhai no kimochi*). Getting past this attitude is the biggest challenge for internationalization."

Though some ALTs seemed to enjoy this unusual attention, in the long run many resented the concomitant lack of privacy and seeming denial of their individuality. They were irritated that their daily whereabouts seemed to be public knowledge, and they expressed annoyance when students would ask overly personal questions during the obligatory self-introduction and question-and-answer session in a new class. Some even went so far as to publish lists of the questions they would refuse to answer. Others wrote letters, such as the one below, to the *JET Journal* or to the English language newspapers in Japan complaining about their treatment:

> As the local foreigner I am expected to attend every international event that occurs in my city. Far from an exchange of culture these gatherings have a tendency to be one-sided affairs where my foreignness is put on display for all to see. Rather than an increased understanding of different cultural groups, such international gatherings tend to reinforce slanted views and skewed perceptions about other cultures because they negate the person and focus on the culture and country of origin which effectively puts the "Gaijin on Parade." . . . While on parade my only viability comes from my non-native status, causing me to feel as if I am being paraded around for no other purpose but to fulfill the visual component of an international meeting, talk, gathering or party.[26]

Indeed, outsiders or marginal people in any organization or small, tight-knit community may be treated similarly.[27] Because JET participants were visible as members of a category, their actions carried extra symbolic consequences; their behavior was interpreted as representative of that category—indicating not their individual personalities but "the way their nationality is." One ALT offered a humorous account of the phenomenon:

> "Which do you prefer, tea or coffee?" This question is one of many I face in my capacity as an ALT: representative of a foreign country and counsel on all matters pertaining to that country's society, economy, history and general trivia. As JETs it is true: we are ambassadors of a sort. On this, what I call the "Morning Break Question," I stick to a middle of the road answer. I like both. It's true, and nothing to be ashamed or embarrassed about. However, when I answer in this way I am invariably met with a stunned response. One colleague, Mr. H, was fairly shocked at my answer. He went on to explain, "Well, as you know, all Americans prefer to drink coffee, and tea is the drink of the English. How about Australians?" "Well, we drink both." "Ah-ha," my friend nodded wisely. "So in Australia you are half British, half American way."

She also described occasions on which teachers expected her to conform to the stereotype of Australians as heavy beer drinkers and further questioned her on which way the washing machines spin in Australia and whether snowmen are made with two balls (as in Japan) or three (the American model). While she appreciated the teachers' desire for knowledge, a nagging doubt persisted:

> Nevertheless I can't help but notice how my answers are taken to reflect Australians as a whole. If I say or do something in a certain way, then it is the Australian way. Very often, no matter what I might say in protest, such a conclusion will be drawn. It's almost like a full-stop; end of conversation. . . . Surely saying "All Americans drink coffee" or "All Australians drink beer because their former Prime Minister is in the Guinness Book of Records for the fastest swilling of a yard glass" are harmless enough examples in themselves. Yet what of the principle, the mindset behind them? Is it not the same mindset that leads one to say that all people from X country are fascists or homicidal or warmongering or carry guns? To a black extreme, isn't that the basis of propaganda, and what makes it work? Clearly I'm stretching the point . . . and there are no clear-cut earth-shattering conclusions for me to make here either. It is simply another of the many things I have been forced to think about ever since I became Therese the beer-swilling, two-ball snowmanmaking, tea AND coffee-drinking Australian, instead of just plain old Therese.[28]

Therese might also have noted that this tendency to see individuals as embodying national distinctiveness does not apply exclusively to foreigners. The Japanese media elevated Hideo Nomo, their first countryman to make a successful debut in U.S. major league baseball, to goodwill ambassador and representative of all things Japanese.

The ALTs were also treated as symbols on those occasions when, regardless of their experience or expertise, they were asked to talk on the inescapable theme, "[fill in the country's] view of Japan." In these situations they were expected to be speaking not just for themselves but for their nationality more generally. Some ALTs seized on such opportunities to represent all JET participants or all foreigners and to critique Japanese society; they welcomed the sense of power and prestige that comes with being in the limelight. Yet nagging doubts about the grounds for their special treatment always remained.

Moreover, their token and symbolic status constantly threatened to assume sole importance. The ALTs often captured attention for reasons wholly unrelated to their job performance. For example, even though approximately 15 to 20 percent of JET participants have had some teaching experience prior to coming to Japan, JTLs do not, by and large, use them any differently than they use those without teaching experience. The reluctance of many prefectures to match ALTs with teaching credentials to schools where their talents can be employed is particularly striking in light of complaints by some JTLs that the ALTs are too young and inexperienced and that the government should send qualified teachers.

Yet another feature of being treated as symbols was that JET participants had to prove themselves as individuals in every new context. In particular, those who had been in the program for two or three years complained that the Japanese whom they met rarely picked up on such nonverbal cues as dress, demeanor, and the like as indicators of their level of acculturation; instead, only their physical appearance was noted. As a result, whenever they left the communities and schools in which they were known, they were unwillingly thrust back into the role of the generic gaijin. Most ALTs also found that displays of competence in mastering Japanese language and culture were commented on and treated as special precisely because they were unexpected. They were praised most often for their ability to speak any Japanese, regardless of fluency, and to use chopsticks. The compliments themselves underscored the perceived rarity of the accomplishment, and ALTs quickly tired of repeatedly enacting this ritual.

The roots of the impulse to extend "guest treatment" (*kajō sābisu*) to light-skinned Westerners run very deep. Consciousness of the military and economic might of Western countries from the Meiji period on has certainly played a part in fostering these attitudes, but the late Hiroshi Wagatsuma, in an essay on the social perception of skin color in Japan, also notes a long-standing inferiority complex toward white skin that has led the Japanese to a certain ambivalence in their interactions with whites.[29] There are accounts of the Dutch being paraded in front of the emperor (*ijin gyōretsu*) in the early years of contact with the West; and even in Japanese folk religion, Westerners were viewed as gods.[30]

Not surprisingly, then, Japanese teachers and administrators were invariably puzzled at the ALTs' distress at what they considered to be well-meaning gestures. One JTL told me, "JET participants complain about compliments and gestures of gratitude that we would never think twice about." Indeed, the Japanese intended the compliments about the ALTs' use of chopsticks or their language proficiency more as encouragement than as praise. They had to find *something* to compliment, since it was only good etiquette to extend preferential treatment to "the honorable visitors." Being polite and hospitable illustrated the high esteem in which Japanese held Westerners. Instead of interpreting these expressions as tiresome and insincere praise, the ALTs ought to have seen them as signals to redouble their efforts to master Japanese language and customs, for the praise usually decreased when the achievements became genuine.

As for lack of privacy, this was simply a price paid by all visitors from outside the community, foreigners or not. When the urbane Japanese hero of Natsume Soseki's *Botchan* is posted to a rural middle school and experiences the shock of being the newcomer, he too finds his every move observed and remarked on by his students. Finally, he despairs: "How annoying it is to have to live in a small town and be an object of criticism! It seemed as if all the students were spies watching every move and act I made. Dejection came upon me. Let the boys do and say as they will, I am not a man who will give up on account of their interference the plan he has set his heart on. But my heart began to fail me when I thought why I had come down to such a small miserable town where the tip of your nose finds limitation whenever you move about."[31] The treatment that JET participants blamed primarily on a reaction to their skin color is perhaps better understood as a magnification of long-held attitudes toward outsiders in general. The foreigners in the neighboring village have simply been replaced by the foreigners from abroad.

Those who cast these actions in conspiratorial terms, as ALTs often did, thus ignore the extent to which the distinction between "inside" (*uchi*) and "outside" (*soto*) underlies all social interaction in Japan. To be "good" by Japanese standards is to be loyal to the group, and such loyalty may require that outsiders (both Japanese and foreign) be excluded. Defending organizational boundaries is a form of virtuous, not sinister, behavior. When accused of discrimination by the ALTs, Japanese teachers and administrators have countered that insofar as it exists it is "accidental," since the intent is benign.

Well-intended or not, such praise and attention indisputably act as a distancing mechanism. The flip side of preferential treatment is that the ALTs are rarely integrated more than superficially into social routines and groupings at their schools. With only a few exceptions, no one in the schools I visited expected that ALTs would truly become part of the social fabric. Most of the ALTs with whom I talked reported that they were denied certain kinds of information, informed after the fact or not at all about meetings that concerned them, not consulted about decisions affecting their jobs, and excluded from the group in ways both symbolic (e.g., greetings not extended) and physical (e.g., desk placement). In one school the vice-principal referred to their ALT as *uchi no gaijin* (literally, "our outsider"), a fascinating juxtaposition of terms that demonstrates the liminal status of the ALT in the eyes of Japanese school personnel.

To be sure, the degree to which an individual JET participant is included in school routines varies significantly, depending both on the makeup of the particular school and on the ALT's personality and linguistic and cultural skills. In some cases, ALTs are used quite effectively and participate in a wide range of school activities, and they may have enormous influence over the content of their team-taught classes. But they too will eventually find themselves confronting the limits of integration. Their designation as a well-paid, short-term assistant sent by the board of education defines the parameters within which integration and exclusion play out. For example, ALTs by and large are not permitted to make decisions affecting the overall English course at their schools. One JTL noted that Japanese teachers always see the ALTs as connected to the board of education: "ALTs ask not to be treated like guests but because they come from the board of education we naturally treat them like guests [raising both hands and bowing]. The ALTs don't understand that, because they are only here for a year. We can't help but treat them like that, especially the first time they come."

There are also practical reasons for keeping the foreigners at a distance. So finely attuned are Japanese sensitivities to interpersonal relations that the ALTs almost inevitably appear to be bumblers. It is simply a lot more work to include them because they don't catch many of the subtle messages that are so vital to the smooth workings of small groups in Japan. One JTL explained, "Our first ALT was a British fellow and everyone hated him. He never greeted the students and they could tell that he wasn't sincere even though he didn't speak any Japanese. Now our ALT is great and gives us lots of ideas for team teaching. But we never consider him a real part of the group, because if we invite him out drinking with us the atmosphere changes." When an ALT has limited Japanese skills, the flow of conversation must be constantly interrupted. Although these interruptions are often motivated by a sincere desire to put the ALT at ease and explain what is being said, they also serve to reinforce differentiation. In many ways, this is a core problem of all cross-cultural interaction—the very act of attempting to learn how to integrate someone can underscore his or her status as outsider. In some cases, the arrival of an ALT seemed to actually heighten the sense of "Japaneseness" among teachers and the anxiety about maintaining boundaries. There seemed to be an assumption that learning about a second culture would lead to a corresponding loss of Japaneseness.[32]

Of crucial importance in determining the extent to which an ALT becomes part of school culture is his or her own disposition. Integration into any group is, after all, a mutual process. In Japan, being a good member of the group entails a willingness to engage in reciprocal courtesies. When the Japanese had tried to integrate the ALTs, I often found that the ALTs were unwilling to make the kinds of personal sacrifices (such as staying late at school) necessary for maintaining proper human relations. One JTL, for instance, recounted that when he had asked for $150 for the end-of-the-year party, the ALT had refused to pay because it was too much money—but then later complained that he was not made to feel welcome in the school. When I asked the JTL how teachers felt when ALTs turned down such invitations, he replied: "If they accept you as one of their members, it's impossible to turn it down, but if you are a guest like most ALTs, it's OK!" Nondrinking ALTs also had real difficulties with after-hours socializing if it revolved around alcohol consumption, particularly when the bill came (was it fair to pay an equal share when one had had only a couple of glasses of juice?).

Those ALTs who refused to meet Japanese expectations of proper behavior sometimes felt that they were responding realistically to the temporary nature of their position. "If I stay at school till midnight every day I will not become head teacher," observed one ALT. In addition, many of the ALTs were clearly reluctant to give up their special status and take their place at the bottom of the totem pole, as a Japanese newcomer would.

Contrasting Formulations of Ethnicity

On a follow-up trip to Japan in 1996, I had the opportunity to visit Kyoto's Ryoanji Temple. As luck would have it, as I approached the famous rock garden I encountered a group of at least a hundred high school students on a school trip. Just as I was beginning to contemplate how this development would transform the serenity of the place, a teacher in charge of the group suddenly stopped all bystanders in our tracks by screaming at one of the male students, "What do you think you're doing? Can't you read?" I realized that in trying to get a better picture, a hapless boy had accidentally stepped on the pebbles in the garden. He had had the doubly bad luck of being right next to a sign that read "Please do not walk on the rocks" and of being spotted by one of the accompanying teachers. Raising his voice even further, this teacher repeatedly challenged the boy, "What will all these foreigners think? Aren't you Japanese? (*Nihonjin yarō?*) Well, aren't you?" until finally, head bowed in embarrassment, the boy nodded in agreement.

While this incident had nothing to do with the JET Program per se it reminded me not only that public education can be harnessed to reinforce

national identity but also that the very presence of diversity can paradoxi-
cally heighten consciousness of that identity. Indeed, most responses to the
ALTs were grounded in the sense of separateness and the very different
formulations of ethnicity held by Japanese at all levels. The Japanese tendency to assume that linguistic and cultural competence, much less identity, was a priori beyond the grasp of foreigners lay in sharp contrast to the
tendency of the JET participants (particularly strong among the exuberant
Americans) to assume that Japanese not only could, but darn well should,
learn English and become cosmopolitan. The implications of what seems to
the Japanese to be commonsense behavior are summed up nicely by
Harumi Befu:

> Once dissatisfaction is fixed in the foreigner's mind because of his per-
> manent exclusion from the category into which he wishes to be in-
> cluded, the label of *gaijin* will necessarily sound pejorative when thrust
> on him against his will. Here is a classic case of mutual misunderstand-
> ing: a foreigner's wishful thinking is that internationalization obliter-
> ates the line between him and the Japanese, whereas for the Japanese
> internationalization compels them to draw a sharper line than ever be-
> fore between themselves and outsiders.[33]

Most JET participants saw internationalization in terms less of building
bridges between people than of breaking down the walls between them.
The Japanese teachers and administrators, however, saw internationalization as the development of techniques to improve understanding and communication between cultures and groups that they assumed would always
be fundamentally different.

We have seen that there is surprising variation in the receptivity of local
schools to the JET Program. Clearly, some schools and teachers take the
goals of improving foreign language education and broadening attitudes
very seriously, and they put JET participants to very good use. Yet there
was a considerable gap between the expectations of national-level policymakers and the capacity of those at the local level to handle a top-down resource. The organizational and cultural priorities of Japanese schools often
led local teachers to engage in behaviors that were perfectly commonsensi-
cal to them but ran directly counter to the program's stated aims of improving conversational English and integrating foreigners into Japanese
society. Thus it was often unclear how—and if—the ALTs fit into the day-
to-day priorities and social routines that characterize Japanese schools.
This naturally resulted in considerable frustration and disillusionment for

the ALTs, who developed various strategies both to protest and to milk the system.

The JET Program therefore has produced a kind of conflict that is unusual in the public education system in Japan. Most academic accounts of its postwar history assume that the higher the administrative level, the greater the degree of overt conflict; they find that conflict is sharpest at the national level, where the sides are clearly drawn and most institutionalized.[34] At the small group level in local schools, by contrast, there is much greater pressure to work together, and ideological considerations are seen to take second seat to the more practical concerns of cooperating to run the school. Here, however, the level of agreement is highest at the symbolic level: virtually everyone agrees on the importance of *kokusaika*. It is only when an attempt is made to give a concrete shape and form to that vague concept that conflict emerges, usually at the very lowest levels of the system. Masao Miyoshi describes a similar process at work in U.S.-Japan trade negotiations: conflict arises not because interaction is resisted but because no agreement can be reached on its ground rules.[35] The JET participants are problematic precisely because many (though not all) assert universal ethical principles that contradict and can damage the norms of group process.

Given that ALTs and JLTs often hold divergent views of the goals of the educational process itself, it is surprising that battles do not erupt more frequently. That overt conflict is minimal is a testimony to the extraordinary capacity of Japanese teachers and school-level administrators, relying on situational adaptation, to absorb the potential shock of the ALTs' arrival. One might expect that the introduction of an outsider into the tight-knit culture of the school would result in serious disruption, radically altering the chemistry of the community; but instead all the other elements, from the principal down to students, reconfigure themselves to minimize the effects of the outside agent. The high level of sympathy among Japanese teachers for the general slogan of "internationalization" and the cultural tendency to treat foreigners as guests have been crucial in partially neutralizing the disruptive potential of the educational imports.

6 The Learning Curve

JETting into the New Millennium

It takes three years for dripping water to make a mark on a rock
(*Ishi no ue ni sannen*).

Japanese proverb

On 7–8 October 1996, hundreds of people converged on the Keio Plaza
Inter-Continental Hotel in Tokyo for two days of ceremony and sympo-
siums held to commemorate the tenth anniversary of the Japan Exchange
and Teaching Program. Walter Mondale, the U.S. ambassador to Japan at
the time, presented the commemorative speech, and the three sponsoring
ministries gave out dozens of "meritorious service awards." Panelists who
had played key roles in the development of the JET Program discussed
such topics as the changing roles of assistant language teachers, the internationalization of local communities, and future issues for the JET Program. By the following spring, CLAIR had published a 360-page tome titled *The JET Programme: Ten Years and Beyond*, which boasted in its
foreword that JET was "one of the largest human exchange programs in
the world."[1] The overall tone of the commemorative events was celebra-
tory, and the moral of the story seemed clear: through programs like JET,
Japan was gradually coming of age in learning how to cope with "internationalization."

The tenth anniversary provides a useful opportunity to assess the
major continuities and changes in the JET Program over its history. This
long-term perspective is invaluable for it allows us to distinguish the essential and fixed features of the program, and the cultural ideologies and
political priorities that support them, from those that are transient and
malleable. Such a perspective is crucial for understanding how the JET
Program managed to rise above the difficulties that plagued its formative
years.

This chapter therefore revisits policy developments at CLAIR and the
Ministries of Home Affairs, Education, and Foreign Affairs since the early

1990s. As noted earlier, one of the most striking features about the JET Program at the national level is the complex relationship among the several bureaucracies involved, each with distinct interests in seeking internationalization. For each of these ministries and their subordinate branches, we must assess the learning curve as it pertains to the main (if vague) goals each envisions for the JET Program—improving the "internationalization" of local communities (CLAIR/Home Affairs), reforming English education (Education), and enhancing foreign understanding of Japan (Foreign Affairs).

My argument in this chapter is twofold. First, improvements have occurred surprisingly quickly, thanks to a combination of top-down leverage, the mobilization of knowledge, and the ability of local teachers and administrators to put themselves in the position of learners without relinquishing autonomy. National-level officials have tackled, with some degree of success, virtually every problem raised by the JET participants, and they have pressured local officials to do the same. Second, in examining the program's implementation broadly and over the long term, one can see a subtle yet powerful cultural drift at work. In shaping program policy and structure, the view of the JET Program as a vehicle for improving foreign understanding of Japan clearly has gained the edge.

CLAIR AND THE MINISTRY OF HOME AFFAIRS: PERFECTING PROGRAM POLICY

My most recent visits to CLAIR in 1995 and 1999 were eye-opening. Now situated on the twenty-fourth floor of the Shin Kasumigaseki Building in the heart of Japan's government district, and affording a breathtaking panorama of Tokyo, the office was a far cry from the crowded room in the prefectural office building (*todofuken kaikan*) where the agency got its start in 1987. CLAIR's staff had increased tenfold, and most concerned themselves with other dimensions of the Ministry of Home Affair's growing international presence. The atmosphere, too, had changed considerably. The pace was noticeably less frantic, and conversations with CLAIR officials confirmed that heated disagreements between program coordinators and Japanese staff were rare. As one program coordinator put it, "Now we fight about where we're going to eat lunch." The program was by no means on autopilot, and the CLAIR staff clearly remained dedicated and hardworking, but much of their task had become routine.

Subsuming the World under JET: Program Expansion

The smooth workings of the office are particularly striking given the rapid expansion of the JET Program. By 1999 the total number of participants was double the initial target of 3,000. Most of this growth has been achieved by steadily increasing the numbers of ALTs from the six core English-speaking countries. It seems quite likely that the program will continue to expand, as the secretary-general of CLAIR confirmed in 1997: "Seeing that our survey shows that the number of JET participants requested are increasing every year, we take it that there still exists substantial potential demand. In order to meet such demand from local public bodies, it is necessary to increase steadily the number of participants."[2]

Several trends in this overall expansion are worth highlighting. The most significant growth in recent years has taken place in municipalities rather than prefectures (see table 6). In the first year of the program, 72 percent of JET participants were assigned to prefectural boards of education, and municipalities employed only 18 percent. By 1997, however, the prefectural share had fallen to 47 percent while those in municipalities had risen to 46 percent (the remaining participants in both cases were employed in private schools or in special district offices). This meant that by the tenth year of the program, fully half of Japan's municipalities employed a JET participant. For instance, when Chiba Prefecture began the JET Program in 1987, fewer than 20 percent of its eighty municipalities participated. Ten years later, 81 percent of the municipalities were inviting ALTs each year, and Chiba prefectural officials were talking seriously about ways to reduce the financial burden on the smallest villages that wanted an ALT but simply couldn't afford to add even one additional staff member. In Toyama Prefecture, an ALT is now posted to every single public high school, and there is one ALT for every two junior high schools. Local officials' thirst for JET participants shows little sign of abating. Shiga Prefecture plans to increase their eighty-one JET participants by 50 percent in the near future, and continued expansion is planned for every prefecture in Japan. The goal of placing a JET participant in every single municipality in the nation, which seemed so idealistic ten years ago, is now well within reach.

Revisiting Nationality

The diversification of participating countries has also been astounding. I vividly remember attending a session for coordinators for international

Table 6. The Number of Host Institutions, 1987–96

Host Institution	1987	1988	1989	1990	1991	1992	1993	1994	1995	1996
Prefecture	47	47	47	47	47	47	47	47	47	47
Designated City	10	10	11	11	11	12	12	12	12	12
City	76	139	220	264	350	343	371	388	410	440
Town	36	134	253	337	503	663	774	884	980	1,063
Village	4	11	22	30	65	87	108	127	138	164
Total	173	341	553	689	976	1,152	1,312	1,458	1,587	1,726

SOURCES: Adapted from *The JET Programme: Ten Years and Beyond* (Tokyo: Council of Local Authorities for International Relations, 1997), 356; advertising brochure, *The Japan Exchange and Teaching Programme, 1998–1999* (Tokyo: Council of Local Authorities for International Relations, 1998), p. 2.

relations at the 1990 Renewers' Conference in which the issue of the nationalities of JET participants was brought up. One American CIR complained, "My prefecture has international relations primarily with China and Brazil yet there's no one to deal with them. I kept asking my boss, 'Why did you hire me?' I almost talked myself out of the job." The program coordinator facilitating the session replied that they had repeatedly brought up this point with Japanese officials at CLAIR, but the idea had never gone very far. She concluded, "We still come up against a lot of racism and 'the West is best.' You can imagine the politics involved." Another CIR wondered if it would be possible to have CIRs who don't speak English at all. Again, the program coordinator replied that it had been proposed, but to little effect; indeed, the little progress that had been made was almost accidental. "Even with the French and German participants, he [then–Prime Minister Takeshita] made promises that shocked the ministries and for diplomatic purposes they had to be kept." As the discussion concluded, many observed that CIRs can do much to promote the idea that internationalization is more than just hiring Westerners and that they all should encourage their local offices to hire people from non-Western countries.

Such exhortations would be unnecessary today. By 1997 fully 35 percent of CIRs hailed from non-English-speaking countries. Beginning with China in 1992, which was soon followed by Korea (1993) and Russia (1994), ten additional countries have been invited to send CIRs to select prefectures and municipalities. More recently, individuals from Italy, Mexico, and Israel have joined the program. Especially significant was the dispatching of an Israeli to Yaotsu-cho—the hometown of the late Sugihara Chiune, who as Japan's acting consul in Lithuania during World War II issued visas to more than 6,000 Jews fleeing Nazi oppression and who thereby saved many lives.

In addition, an entirely new category of JET participant, the Sports Exchange Advisor (SEA), was created in 1994. A local government can forward a request for a specific type of professional athlete to the Ministry of Foreign Affairs, which then begins inquiries through its diplomatic channels to locate a suitable candidate. Alternatively, ministry officials may locate a potential applicant abroad and then set out to find a municipality willing to host him or her. Some of this expansion has been tied to the hosting of international sporting events. By 1996, for instance, Nagano Prefecture, home of the 1998 Winter Olympics, was employing forty-two CIRs and SEAs, double the number of any other prefecture. The proportion of CIRs and SEAs to ALTs has been steadily growing, from approximately 4 percent of total JET participants in 1987 to 10 percent in 1997.

Obviously, the Ministry of Foreign Affairs has played a crucial role in facilitating this expansion. In fact, countries have been lining up at the door to gain admittance to the program, as the director of the Cultural Affairs Division has noted: "Governments of many countries, including both those which have sent JET participants and those which have not, are interested in and think highly of JET. For example, JET sometimes becomes a topic of conversation at bilateral top-level meetings or meetings of foreign ministers and desire is sometimes expressed to the effect that they also want to send their youths on the JET Programme or that they want to have the number of their participants increased."[3] But this growth is also clearly in line with the Ministry of Home Affair's interest in using the JET Program to improve international linkages among local communities. Discussion is currently under way at CLAIR to create new categories for participants with artistic or cultural talents. These new developments highlight the pressing need for a careful ethnographic study of the CIR and SEA components of the JET Program.

The Re-Asianization of Japan

The inclusion of Korean and Chinese JET participants is a manifestation of larger regional dynamics. After deliberately remaining aloof from Asia for four decades, Japanese leaders are being forced by new economic realities to turn their attention back to their nearest neighbors. Under low-key government leadership, Japanese corporations are increasingly shaping an interdependent regional system of trade, finance, and production.[4] While many Asians are understandably uneasy about Japan's expanding role, Japan's image in the region is nevertheless much better than it was two decades ago. One high-level government study group suggested that Japan could become a "culturally oriented industrial state" (i.e., a state possessing the economic but not military status of a major power) by creating new economic relations with its Asian neighbors.[5]

South Korea is increasingly viewed not as an ancillary element in U.S.-Japan relations but as a significant political and economic partner (and competitor) in its own right. Japan has recently made overtures toward overcoming the legacy of its past colonial rule by apologizing for past transgressions and offering economic compensation. And while Chinese bitterness lingers over Japan's joining with Western countries in imposing sanctions over the Tiananmen incident, Japan still stands as China's top loan source and second only to Hong Kong as a trading partner.[6] Within this context of growing economic integration, the JET Program has played an important role on the individual level, both fostering new ties and building on old ones. Thus when Chinese CIR Huang Bao zhong arrived in Kagawa Prefecture in 1992, he was only the most recent in a long line of exchanges between Kagawa and Shaanxi, beginning over 1,200 years ago when Kukai (Kobo Daishi) studied at Quinlong Temple in the T'ang capital of Chang'an (now Xi'an) and brought back to Japan something of Chinese Buddhist culture and art. Even the governor and senior treasurer in the prefecture took an interest in Bao zhong's stay, and after returning to China he was closely involved in preparing for the 1994 signing of a friendship agreement between the two districts. Since that time, Shaanxi and Kagawa have sponsored at least ten exchange events each year.[7]

To be sure, the JET Program still caters primarily to recent college graduates from six English-speaking countries: the United States, the United Kingdom, Canada, Australia, New Zealand, and Ireland. Yet even among these core countries there has been a significant change, as their own internal diversity is increasingly being represented in successful JET applicants. One longtime participant in the New Zealand selection process notes, "Where at first they were almost totally of European origin, Kiwi JETs are now of Pacific, Chinese, African, Middle Eastern, West Asian and even Japanese ancestry. The success of these candidates is in itself effectively communicating to Japan something about New Zealand."[8] This a far cry from the program's early days.

But such growth in scale and diversity is bringing new problems. Now that a JET participant is no longer the only foreigner in his or her school or office, competition and friction between co-workers may arise. There have been some reports of fallings-out between JET participants who share the same office or school but who have different attitudes toward Japanese culture. Having other ALTs so close can also encourage a dangerous tendency to rely too heavily on each other, as one former MEF (Mombushō English Fellows) Program participant noted:

> Because the number of JETs is so great now—I mean, you can swing a bat virtually anywhere in Japan and hit two or three or them—just having someone nearby has changed the whole feeling of the program. When I was on MEF it was me alone in one prefecture so if I had a problem, I called a friend in the next prefecture. That was as close as it got. Otherwise, I had to rely on the Japanese to help me out, which, for me, in retrospect was wonderful. Even at the time I never felt completely isolated or lonely, but now I think most JETs, unless they really

make an effort to rely on the Japanese, can pretty easily get all the help and information they need either through foreign friends on the program or through all the English information the prefecture puts out. It seems like the prefectures have done so much to make the participants comfortable that maybe the result is there's not much need for them to communicate with the Japanese.

And as a larger number of countries participate, the criticism of the American focus of the program has intensified. A high-ranking official in the German embassy in Tokyo had this to say in the summer of 1995:

> The ALTs from Germany are of very high quality for the simple reason that there are so many applicants for each position [there were only four assistant German teachers in 1995]. When we contacted Gaimushō and Mombushō officials about increasing the numbers, they told us that the original JET Program was only meant for English language education and that we should be happy to be able to participate at all. "So don't complain about the small number from your country"—that was their message. But I continue to go there and tell them that internationalization should have tangible results, and if it is done, it should not mean tightening your relations with the U.S. I mean, there are a few other countries in the world—insignificant of course [laughter]—but they are there. So we've strongly raised the objection against internationalization being a camouflage for the improvement of U.S.-Japan relations.[9]

The growing presence of Korean and Chinese CIRs has also led to calls to increase the use of Japanese as the common language among JET participants. Complaints such as the following began to be lodged with CLAIR: "American English is not the only language; American culture is not the only culture; even the United Kingdom or New Zealand has a culture entirely different from American culture; when it comes to Chinese or Koreans, they have a different language and a different way of thinking; this is Japan, and being in Japan where the common language is Japanese, they should use Japanese among them."[10] Kim Chishyku, a Korean CIR in Fukuoka Prefecture from 1995 to 1997, agreed on the need "to see more consideration given to JET Programme participants from non-English speaking countries."[11] As more and more Asian participants join the JET Program, the huge gap between their linguistic competence in Japanese and that of most participants from Western countries will likely receive even more attention. CLAIR has already responded to this change by printing a Japanese version of its monthly newsletter.

The growing diversity of participating countries also makes it more likely that JET participants will interact with and learn from different peoples within the program, and it is increasingly common for ALTs to report that the best part of the program was getting to know their colleagues of other nationalities. Some American participants have also been taken somewhat aback to discover that their compatriots from other parts of the world do not always have a high opinion of them. An interesting submission to the *JET Journal* in 1995 described the surprise of one American ALT at hearing the term "American American" applied to some loud, boastful, and self-absorbed JET participants from the United States. "What I did not expect to be confronted with," she wrote, "was how some other westerners stereotyped Americans."[12] Her defensive letter in turn provoked a number of responses, including one from a Welsh JET: "in my experiences, non-Americans are far more informed on world issues than their inward-looking American counterparts. . . . Your article just strengthens my belief in the inadequacies, intellectual and cultural, of many American people."[13] The result was an escalating game of "Which is the most ethnocentric nationality?"

The gradual addition of non-Western countries in the program suggests that Japan is now willing to look beyond the United States and other Western nations in coming to terms with internationalization, and the proportion of American participants will no doubt continue to decline as Japan broadens the scope of its "JET relations." But it is important not to overstate the trend. In the postwar era Japan has largely defined itself in relation to the United States, and by and large this mind-set persists.[14] Japan will likely view the United States as the embodiment of "Western" culture and perceive "American English" as the most desired form of English for the foreseeable future.

An Administrative Coup: Pension Rebates

One of the most dramatic turnarounds in program policy occurred in 1995 when the Health and Welfare Ministry, following a vote in the Diet, issued guidelines that would allow short-term foreign employees of Japanese government offices to collect a partial rebate on their pension contributions when they left Japan. The decision was hailed as a breakthrough by CLAIR officials and JET participants alike, and it came after years of sustained pressure.

The possibility of pension reform had seemed slim indeed in the early years of the program. The Ministry of Education had no interest in pursuing the cause, and Wada Minoru tended to see JET participants' dissatisfaction as yet another example of their complaining about issues far beyond their understanding: "The JETs and the program coordinators should not get mad over the pension. It's not their specialty so they can't judge the issues involved. It involves very complex legal issues and it's not just an ALT problem. It's part of the larger foreign worker problem." Yet CLAIR officials not only supported the ALTs but tried to use the Association of JET Participants, and the "foreign pressure" it represented, to further the cause, as a former AJET chair attested:

> I remember on one of my visits to CLAIR the secretary-general took me into his back room and said, "Look! They won't listen to us. I hope you'll put some heavy pressure on this person in this ministry. Here's his address: Write to him." So I told the AJET prefectural representatives to report this to their constituencies. I think it was the beginning of a bombardment scheme, though whether or not it had the intended effect, or if many letters were actually written, I'll never know. I would like to think that we helped.

AJET's letter-writing campaign did eventually put the problem on the radar screen of Health and Welfare Ministry bureaucrats. Behind the official administrative silence about pensions, which was long interpreted as a refusal to entertain the idea of change, the wheels were slowly turning.

Conference Woes and Successes

Perhaps the most striking indicator of CLAIR's increasing efficiency and responsiveness to the concerns of JET participants is the evolution of the national-level conferences. Most contact with JET participants and local Japanese officials occurs by phone, fax, email, or mail. Each year, however, there are several events that bring together many of the major players in the JET Program (except students) for several intense days. These national-level conferences include the Tokyo orientation (held during the first week of August to welcome new JET participants), midyear block seminars (regional conferences designed to improve strategies for team-teaching and work relations), and the spring renewers' conference (to reinvigorate JET participants who have chosen to extend their contracts for an additional year).[15] Especially during the early years of the program, CLAIR and ministry staff typically spent months preparing for these conferences, and they worked furiously during them.

Though the purpose of each of these conferences is slightly different, the format and flavor are strikingly similar. All JET participants are provided with free transportation, meals, and hotel rooms, giving the entire affair the feel of a corporate working retreat. The program usually involves an opening and closing ceremony, as well as keynote speeches by a Japanese ministry official and an invited guest; but the bulk of the time is spent in workshops on topics ranging from team-teaching techniques to office relations. Over a period of ten years I attended five of these conferences: a Tokyo orientation, two midyear block seminars, and two renewers' conferences. Because of the logistical difficulties of convening such large numbers of people and the potential for public confrontations among them, they often make visible the conflicts among the various constituencies in the JET Program.

The very first problem that had to be resolved was control of the agenda. Early on it was decided that a strict division of labor between CLAIR and the Ministry of Education would minimize friction, with the result that each conference is divided into two consecutive sessions: the first, on team teaching and educational matters, is sponsored by the ministry; the second, on broader program-related issues, is sponsored by CLAIR. Compartmentalization of duties is rigid, and face-to-face interaction between ministry and CLAIR officials is kept to a minimum. At times this reached almost comical proportions. At the 1989 Tokyo Orientation, the agencies' offices were forty floors apart in the hotel, and one CLAIR official told me that the two sides met with each other exactly once during the entire week.

Negotiating AJET's role in the conferences proved to be much more problematic. Relying on feedback from its members, AJET compiled a long series of complaints, most of which centered on the content of the workshops and the selection of speakers. The *AJET Magazine*, for example, carried a critical review of the midyear block conferences in 1988:

> The Kanto Block Conference . . . was a haphazard, ambulatory attempt at professional orientation. Speakers were selected at random by some far-removed body/bodies with scant knowledge of whom they were conscripting for workshops. Residents of 500,000 + populated cities were talking on "Life as a Rural JET"; those who had never administered a Teacher's Seminar were delivering presentations on it; in short, planning and organization were poorly done, and the ensuing conference rendered about as entertaining as a circus and about as professionally beneficial as one. . . . Why were we not consulted upon for content

and logistical support? . . . Aside from CLAIR, AJET appears to be receiving little recognition and cooperation from any other administrative body despite the enormous effort we contribute on the program's behalf.[16]

AJET particularly resented being shut out of the process of selecting speakers and presenters at the ministry-sponsored workshops. Craig, a program coordinator from Britain, explained, "The first year Mombushō just contacted the ETCs [English teachers' coordinators] and asked them to submit a list of ALTs, but the ETCs don't know what ALTs do, so they'd send a list of their drinking buddies or the first five letters of the alphabet—it was disastrous."

The lack of consultation with AJET only fueled the conspiracy theories that had begun to circulate among JET participants. The magazine's critique continued:

> Is somebody afraid that the conferences will become too professional or beneficial should we get actively involved in the planning process? Doesn't there appear to be desired stagnation? Perhaps the benefits an organized JET Programme could effect upon the education system are purposely shunned. . . . If we are here to balance the exportation of walkman units, automobiles, and semiconductor chips, why would there be a need for anything more than a half-hearted attempt to assemble us for a few days of semi-structured, innocuous chatter?[17]

CLAIR and Ministry of Education officials, however, saw the situation differently. They believed that it was necessary to go through the "appropriate channels" in selecting speakers. One ministry official insisted, "The ALTs don't understand our administrative structure. We have to allow prefectural officials to recommend their own speakers. We can't order them to choose certain people."

Other difficulties in the interactions between Japanese officials and JET participants began to arise almost immediately. One of the first things that ALTs noticed about the midyear block conferences, for instance, was that relatively few Japanese teachers of language attended. Having worked in schools for several months, most ALTs had come to the conclusion that the "problem" with team teaching lay with the system of entrance exams and the resistance of Japanese teachers rather than with their own limited training. Consequently, they dismissed the workshops on how to do effective team teaching as simply preaching to the converted. Leslie, an American ALT, summed up the general frustration: "It ticks me off. We spend a week in Tokyo learning all this crap about team teaching and then again at the block conferences, and they [the JTLs] don't have the foggiest idea what's up. It puts the obligation on us to teach them what team teaching is all about. I mean, it puts you in a really tough position. Why don't they send more Japanese teachers to these conferences?"

The small number of Japanese participants exacerbated yet another problem: those Japanese teachers and administrators who did attend often felt overwhelmed by the aggressive, sometimes confrontational, styles of the foreigners. In December 1988 the *Daily Yomiuri* even ran an article ("ALTs Overwhelm Japanese at Kanto Block Seminar") that focused on this point, noting that "as is often the case with the discussion conducted in English, the ALTs were quite vocal in expressing their opinions while the Japanese barely uttered a word."[18] In some cases, JTLs or ETCs were put on the spot and asked to defend (in English) their teaching practices. Answers that justified current approaches by invoking "Japanese custom" were privately, and sometimes publicly, ridiculed by ALTs. The Japanese tendency to treat their own cultural forms as places where analytic thought and discourse must or should stop made little sense to most ALTs, who preferred to treat cultural explanations as critically as any other. Yet underlying their critiques was the ALTs' assumption that their own organization of thought was somehow more sophisticated than the "naive" thinking of Japanese who spoke of "Japanese history" or the "island mentality."[19]

My own observations of workshops during 1988 and 1989 as well as conversations with JTLs and ETCs who attended confirmed that overall, they had the tone of extended gripe sessions for JET participants who, having suffered in various ways in Japanese schools and boards of education, were suddenly granted a sympathetic audience. But informal gatherings in which ETCs or JTLs were in the majority could be equally cynical and pessimistic. At lunch at one conference I retired with a group of JTLs and ETCs I knew, and listened to a different set of gripes. "Everyone talks so fast, I can't follow the train of thought," complained one, to many murmurs of agreement. "Yeah, the moderator kept telling them to slow down, but they wouldn't," added another. "Why do ALTs raise their hand before someone's finished talking?" another wondered. "We think it's more polite to wait till the speaker is finished and then raise our hand." Another teacher grumbled that ALTs had "too much energy."

I do not mean to imply that there were no ETCs and JTLs who could hold their own in the public discussions, but in the early years of the conferences they were few and far between. In 1989 ministry officials decided that a good way to inject more "dialogue" into the midyear conferences was to require every ALT, JTL, and ETC in attendance to write a one-page essay on "what effective team teaching means to me." These were copied and distributed to all participants, but the resulting collection of papers was so bulky and heavy, and so varied in quality, that for most JET participants it simply became the butt of running jokes; the clumsy attempt only seemed to fuel nagging doubts about Japan's commitment to internationalization. How could a conference to change English education be useful when there were virtually no Japanese teachers engaging in dialogue?

Another problem was that the JET participants quickly turned into fierce critics of the speeches by Japanese officials. Cultural standards of speechmaking clearly influenced their opinion. To CLAIR and ministry officials, these were primarily symbolic occasions and thus were properly governed by protocol. Relevance, humor, liveliness—these are not the qualities by which ceremonial speeches are ordinarily judged in Japan. Moreover, in Japan seniority is often more important than charisma when speakers are chosen for events such as these, but CLAIR and Ministry of Education officials soon learned that senior officials were rarely a hit with the JET participants. At one conference I attended, the speaker talked for an hour about the pre–World War II era, much to the dismay of ALTs in the audience. Indeed, the conference speeches by ministry officials were virtually the same year after year, and their rehashed abstractions and advice had little appeal after the Tokyo orientation. Wada himself was often taken to task by ALTs for repeatedly giving a standard speech on team teaching, though he became quite adept at counterattack:

> I want you to remember my name correctly. Wada is a very nice name because *Wa* means "peace" and *Ta* means "paddy field." I am the type of person who likes peaceful paddy fields. Some ALTs have called me Mr. *Yada* [Mr. Yuck], and I wondered why. One reason is I gave a very long speech to ALTs last year. According to Western logic, you like to have a question-and-answer type discussion, but in Japan we like to talk and talk and talk. Today I'm going to talk for more than one hour. I hope ALTs will get used to this kind of presentation.

Wada rightly recognized that some ALTs found the absence of a question-and-answer session—a common feature of Japanese speechmaking—quite irksome. They objected not because they had burning questions that had to be asked in public but because they believed they were engaged in a symbolic struggle over the "right" to ask questions. Stopping them from asking questions was thus seen as an affront to democracy: what Yoshio Sugimoto has called "friendly authoritarianism" was affirmed and individual opinion devalued.[20]

For Japanese officials, the most challenging problem posed by the conferences was to manage and control the behavior of JET participants. In particular, they struggled with the apathy and cynicism of renewing JET participants who were making presentations at the Tokyo orientation. In 1988 a number of those invited to do workshops did not even shown up at their sessions, leading Wada to write a letter to the *AJET Magazine* the following month: "At this point I have to be honest with you in adding something unpleasant about a happening which is unprecedented in my many years' cooperation with MEFs, BETs and ALTs. Some ALTs, most of whom were renewers, 'evaporated' from the workshops in the heat of the summer. . . . To be frank, my trust in you nearly collapsed when I found out about the poor attendance of the renewers in the workshops."[21] The following year the cynicism of workshop presenters, all of whom were renewers, had become such an issue that the program coordinators at CLAIR had to explicitly ask them to be less negative in speaking to incoming participants: "Remember that they've just got off the plane and have high expectations. Try to present a realistic but positive picture. Last year I heard people saying, 'Gosh, after I heard these renewers talking, I wanted to leave.'"

Another serious problem was that many JET participants treated the conferences more as a social event than as a business meeting. One CLAIR official complained to me that JET participants were so enamored with the nightlife that they would wear T-shirts and shorts to the business meeting in the day and then dress up to go out at night! A more fundamental problem was simple nonattendance, particularly at the midyear block seminars and the renewers' conferences. Though all of the conferences qualified as a fully paid business trip, a not insignificant minority of ALTs viewed the sessions as a waste of time and skipped them altogether, using the opportunity instead to reunite with friends and enjoy some relief from the constant stress of being a gaijin in an all-Japanese community. Some officials seriously proposed holding the conferences in more remote locations, where there would be fewer tempting diversions, but because of logistics and other considerations these proposals never won out.

Even worse, a very small number of JET participants caused property damage at these conferences. At the 1989 Renewers' Conference in Kyoto, an ALT (who had been drinking) smashed a huge glass window while playing baseball in his hotel room. He agreed to pay for the damage, but the incident caused acute embarrassment to program officials. At another conference CLAIR ended up paying nearly $2,000 for drinks from hotel room refrigerators when JET participants checked out without paying their tab.

CLAIR and Ministry of Education officials found the solution to these various difficulties not in large-scale interventions or drastic overhauls of conference format and agenda but in incremental improvements. First, they looked very closely at the written evaluations for each conference, as well as analyzing all the conferences at annual "evaluation meetings" at CLAIR. Thus every year they received a great deal of input from participants as to what did and did not work. In addition, from the very start Japanese officials at CLAIR gave the program coordinators fairly wide latitude to make changes; indeed, to a remarkable extent the program coordinators have run the show.

The workshops themselves were improved in several ways. JET participants were required to apply to be presenters, and the Ministry of Education advised prefectural administrators to meet with AJET prefectural representatives before approving their applications. In addition, teams of JTLs, ALTs, and ETCs were assigned to moderate each session and were specifically instructed to ensure that Japanese points of view were aired and fairly represented. Criticisms of the keynote speeches helped make clear who was a hit, who bombed, and why, resulting in an annual search for speakers who would be popular with JET participants. The ministry began to rotate its speakers more often and to stress variation in the speeches. At one renewers' conference, CLAIR even brought in a Zen monk as the keynote speaker. A brief experiment with a question-and-answer session after the keynote speeches was dropped after one year when it proved to be too uncomfortable for the Japanese speakers, but a permanent Q&A box was established at each conference so that written questions could be submitted to CLAIR. A program coordinator was put in charge of drafting official responses, which were subject to approval by Japanese officials.

Integrating Japanese teachers and administrators into the conferences proved to be a stiffer challenge, and JET participants outnumber their Japanese counterparts to this day. Few JTLs were clamoring to attend these conferences, and ETCs were also reluctant to act as presenter or moderator in sessions governed by the rapid-fire comments, sarcasm, and humor of college-age English speakers. Over the years, however, the Ministry of Education has gradually increased the numbers of JTLs that prefectures are required to send to the Tokyo orientation and the midyear block seminars

244 / The Learning Curve

and also now expects ETCs to play a substantial role in workshops. Ministry officials promote these conferences as a chance to "travel abroad in your own country" and to "learn how to give a lecture in English" or to "learn how to participate in a Western-style discussion." Wada put it this way: "Honestly speaking, the majority of Japanese don't know how to give a speech or moderate a discussion in English. I believe ETCs and JTLs should learn how to do this in this age of internationalization." Not surprisingly, many ETCs and JTLs pulled into the conferences spent weeks brushing up on English and preparing their ideas and comments. By 1993–94, it was obvious that Japanese teachers and administrators were becoming more assertive in the workshops. In one conference in Ishikawa Prefecture, a JTL even stood up and admonished the ALTs: "Look, do you want us to be involved in this conference or not? If so, then stop talking so quickly and help us understand. Otherwise, you totally dominate the workshop and we have no reason to be here."

Solving the twin problems of poor attendance and irresponsible behavior by JET participants has proved more difficult, but a number of approaches have met with some success. First, the program coordinators leveled a variety of warnings and pleas; as one secretary-general of CLAIR told me, "Because the program coordinators are a kind of 'in-group' for JETs, they can say these kinds of things in a way that won't sound as harsh as if Japanese were to say it." When these exhortations had no effect, CLAIR required all JET participants to sign in on the first day of the conference; but some simply left after signing in. Finally, at one renewers' conference an unannounced attendance check was done, revealing that over 25 percent of ALTs were missing. As program coordinators apologized profusely for treating the JET participants like kindergartners, the ALTs were informed that this time the names of all those not present would be forwarded to their prefecture or municipality, and ultimately to their base school; the offenders were then required to write a letter to their principal or ETC explaining their absence.[22] The strategy led to more problems, however: JET participants who had missed the session for legitimate reasons became defensive, and local Japanese supervisors were put in the awkward position of having to respond to the transgression of their ALT. This last tactic was not used again, though attendance is still taken at some conferences.

On at least one occasion the new, tough approach exposed a fascinating rift between program coordinators and senior Japanese staff at CLAIR. On the second day of the 1989 Renewers' Conference, Ann, a program coordinator, announced the transgressions of the night before—a gate to a parking lot had been broken by ALTs who were seen drinking while sitting on parked cars, an expensive ashtray had been knocked over and broken, and an ALT returning from a party had thrown up in her taxi just as the driver pulled up to the hotel. She exited hastily, leaving the taxi driver to demand that the hotel staff make her return to clean up the mess. The following morning at the plenary session, Ann reported that the Japanese staff of CLAIR had decided that this kind of behavior could not be tolerated: "I was asked to tell you that such actions affect the reputation of the JET Program and in your contracts there's a clause about morality. The Japanese staff has made the decision that if something happens during the next two days your contract will be terminated." At this point, there was scattered applause, indicating at least some approval of taking harsher measures against peers who act irresponsibly. That afternoon as I made the rounds with the counseling section chief of CLAIR, he commented: "We can't even imagine what kind of people these are. Whoever broke the parking gate should be terminated. If we can find evidence, we will. The local institutions, you know, are too lenient. Sometimes we'll advise them on a particular person and you'd naturally think that person wouldn't be renewed, but then we see their name on the renewers' list."

But there was a considerable gap between words and deeds. Hotel video cameras had actually filmed the perpetrators returning to their rooms after damaging the gate, and several of the Japanese staff and program coordinators confronted these JET participants. They initially denied their involvement, but after seeing the video they confessed, and eventually apologized; they then were lectured on proper conference comportment by the Japanese staff. At the end of this encounter the secretary-general of CLAIR told them *otsukaresamadeshita*—literally, "you must be tired after this ordeal"—and sent them on their way. His leniency absolutely infuriated the program coordinators, who confronted the secretary-general in what one described as a "heated exchange," asking why he had "wimped out" and demanding that he carry through on his threat to terminate the contracts of the guilty parties.

In this case, CLAIR officials were caught between the hard-line attitude of the program coordinators and their own cultural tendency to avoid confrontation and to be satisfied with an apology. Moreover, their threat was empty, as the secretary-general of CLAIR later admitted: "Actually, CLAIR has no power to hire and fire. So the threat is in a sense a bluff, although I suppose we could advise the local host institution to do it. But at the local levels if they fire someone, then it's looked at as a real dark spot; so the most common response is to wait it out." In the end, CLAIR did notify the prefectures of the transgressions of these ALTs and urged that their contracts not be renewed, but no further pressure was applied. The program coordinators, however, were very distressed that a few bad apples had given all ALTs a bad reputation. Scott, an incoming program coordinator, felt strongly that a severe speech about professionalism ought to be given to ALTs at the next conference; after the approval of the secretary-general was secured, this was done.

The conferences have thus evolved largely by trial and error, and chronic problems persist. Although the number of JTLs participating has increased they are still in the minority, and there are always a few workshop leaders who have been picked by the ETCs for reasons no one can fathom; the keynote speeches are still uneven in quality; and attendance at sessions remains a nagging concern. The overall tone of the conferences, however, has improved greatly, and in general the JET participants seem more sensitive to Japanese concerns. Robert Juppé, a longtime program participant and observer, offered this assessment in 1996:

> I can remember a workshop on textbooks and the JTL had given a very befuddling kind of talk—very vague, and he didn't quite know what to say. And then this ALT got up, a real overcharged, hyperactive guy, and gave an impassioned talk about the problems with the textbooks and the whole mood turned into how bad the textbooks were, and I hate this chapter, and why do we have to use them? It was just one after another, and it finally hit a crescendo, and one woman stood up and said, "We HAVE to get rid of the textbooks" and a quiet descended over the room. And I'm in the back thinking, "What an absurd workshop. This defies the term." And then Mr. Wada stood up at the end and said if ALTs don't adopt a more mature attitude, we're going to stop holding these midyear conferences.
>
> That was in 1988. Now I look and the same topic is there—how to use the textbook effectively—but the discussions seem so much more effective and focused. You'll get the occasional character who'll stand up and say, "These texts are all censored, and I won't have anything to do with them," but overall the ALTs seem more willing to adapt, and they work harder with the JTLs to get them to understand team teaching. Even the JTLs are more forthright now, and once in a while, they'll stand up and say, "Look, I can't follow this. If you want me to stay and contribute, slow down!"[23]

The Assimilation of AJET

In perhaps its boldest move, CLAIR defused AJET criticism by allowing the association's members to attend special AJET-sponsored sessions at the renewers' conference the day after the official program ended. This offered AJET an opportunity to hold elections, to allow its special interest groups to meet, and to discuss topics such as "learning the Japanese language" that weren't on the official program. AJET also won the right to sponsor an independent speaker at this session, and the organization has worked hard to bring in people who would offer a critical perspective on Japanese culture; past speakers include the academic Gregory Clark and the journalist Karel van Wolferen.

CLAIR not only allowed AJET this extra day at the conference but also subsidized the entire affair, and in the long run this may have been one of the most effective strategies for preventing AJET from developing into a full-fledged resistance group. In fact, the financial support for AJET's activities had begun in the early years of the program, as one former AJET chair recalled:

> I used to go over to CLAIR on a weekly basis for an informal meeting with the secretary-general, just to fill him in on what AJET was doing. Strictly informational. And as I was leaving he would say, "You mean you're not asking for anything?" and I'd say "No, I just wanted to keep you up to date on our activities." I think he really appreciated that, and after a while he started saying, "Well, if you ever need something, let me know." Pretty soon we got into some projects that needed financial support, and so a program coordinator gave me this account number, and it was like money from CLAIR would just show up in this account to be used on certain projects of joint interest. It seemed unlimited, though I never knew since I didn't request much. But in the end I think AJET was weakened by getting money. It was a crutch.

The leverage provided by financial assistance was particularly useful when confrontations threatened. In 1994, for instance, hoping to get a critical perspective on Japanese bureaucracy, AJET approached Masao Miyamoto, a former bureaucrat at the Health and Welfare Ministry, who had been fired after writing a scathing tell-all critique of the culture of Japan's bureaucrats.[24] Celebrated as something of a hero abroad but reviled by government ministries in Japan, Miyamoto immediately accepted the invitation, only to find out that Ministry of Education and CLAIR officials had vetoed it as soon as they discovered AJET's plan. The curriculum specialist at the ministry explained their disapproval: "Miyamoto is not representative of the dominant way of thinking in Japan. If we were to allow someone like him to speak, JET participants would get a very skewed impression of what Japan is like." In handling this issue, unlike the gay rights controversy discussed in chapter 3, CLAIR had considerable leverage over

AJET. They threatened to cut off funding, including the extra overnight hotel stay, for the AJET-sponsored session, and AJET leaders quickly dropped the invitation to Miyamoto.[25]

The larger story of AJET is that it has, in a sense, been transformed by its own success, as former AJET chair Robert Juppé noted:

> I always use the Solidarity parallel. In the first year of the JET Program, membership was close to 80 percent. Now it's around 30 percent and people say, "Well, we've accomplished everything we set out to do—what do we do now?" And they're right. AJET in a way did all that. There were initially a lot of kinks in the program, things that needed ironing out, and AJET worked hard on it, CLAIR helped out a lot, and now the program's at a point where it's down to dotting the i's and crossing the t's. It's become so refined, and every year they have evaluation meetings, and they'll change the orientation to reflect feedback.[26]

While infighting and the high cost of AJET membership in the early years were contributing factors, the biggest reason for the decline in membership was that CLAIR and the Ministry of Education eventually adopted most of AJET's ideas (as former AJET leaders generally recognize).

Nevertheless, AJET continues to play an important role in the operation of the overall program. In 1999 AJET still had more than 2,300 members—roughly two-fifths of the entire population of JET participants. There were fifteen special interest groups, nine nationality interest groups, and numerous popular support activities such as Tatami Time Share, a system enabling JET participants to share accommodations while traveling. AJET has been active in Earth Day activities, and an eighteen-month AJET-sponsored charity drive raised in excess of 3 million yen for survivors of the Great Hanshin Earthquake. *The Team Taught Pizza*, a resource manual for ALTs and JTLs, has sold thousands of copies and has gone into a fourth printing. But the confrontational and critical stance that was AJET's hallmark in the early years of the program has disappeared. By the tenth anniversary of the JET Program, AJET seemed to have become another branch of CLAIR.

Taming Expectations and Honing Policies: The Program Coordinators Revisited

In examining the learning curve at CLAIR, one cannot help but be struck by the steady adjustment of expectations. One longtime participant in the program mused:

> I think a lot of it has to do with getting expectations right from the start. They have really been able to downplay the teaching aspect of the

job enough. They've tempered the orientation so you know you're not going to be a crusader. There used to be such an expectation of importance, and, you know, the ministers would all get up and say, "You're wonderful. You're going to change, totally transform, our society." So people got this idea that they were big shots and then they'd get out to some homely little school building in the countryside and they'd say, "Wait a minute. What happened to my importance? I'm supposed to be a V.I.P. Where's my air conditioner?" Now they're constantly reminding them that reality is going to hit in two days, never mind the five-star hotel. Also, there's so much more information out there now for new people. They can correspond with their predecessors; the predeparture orientation is more developed, there are videos on JET . . .[27]

Host institutions, too, have acquired what, for lack of a better term, might be called "JET know-how." Helped by the accumulation of experience, more detailed guidelines from Tokyo, and numerous opportunities to talk about and reflect on their "JET experiences" with colleagues, they have a much clearer sense of what the JET participants' expectations are and how to solve and avoid problems.

The role of the program coordinators in fostering more realistic expectations and proposing and carrying out improvements in program policy cannot be underestimated. Consider the issue of placement. When Scott Olinger arrived as a program coordinator at CLAIR in 1990, the process of assigning JET participants to prefectures was, in his words, "haphazard." He proposed to tighten the process by allowing JET applicants (1) to indicate their preference for rural, town, suburban, or urban areas; (2) to choose regional blocks as well (Hokkaido/Tohoku, Kanto, Hokuriku, Chubu, Kinki, Chugoku, Shikoku, or Kyushu/Okinawa); and (3) to list up to three specific prefectures or designated cities. This proposal was quickly accepted by Japanese officials at CLAIR and was put into place in 1991, taking much of the guesswork out of placement.

Another issue that initially caused problems was the treatment of married JET participants. Philip recalled one couple who had applied to be in the JET Program when they were engaged. They were assured by the Japanese consulate in the United States that if they were both accepted and got married before their departure, they could be placed in the same prefecture. But the consulate forgot to inform CLAIR of the couple's intentions—and because their applications showed different last names, they were placed in separate prefectures.

One ended up in Hyogo and the other in Koochi, which geographically are very near but there is an ocean between them and at that time the bridge [the Seto-Ōhashi Bridge] hadn't been built. Of course, they both wanted to be on the program but they also wanted to be together. It was a mess. They felt they had been misled because the consulate assured them they would be together. CLAIR was very much in the middle because CLAIR had never been told by the consulate they were married. But of course neither prefecture wanted them to quit. Ultimately, one was moved to an island nearer to the other prefecture where they could commute back and forth on weekends and the prefectures were persuaded not to schedule classes on Friday afternoon. But that was a difficult problem. And two or three years later the same thing happened again and in this case one absolutely refused to live apart and ultimately quit the program. And the prefecture wanted their money back and all that. These sorts of things were very, very difficult. There was nothing we could do, really.

And once again, cultural difference compounded the difficulties. In Japan, it is not uncommon for married men to go off to various parts of the country for long periods of time to work, leaving their families behind (*tanshin funin*). While it was relatively rare for a husband and wife both to be accepted to the program, CLAIR officials initially had little sympathy for the argument that the two absolutely had to be placed close to one another. When only one partner was in the program, he or she would arrive with spouse (and sometimes children) often to find no reservations for the family members at the hotel for the Tokyo orientation and none on the train or bus to the hosting prefecture; much bad feeling would ensue. The program coordinators worked hard to convince CLAIR officials to place married JETs as early in the process as possible so there would be time to clarify procedures and temper expectations. One recommendation was that married JETs leave their dependents at home for the first two weeks, but this advice was sometimes resented and even ignored, leaving the program coordinators scrambling to secure additional accommodations.

Each of these improvements had only a slight impact; but taken together over the years, they markedly increased administrative efficiency and certainly contributed to the high morale among new participants that is so noticeable today. Another cumulative effect has been a new openness among CLAIR officials in discussing the strengths and weaknesses of program policy. Consider, for example, this striking disclaimer about the CIR position that appeared in application materials in 1995:

> The Japanese concept of "coordinator" differs from the Western perspective. As a result of a different contractual status, the CIR is essentially outside the body of mainstream employees. Advice, suggestions, and assistance offered by the CIR may in fact be viewed as the contribution of an outsider. While on the one hand this seems restrictive, on

the other hand it provides for considerable leeway in the decision-making process. In all fairness to applicants, employers and the success of the programme, it may well be more realistic to describe the CIR as "Assistant, International Division."[28]

Even JET promotional videos began to include critical as well as positive comments from participants. Now that the JET Program had a proven track record, it was in CLAIR's best interest to find ways to screen out candidates with unrealistic expectations.

But the growing confidence on the part of Japanese staff also raises the possibility that insularity may increase. Program coordinators today are less likely to be involved in the big decisions regarding program policy than they were in the early years of the program. Japanese officials have moved to minimize their voice in selecting their own successors, and it is now widely accepted that the job is held for two or three years at most. As CLAIR officials outgrow their initial position of humble apprentices to become "diversity experts," it is becoming clear that the sharing of ideas with program coordinators does not mean granting them equal footing in the arena of decision making.

THE MINISTRY OF EDUCATION AND THE REFORM
OF ENGLISH EDUCATION: LOW-KEY PERESTROIKA?

CLAIR has achieved some success in fashioning a program that is attractive both to local officials and to foreign participants; what of the Ministry of Education's attempts to disseminate a top-down innovation throughout the entire public secondary school system? The question is intriguing not only because of the ministry's initial ambivalence about the program but also because of its well-entrenched reputation as a bastion of conservatism and rigidity. That image is captured in a political cartoon run in the *Japan Times* as recently as April 1997. Four identical male ministry bureaucrats dressed in dark suits are shown musing, one by one: "Why should we in the Ministry of Education waste taxpayer money funding research on cloning humans when we've already developed a perfectly good system for producing clones in the classroom?"[29]

The ministry's record of engagement with the JET Program over the past decade suggests that the picture is a good deal more complex than this cartoon implies. First of all, the official guidelines and rhetoric emanating from national-level officials are clearly consistent with the goal of making English education more communication-oriented. For example, the ministry's *Handbook for Team Teaching*, published in 1994, stresses the idea that the team-teaching classroom involves a substantial departure from traditional methods. Its demonstration videos highlight this point as well: one team-taught class features a lively session in which an ALT uses a make-believe bottle of *"natto* juice" (*natto* is fermented soybeans) to teach a lesson on likes and dislikes.

Consider, too, the following statement of the goals of the program by Wada Minoru at a midyear block seminar in 1989:

> First, we should try to develop students' communicative competence and performance and their awareness of different cultures. Up to this moment, the majority of Japanese students cannot communicate in English, and they don't know about different customs, values, and lifestyles. In order to internationalize, we must work toward these ends. Second, we must develop the above skills in JTLs. There is a big gap between what Japanese teachers are doing and what the Mombushō wants to accomplish, and in order to bridge this gap we need ALTs. All 35,000 JTLs throughout Japan follow almost the same teaching procedure, one that focuses on linguistic competence—grammar, sentence patterns, and pronunciation of new words. These teaching methods have been firmly established through a long history, and JTLs are very stubborn, though not entirely wrong, in sticking to them. I believe we need to change them, and if JTLs become more receptive to the ideas of communicative competence, then they have become more "internationalized."

Wada went on to assess JTLs' receptivity to change critically: "The biggest problem with JTLs is that they are not accustomed to accepting new ideas. They also get upset about the new ideas the ALTs suggest. I strongly urge them to be more attentive to new ideas. . . . I say to those who are hesitant that this is a good chance to break the vicious circle of teachers not wanting to team-teach because they don't want to use English because they can't speak it because they won't try. . . . I believe some of the Japanese here are becoming angry with me."[30] After this speech the ALT sitting next to me turned with a skeptical look. "I don't know," he said. "His speech sounded good, but maybe he was just telling us what he thought we wanted to hear."

The question of what the Ministry of Education has done for the JET Program, beyond making speeches, is worth exploring further. As we will see, the ministry unmistakably (albeit slowly) has taken concrete steps to help realize what it perceives to be the program's goals.

The First Foreigner in the Ministry of Education

Arguably, one of the ministry's most revolutionary moves came in 1990 when the Upper Secondary School Division hired a former ALT and AJET chair from Chiba-ken to serve as an ALT consultant. When Robert Juppé, Jr., moved into his cramped quarters in the High School Education Section, he became the first foreigner the Ministry of Education had ever employed.[31] Bureaucratic rivalry with CLAIR and the Ministry of Home Affairs played a part in the hiring. Wada informed me that the Upper Secondary School Division believed CLAIR to be primarily concerned with the CIR component of the JET Program, and they questioned CLAIR's ability to provide effective guidelines to ALTs about team teaching.

Once inside the ministry, Juppé gained an insider's view of the making of ALT and team-teaching policy, and the portrait that he paints is of an office of very competent individuals, many of whom have progressive ideas but are also extremely conservative in *administering* change. Juppé recalled his first reaction to being summoned for the pro forma "job interview": "At the time Mombushō had a horrible image among JETs. They were called the faceless blue suits. Like the politburo up there—these white shirts, similar neckties, and I thought, good heavens, I'm going to go into this. The worst thing that could happen is to fall over into their camp and start representing their interests." Over the next three years, however, Juppé developed a close working relationship with the officials in his office, where he was widely respected for his work ethic and for his ability to generate creative, cutting edge proposals while maintaining a healthy respect for protocol.[32] In addition to fielding calls and complaints from ALTs, he was often sent out to conduct training sessions on team teaching for JTLs, and he participated in the ministry-sponsored intensive one-month study programs (*shidōsha kōza*) for select JTLs. Most important, in the eyes of ALTs Juppé gave the Ministry of Education a human face, and his reputation and accessibility helped it immeasurably in forestalling their criticism. Juppé became known among ALTs as the "team-teaching guru" for his dedication to improving the classroom dimensions of the program; when he moved on in the spring of 1996, after giving the keynote speech at the renewers' conference and receiving a standing ovation, many commented that it felt like the passing of an era.

Yet by the end of his tenure, even Juppé's contagious optimism had become tempered by the administrative conservatism in his office. He recalled that when he first came to the job, brimming with enthusiasm, he would write detailed summaries of each confidential ALT call that came into the office and painstakingly translate them into Japanese for the benefit of his co-workers. Only later did he realize that no one ever read them: his boss was primarily interested in the *number* of calls that came in. In order to facilitate communication among incoming ALTs with teaching experience, he asked that asterisks be placed by the names of Tokyo orientation workshop presenters who had teaching credentials. But when ministry officials heard of his idea they immediately overruled it, arguing that all JET participants must be treated equally. Juppé found early on that most of his proposals to reform the structure of the three national-level conferences were politely, but routinely, ignored. He finally came to accept that, like the program coordinators, his main role was to serve as a buffering agent.

Team-Teaching Laboratory Schools

At roughly the same time that they hired an ALT advisor, the Ministry of Education embarked on a long-term project to conduct research on team teaching and to create centers of local expertise in the method. Under the plan, each prefecture selected one school to model team teaching on a two-year cycle. At the end of the two years, the model school conducted an open house (consisting of demonstration classes, discussion groups, and research reports) and published a record of its accomplishments; these were gathered by the ministry and used in making policy and in advising local boards of education. The ministry compiled summaries of the results from each of the twenty-four junior high schools and twenty-three senior high schools that participated in the first cycle and published them in a special "team-teaching" edition of its journal *Curriculum Materials for Secondary Education*, thus making the results available to all teachers.[33] By the year 1997, the fourth and final two-year cycle had been completed: in each prefecture, four junior or senior high schools had been designated as "special research schools" (*kenkyū shiteikō*).

The schools usually found that being chosen to serve as prefectural model was a mixed blessing. The amount of extra work was considerable, with the added pressure of having to make a highly visible public presentation at the end. Moreover, there was some question about the program's utility; ALTs often complained that the model classes presented were so far removed from real classrooms as to be virtually pointless. Yet many JTLs did report significant professional growth, crediting the concerted focus on improving team teaching over an extended period and the opportunity to conduct mini–research projects on team teaching in their schools.

In addition, Ministry of Education curriculum specialists spend a large part of their time traveling to prefectures all over Japan to give advice on team teaching to ETCs and JTLs. These frequent interactions both keep officials apprised of local developments and foster a hands-on relationship that is helpful when implementing top-down reforms. The entire system thus represents a useful model for in-service training.

The success of any top-down innovation depends in part on the extent to which those at the lower levels, who are directly responsible for its implementation, are involved in the planning stages and have the same understanding of the project as those at the upper levels, who are making policy. This is especially true of interventions that are ambitious in scope and require radical change. In this case, however, the Ministry of Education could not involve JTLs at all in the initial phase, because planning had to be coordinated with other ministries. Thus, the success of the JET Program ultimately hinged on whether the capacity and willpower to adapt could be generated among local teachers: in-service training efforts were directed toward this end.

The New Course of Study and Textbook Revision

In 1994 the Ministry of Education put in place new curriculum guidelines (*shidō yōryō*) that gave junior high schools the option to have English classes meet four days a week instead of three and authorized new high school classes emphasizing listening and speaking skills. Under the new oral communication guidelines, high schools can now choose from Oral Communication A, a conversation course; Oral Communication B, a listening course; and Oral Communication C, a course focusing on formal thinking and speaking. So far very few schools have adopted the C course, as its goals are unclear, but Oral Communication A and B have proven to be quite popular. According to the head of a ministry committee formed in the early 1990s to assess trends and prospects for foreign language education in Japan, the JET Program provided an important impetus for these changes.[34]

Yet these new guidelines by no means implied that Ministry of Education officials were willing to entertain the possibility of using materials other than the approved textbooks for communication-oriented language learning. Wada explained to ALTs: "The textbooks are not always useful for communication and we need to rewrite them, but Japanese teachers like to teach textbooks. You need to use the texts indirectly. If ALTs continue to reject textbooks, I'm afraid Japanese teachers don't want to invite you to their schools, so try to compromise." Part plea and part threat, his comment highlights the delicate line that the ministry has had to walk between acknowledging the ALTs' complaints about the drawbacks of the textbooks and appeasing JTLs who insist on the grammar translation method (either because they prefer it or because they believe it essential to prepare their students for the entrance exams).

ALTs outside the Classroom

In addition to overtly intervening to improve the team-teaching class-room, Ministry of Education officials have also encouraged host institutions and schools to use ALTs to change the climate of English education in more subtle ways. ALTs are increasingly used by prefectural boards of education to help conduct job interviews for prospective JTLs, and both ETCs and JTLs report that the perception that conversational ability counts is markedly affecting new hires. One veteran JTL recalled: "Last semester we had two teachers for teacher training. The first one had been in Britain for a year, and she had beautiful pronunciation and the students evaluated her really highly. But the second one didn't. I think new English teachers in Japan are increasingly going to be judged by a higher standard because of ALTs." ALTs are also being asked more frequently to serve as judges at English speech contests, which are ubiquitous at the secondary school level in Japan. In many cases the criteria used by ALTs to assess students' delivery differ from those used by the Japanese judges.[35] How and whether the Japanese approach will survive in the face of the communication-oriented criteria of the ALTs is an interesting question for the future.

Another unintended effect of the JET Program may be the gradual eradication of so-called Janglish, English that doesn't make sense to a native speaker. Now that the "English police" are scattered through every community in Japan, there is scarcely a T-shirt or sign that can escape their watchful eyes.

Progressive Ideas, Conservative Administration

Taken together, the above efforts suggest that the JET Program may have produced low-key perestroika at the Ministry of Education: officials there are now irrevocably committed to promoting conversational skills in foreign language education. Two developments in the late 1990s provide a hint of where reform efforts may be directed in the coming years. The first was the arrival of two assistant Korean teachers (AKTs) and three assistant Chinese teachers (ACTs) in August 1998. Previously, China and Korea had been involved solely on the CIR side of the JET Program; but as economic and political ties with Asian countries have strengthened in recent years, there has been growing pressure to offer Korean and Chinese as foreign language electives in public schools. In fact, in 1997 the most popular non-English foreign language studied in high school was Chinese, with 15,390 students studying at 303 schools (201 public and 102 private).[36]

The second development is that Ministry of Education officials now talk openly about the possibility of introducing English classes in public elementary schools. In 1996 a high-profile ministry task force recommended that the teaching of English at elementary schools be seriously considered, and several pilot projects in this area have been completed. Ministry surveys also revealed that in 1998 roughly one-half of all ALTs had conducted some form of English or "international understanding" class at an elementary school. Though formalizing this arrangement would involve surmounting formidable legal and logistical barriers as well as resistance from some elementary school teachers, the new course of study in 2002 at the elementary level will see a new addition to the curriculum—general studies (*sōgō gakushū*). It will be up to each school to develop its own integrated study course covering areas of international understanding, the environment, information technologies, and social welfare.

Skeptics will undoubtedly argue that even if such efforts are sincere, they will bear little fruit so long as the current entrance exams and textbook-screening process remain in place. Certainly most ministry officials see the entrance exams as a powerful motivators of student achievement, and that system is unlikely to be overhauled in the foreseeable future—particularly since it is largely controlled by university officials who make up exams for their department. But the content of entrance exams may be changing. For example, in what was widely hailed as a major step forward, Tokyo University decided to include a listening component on their entrance exam in English; and as JTLs have become more comfortable with the practice of team teaching itself, they have more forcefully questioned how to evaluate oral communication classes effectively. As Wada remarked, "ALTs are one part of the process of changing English education. We must change the textbooks, teacher training, guidelines. But we can't change the whole education system so quickly. If we compare with ten years ago, we've made lots of progress."

To many observers, however, that "progress" seems painfully slow. Given that methods of assessment play a powerful role in shaping teaching strategies, the inclusion of a listening component on entrance exams could be viewed as an important marker of change in Japanese foreign language education. Yet in 1996, while 41.4 percent of national universities reported that at least one department in the university required such a listening component, the figure at private universities was only 18 percent, and for local public universities (operated by prefectural or municipal governments) it was even lower (9.6 percent).[37] Moreover, the consensus among virtually all the major players in the JET Program is that the Ministry of

Education has been the most resistant to change: in spite of ringing public endorsements of communication-oriented language teaching, ministry officials and their spokespersons at the prefectural level, the ETCs, seem determined to find a way to wedge the team-taught class into the existing system without making any major structural changes. We should also remember that foreigners are still prohibited from becoming certified to teach in public schools; and though recently more high schools have begun to offer German, French, Korean, and Chinese, English continues to be the foreign language of choice at all levels. In short, the JET Program, while important, hardly compares with the other two major transformations in Japanese education, which took place during the early Meiji period and during the Allied Occupation.

THE MINISTRY OF FOREIGN AFFAIRS AND THE ALUMNI RIPPLE EFFECT

Though its effects on English education have been gradual and mixed, the JET Program has achieved phenomenal success as a cultural exchange program. Many of the JET participants, even those who are preoccupied with changing the Japanese system, come to feel close to Japan. In a 1992 CLAIR survey on the living conditions of JET participants, for example, nearly 50 percent of the 2,172 respondents indicated that they would absolutely recommend JET to a friend, while another 45 percent said they probably would. In addition, the renewal rate among JET participants, after hovering slightly above 40 percent for the first few years of the program, has now soared well above 50 percent (see table 7). As noted in chapter 4, fewer than 1 percent now leave Japan before their contracts expire. And in spite of their sharply differing styles of social relations and education, many JET participants and their Japanese hosts do hit it off and form enduring friendships.[38]

If we focus on the alumni ripple effect, the JET Program appears to have succeeded beyond the wildest dreams of its originators.[39] Although it was conceived narrowly as a bargaining chip in U.S.-Japan bilateral trade negotiations, JET has grown to include numerous countries. Hundreds of its alumni have returned home to study Japan-related topics in graduate school, with a level of preparation that is, in the words of one longtime Japan expert, "something we could only have dreamed of ten years ago."[40] Other JET alumni have stayed in Japan, working in various capacities, or have found Japan-related work in their own country; there have even been dozens of cross-cultural marriages.

Table 7. The Numbers of Participants and Renewers, 1987–96

Year	Number of Renewers	Ratio of Renewal[a] (percent)	Number of New Participants	Total Number of Participants	Number of Nonrenewers
1987			848	848	
1988	376	44.3	1,067	1,443	472
1989	651	45.1	1,336	1,987	792
1990	823	41.4	1,461	2,284	1,164
1991	1,033	45.2	1,841	2,874	1,251
1992	1,432	49.8	1,893	3,325	1,442
1993	1,698	51.1	2,087	3,785	1,627
1994	2,113	55.8	2,072	4,185	1,672
1995	2,157	51.5	2,471	4,628	2,028
1996	2,619	56.6	2,411	5,030	2,009
Total	12,902	48.9[b]	17,487	30,389[c]	12,457

[a] This ratio indicates the proportion of participants who renewed their contract from the previous year.

[b] The average ratio of renewal.

[c] The total number of one-year tenures completed.

SOURCE: Adapted from *The JET Programme: Ten Years and Beyond* (Tokyo: Council of Local Authorities for International Relations, 1997), 356.

CLAIR and the Ministry of Foreign Affairs have approached alumni relations with great enthusiasm, thereby indicating their high priority among Japanese policymakers. As early as 1988 CLAIR was toying with the idea of holding a "non-renewers' conference" in order to ensure that nonrenewing JET participants would leave Japan with a good taste in their mouths. One program coordinator recalls,

> We came up with this idea of having a meeting, like a closing to the whole year. Well, the Japanese were really enthused about it. They wanted the crown prince to come and the secretary-general had actually visited the Imperial Palace to try to arrange it. That didn't work out, and then they wanted the prime minister. They were HOT on the idea! We had the money to cover the program, and then we started running into problems of agenda and cost to the prefectures. The prefectures would have to pay for sending them to the conference and they started to balk, saying we're not going to pay for a JET to come up there just for a party or for one night or whatever.

The idea was effectively dropped for a number of years, but it resurfaced in 1995, largely through the efforts of program coordinators. In 1996 the first annual Non-Renewers' Conference was held.

The idea of forming a JET Alumni Association met with a more immediate positive reception; indeed, its formation arguably provides the best example from the program's history of how JET participants and their Japanese hosts can work together on new projects that are beneficial both to the program and to society as a whole. Much of the groundwork for JETAA was done by an AJET representative, Scott Olinger, who became a program coordinator at CLAIR. The first significant gesture toward alumni concerns was an AJET publication titled *The Non-Renewer's Handbook*, which gave advice on jobs, graduate schools, and other matters pertaining to life after JET. When Olinger arrived at CLAIR, he convinced officials there that a more formal organization was needed to assist JET participants in making the transition back home and in providing information and contacts regarding what to do next. By January 1999, more than 9,000 former JET participants were members of forty-two regional JETAA chapters located in eleven participating countries, and each year representatives from regional chapters gather for a JETAA International Conference. The only snag concerned funding for the JETAA regional groups. Particularly in cities where the Ministries of Foreign Affairs and Home Affairs both had offices, there was competition for sponsorship of JETAA chapters. And the JET alumni themselves were suspicious of both, fearing that if they accepted ministry funding for outreach activities they then would be forced to accept ministry policies. In the end each chapter set itself up as a nonprofit organization, and this arrangement has worked quite well.

While the activities of each JETAA chapter vary considerably, they usually include assisting in recruiting and interviewing, participating in Japan-related community outreach activities, holding social gatherings in conjunction with the consulate, and assisting JET alumni in their job searches. Scott Olinger told me that at the outset he hoped "these groups would become active in promoting a better, realistic understanding of Japan in their communities." CLAIR very generously funded and supported the creation of a quarterly newsletter, *JET Streams*, for JET alumni, as well as an annual alumni directory. An annual essay contest was begun in 1993, and enterprising alumni have ensured that the JET Program is well-represented in cyberspace. In fact, when Olinger did a cursory search in 1998 he found 182 references to the JET Program on the World Wide Web. Prefectures have also jumped at the opportunity to establish their own alumni groupings within the framework of JETAA. Hyogo-ken was thrilled when a JET alumnus from the prefecture was appointed vice-consul for his country's consulate in the Kansai region of Japan, of which Hyogo is a part.

The establishment of JETAA has significantly affected the recruitment of new participants as well. In general, all aspects of the process that occur before the applicants arrive in Japan—advertisement, selection, and predeparture orientation—are vastly superior to what they were in the early years of the program, in part due to the assistance of JET alumni. They are active in promotional activities and predeparture orientations, and most selection committees utilize the services of one or two.

Despite its shaky start, the JET Program seems to have generated a tremendous amount of goodwill among college faculty in Japan-related fields in the participating countries. At those times when job prospects for graduating seniors in many of the participating countries are not promising, JET offers students an attractive option—both for those interested in pursuing Japan-related careers and for those interested in a cross-cultural learning experience before entering graduate school or tackling the job market at home. Two graduate institutions in the United States have even instituted scholarships specifically for JET alumni: the Monterey Institute of International Studies offers a JET Alumni Scholarship for its TESOL (teaching of English to speakers of other languages) program, and the Japan-American Institute of Management Science at the University of Hawaii offers scholarships for its Japan-focused management programs. Indeed, the benefits of the program on the individual level, in cultivating international goodwill and establishing cross-cultural ties, may far exceed those on the national scale, gained in pursuit of the ambitious goals of reforming Japanese society and education.

The Japanese enthusiasm for the JET Alumni Association makes perfect sense, for in Japan enduring ties of group membership have an important cultural function. Japanese regularly meet for school reunions, even of their elementary school graduating class. Japan's Fulbright alumni network is renowned for its level of activity and its dedication to fund-raising, going so far as to sponsor additional Fulbright scholars abroad. Members act, in large part, from a genuine concern for reciprocity and a desire to return something to those who made their experience possible. But culture can also be mobilized for political ends, and we can also see a strong component of national self-interest in the promotion of JETAA. Ideally, each chapter provides a solid constituency of pro-Japan youth in each of the participating countries.

A wide range of program policies support this goal. For example, most of the overseas advertisements for the JET Program stress that it promotes "international exchange" and provides the opportunity to learn about Japan; teaching in the schools is mentioned almost as an afterthought. The three-year limit on participation, the age limit of thirty-five, and the tendency of the Japanese side to appease the foreign participants and to judge program success in terms of their "level of happiness" also make the most sense if viewed in light of this goal of enhancing foreign understanding of Japan. When the possibility of eliminating the age limit and extending the period of stay from three to four years was brought up at one symposium at the tenth anniversary celebration, a Ministry of Foreign Affairs representative responded: "From the standpoint of having these people as assets to Japan's foreign relations, extending the length of service from three to four years means more or less slowing down increase in the number of such people through decrease in the number of invitees. Also, with regard to the age limit of thirty-five, it is possible that it was considered better to invite younger people than older ones from the viewpoint of building up diplomatic assets for the future."[41] CLAIR and ministry officials have even begun to complain that the renewer rate is too high, as veterans are taking up spaces that could be filled by new applicants. This is striking admission of their focus on the foreign relations goals of the JET Program, even to the detriment of educational ends.

Japanese Language Policy

The evolution of Japanese language policy nicely illustrates the cultural drift in program implementation. One of the striking silences in JET Program policy during its fledgling years was the sparse encouragement for learning the Japanese language. As one ALT pointed out in an evaluation meeting at CLAIR in 1990, "Nothing in the JET Program suggests that anyone in Mombushō views Japanese language acquisition as an important thing." Although CLAIR sent audiotapes on beginning Japanese to all participants before they came to Japan, there was no follow-up. Indeed, all three ministries have resisted the idea of including workshops on the Japanese language at the Tokyo orientation or at other conferences. Wada Minoru explained to me the Ministry of Education's position: since the official job of the ALTs is to teach their native language, Japanese language study should be undertaken privately by each participant.[42]

Many ALTs, however, saw the study of Japanese language and culture as one of the primary goals of their stay in the country. Few are certified teachers or have experience teaching English as a second language. Given that Japanese officials repeatedly exhort them to respect Japanese culture and schools, they have argued that, at the very least, there should be official encouragement to study Japanese as a means to accomplish this. Frustrated by the perceived lack of support from the Ministry of Education for one of their main aims, JET participants requested a special AJET-sponsored session on learning Japanese at the 1989 Tokyo Orientation. Nearly two hundred people attended, even though it was held at 7:00 A.M.

After years of protests, CLAIR finally began to move on the issue; in 1990 it produced a text and tape called *Japanese for CIRs*, which was an extremely useful introduction to conversational Japanese needed in the workplace. But the majority of JET participants still had no formal support. It wasn't until 1992, five years into the program, that CLAIR and the Ministry of Foreign Affairs began to plan a series of three Japanese language learning opportunities that would be open to ALTs during their stay in Japan. But the outcome was not at all what JET participants had expected. Instead of producing courses that would assist JET participants in conversational Japanese, all three initiatives were ultimately tied to producing qualified teachers of Japanese abroad.

The first course, CLAIR's Correspondence Course in Japanese, was an attempt to provide language learning opportunities for JET participants without removing them from their job sites. Once the proposal was funded by the Japan Lottery Association, the secretary-general at CLAIR asked Bonjinsha, a reputable publisher of Japanese language materials, to publish and administer the course. A professor of linguistics at Osaka University was chosen to oversee its design, and several other experts in Japanese linguistics contracted to write chapters for the course. After much of this legwork had been done, Peter Evans, a program coordinator, was brought on board to assist in the final editorial work. His main complaint when he began working at CLAIR had been the JET participants' lack of interest in learning Japanese (over 60 percent report that they study Japanese less than three hours a week or not at all), which he saw as a cultural failing on their part.

When the draft of the course finally arrived at CLAIR, though, it was a far cry from what the program coordinators had sought. Evans recalled, "Basically, it was a graduate level course in linguistic analysis of Japanese. It was all *wa* and *ga* and the use of particles. There was no Japanese script at all." In addition, the material was poorly edited, as Bonjinsha had published little in English prior to this project. But CLAIR's agreement was that the program coordinators would review the draft only for spelling errors.

To make matters worse, CLAIR had miscalculated how strenuously prefectures would resist paying for language study by JET participants. Cost for the course had been set at 60,000 yen (approximately $500) per person, to be split between the individual and the host institution, but over 80 percent of host institutions initially refused to fund their share. With deadlines looming, CLAIR officials were forced to resort to strong-arm tactics. Evans remembered:

> There was a lot of arm-twisting. We had a chart of which prefectures were giving us trouble and *bucho* [the division chief] would get on the phone and engage in the most overt type of persuasion I witnessed during my time at CLAIR. It completely changed my view of what CLAIR can and can't do. They can force prefectures if they want to, and they were very creative with their offers for how prefectures could pay. CLAIR offered to wait for payment until next year's budget kicked in or to reduce monthly allocation tax payment by the 30,000 yen cost of the course. A few holdouts were offered the possibility of paying but then having their lump sum increased a bit.

By the end of the phone campaign, every prefecture had verbally committed to the project.

But that commitment hardly guaranteed success. For JET participants, the first year of the correspondence course was a disaster. It offered nothing at all of practical value, such as how to order from a menu or answer phone calls in the office. In addition, the homework had little relevance to the text, and JET participants were never told how it was graded. After the first marking period, 85 percent of participants had received As and 15 percent Bs—a direct result of the overseer advising Bonjinsha to be lenient so that students would not become discouraged. Evans told me, "It was the worst grading situation you could imagine. They were giving letter grades to each question, but students would get final grades that didn't reflect grades on individual questions." And they were not shy about making their opinions known: "In September alone I had 100 phone calls of complaints on this issue. People were angry and were saying things like, 'I'm gonna tell everybody I know not to do this.' We did a survey during that first year and found that just under 4 percent were satisfied, 5 percent had no opinion, and the other 91 percent were dissatisfied. There were 3 months when I did 100 hours of overtime. The whole process just shows how inefficient CLAIR was. I always hold this case up as the worst example of politico-bureaucratic decision making." Not surprisingly, applications for the second year of the course dropped precipitously.

In response to these problems, CLAIR held an evaluation meeting at which, in the words of one participant, "the whole course was ripped apart." The authors were all qualified specialists in their field, but CLAIR and Bonjinsha officials clearly had misinterpreted what JET participants wanted. The secretary-general at the time was generally supportive of these critiques, and he agreed to allow CLAIR to produce the text at their own office. Evans reflected,

> That gave us control over production schedule and some on content, though mostly it was window dressing. I became the prime mover of the project and completely bypassed the chain of command so that I could work directly with the secretary-general. He was sympathetic but only in the language of "there are improvements that can be made." I even learned phrases like "labial dental" and "fricative" in Japanese. I tried to wed pragmatic and linguistic approaches, and we asked authors to rewrite their sections. It improved somewhat but it never became the functional introduction to Japanese we had hoped for.

That the approach taken diverged so sharply from what most JET participants had expected suggests that more than the need to prepare for "exam hell" influences Japanese methods of language instruction. Although the correspondence course had a very different purpose, the usual Japanese emphasis on learning through focusing on form and repetition of discrete grammatical items found its way into the curriculum. The project thus replicated the major problems plaguing the teaching of foreign languages in Japanese schools, and to JET participants it seemed to demonstrate that CLAIR was simply paying lip service to communication-oriented language teaching.

But the course's design also reflected CLAIR officials' perception of its ultimate utility, which was in training those who enrolled to teach the Japanese language abroad. This idea, in keeping with JET's purpose as a foreign relations strategy, had initially been raised by officials within the Ministry of Foreign Affairs; the JET participants appeared to be a ready-made pool of potential language teachers, easily tapped. In addition to the correspondence course the ministry thus initiated the second course, a two-month program of Japanese language study in Tokyo for selected JET participants who desired to teach Japanese on their return home. Attendees received scholarships that covered the entire cost of the program, but they were required first to have completed not only CLAIR's correspondence course but also the third course: a short-term intensive program in Japanese language at the Ministry of Home Affair's state-of-the-art intercultural training facility on the shores of Lake Biwa in Shiga Prefecture.

Without question JET participants are offered more options for learning Japanese today than they were during the program's start-up period, and Japanese officials can honestly claim to have responded to the complaints about inadequate language training and support. Yet while fulfilling the letter of the JET participants' demands, they ensured that the solution better suited Japanese conceptions of internationalization. Ironically, by targeting these language courses at the minority of JET participants who might want to teach Japanese after returning home, CLAIR and Ministry of Foreign Affairs officials have ignored the ALTs' much larger need: the skills to aid their integration into Japanese schools and local communities. Only in 1999 did serious work begin on a proposal to offer a correspondence course that truly stresses conversational Japanese.

Cultural Exchange and the National Interest

I do not mean to suggest that the idea of JET as a cultural exchange program is a bad one. Given Japan's often vexed relations with other governments in matters of global economic or political affairs, it is refreshing to know that many JET participants and their Japanese hosts forge meaningful personal relationships with each other. In addition, regardless of their take on Japan, JET alumni are able to put a realistic, human face on a society that is all too often stereotyped by foreign media.

Clearly, the JET Program is an example of smart foreign policy, and key ministry officials believe that the program's main purpose is to serve national interests. On the occasion of the tenth anniversary celebration, Hisaeda Joji, director of the Second Cultural Affairs Division at Gaimushō, stated in no uncertain terms:

> From the viewpoint of the Ministry of Foreign Affairs, it is significant as part of Japan's national security policy that these youths go back to their respective countries in the future and become sympathizers for Japan. In the case of the United States and France, for instance, they often get criticized by many countries for promoting their own independent international policies. All the same, they will carry through these policies, because these nations have sufficient national strength. . . . In Japan's case, the nation is far from possessing such strength to carry out policies in defiance of world opinion. Therefore, highly deliberate, even artificial efforts are required to create sympathizers for Japan as part of national security policy. From this point of view, we consider the JET Programme is an extremely important and at the same time effective policy instrument.[43]

It is precisely this mind-set, however, that program coordinators and JET participants fought, arguing on many occasions that *kokusaika* was not *nihonka*: that is, "internationalization" was not the same as "Nipponification." It also underlies their frequent accusation that the "exchange" dimension of the Japan Exchange and Teaching Program has been short-changed in its implementation.

Of course, Japan is not unique in using cultural programs to suit national purposes; the Peace Corps, the British Council, and other quasi-governmental international exchange organizations have often been accused of being tools of their respective governments. What is most interesting here is how clearly we can see that the justification for the program has shifted during its implementation. The public proclamations about opening up Japan and demonstrating that foreigners can be part of the group have gradually given way to a preoccupation with encouraging foreign guests to greater sympathy toward and understanding of Japan. The JET Program is not ultimately concerned with fostering some idealistic movement to create a global village or to blur absolute lines of national sovereignty; instead, it focuses on getting Japan better press and getting Japanese better understanding of outsiders, enabling them to avoid unanticipated counterreactions and thereby raise their own relative status in the world.

7   Final Thoughts

Social commentators of all political stripes, both inside and outside Japan, delight in observing that Japan is on the verge of a momentous transformation, a series of changes "so far-reaching in their import that Japanese society 'as we know it' is being transformed irrevocably." But as Robert Smith has noted, the real question is not one of tradition versus change but of which version of change is acceptable.[1] The Japanese have been effective managers of economic change over the past few decades, but managing economic and technological change is not the same as managing diversity. Thomas Rohlen makes the sobering point that "Japan has never before in history succeeded in being an international leader in cultural, scientific or political terms."[2] Is Japan's handling of the Japan Exchange and Teaching Program an indication of its readiness to assume a new, higher profile in international affairs? What does it tell us about the prospects for cultural and educational change in Japanese society?

Through the lens of the JET Program, we see competing interpretations of "internationalization." In its links to foreign policy objectives at the national level, the program makes a certain kind of sense, but the relevance of foreigners to the daily priorities of local boards of education and schools is ambiguous at best. Indeed, in its practical implementation JET appears to be much more fragmented, loosely structured, and marked by competing goals and communication breakdowns than we might expect. The fit between national-level objectives and local realities becomes increasingly problematic as the program moves down through the various layers of the education system—as those administering the program take progressively greater liberties with official policy. The actions of local school personnel in some cases run directly counter to the public objectives of the program.

For instance, while there is no doubt that the large numbers of assistant language teachers have created some impetus for change in the goals and methods of teaching English in Japan, the contradiction between the ideal of teaching conversational English and the reality of preparing for entrance exams remains acute. And the image of Japanese becoming more open to foreign cultures and accepting a more pluralistic view of their society must be tempered by our recognition that JET participants at all levels of the program receive preferential treatment and that the presence of an ALT in local schools sometimes leads Japanese teachers to maintain identity boundaries more intensely. If we judge the program by its success in achieving its formal goals—promoting conversational English and the acceptance of diversity—then the policy lever being applied to its implementation seems inadequate.

Clearly, the events and analysis presented above refute any notion of a monolithic Japanese response to outsiders, such as has been popularized in *nihonjinron* accounts of Japanese culture and society. There is no single notion of internationalization in Japan, nor is there any single body that could implement such a policy. The story is rather one of competing ideologies and interests, miscommunication, and the reinterpretation of program objectives at each administrative level. In short, we find an extraordinarily complex picture of internal conflict and variation. Spanning three Japanese ministries, eighteen countries, dozens of consulates, forty-seven prefectures, thirteen designated cities, hundreds of municipalities, and thousands of schools and local government offices, the JET Program hangs together—but only in the most ungainly manner.

But its hanging together is at least as significant as its unwieldiness, for the diversity in Japanese approaches to the JET Program is held within a single process, a shared framework of meaning. There has been very little public controversy within Japan over the program itself, and the government has achieved an extraordinary degree of compliance with its policies and procedures. Requests from prefectures and municipalities for ALTs have remained high, and through its bureaucratic arm, the Japanese government has placed more than 20,000 foreigners in schools all over the country. In the thirteen years since the program began, ALTs have visited and team-taught on at least one occasion in virtually every one of Japan's 16,000-plus public secondary schools.

In this top-down attempt to orchestrate societal change, the government's success had less to do with its coercive power than with the degree of receptivity and shared consent that already existed among educators at the lowest levels of the system. Far from being a command system, the entire process seems to have worked through a combination of firm persuasion at the top and a general willingness on the part of prefectures, municipalities, and schools to accept the authority of the next level up even while pursuing their own interests. Nor was there public outcry from JTLs, who were asked to team-teach with threatening foreigners without ever having been consulted about the program. Their receptivity seems remarkable, particularly given the current wisdom in the United States that top-down interventions rarely get through the classroom door. Although JTLs are often taken to task for digging in their heels and resisting communication-oriented approaches, over the long term these local teachers have shown a surprising willingness to act as learners. They have mobilized knowledge and striven for perfection and mastery, while not relinquishing autonomy; the result is that those placed in the difficult position of managing face-to-face contact with the JET participants have learned quickly, if not always smoothly.

In spite of great private ambivalence and even dissatisfaction with the program, Japanese at all levels continue to salute the flag of internationalization, and some put forth great effort to make it work. We find actors in all parts of the system mouthing the same words used by government officials to justify the program in the first place: "This is something Japan must do to survive in the new international world order" (*kokusai shakai no naka ni ikiru tame ni*). Yet what Japan does in giving "internationalization" cultural form and meaning begins with deeper assumptions about selfhood and social relations. For a millennium, foreign elements have been incorporated into the Japanese value system and subsequently transformed in ways that astonish their originators. Likening the outcome of Japanese importation of Chinese culture to the process by which soybean cake emerges after brine (Chinese civilization) is added to clear soup (Japanese culture), Hidetoshi Kato has observed that there is very little "authentic" about Japanese culture; indeed, he locates the essence of the Japanese way of life in the ability to transform outside influences.[3] Numerous scholars have shown that fundamental abstractions like capitalism or democracy, on the one hand, or mundane institutions like baseball, Disneyland, or even department stores, on the other, undergo a sea change after being adopted by Japanese—they are infused with indigenous meanings that arise from a more sociocentric conception of the self.

While the concept of the JET Program has worldwide scope, its implementation remains very "Japanese" in a number of ways, with mixed results. First, the attention given to form, detail, and careful planning leads to a degree of regulation that frequently clashes with the expectations of the foreign youth that internationalization will be spontaneous, informal, and more free-flowing. The program is standardized and ritualized in everything from how CLAIR has targeted every local government entity in Japan to how team-taught classes and international festivals are conducted. There is a danger that one "correct" way of doing internationalization will be assigned and scripted from the top.

Second, as I have argued, internationalization takes on a very different meaning in a relation-based social order than in those that are more rule-based. That Japanese privilege situational ethics and go to great lengths to maintain harmony in face-to-face interaction contrasts with the tendency of most JET participants to confront and debate differences and to regulate behavior according to general principles. The centrality of social relations in the Japanese worldview is manifest in a number of ways, including approaches to program evaluation. These evaluations, which are numerous at every level,[4] exhibit an interesting pattern. They rely above all on tabulating the percentage of renewers, the percentage of ALTs who quit early, and the number of phone calls to CLAIR to measure the effectiveness of the program. Virtually every evaluation takes the form of a questionnaire designed to discover whether all parties—the JET participants and their Japanese hosts (administrators, teachers, and students)—are satisfied with the program. The core question is "Are you happy?" Conspicuously absent from most of these surveys is any attempt to objectively measure the effects of the program.

Finally, internationalization is primarily perceived by Japanese as accommodation to external demands, in particular to demands from Western countries. Kazukimi Ebuchi offers the provocative insight that "to internationalize" is defined in most English dictionaries as a transitive verb—that is, it involves action on others—whereas most Japanese dictionaries categorize *kokusaika* as a passive verb, indicating the process of becoming accepted by the rest of the world (*sekai ni tsūyō suru yō ni naru koto*).[5] Even though teachers and administrators with whom I talked almost invariably defined internationalization as becoming more forthright, assertively defending one's arguments, and generally holding one's own with foreigners in a discussion, the unthinking response in interactions with foreigners is appeasement. As Walter Edwards has remarked, great difficulties remain in overcoming "the long-standing anxiety over Japan's position vis-à-vis the West."[6] In this respect, it is telling that the many changes in JET Program policies over the past thirteen years have almost always come in response to demands made by the program coordinators and JET participants. The parallels between this process and what Margaret Gibson has called "accommodation without assimilation" on the part of some immigrant groups in the United States is striking.[7]

In one respect, the JET Program has brought extraordinary change. One can now go into virtually any public high school in Japan and witness team-taught English classes that depart radically from traditional teaching practice. Sometimes, it seems as if the atmosphere of the ubiquitous private English conversation schools has pervaded public secondary school English classes. Yet in reality this change is, for the most part, limited to specific contexts and shielded from the rest of the system, suggesting that it is a sign of an adaptive and pragmatic response and not a fundamental alteration of the culture. That the implementation of JET reveals internationalization to be defined by most Japanese as linking up with the rest of the world (rather than as Japanese themselves changing and integrating foreigners into their own society) should remind us that the limits of pluralism in Japan do remain fairly narrow; keeping foreigners at a polite distance rather than socializing them to become part of daily routines is a process at which a majority of Japanese still excel. By defining internationalization as situational accommodation to Western demands, the JET Program provides a means by which Japan can "do" Western-style internationalization (however defined) while at the same time protecting local meanings and institutions. What the Japanese have done is to meet the guests at the door with a great display of hospitality. Assured that they are only short-term guests, the hosts then focus not on whether the foreigners are integrated into Japanese society but on whether they are treated hospitably and enjoy their stay.

In effect, the implementation of this plan relies on two different frameworks. Strikingly, virtually everyone continues to go along with the *tatemae* (official) version of the program while at the same time devising various ways to subvert it whenever local priorities and institutions are at stake. The Japanese appear to be much more willing to live with the resulting contradictions than are the JET participants, whose unhappiness with the situation creates difficulties that require a considerable amount of time to manage. Indeed, the larger significance of the JET Program may lie in how it enacts the interplay between forces for continuity and for change in Japanese society. The theme of reluctant adaptation is an old one in Japan, and the parallels between "internationalization" in the Heisei era and "democratization" and "modernization" in earlier eras are certainly more than coincidental. In spite of the profound technological and economic changes that have characterized the past century, Japanese have responded similarly to the pressure applied by the foreign consultants brought over during the Meiji period, the Allied Occupation forces and their educational consultants in the late 1940s, and the JET Program participants today.

In Japan, the reinforcing of ethnic identity in response to external contact seems almost automatic, and I believe that the Japanese to some extent display what Edward Spicer refers to as a "persistent identity system."[8] Spicer suggests that some cultural systems, such as those of the Jews, Basques, Navaho, and Amish, have demonstrated their ability to survive over time in different cultural environments. They are characterized by what he calls "oppositional process": that is, they have continued to resist, throughout their history, attempts to incorporate or assimilate the groups into a larger whole. Though Spicer's model seems to be designed to explain the persistence of certain ethnic groups within a larger nation-state, here the same process seems to apply to a nation's relations to the larger world system.

At first glance, the notion of a persistent identity system seems hopelessly rooted in a static, timeless concept of culture. But Spicer argues that since these systems develop as a response to attempts at incorporation by outside forces, flexibility and effectiveness in coping with change are key characteristics.[9] What this suggests is that "Japaneseness" may change over time and with increasing external contact.[10] New exogenous linkages may, in direct cultural compensation, generate new standards of identity. More specifically, attempts at "mass internationalization" such as the JET Program suggest that the criteria for demonstrating Japaneseness in the latter part of the twentieth century may increasingly include the ability to interact with foreigners and the capacity to specify and defend Japanese culture in ways that avoid a blanket indictment from foreigners, particularly Westerners. In turn, such programs foster these abilities: the JET Program is helping Japanese learn how to talk about diversity in ways that are more acceptable in international venues. In conjunction with other policies and forces that increase external linkages, the program is likely to foster the development of a new generation of young people in Japan who do not have a hang-up about Westerners, who can hold their own in debates, and who are not afraid to say "No!"

It is significant that Japanese ministry officials, administrators, and teachers almost unanimously feel that the JET Program has ushered in tremendous change. One Ministry of Education official, for instance, pointed out that English teachers' coordinators are finally getting over the "gaijin complex": "I think all the prefectures and schools are getting stricter with ALTs. The honeymoon period is over. When ALTs first came they bent over backward and almost treated them like gods. They couldn't change their commonsense response and just treat them normally. But now they realize that outsiders are not strange and we're learning to say clearly what is good and bad. They've learned not to panic when ALTs make unreasonable demands." An ETC concurred: "Ten years ago we couldn't have dreamed about having this kind of talk about ALTs." In spite of the complaints of some JET participants that one-shot visits to either a school or a classroom are meaningless, JTLs and students really do believe that seeing and interacting with one foreigner can make a difference. That virtually every public secondary school student in Japan has a chance to see, hear, and talk to a foreigner is an accomplishment not to be underestimated; and it is worth remembering that it never could have been achieved without the massive resources that only the central government can mobilize.

Furthermore, common sense tells us that achieving physical diversity may be only the first step in a much longer process. An official in Shiga-ken's International Affairs Division wrote in an essay of three phases in the development of the JET Program—the era of astonishment, the era of acclimation, and the era of understanding. In the first stage, "The schools and towns hosting ALTs found themselves bewildered. They took it upon themselves to do vast remodeling work on their apartments, installing showers and even bilingual televisions, which were still a rarity at the time. To the people of the town, it seemed as if the aliens had landed. Amidst all the commotion, countless troubles occurred due to cultural differences." With the passing of a few years, however, came acclimation, and previously apprehensive schools and towns began to show interest. JET participants were requested all over the prefecture, and their numbers soared. "Even in towns with a population of less than ten thousand, one can find a JET participant riding his or her bicycle around town or shopping in the local supermarket in everyday life. Becoming accustomed to seeing foreign people has surely caused great strides in the internationalization of the eyes of the local people." But the real challenge remains: "Even with this internationalization of the eyes of the people, lack of mutual understanding of each other's cultures still poses the same problems that it did ten years ago. . . . It is our goal to move on from the stage of internationalization of the eyes to internationalization of the mind, true mutual understanding."[11] The reaction to newcomers anywhere, especially those perceived as tokens, often follows a similar pattern: only after the initial excitement dies down, and a different kind of relationship is negotiated, do the possibilities for some lasting impact emerge. At the very least, a longitudinal view of the JET

Program suggests that claims for the unchanging nature of Japanese national character are untenable.

Yet those possibilities should not be overstated. For a Japanese secondary school student, exposure to a JET participant for a number of class periods is not likely to lead to the kind of personal change often triggered by a long-term sojourn, or even a short-term homestay, abroad. Nor should we confuse a decrease in overt preferential treatment with a willingness to accept foreigners as equal members of the group. Becoming acclimated to foreigners does not necessarily imply giving up Japanese identity, nor does it mean that the pressure in Japan to conform to a cultural center, along with the corresponding search for deviants, will end. One Ministry of Education official put it bluntly: "If we lose our identity, who are we? We must guard our identity while at the same time preparing to live in an international society."

In many ways, the friction surrounding the JET Program is not unlike that accompanying the opening up of Japan to foreign companies. In both cases considerable foreign pressure was brought against Japan's insularity. Both the teaching program and trade liberalization have the government's official blessing but run into trouble when foreigners are brought into fixed social patterns. The entrenched attitudes and behavioral habits that form invisible barriers to change prove difficult to overcome. Yet in neither case have Japanese officials given up. Japan is inextricably linked to the global economy and has a very public goal of becoming more cosmopolitan. While the process of opening Japan's markets may be slow, it is nonetheless steady: in this regard, the difference between the 1990s and the 1960s is astonishing. The challenges of managing diversity in schools and offices across the country may be formidable, but Japan's extraordinary capacity for learning justifies our optimism that the JET Program may follow a similar course.

Epilogue

Mirror on Multiculturalism in the United States

What insights does Japan's struggle to cope with diversity hold for understanding the discourse and practice of multicultural education in American society? It might seem at first that we can learn little from a country that still ranks as one of the most ethnically homogeneous nations in the contemporary world, where an ideology of blood still holds considerable sway. It is tempting to repeat the familiar refrain that Japan is twenty or thirty years "behind" the United States in coming to terms with diversity. After all, unlike Japan, Americans have considerable experience living in a pluralistic society, and some form of multicultural education has been integrated into the curriculum of most elementary schools. Academia is awash in multiculturalism; even at the corporate level, calls for "diversity training" are becoming more pronounced. Thus, when we hear that it was not until May 1997 that the Japanese government finally recognized the Ainu as a distinct ethnic group, it is all too tempting to shake our heads in disbelief at the level of overt racial intolerance.

Such a view is dangerous, not only because it ignores the persistent gap in the United States between the rhetoric of equality and social justice and the reality of racism and intolerance but also because it profoundly fails to recognize that our own discourse and practice of multiculturalism are every bit as embedded in a cultural and symbolic order as are the form and meaning of "internationalization" in Japan. Thus, the American ALTs in the JET Program find it easy to protest against the injustice of patterns of group affiliation based on racial and ethnic criteria in Japan without realizing that their own ideology of individualism carries with it an intolerance of a different kind.

The popularity of the "salad bowl," the "quilt," and other metaphors stressing persistent differences notwithstanding, multiculturalism in U.S.

society in fact exists within a homogenizing framework of meaning. Francine Ruskin and Hervé Varenne elaborate:

> We cannot ignore the possibility that America is indeed an overarching structure that organizes the most powerful events in the United States, be they political or educational. To ignore the possibility is to condemn oneself to blindness and a particularly insidious form of righteous false consciousness that insists on the need for certain kinds of awareness (e.g., awareness of cultural differences) without giving itself the means of framing this awareness. . . . The melting pot has worked. There is an American culture. It is necessary to learn the means of recognizing its presence, particularly in those settings where it hides itself. And then, when necessary, one must examine one's own productions so as to escape its overwhelming power.[1]

It is precisely in mirroring this set of unexamined assumptions about selfhood, ethnicity, and change, which Michael Olneck terms multiculturalism's "symbolic order," that the Japanese case can be instructive.

To make such a claim is not to say that everyone sees multiculturalism the same way. Conservative positions that view all but the most benign forms of multiculturalism as undermining national unity and leading to social and political fragmentation clearly differ from radical critiques that charge multicultural education with failing to confront established cultural categories or power relations. But just as the variation in Japanese responses to "internationalization" can be located within an overarching symbolic system, so too do American discourse and practice vis-à-vis diversity rest on a set of fundamental assumptions about self and social relations.

The reactions of American JET participants to Japanese culture and education suggest that believers in individualism have great difficulty accepting the legitimacy of cultural differences; thus, multicultural movements may not be as tolerant of group identities as they claim to be. There is often a considerable discrepancy between their professed respect for cultural differences and their actual behavior. Most strikingly, they generally expect and demand that Japanese approaches to language teaching and internationalization conform to their own. In various ways, most of them construe Japanese culture and education as a "problem" and as in need, at some level, of "development." Wherever Japanese practice diverges from the American ideal, it is seen to fall short of being progressive or international. Though there are some apologists for Japanese culture among the JET participants, they are clearly a minority.

In addition, the American JETs treat ethnicity as a personal religion: that is, each person is cast as defining him- or herself by using available ethnic labels. One can be 10 percent Cherokee, or 20 percent Chinese—or, as the media never tire of reminding us in Tiger Woods's case, several different things all at once—but in every case the focus is an individual's ownership of ethnicity. Although it appears that a person belongs to one or more ethnic groups, for the most part these are groups on paper, or groups in name only. They are a far stretch from the Japanese groups in action, which demand constant loyalty and in return provide a sense of belonging. It is hard to escape the conclusion that the United States is an atomized society playing games with ethnic labels.[2] To be sure, the labels have meaning for the individuals concerned; but they rarely are accompanied by a whole set of obligations and expectations for behavior of the kind attached to ethnic affiliation in Japan.

The voluntary and associational character of contemporary group life in the United States thus carries important implications for the kind of pluralism being nurtured. Affiliating within ethnic groups now is not primarily a matter of ascribed, inclusive identity. Instead, as Michael Olneck argues, "Multiculturalists render ethnicity consistent with the core American norms of individual choice and individual expression . . . by representing ethnic identity as an option or voluntary choice. . . . By affirming and centering the autonomous individual whose cultural identity is a matter of relatively unrestrained choice, multicultural education locates ethnicity well within the established symbolic order through which Americans perceive and interpret society."[3] This helps explain why American JET participants so strongly resent being singled out as gaijin: to confer and deny ethnic identity on the basis of blood is anathema in the American ideology, which tends to define "Americanness" as a matter of having the right attitudes. Our own version of multiculturalism thus reflects a radical individualism that fails to take seriously the identities and claims of groups *as* groups.

That American JET participants insist on the necessity of increasing cultural awareness among Japanese teachers and students also suggests that multicultural discourse tends to frame the educational task largely in terms of affecting the individual. James Banks, for instance, stresses the importance of moving from a "contributions" stage, in which the distinct achievements of minority individuals are recognized by the larger society, to a level of social action/empowerment,[4] taking for granted the idea that change must occur at the level of individual attitudes. As one critic has pointed out, because of that assumption such stage theories run "the risk of masking political and socioeconomic conditions that contribute to real inequality in contemporary plural societies."[5]

The challenges facing Japan and the United States in coping with diversity are in many ways opposites. Yet for those working within each country, the superiority of their own system's logic is taken for granted. In Japan the challenge is to internationalize in a way that requires citizens to open up their language and culture to foreigners, perhaps even teaching them the subtle complexities of what it takes to be a loyal group member. In a more robust version of *kokusaika*, JET participants should learn to adapt to Japan; but foreigners often are the first to recognize this, because the Japanese are so concerned with the outer form and with hospitality. One CLAIR official put it this way: "The hardest part is to get rid of the way of thinking that says, 'Now it's time to do internationalization' (*kamaete, kokusaika no jikan*)." In the United States the challenge is to internationalize in a way that recognizes that other nations' approaches have value and avoids reducing cultural differences to matters of individual choice and attitude. JET participants need to take seriously the task of learning Japanese culture and language and integrating themselves into social routines. Too often they simply criticize Japan rather than admit that they must accept some of the consequences of the Japanese model of social relations.

The history of the JET Program ultimately offers insights into what is fundamental to ethnicity and what is not, and it suggests that concepts such as "internationalization" and "multiculturalism" are rarely employed critically. The idea that simply speaking English, having a foreign pen pal or a sister city, or inviting a foreigner to a local school constitutes internationalization is very widespread in Japan. And a similarly reductionist mind-set can be found in the United States, where the presence of one individual with an ethnic name or a darker skin color is seen as proof of diversity. At one level, the JET Program seems little different from the food, folkways, and holidays approach to multicultural education in American schools or from the reliance on multicultural studies programs and expanded college reading lists to add "ethnic content."

But the seeds of cross-cultural learning must be planted somewhere, and perhaps taking up the cause of internationalization is a necessary first step. Moreover, we cannot assume that intercultural education programs *only* reflect prior cultural values, as if their meaning could be read from a preordained script. People are not only slaves of ritual, symbols, and culture but molders of them as well.[6] The coming together of diverse peoples, despite their mutual reluctance to change, may lead to the creation of something new; we can learn from others without sharing their commitment to a way of life. Clifford Geertz reminds us: "We must learn to grasp what we cannot embrace. The difficulty in this is enormous, as it has always been. Comprehending that which is, in some manner of form, alien to us and likely to remain so, without either smoothing it over with vacant murmurs of common humanity, disarming it with each-to-his-own indifference, or dismissing it as charming, lovely even, but inconsequent, is a skill we have arduously to learn, and having learnt it, always very imperfectly, to work continuously to keep alive."[7] In the final analysis, the beauty of the JET Program and other programs like it is that they open up a public space for dialogue that is grounded in real-life encounters with diversity. The conversations that evolve are shaped by unseen historical, cultural, and political forces, but they retain a creative dynamism of their own. The best of these conversations remind us of the possibility of achieving intercultural understandings that lie somewhere between facile affirmations of human universals and righteous claims of absolute difference.

Notes

PREFACE

1. Advertising brochure, *The Japan Exchange and Teaching Program(me)* (Tokyo: Council of Local Authorities for International Relations, 1991), n.p.

CHAPTER 1. JAPAN'S IMAGE PROBLEM:
CULTURE, HISTORY, AND GLOBAL INTEGRATION

1. Advertising brochure, *The Japan Exchange and Teaching Program(me)* (Tokyo: Council of Local Authorities for International Relations, 1991), n.p.

2. With the addition of France and Germany as participating countries in 1989, the more inclusive acronym ALT, or assistant language teacher, was coined to refer to the first category of participants, and the acronyms AFT (assistant French teacher) and AGT (assistant German teacher) also came into use. In practice, however, the acronym AET was long used to refer all participants, much to the chagrin of ALTs who did not teach English.

3. Of these 848 participants, 592, or fully 70 percent of the total, were from the United States; 150 were chosen from Britain, 83 from Australia, and 23 from New Zealand. The following year Canada and Ireland were added to the list of participating countries, and France and Germany joined in 1989.

4. Teresa Watanabe, "Importing English: Teacher Exchange Offers Tough Lesson," *San Jose Mercury News*, 15 August 1988; "Apathy Rampant in JET Program," *Japan Times*, 11 October 1988; "Teacher Torture," *Tokyo Journal*, March 1989; Karen Hill Anton, "Japan Pulls in Welcome Mat with Racial Insensitivity," *Japan Times*, 13 April 1989.

5. *The JET Program(me): Five Years and Beyond* (Tokyo: Council of Local Authorities for International Relations, 1992), 80, 166.

6. Anniversary events included a two-day symposium on 7–8 October 1996 on the role of the JET Program in promoting internationalization, the announcement of "Meritorious Service Awards" by each of the sponsoring

ministries, and publication of a tenth anniversary booklet chronicling and assessing the JET Program's first decade.

7. Nosé Kuniyuki, interview with author, Tokyo, 4 June 1993.

8. See, for example, Frank Gibney, "Time to Lay Ieyasu's Ghost to Rest," *Japan Times Weekly International Edition*, 10–16 June 1996, p. 9.

9. Ronald Dore, "The Internationalisation of Japan," *Pacific Affairs* 52 (1979): 601.

10. See Haruhiro Fukui, "State in Policymaking: A Review of the Literature," in *Policymaking in Contemporary Japan*, ed. T.–J. Pempel (Ithaca, N.Y.: Cornell University Press, 1977), 22–59.

11. John O. Haley, "Governance by Negotiation: A Reappraisal of Bureaucratic Power in Japan," *Journal of Japanese Studies* 13 (1987): 343–57; Steven R. Reed, *Japanese Prefectures and Policymaking* (Pittsburgh: University of Pittsburgh Press, 1985); Leonard J. Schoppa, *Education Reform in Japan: A Case of Immobilist Politics* (New York: Routledge, 1991).

12. Thomas P. Rohlen, "Conflict in Institutional Environments: Politics in Education," in *Conflict in Japan*, ed. Ellis Kraus, Thomas P. Rohlen, and Patricia G. Steinhoff (Honolulu: University of Hawai'i Press, 1983), 136–73.

13. During the past two decades, research on policy implementation has increasingly recognized the importance of taking into account the perspectives of those who are actually charged with implementing policy innovations. Systems management and bureaucratic process models have fallen into disfavor as more attention is focused on the issue of whether or not the goals and resources of policymakers fit the needs and perspectives of those actually affected by top-down policies. In this vein, Lee Sproull offers a framework that focuses not on the properties of programs but rather on the processes by which organizational attention is captured, external stimuli are interpreted, response repertoires are invoked, and behavioral directives are communicated; see "Response to Regulation: An Organizational Process Framework," *Administration and Society* 124 (1981): 447–70. Karl Weick, pointing out the lack of structure and determinacy and the dispersion of resources and responsibilities, argues that commonality of purpose in educational organizations cannot be assumed; "Educational Organizations as Loosely Coupled Systems," *Administrative Science Quarterly* 21 (1976): 1–19.

14. See W. G. Beasley, *Japan Encounters the Barbarian: Japanese Travellers in America and Europe* (New Haven: Yale University Press, 1995), for a fuller treatment of these missions.

15. John Bennett, Herbert Passin, and R. K. McKnight, *In Search of Identity: The Japanese Overseas Scholar in America and Japan* (Minneapolis: University of Minnesota Press, 1958), 27.

16. Hajime Nakamura examines the various ways Japanese modified Indian and Chinese Buddhism, which teaches how to transcend worldliness, to focus on comprehending absolute truth within secular life; see "The Tendency to Emphasize a Limited Social Nexus," in *Ways of Thinking of Eastern Peoples: India, China, Tibet, and Japan*, ed. Philip P. Wiener (Honolulu: East-West Center Press, 1964), 496–513.

17. Roger Goodman, *Japan's "International Youth": The Emergence of a New Class of Schoolchildren* (Oxford: Clarendon Press; New York: Oxford University Press, 1990), 193.

18. Thomas Rohlen, "Learning: The Mobilization of Knowledge in the Japanese Political Economy," in *The Political Economy of Japan,* ed. Yasusuke Murakami and Hugh T. Patrick, vol. 3, *Cultural and Social Dynamics,* ed. Shumpei Kumon and Henry Rosovsky (Stanford: Stanford University Press, 1992), 324.

19. Herbert Passin, *Education and Society in Japan* (New York: Teachers' College Press, 1965), 21.

20. Beasley, *Japan Encounters the Barbarian,* 157.

21. Rohlen, "Learning," 326.

22. Quoted in Beasley, *Japan Encounters the Barbarian,* 1.

23. H. J. Jones, *Live Machines: Hired Foreigners in Meiji Japan* (Vancouver: University of British Columbia Press, 1980).

24. Helen Hardacre, *Shinto and the State, 1868–1988* (Princeton: Princeton University Press, 1989); Takashi Fujitani, *Splendid Monarchy: Power and Pageantry in Modern Japan* (Berkeley: University of California Press, 1996).

25. There have been numerous cases of outright opposition to ceremonial uses of the flag and anthem—particularly in Okinawa, which was the only major island to experience ground fighting and which remained under U.S. control until 1972.

26. See Harum Befu, "Symbols of Nationalism and *Nihonjiron,*" in *Ideology and Practice in Modern Japan,* ed. Roger Goodman and Kirsten Refsing (New York: Routledge, 1992), 26–46.

27. I am indebted to Thomas Rohlen for this image.

28. Two major perspectives can be discerned in the academic analysis of ethnicity. The first sees ethnicity as powerful and irreducible attachments emanating out of what Clifford Geertz described as "the assumed givens of social existence": namely, congruities of blood, speech, and custom. This view assumes the primacy of cultural attributes in defining ethnic groups, and the key question becomes discovering the nature of the shared culture on which ethnic identity is based. See Geertz, "The Integrative Revolution: Primordial Sentiments and Civil Politics in the New States," in *The Interpretation of Cultures* (New York: Basic Books, 1973), 259. The other looks not to these "primordial instincts," which may be strengthened by isolation, but to an interactive model. Fredrik Barth and others have argued that ethnicity is a social creation that may in fact go hand in hand with cultural contact, which creates the need to defend ethnic boundaries. Language and culture, in this view, become byproducts of social organization. Far from being eternal and mysterious, ethnicity becomes predictable and changeable. See Barth, ed., *Ethnic Groups and Boundaries: The Social Organization of Culture Differences* (Boston: Little, Brown, 1969).

These two perspectives are certainly not mutually exclusive. In times of perceived threat, ethnicity clearly becomes more salient and purposive. Similarly, the shared culture cannot be ignored, even if we recognize that cultures are never completely holistic entities. As Joshua Fishman has noted, if there can be no heartland without boundaries, there can also be no boundaries without a heartland; *Language and Nationalism: Two Integrative Essays* (Rowley, Mass.: Newbury House, 1972).

29. Walter Edwards, "Buried Discourse: The Toro Archaeological Site and Japanese National Identity in the Early Postwar Period," *Journal of Japanese Studies* 17 (1991): 1–23.

30. Jennifer Robertson, *Native and Newcomer: Making and Remaking a Japanese City* (Berkeley: University of California Press, 1991), 14.

31. Takie Sugiyama Lebra, *Above the Clouds: Status Culture of the Modern Japanese Nobility* (Berkeley: University of California Press, 1995), 14; David Titus, "Accessing the World: Palace and Foreign Policy in Post-Occupation Japan," in *Japan's Foreign Policy After the Cold War: Coping with Change*, ed. Gerald Curtis (London: M. E. Sharpe, 1993), 68–69.

32. For a broader discussion of this general phenomenon, see Ulf Hannerz, *Cultural Complexity* (New York: Columbia University Press, 1992).

33. See Kosaku Yoshino, *Cultural Nationalism in Contemporary Japan* (New York: Routledge, 1992).

34. Akira Nakanishi, "*Ibunka rikai to kaigai shijo kyōiku/kikokushijo kyōiku*" (Intercultural understanding and education for overseas and returning children), *Ibunkakan Kyōiku* (Intercultural Education) 2 (1988): 21.

35. Dore, "The Internationalisation of Japan," 606.

36. See, e.g., Choong Sun Kim, *Japanese Industry in the American South* (New York: Routledge, 1995); James Fallows, "Getting Along with Japan," *Atlantic*, December 1944, pp. 60–62.

37. Edward Lincoln, for instance, concludes that although the strategy of providing soft loans (to impose discipline on the host country) has theoretical merit, "the extent of the commercial interests in shaping Japan's aid program is pervasive, enduring and generally nontransparent"; *Japan's New Global Role* (Washington, D.C.: Brookings Institution, 1993), 133.

38. According to the Justice Ministry, at the end of 1995 the number of "registered alien residents" totaled 1,362,371, accounting for 1.09 percent of the population; 666,000 were Korean. See "Justice Ministry Report," *Japan Times Weekly International Edition*, 15–21 July 1996, p. 2. See also George DeVos, *Social Cohesion and Alienation: Minorities in the United States and Japan* (Boulder, Colo.: Westview Press, 1992), 176–205; on the *burakumin*, see 171.

39. In 1988 Watanabe Michio, speaking at a political action meeting, accused blacks of indifference to bankruptcy; in 1990 Kajiyama Seiroku compared the arrival of foreign prostitutes in Japan to blacks moving into white neighborhoods in the United States.

40. See William Cummings, *Education and Equality in Japan* (Princeton: Princeton University Press, 1980); Thomas Rohlen, *Japan's High Schools* (Berkeley: University of California Press, 1983); and Merry White, *The Japanese Educational Challenge: A Commitment to Children* (New York: Free Press, 1987).

41. Nikolas Kristof, "Japanese Schools: Safe, Efficient, But Boring," *New York Times*, 18 July 1995.

42. Masami Yamazumi, "State Control and the Evolution of Ultranational-istic Textbooks," in *Japanese Schooling: Patterns of Socialization, Equality, and Political Control*, ed. James J. Shields, Jr. (University Park: Pennsylvania State University Press, 1989), 235.

43. Teruhisa Horio, *Educational Thought and Ideology in Modern Japan*, trans. Steven Platzer (Tokyo: University of Tokyo Press, 1988), 174.

44. Ienaga had lost two previous lawsuits dating back to 1965; and in this third and final ruling the Supreme Court did uphold the constitutionality of the textbook screening process. See Tomoko Otake, "Historian Wins Text-book Suit," *Japan Times Weekly International Edition*, 8–14 September 1997, p. 1.

45. See Yasuko Minoura, "Life in Between: The Acquisition of Cultural Identity among Japanese Children Living in the United States" (Ph.D. diss., University of California at Los Angeles, 1979); Merry White, *The Japanese Overseas: Can They Go Home Again?* (New York: Free Press, 1988); Tetsuya Kobayashi, "Educational Problems of 'Returning Children,'" in Shields, *Japanese Schooling*, 185–93.

46. Goodman, *Japan's "International Youth."*

47. Japan-U.S. Friendship Commission, "Commission Funds Center to Promote Study Abroad in Japan," *The Commissioner*, spring/summer 1997, p. 1.

48. Rohlen, "Learning," 362.

49. Lynn Earl Henrichsen, *Diffusion of Innovation in English Language Teaching: The ELEC Effort in Japan, 1956–1968* (New York: Greenwood Press, 1989), 121.

50. Inazo Nitobe, "The Teaching and Use of Foreign Languages," *Sewanee Review* 31 (1923): 338–39. While Nitobe found this tendency deplorable, it is also worth noting that Japanese sensibilities call for humbling oneself and downplaying one's proficiency no matter how great it might be.

51. Ibid., 338.

52. Roy Andrew Miller, *Japan's Modern Myth: The Language and Beyond* (New York: Weatherhill, 1982), 233.

53. Masayoshi Harasawa, "A Critical Survey of English Language Teaching in Japan: A Personal View," *English Language Teaching Journal* 29, no. 1 (1974): 71–72.

54. Popular belief in the inadequacy of language instruction is fueled by such media events as a 1989 prime-time television special called *We Don't Need This!* (*Konna Mono Iranai*), in which a panel of distinguished guests explored the reasons for Japan's poor performance in English education.

55. A 1986 survey by the Economic Planning Agency revealed strong support (70 percent) for what Kenneth Pyle calls "superficial internationalization" (information exchange, increased tourism, etc.) but weak support (30 percent) for more far-reaching measures such as greater numbers of foreign employees and marriage to foreigners; see Pyle, *The Japanese Question: Power and Purpose in a*

New Era (Washington, D.C.: AEI Press, 1992), 113. Harumi Befu and Kazu-fumi Manabe found a high willingness to allow foreigners to be integrated into educational and economic institutions, but a reluctance to admit them into the spheres of politics and kinship; "An Empirical Study of Nihonjinron: How Real Is the Myth?" *Kwansei Gakuin University Annual Studies* 36 (1987): 97–111.

56. There were numerous other national-level actors whose policies and decisions affected the JET Program on occasion—the Prime Minister's Office, the Justice Ministry, the National Audit Board, the Finance Ministry, and the Health and Welfare Ministry.

57. For a good overview of key concepts in the anthropological study of organizational culture, see Tomoko Hamada and Willis E. Sibley, eds., *Anthropological Perspectives on Organizational Culture* (Lanham, Md.: University Press of America, 1994).

58. See Conrad Kottak and Elizabeth Colson, "Multilevel Linkages: Longitudinal and Comparative Studies," in *Assessing Cultural Anthropology*, ed. Robert Borofsky (New York: McGraw-Hill, 1994), 396–412.

59. Harumi Befu, "The Internationalization of Japan and *Nihon Bunkaron*," in *The Challenge of Japan's Internationalization: Organization and Culture*, ed. Hiroshi Mannari and Harumi Befu (Tokyo: Kodansha, 1983), 262.

60. Masao Miyoshi's argument that U.S.-Japan trade negotiations must attend carefully to history is relevant to policy innovations such as the JET Program as well. He writes, "What we need is historical understanding as to why what looked like Japan's deceptions to the Americans are rooted in history, or why—if it must be so phrased—a 'deception' is perpetrated, or how differences have come about in the manner of achieving the same goals, why individuals are motivated differently in different societies, or even why a nation is so self-enclosed. In short, what historical forces shape a given society into a different organization with a different imaginary and a different articulation?" Miyoshi, *Off Center: Power and Culture Relations between Japan and the United States* (Cambridge, Mass.: Harvard University Press, 1991), 80.

CHAPTER 2. THE SOLUTION: TOP-DOWN
"GRASSROOTS INTERNATIONALIZATION"

1. Karel van Wolferen, *The Enigma of Japanese Power: People and Politics in a Stateless Nation* (New York: Vintage Books, 1990), 361.

2. Richard Samuels, *The Politics of Regional Policy in Japan: Localities Incorporated?* (Princeton: Princeton University Press, 1983), 46.

3. Tsuchiya Yoshiteru is quoted in *Chiiki ni okeru kokusai kōryū* (International exchange in local areas), special issue of *CLAIR*, a magazine for local government bodies, March 1987, pp. 2–3. It is interesting to note that deficiencies in other languages were not viewed as impeding internationalization in the same way that English was.

4. Eto Shinkichi, interview by author, Tokyo, 3 June 1995.

5. Nosé Kuniyuki, interview with author, Tokyo, 4 June 1995.

6. In actuality, the Ministry of Home Affair's claim to have some jurisdiction in educational matters was not as farfetched as it might initially seem. Eto elaborates (interview):

> While the Ministry of Education has the right to make general educational policy, the Ministry of Home Affairs also has an implicit right to get involved in educational matters. It works this way. The number three man in most prefectures, directly under the governor and the vice-governor, is the *sōmu bucho*, or head of the general affairs section. This person is almost always appointed by Home Affairs—usually it's a young, career-oriented official. This person, in turn, has the de facto right to select the board of education (*kyōiku iinkai*), which is a group of prominent citizens who advise the superintendent of education. Normally, they're just sleeping, but in any event this was one rationale used by Home Affairs for justifying its involvement in educational matters.

7. Nosé, interview.

8. Steven R. Reed, *Japanese Prefectures and Policymaking* (Pittsburgh: University of Pittsburgh Press, 1985), 27. One interesting outcome of this system of local allocation is that prefectures or municipalities with high revenue from local sources receive a smaller percentage of state support than do poorer local governments.

9. I am grateful to Kevin Newman for pointing out this view of the JET Program. Roughly 50 percent of JET participants report that they are able to save at least 25 percent of their salary, according to the "1990 JET Questionnaire: Evaluation of Living Conditions."

10. *The Sasakawa Peace Foundation* (Tokyo: Sasakawa Peace Foundation, 1991), 11.

11. Nosé, interview.

12. For a discussion of recent developments in Japan's cultural diplomacy, see Maureen Todhunter, "International Cultural Exchange in Japan's Foreign Policy Today," in *Japan and the World*, vol. 1 of *Proceedings of the Seventh Biennial Conference of the Japanese Studies Association of Australia* (Canberra: Australia Japan Research Centre, 1991), 98–105.

13. John Creighton Campbell, "Japan and the United States: Games That Work," in *Japan's Foreign Policy: After the Cold War*, ed. Gerald Curtis (New York: M. E. Sharpe, 1993), 53.

14. Nathaniel Thayer, "Japanese Foreign Policy in the Nakasone Years," in Curtis, *Japan's Foreign Policy*, 96.

15. Nakasone is quoted in Takashi Inoguchi, "The Legacy of a Weathercock Prime Minister," *Japan Quarterly* 34, no. 3 (1987): 367.

16. Aurelia George, "Japan's America Problem: The Japanese Response to U.S. Pressure," *Washington Quarterly* 14, no. 3 (1991): 7.

17. Leonard J. Schoppa, *Education Reform in Japan: A Case of Immobilist Politics* (New York: Routledge, 1991), 243.

18. Christopher P. Hood, "Nakasone Yasuhiro and Japanese Education Reform: A Revisionist View" (Ph.D. diss., University of Sheffield, 1998).

19. Staff report quoted in Lynn Earl Henrichsen, *Diffusion of Innovation in English Language Teaching: The ELEC Effort in Japan, 1956–1968* (New York: Greenwood Press, 1989), 1.

20. Richard Rubinger, interview by author, Kyoto, 23 May 1989. A contemporary equivalent to this approach does exist in an intensive one-month "seminar" (*shidōsha kōza*) for Japanese teachers of English sponsored annually by the Ministry of Education. The idea is that these teachers will return to their districts and demonstrate leadership in foreign language training, but the teachers are often too young to be able to influence the tightly woven professional network of local English teachers.

21. Caroline Yang, interview with author, Tokyo, 23 March 1989.

22. Ironically, because of this relative neglect of conversational English, the private sector was the source of dynamism and change in foreign language education in Japan.

23. Wada Minoru, interview with author, Chiba Prefecture, 4 June 1995.

24. Ibid.

25. The Japanese term has always been *eigo shidōshuji joshu*.

26. Wada Minoru, interview with author, Tokyo, 18 January 1989.

27. Advertising brochure, *The Japan Exchange and Teaching Program(me)* (Tokyo: Council of Local Authorities for International Relations, 1987), n.p.

28. To be sure, there are voices within Japan criticizing the rigidity that comes with top-down programs. Some have even argued that the Chinese character for "country" (*koku*) in the term "international understanding" (*kokusai rikai*) should be changed to "people" (*min*).

29. With a keen eye for the symbolic, Ministry of Home Affairs officials noted that in French, *clair* means "clear" and "distinct"; thus, the acronym connotes a clear and distinctive vision for internationalization. They might also have observed that the adjective is masculine rather than feminine.

CLAIR has gone through several incarnations since its inception. The original name for this office was the Conference of Local Authorities for International Relations (Kokusaika Suishin Jichitai Kyōgikai), but as its functions began to expand beyond the JET Program, CLAIR acquired status as an incorporated foundation (*zaidan hōjin*) and changed its name to "Council" on 17 June 1988.

30. One hundred twenty-four persons, or roughly 50 percent of MEF and BET participants, chose to renew under JET.

31. See Masao Miyoshi, *Off Center: Power and Culture Relations between Japan and the United States* (Cambridge, Mass.: Harvard University Press, 1991), 86–87.

32. Under the MEF and BET programs, some local Japanese supervisors had circumvented Ministry of Education guidelines by telling the foreign participants to take "secret holidays"—for example, on a Monday.

33. Nosé, interview, 4 June 1995.

34. Other embassies did employ those with some knowledge of Japan but rarely with firsthand experience teaching in Japanese schools.

35. *CLAIR Newsletter*, October 1988, p. 2.

36. Fumiko Harada, chair, Ohio-Saitama English Teaching (OSET) Program, personal correspondence with author, 17 July 1995.

37. This figure varies somewhat from consulate to consulate depending on the number of applicants in a given year in a particular region. In 1992, for example, 300 applicants requested a Boston interview, and 218 interviews were granted (206 for ALTs and 12 for CIRs). Out of this pool, 89 ALTs and 6 CIRs were selected.

38. There were also a few interesting cross-cultural moments. A Japanese member of our group gave a particularly low score to an interviewee who furrowed her brow as she spoke, arguing that this mannerism would be viewed negatively in Japan. In another case, a woman was rejected because of a very noticeable facial scar that Japanese members of the consulate found problematic.

39. Cliff Clarke, interview with author, Palo Alto, Calif., 13 May 1988. Interestingly, however, the CIEE committee initially rejected (and only later recalled) the application of Robert Juppé, Jr., who went on to become the first foreigner ever hired by the Ministry of Education. It is worth noting as well that the frustration voiced by CIEE representatives with the start-up of the JET Program no doubt stemmed in part from losing a very lucrative contract.

40. A paucity of Japanese language programs also accounts for the virtual absence of applicants from Britain for the CIR position, which requires knowledge of the Japanese language.

41. The results of the 1995 JET Program questionnaire reveal that the Japanese language competence of new participants has improved, but only slightly, since the early years of the program. By 1995, 52.7 percent of JET participants rated their conversational ability in Japanese prior to coming on the program as nonexistent; 22.4 percent called themselves beginners; 16.8 percent placed themselves in the intermediate stage; 6.6 percent viewed themselves as advanced; and 1.4 percent characterized themselves as fluent. These figures, however, include CIRs, who are required to have some Japanese language competence.

42. A major drawback to this method of assessment was that 165 participants had not submitted photographs. This directory, incidentally, was originally compiled by AJET and called the "AJET Lookbook," but the publication was soon appropriated by CLAIR.

43. There was also a miscellaneous group (5 percent) who came to Japan for other reasons, including quite by accident.

44. Nakasone is quoted in Inoguchi, "Legacy," 365.

45. The sense of resignation is apparent in the orientation manual sent to local governments in 1988, which explained the rationale for the program as follows:

As a result of the increasingly high status of our country in the international community, the manner in which we relate to other countries is in the process of changing drastically. While internationalization up until now has primarily involved diplomacy and trade at the national level, at the present time the manner in which citizens at each stratum of society are engaging in internationalization has come to be questioned. In light of this fact, from this point on, the responses of local governments to internationalization will become an important topic that, like the aging of our population or the emerging information age, cannot be avoided. *Gaikoku Seinen Shōchi Jigyō Ukeiredantai yō Manyuaru* (JET Program host organization's orientation manual) (Tokyo: Council of Local Authorities for International Relations, 1988), 112–13.

46. See John D. Montgomery, "Beyond Good Policies," in *Great Policies: Strategic Innovations in Asia and the Pacific Basin*, edited by John D. Montgomery and Dennis Rondinelli (London: Praeger, 1995), 1–13.

47. Wada, interview, 18 January 1989.

CHAPTER 3. THE START-UP YEARS:
THE "CRASH PROGRAM" NEARLY CRASHES

1. The explanation I was given for this policy was that it prevented any problems regarding JET participants' ability to carry the luggage necessary for their stay in Japan.

2. The foreign minister spoke first, followed by the education minister; the home affairs minister was last. In subsequent years, a lesser official from each ministry was sent to pass on greetings.

3. John Creighton Campbell, "Policy Conflict and Its Resolution within the Governmental System," in *Conflict in Japan*, ed. Ellis Kraus, Thomas P. Rohlen, and Patricia G. Steinhoff (Honolulu: University of Hawai'i Press, 1984), 295–334.

4. Robert Juppé, "For the Jets, by the Jets," *AJET Magazine*, 1 August 1988, p. 1.

5. The renewers' conference itself was initially an AJET event; CLAIR decided in 1988 to adopt it as an official conference for all renewing participants.

6. The following accounts of the Australian tax problem and the controversy over health insurance and pensions were pieced together through interviews with CLAIR officials, prefectural administrators, and JET participants and from reports on the issues in the *AJET Journal*. A similar problem erupted in 1989 over the tax status of Canadian participants.

7. Gregory V. G. O'Dowd, "Australia—Don't Miss the JET!" *Japanese Studies: Bulletin of the Japanese Studies Association of Australia* 12, no. 1 (1992): 38.

8. John Moran, "Insurance Blues," *JET Journal*, autumn 1989, p. 72.

9. In 1989 France and Germany had 2 CIRs each; by 1991, the figures were 12 and 13, respectively; and by 1995 they each had 20 CIRs. The numbers of assistant French teachers and assistant German teachers remained in single digits throughout this period.

10. Shunsuke Wakabayashi, "Amateurs Doing Their Best," *Japan Times Weekly International Edition*, 12 September 1987, p. 8.

11. Letters to the editor in the *Japan Times*: Kimberly Kennedy, "Professional Teachers Not Needed Yet," 9 September 1987; Michelle Long, "Sorry English Education," 6 September 1987; Andrew Barnes, "Re-evaluating JET Program," 9 September 1987.

12. Iizuka Shigehiko, "We Welcome JET Teachers," *Japan Times*, 11 January 1988.

13. Minoru Soma, "The JET Program," *Japan Times*, Readers in Council, 27 March 1988.

14. Daniel Lester, "A Proposal to Improve English Teaching," *Japan Times*, Readers in Council, 18 April 1988.

15. Indeed, at the 1987 Tokyo Mid-Year Block Seminar, two months after Wakabayashi's letter appeared, a senior Japanese official on the stage loudly addressed the JET participants as "boys and girls," setting a disastrous tone at the conference's outset. I also encountered this assumption at the JET Program Renewers' Conference in 1993. The speaker, a Ministry of Home Affairs official, ended his talk by exhorting the hundreds of JET participants in the audience with the slogan, "Be Ambitious, Boys and Girls." There was awkward silence, then scattered laughter, as he sat down. The next CLAIR speaker, apparently realizing the danger, hastily pointed out that the slogan "boys be ambitious" had been made famous by Dr. William Clark in Hokkaido and every Japanese student knows it—"it doesn't mean that you are boys and girls—you're much older than that."

16. Merry White, *The Material Child: Coming of Age in Japan and America* (Berkeley: University of California Press, 1993), 10–11.

17. In recent years, CLAIR has adopted a more flexible policy on the age limit, and several applicants over the age of thirty-five have been accepted as JET participants. CLAIR officials scratched their heads, however, when they received an application from an eighty-four-year-old woman!

18. Morita Kiyoshi, "Beijin kyōshi ni bōgen, taigaku sawagi: Eigo kyōikukan no sa ga haike ni" (Verbal abuse of American teacher leads to student expulsion, controversy: Behind incident lies gap in views of English education), *Yomiuri Shimbun*, 5 November 1988.

19. Kathleen Brown. "A Note from 'B-san,'" *AJET Magazine*, no. 4 (December 1988–January 1989): 12.

20. Ibid., 13.

21. "Mie Incident," *CLAIR Newsletter*, October 1988, p. 1.

22. "Teacher Torture," *Tokyo Journal*, March 1989.

23. Patricia Smith, "Jet Brag," *Tokyo Journal*, June 1989.

24. Karen Hill Anton, "Japan Pulls in Welcome Mat with Racial Insensitivity," *Japan Times*, 13 April 1989.

25. The Minority Support Group was not officially sanctioned by CLAIR or the Ministry of Education but rather was formed and sponsored by AJET. That two program coordinators and the head of the Counseling Division of CLAIR attended this meeting indicates the concern over this issue.

26. A prefectural official in Osaka offered this recollection: "I remember in the early years of the program receiving a call asking me if I would 'undertake the burden' (*hikiukete kurenaika*) of hosting an African American participant. I thought that their phrasing of the request was really odd, so I told them, 'Of course, we welcome African American participants. Send us as many as you want.'"

27. See especially magazines published by quasi-governmental agencies and "Japan Welcomes More JETers," *Japan Pictorial* 12, no. 1 (1989).

28. Mary Canz, "Foreign Teachers Find Fame," *San Francisco Examiner*, 18 December 1988; Keiko Kanbara, "How to Make English More Fun for Japanese High School Students," *Christian Science Monitor*, 28 December 1988.

29. See Gerald K. LeTendre's three-part series in the *Daily Yomiuri*: "AETs, Schools Find Working Together Brings Benefits to Fukui," 30 June 1988; "AET's Must Vary Activities to Succeed," 7 July 1988; "Students Learn to Switch Cultures," 14 July 1988. Ironically, however, when LeTendre submitted a condensed version of these articles to CLAIR for publication in the *JET Journal*, he received a rejection notice stating that because he was based full-time in an "international high school," his experiences would not be relevant to the majority of assistant English teachers. Apparently, CLAIR did not want to risk further raising the ire of the many AETs who were being shuffled around to numerous schools under the "one-shot" school visitation system.

30. John Flanagan, "English Teaching Project Feeling Growing Pains," *Japan Times*, 2 August 1988; John Flanagan, "English-Teaching Program a Success After Overcoming First-Year Trouble," *Japan Times*, 3 June 1989.

31. Edith Terry, "Just Replacing Tape Recordings, Canadian Teachers in Japan Find: Teaching in Japan Can Be Frustrating Experience," *Toronto Globe and Mail*, 12 January 1989.

32. Teresa Watanabe, "Importing English: Teacher Exchange Offers Tough Lesson," *San Jose Mercury News*, 15 August 1988.

33. Satoko Nozawa, "Apathy Prevails in English Classrooms," *Daily Yomiuri*, 18 May 1989.

34. "School English Teaching Program Faltering: Union," *Mainichi Daily News*, 27 October 1988.

35. Morita, "Beijin kyōshi ni bōgen, taigaku sawagi."

36. "'Honmono eigo' juken ni fuyō? Seito hannō mo toboshiku, shitsui no tochū kikoku mo," *Kyoto Shimbun*, 26 October 1988.

37. The December 1988 issue of the *CLAIR Newsletter* contained this note under the heading "Media" on page 1:

> It has not gone unnoticed that the JET Program has been receiving some unfavorable press recently. Many JETs have voiced complaints at being misquoted in local newspapers or having had the meaning of what they've said distorted. Time and again newspaper reporters focus on the negative aspects of the Program or conveniently present half-truths which tend to emphasize grievances rather than show the program in an accurate light[:] . . . as a word of advice, be wary of giving frank opinions not only to newspaper reporters, but also to people with whom you are unfamiliar. Criticism in Japan is not easily forgiven and it only takes one throw-away remark to destroy months of hard-earned trust and respect.

38. *The JET Program(me): Five Years and Beyond* (Tokyo: Council of Local Authorities for International Relations, 1992), 78.

39. "Under the Influence," *CLAIR Newsletter*, no. 7 (December 1989): 1.

40. *The Japan Exchange and Teaching Programme General Information Handbook* (Tokyo: Council of Local Authorities for International Relations, 1995), 17–18.

41. Matsuda Hisako, "Totsuzen no shi: Shigoto, scito wo ai shi . . . naze?" *Kyoto Shimbun*, 26 January 1990.

42. Nancy Sato has argued that the term "relations oriented" rather than "group oriented" best captures the dynamic between the individual and the group in Japanese society. See "Honoring the Individual," in *Teaching and Learning in Japan*, ed. Thomas Rohlen and Gerald LeTendre (New York: Cambridge University Press, 1996), 119–53. Robert Smith observes that "much of the definition of a 'good person' involves restraint in the expression of personal desires and opinions, empathy for the feelings of others, and the practice of civility"; *Japanese Society: Tradition, Self, and the Social Order* (New York: Cambridge University Press, 1983), 44–45.

43. Takie Sugiyama Lebra, *Japanese Patterns of Behavior* (Honolulu: University of Hawai'i Press, 1976), 209.

44. William Horsley, "An Outsider's View of CLAIR's Activities," *Jichitai Kokusaika Forāmu* (Forum on Internationalization for Local Governments), no. 11 (November 1989): 21.

45. Caroline Yang, interview with author, Tokyo, 23 March 1989.

46. Jackson Bailey, "Student Exchanges and the Use of Technology," in *Between Understanding and Misunderstanding: Problems and Prospects for International Cultural Exchange*, ed. Yasushi Sugiyama (New York: Greenwood Press, 1990), 96.

47. The "wrong" reasons included (1) you like Japan but not the JET Program (look for other employment), (2) you don't like the JET Program but the money is good and there's lots of free time (if money is your main consideration there are more lucrative means of employment), (3) you think the problems you had this year will probably not occur next year (problems have a habit of not going away), and (4) you want to renew to postpone making a difficult career decision (procrastination should not be a reason for renewing). *CLAIR Newsletter*, no. 7 (December 1989), p. 2.

48. Since 1992, CLAIR has allowed a few individuals to renew for a fourth year, so the policy is not ironclad; but such a request usually requires extenuating circumstances and strong support from local officials, program coordinators, or both.

49. The renewal rate was 44.3 percent in 1988, 45.1 percent in 1989, 41.4 percent in 1990, and 45.2 percent in 1991 (*JET Program(me)*, 162).

50. Minutes of First Evaluation Meeting, 1989–90 JET Program (given to me by a program coordinator).

51. Horsley, "An Outsider's View," 21.

52. Given the secrecy of personnel decisions in Japanese bureaucracies, this story about his reassignment was impossible to verify. I did speak with Nakamura after he had been transferred, and he confirmed that he had wanted to stay on at CLAIR longer. Indeed, he confessed that he had really wanted to join

the Ministry of Foreign Affairs but was afraid he would be posted to some remote part of the world and so had joined the Ministry of Home Affairs instead. Now he regretted the decision. The following year he resigned from the ministry to practice law.

53. G. Victor Soogen Hori, "Teaching and Learning in the Rinzai Zen Monastery," in Rohlen and LeTendre, *Teaching and Learning in Japan*, 20–49.

54. Donna Haraway, *Primate Visions: Gender, Race, and Nature in the World of Modern Science* (New York: Routledge, 1989), 12–13.

55. H. J. Jones, *Live Machines: Hired Foreigners in Meiji Japan* (Vancouver: University of British Columbia Press, 1980), 30–40, 116–26.

56. Gaimushō, Bunka Kōryūbu, Bunka Dainika (The Ministry of Foreign Affairs, Second Cultural Affairs Division), "An Interim Evaluation of the JET Program" (in Japanese), *Shiryo*, no. 87–4 (5 February 1988).

57. See, for example, the special issue of the Ministry of Home Affair's magazine devoted entirely to celebrating the inauguration of the JET Program: *Kurea: Jichitai no tame no kokusai ka jōhōshi* (CLAIR: A Journal Promoting the Internationalization of Local Governments), 10 November 1987.

58. The profile of resigners over this five-year period closely matched the overall profile of JET participants in terms of nationality, sex, and type of position; *JET Program(me)*, 80.

59. For an extended and insightful discussion of the cultural foundation of learning in Japan, see the essays collected in Rohlen and LeTendre, *Teaching and Learning in Japan*.

CHAPTER 4. MANAGING DIVERSITY: THE VIEW
FROM A PREFECTURAL BOARD OF EDUCATION

1. To acquire a sense of the "typicality" of arrangements in this prefecture, I visited boards of education or international relations divisions in government offices in ten others: Fukuoka, Hyogo, Iwate, Kanagawa, Kumamoto, Osaka, Saitama, Shiga, Kyoto, and Toyama. I also interviewed officials in two designated cities, Kyoto City and Osaka City.

2. Tanabe-san later confessed that his boss had told him to handle everything, and thus he had spent his first two hours at work that morning frantically looking up English words in his dictionary.

3. I eventually learned that my mentor at the university had played a very important role in publicly supporting the prefecture's position on a major educational reform issue, and as a result prefectural officials were very much indebted to him. That he had been willing to spend some of this built-up goodwill on a naive graduate student from abroad was a humbling thought. In any event, over the course of the next eighteen months I met every two months with Tanabe-san and Sato-sensei over coffee and attended numerous seminars, orientations, and informational meetings for JET participants, Japanese teachers of English, and local Japanese administrators.

4. Thomas P. Rohlen, "Conflict in Institutional Environments: Politics in Education," in *Conflict in Japan*, ed. Ellis Krauss, Thomas P. Rohlen, and Patricia G. Steinhoff (Honolulu: University of Hawai'i Press, 1984), 159.

5. Jackson Bailey, "Student Exchanges and the Use of Technology," in *Between Understanding and Misunderstanding: Problems and Prospects for International Cultural Exchange*, ed. Yasushi Sugiyama (New York: Greenwood Press, 1990), 97.

6. The road to widespread use of foreign teaching assistants had not been smooth. In 1976 only six prefectures expressed an interest in having a foreigner come, even though fourteen had been recommended to the Fulbright Commission. After the Ministry of Education took over the program, it placed foreigners in prefectures with which it had close ties and sought to gradually expand the program over the years by using these "veteran" prefectures as models. In a few cases, some major scandal involving a foreign teacher prompted a backlash, and the prefecture made no requests for several years. Nagasaki, for instance, refused to participate for ten years following a marijuana-smoking incident.

7. A small number of ALTs thought that the one-shot visit could be educationally valid. See, for example, Suzy Nachtsheim, "Bull's Eye: Keeping Your One-Shot Visits on Target," *Language Teacher* 12, no. 9 (1988): 25–26.

8. "Research on the Situation of Foreign Teachers of English in Japanese Schools," *IRLT Bulletin*, no. 2 (1988): 62.

9. *The Japan Exchange and Teaching (JET) Programme General Information Handbook* (Tokyo: Council of Local Authorities for International Relations, 1996), 12.

10. Saito Eiji, "AET o mukaete akirakani natta nihon no eigokyōiku no mondaiten" (The problems of English education in Japan as illuminated by the arrival of AETs), *IRLT Newsletter*, no. 104 (1989): 1.

11. *The JET Program(me): Five Years and Beyond* (Tokyo: Council of Local Authorities for International Relations, 1992), 169–266.

12. Ibid., 169–278.

13. Rebecca Erwin Fukuzawa, "The Path to Adulthood According to Japanese Middle Schools," in *Teaching and Learning in Japan*, ed. Thomas Rohlen and Gerald LeTendre (New York: Cambridge University Press, 1996), 295–320.

14. Such "talent benefits" tend to diminish when the foreigner is not white. One Japanese teacher told me,

Japanese associate speaking English with the image of a white person (*hakujin*). With our first [white] AET [assistant English teacher] students would pay attention even if she was just standing in front of the room. They don't do that with Pat-san [a Japanese American]. When she speaks English it seems strange to us. When we enter the classroom together, students don't change their behavior at all. That's the kind of handicap we faced. Students were a little disappointed when they found out our AET was a Japanese American.

15. In fact, in one new international high school I visited in a neighboring prefecture, the municipal office of education had concentrated no fewer than

eight ALTs in the school, displaying their pictures prominently in the lobby and in community advertisements for the school.

16. In a few instances, however, principals have actually invited an ALT in order to combat discipline problems at the school, the naive hope being that the foreigner might capture students' interest and provide a form of outside pressure (aren't you embarrassed to act like that in front of a foreigner?) that acts as a deterrent to misbehavior.

17. Gregory V. G. O'Dowd, "Australia—Don't Miss the JET!" *Japanese Studies: Bulletin of the Japanese Studies Association of Australia* 12, no. 1 (1992): 39.

18. Anthony Gribben, interview with author, Kyoto, 10 October 1989.

19. Michel Foucault, *Discipline and Punish: The Birth of the Prison*, trans. A. Sheridan (New York: Pantheon Books, 1977), 25.

20. Minutes of First Evaluation Meeting, 1989–90 JET Program (given to me by a program coordinator).

21. According to the "1989 JET Program Living Conditions Survey" (a compilation sent to all JET participants), 63 percent of host institutions provided a telephone, 75 percent provided a refrigerator, 79 percent provided a washing machine, 71 percent provided a television, and 60 percent provided a futon or bed.

22. I am indebted to Scott Olinger for this insight.

23. See Robert Smith, "Gender Inequality in Contemporary Japan," *Journal of Japanese Studies* 13 (1987): 1–25.

24. "Sexual Harassment and Kokusaika," *JET Journal*, autumn 1989, p. 50.

25. "Assembly Votes to Remove Official: Allegedly Pawed 23-Year-Old AET at Village Party," *Daily Yomiuri*, 2 May 1993. The story was also reported on the national news.

26. "1989 JET Program Living Conditions Survey."

27. Toby did go on to work at CLAIR, and at the next orientation he invited himself to the prefectural dinner for new JET participants. Sato-sensei showed no visible anger when he saw Toby, but he complained bitterly to me afterward that Toby "had a lot of nerve to show his face here tonight!"

28. Robert Whiting recounts similar criticisms about the haggling by American baseball players in Japan over minute contract details; *You Gotta Have Wa* (New York: Vintage Books, 1989), 131.

29. *JET Program(me)*, 80.

30. On these school visits, Kevin invariably ended up meeting with the ALT alone instead of with the JTLs as well, though that was not his original intention.

31. Some prefectures effectively used other strategies to deal personally with their ALTs. Toyama Prefecture, for instance, hired a middle-aged Japanese woman with excellent English skills and years of experience living abroad. Based in the prefectural "education center," she single-handedly kept morale high and defused potential problems by virtue of her excellent rapport with the

ALTs; at the same time, the board of education administrators retained key decision-making powers. In Osaka City the municipal board of education created a special position—ALT liaison—and filled it with a very young Japanese teacher of English, a fluent English speaker who had spent considerable time abroad. While his school-based colleagues lamented that he had moved to a position where he couldn't speak his mind freely (*ienai tachiba*), his language skills and his similarity in age and marital status to other ALTs made him a very effective liaison.

32. Frank K. Upham, *Law and Social Order in Postwar Japan* (Cambridge, Mass.: Harvard University Press, 1987), 223. As Clifford Geertz points out, the dominant Anglo-American worldview is based on the notion of an autonomous individual that is a "bounded, unique, more or less integrated motivational and cognitive universe, a dynamic center of awareness, emotion, judgement and action"; "From the Natives' Point of View: On the Nature of Anthropological Understanding," in *Meaning in Anthropology*, ed. Keith Basso and Henry Selby (Albuquerque: University of New Mexico Press, 1976). It logically follows that a society made up of such individuals would be contractual in nature.

33. In any given community, there may be a number of levels of *honne*—at the level of work group, males in the work group, and males of the same age in the work group, for example.

34. *Gaikoku Seinen Shōchi Jigyō Ukeiredantai yō Manyuaru* (JET Program host organization's orientation manual) (Tokyo: Council of Local Authorities for International Relations, 1988), 112–13.

35. Stanley Heginbotham, *Cultures in Conflict: The Four Faces of Indian Bureaucracy* (New York: Columbia University Press, 1975), 156.

36. Ibid.

37. It is difficult to judge how typical the experience of these two prefectural educational administrators was, for I did not have similar access to other boards of education. At one extreme, Sato-sensei had a friend in a neighboring prefecture who was literally at wit's end (Sato-sensei threw his hands up in the air to signify despair) due to the governor's decree that an ALT be placed in every prefectural high school; at the other, a minority of ETCs who were exceptional at English or who have lived abroad found the chance to use their skills very rewarding. I interviewed ten ETCs; Sato-sensei seemed slightly more rigid than some of his colleagues in his approach to team teaching (more adamant about using the textbook) and his handling of conflict (less likely to budge from established policy). The ALTs, too, viewed this prefectural system as fairly strict in comparison with others.

38. Harry Wolcott, *The Man in the Principal's Office* (Prospect Heights, Ill.: Waveland Press, 1974).

39. Michael Blaker, "Evaluating Japanese Diplomatic Performance," in *Japan's Foreign Policy After the Cold War: Coping with Change*, ed. Gerald Curtis (New York: M. E. Sharpe, 1993), 3.

CHAPTER 5. BEYOND THE STEREOTYPES:
THE JET PROGRAM IN LOCAL SCHOOLS

1. Hayano-sensei linked this need for secrecy explicitly to foreign pressure (*gaiatsu*)—the widespread critique of Japan as a nation of "workaholics" and the corresponding implication that citizens in a "developed" nation ought to be able to enjoy leisure time.

2. My own negotiation of access to this school followed a similar pattern. Sato-sensei made the request to the principal, who said he would leave it up to the English Department. Hayano-sensei (the head English teacher) and Ueda-sensei backed my plan to visit the school twice a week as an observer; but the vice-principal objected, saying they had turned down an exchange student the previous year and it would not make sense to admit me. There was some resistance among the English teachers as well. About two weeks later the vice-principal called to say that he and Ueda-sensei had decided to let me visit on an individual basis (*kojinteki ni*). Ultimately, their sense of obligation to Sato-sensei and the board of education's commitment to my mentor at the university unlocked the doors, but I felt compelled to keep a very low profile at first. It took some time for me to gain the confidence of other teachers at the school.

3. By and large Nishikawa was extremely conservative when it came to following protocol. Thus Karen was not allowed to teach by herself, even on the day that Ikuno-sensei called in sick and asked Karen to take the class. When Hayano-sensei double-checked with the head of curriculum, he was told that such solo teaching wasn't allowed, so Kitano-sensei was asked to accompany Karen to class. Karen fumed, "I don't want an audience." Hayano-sensei also recalled having been scolded by the principal for arranging with a teacher at another school for Karen to make a special visit. He was informed that he should have gone through the official channels, involving both principals and the head of the other school's English department.

4. In the one instance when Karen was asked by Ueda-sensei to help put together an exam for his advanced students, the article she recommended for the reading comprehension section was deemed too difficult. His polite refusal prompted Karen to grumble to me, "Why does he ask me to help out if he's just going to reject my ideas?"

5. Harumi Befu, "An Ethnography of Dinner Entertainment in Japan," in *Japanese Business: Cultural Perspectives,* ed. Subhash Durlabhji and Norton E. Marks (Albany: State University of New York Press, 1993), 136.

6. Gerald LeTendre, "Shidō: The Concept of Guidance," in *Teaching and Learning in Japan,* ed. Thomas Rohlen and Gerald LeTendre (New York: Cambridge University Press, 1996), 275–94.

7. Rebecca Erwin Fukuzawa, "The Path to Adulthood According to Japanese Middle Schools," in Rohlen and LeTendre, *Teaching and Learning in Japan,* 317.

8. With respect to the contrasting disciplinary approaches, Yamada-sensei added, "Their school is orderly on the surface, but students do bad things in the community. We have lots of problems inside the school, but because of that,

our students aren't so bad outside of school. They actually look forward to coming to school." ALTs who are placed in schools that do sanction corporal punishment are invariably shocked to witness it; though both atypical and officially outlawed, such behavior is rarely reprimanded.

9. Fukuzawa, "The Path to Adulthood," 304.

10. The typologies of the JTLs were constructed on the basis of the responses to my questions of fifty-four teachers interviewed, observations of their team-taught classes (where possible), and comments from ALTs about their own style of interaction and their classroom demeanor.

11. I witnessed the results of such stress firsthand when I visited a night school for working students who had not been successful in the regular school system. My friend who made the arrangements had apparently failed to warn the JTL that I was coming. When we appeared in the teacher's room and he requested that I be allowed to sit in, the poor fellow's face turned beet red and he went into a coughing fit, fanning himself furiously and opening the window for fresh air. He calmed down and was able to speak after about two minutes, and he even graciously agreed to allow me to visit the class.

12. See Anthony Giddens, *Central Problems in Social Theory: Action, Structure, and Contradiction in Social Analysis* (Berkeley: University of California Press, 1979), passim.

13. Michelle Fine, *Framing Dropouts: Notes on the Politics of an Urban Public High School* (Albany: State University of New York Press, 1991), 154–57.

14. Robert Hicks, "Impressions," *JET Journal*, summer 1995, p. 42. Interestingly, by the end of his stay he had become much more sympathetic toward Japan, thus demonstrating how one's "Japan experience" can change over time.

15. Ben Court, "If Something Goes Wrong, First Look in the Mirror," *JET Journal*, summer 1995, p. 48.

16. Stephane Labranche, "Global Education in a Japanese Senior High School," *Jet Journal*, summer 1994, pp. 44–45.

17. Jeffrey Strain, "More Than Just a Language Teacher," *JET Journal*, summer 1995, p. 106.

18. Lada Toptschan, "Kokusaika or Alienation," *JET Journal*, autumn 1989, pp. 66–67.

19. Takie Sugiyama Lebra, *Japanese Patterns of Behavior* (Honolulu: University of Hawai'i Press, 1976), 125.

20. "Research on the Situation of Foreign Teachers of English in Japanese Schools," *IRLT Bulletin*, no. 2 (1988): 23.

21. Thomas Rohlen and Gerald LeTendre, "Introduction: Japanese Theories of Learning," in Rohlen and LeTendre, *Teaching and Learning in Japan*, 7. On the preschool and elementary classroom, see Catherine Lewis, *Educating Hearts and Minds: Reflections on Japanese Preschool and Elementary Education* (New York: Cambridge University Press, 1995).

22. John Singleton, "Japanese Folkcraft Pottery Apprenticeship: Cultural Patterns of an Educational Institution," in *Apprenticeship: From Theory to*

Method and Back Again, ed. Michael Coy (Albany: State University of New York Press, 1989), 13–30.

23. Yoshie Aiga, "Is Japanese English Education Changing?" *Cross Currents* 17, no. 2 (1990): 139–45.

24. I am indebted to Thomas Rohlen for this insight.

25. Uehara Shuichi, *AET to tsukiau 18 shō* (Eighteen steps for interacting with an AET) (Tokyo: Sankaisha Shuppan, 1988). Other advice includes how to introduce your foreign teacher to the principal, how to throw a welcome party for the ALT, and how to ask the ALT to be a judge at the school's English Recitation Contest.

26. Rebecca Brosseau, "Gaijin on Parade," *JET Journal,* summer 1994, p. 25.

27. The framework of the following analysis relies heavily on Rosabeth Moss Kanter, *Men and Women of the Corporation* (New York: Basic Books, 1977). She writes, "Tokens are ironically both highly visible as people who are different and yet not permitted the individuality of their own nonstereotypical characteristics" (211).

28. Therese Simpson, "The Gospel According to the JET," *JET Journal,* summer 1994, pp. 35–36.

29. Hiroshi Wagatsuma, "The Social Perception of Skin Color in Japan," *Daedalus* 97, no. 2 (1967): 407–43.

30. Teigo Yoshida, "The Stranger as God: The Place of the Outsider in Japanese Folk Religion," *Ethnology* 20, no. 2 (1981): 87–99.

31. Natsume Sōseki, *Botchan,* trans. Umeji Sasaki (Tokyo: Charles Tuttle, 1968), 49–50.

32. Bruce LaBrack, "Is an International Identity Possible for the Japanese?" paper presented at the International Education Center, Tokyo, 21 May 1983.

33. Harumi Befu, "The Internationalization of Japan and *Nihon Bunkaron,*" in *The Challenge of Japan's Internationalization: Organization and Culture,* ed. Hiroshi Mannari and Harumi Befu (Tokyo: Kodansha, 1983), 244.

34. See, for example, Thomas P. Rohlen, "Conflict in Institutional Environments: Politics in Education," in *Conflict in Japan,* ed. Ellis Krauss, Thomas P. Rohlen, and Patricia G. Steinhoff (Honolulu: University of Hawai'i Press, 1984), 136–73.

35. Masao Miyoshi, *Off Center: Power and Culture Relations between Japan and the United States* (Cambridge, Mass.: Harvard University Press, 1991), 77.

CHAPTER 6. THE LEARNING CURVE: JETTING INTO THE NEW MILLENNIUM

1. *The JET Programme: Ten Years and Beyond* (Tokyo: Council of Local Authorities for International Relations, 1997), n.p.

2. Shiikawa Shinobu is quoted in the transcript of "Discussion Meeting," in ibid., 196.

3. Ibid. Several Arab nations have expressed a strong interest in joining the program, but thus far they have been denied.

4. Kenneth Pyle, "Japan and the Future of Collective Security," in *Japan's Emerging Global Role*, ed. Danny Unger and Paul Blackburn (Boulder, Colo.: Lynne Rienner Publishers, 1993), 107.

5. Danny Unger, "Japan's Capital Exports: Molding East Asia," in Unger and Blackburn, *Japan's Emerging Global Role*, 165.

6. Se Hee Yoo, "Sino-Japanese Relations in a Changing East Asia," in *Japan's Foreign Policy After the Cold War: Coping with Change*, ed. Gerald Curtis (New York: M. E. Sharpe, 1993), 303–22.

7. Huang Bao zhong, "Working for Friendship between China and Japan," in *JET Programme*, 335–36.

8. Paul Knight, "Thoughts on an Annual Marathon," in ibid., 350.

9. This official went on to note that the Center for Global Partnership (an organization created in 1991 to honor the late Shintaro Abe, former Japanese minister of foreign affairs) is badly misnamed, as it is primarily dedicated to furthering U.S.-Japan cultural and educational ties.

10. Nakada Masaaki, a CLAIR official, quoted in "Discussion Meeting," 194.

11. Kim Chishyku, "Looking Back upon a Bygone Year and Four Months," in *JET Programme*, 294.

12. Yvonne Thurman, "American Americans," *JET Journal*, winter 1995, pp. 30–31.

13. The letter from the Welsh ALT is reprinted in Yvonne Thurman, "America under Attack," *JET Journal*, summer 1995, pp. 79–80.

14. Public opinion polls, insofar as they can be trusted, continue to show that the United States is by far the country that Japanese like the most and dislike the least. See Masaru Tamamoto, "The Japan That Wants to Be Liked: Society and International Participation," in Unger and Blackburn, *Japan's Emerging Global Role*, 39.

15. At the outset, the Tokyo orientation was a weeklong affair beginning 1 August, the day after the JET participants arrive. In response to the increase in numbers of participants, it has now been divided into two sessions and shortened. Until 1998 the smaller midyear block conferences were conducted in December for ALTs in eight "blocks," or regions, throughout Japan for the purpose of letting ALTs and JTLs reflect on their experiences in schools and share their frustrations and ideas with each other. They are now held separately in each prefecture. The renewers' conference, first conducted by AJET and then taken over by CLAIR, was originally instituted for all renewing JET participants but has since been restricted to first-time renewers.

16. Robert Juppé, Jr., "Debuilding Blocks," *AJET Magazine*, October 1988, p. 2.

17. Ibid.

18. Satoko Nozawa, "AETs Overwhelm Japanese at Kanto Block Seminar," *Daily Yomiuri*, 1 December 1988.

19. See Robert Levy for a discussion of a similar attitude in his fieldwork sites in the Himalayas and the South Pacific; "Person-Centered Anthropology,"

in *Assessing Cultural Anthropology,* ed. Robert Borofsky (New York: McGraw-Hill, 1995), 180–89.

20. See Yoshio Sugimoto, *An Introduction to Japanese Society* (New York: Cambridge University Press, 1997), 245–58.

21. Minoru Wada, letter to *AJET Magazine,* October 1988, p. 2.

22. Kevin, the ALT coordinator whom Sato-sensei had brought into the prefectural board of education, was one of those who had the misfortune of being caught absent from this session, and he was thoroughly embarrassed when Sato-sensei and Tanabe-san were notified. "Since he's the ALT advisor in our prefecture, he has to serve as a role model for others," scolded Sato-sensei.

23. Robert Juppé, Jr., interview with author, Tokyo, 2 June 1996.

24. Masao Miyamoto, *Straightjacket Society: An Insider's Irreverent View of Bureaucratic Japan,* trans. Juliet Winters Carpenter (Tokyo: Kodansha International, 1994).

25. Robert Juppé recalled the incident in more detail:

What happened was in April CLAIR said he couldn't give the talk, so the AJET chair called me and said, "What should we do?" And I said, "Well, why don't you invite him anyway but change the venue?' And they said, "Yes, that's just what we'll do—we didn't think of that." But I guess someone in CLAIR was one step ahead and caught wind of it and they said, "If he's anywhere in the city, we'll cut all your funds." So AJET came back to me and I said, "Well, why don't you do it anyway. AJET has been brought too deep into the fold now. It's almost a branch of CLAIR. Why don't you go back to your independent roots?" I really thought this would be a good chance to provide people with an alternative viewpoint. Well, it wound up that they got another speaker, who did all right, but it was an innocuous topic that didn't cause any friction. Robert Juppé, Jr., interview with author, Tokyo, 27 May 1995.

26. Ibid.

27. Ibid.

28. *The Japan Exchange and Teaching (JET) Programme General Information Handbook* (Tokyo: Council of Local Authorities for International Relations, 1996), 4.

29. Cartoon by Roger Dahl, *Japan Times Weekly International Edition,* 7–13 April 1997, p. 20.

30. Speech given at the Kansai Mid-Year Block Conference in Osaka, December 1989.

31. Bob Juppé was told that because foreigners were prohibited by law from working in a national government office, he was officially hired by Tsukuba University, and he taught at their "attached" high school two days a week. Both his boss at the Ministry of Education and his supervisor at Tsukuba informed him in no uncertain terms that his main responsibilities lay with the JET Program.

32. See, for example, Robert Juppé, Jr., "Time to Structurally Develop Team Teachers," *Tsukuba Women's University Research Bulletin* 2 (1998): 1–17.

33. "Heisei 4–5 nendo Teimu Teichingu Kenkyū Shinshinkō Kenkyū Shūroku" (Summaries of reports from the 1990–92 team-teaching research

schools), *Chūtō Kyōiku Shiryo* (Curriculum Materials for Secondary Education) 4, no. 651 (1994).

34. Koike Ikuo, interview with author, Tokyo, 3 June 1993. This new course of study marked a watershed in another way as well. For the first time the Ministry of Education used *katakana*, the phonetic alphabet used for foreign loanwords, in its guidelines.

35. ALTs are often asked to coach students in the recitation of a particular passage from the textbook (with such titles as "The Titanic," "I Have a Dream," "Save the Rainforests," and "The Hattori Shooting").

36. Huw Oliphant, personal communication, 12 May 1999.

37. Robert Juppé, Jr., personal communication, 1 April 1998.

38. Bruce S. Feiler's *Learning to Bow: Inside the Heart of Japan* (New York: Ticknor and Fields, 1991), reflecting on a year in the JET Program, provides wonderful examples of the kinds of meaningful relationships that can be established, particularly when the visitor is willing to place him- or herself in the position of learner.

39. During my visit to Tokyo in 1996, Ministry of Home Affairs officials, convinced that the JET Program has now become an unqualified success, assured me that its future was secure no matter what the state of the Japanese economy.

40. David Plath, personal communication, 28 November 1992.

41. Hisaeda Joji, quoted in "Discussion Meeting," 203.

42. This hands-off approach to Japanese language learning at the national level was usually mirrored by prefectures and municipalities as well. A few host institutions, however, went their own way. Kumamoto Prefecture offered a three-day Japanese language seminar for all new JET participants.

43. Hisaeda Joji, quoted in "Discussion Meeting," 192.

CHAPTER 7. FINAL THOUGHTS

1. Robert Smith, "The Cultural Context of the Japanese Political Economy," in *Cultural and Social Dynamics*, ed. Shumpei Kumon and Henry Rosovsky, vol. 3 of *The Political Economy of Japan*, ed. Yasusuke Murakami and Hugh T. Patrick (Stanford: Stanford University Press, 1992), 13–31; quotation on 29.

2. Thomas P. Rohlen, "Learning: The Mobilization of Knowledge in the Japanese Political Economy," in Kumon and Rosovsky, *Cultural and Social Dynamics*, 363.

3. Hidetoshi Kato, "Soybean Curd and Brine," in *Listening to Japan: A Japanese Anthology*, ed. Jackson Bailey (New York: Praeger, 1973), 5.

4. The Ministry of Education, for instance, has canvassed the English teacher's consultants at the prefectural level, and CLAIR has done the same with local government officials. Prefectural and local offices of education have surveyed Japanese teachers of English, and the Japanese teachers of English

themselves not infrequently conduct surveys of students regarding the ALTs. As is typical when a "problem" emerges in Japan, outside organizations have also rushed to conduct their own studies.

5. Kazukimi Ebuchi, "Kokusaika no bunseki shiten to daigaku Shihyō settei no kokoromi" (The concept of internationalization: A semantic analysis with special reference to the internationalization of higher education), *Daigaku Ronshū* (Research in Higher Education) 18 (1989): 29–52.

6. Walter Edwards, "Internationalization, *Nihonjinron,* and the Question of Japanese Identity," paper presented at the annual conference of the Japan Association of Language Teachers, November 1988, Kobe, Japan, p. 10.

7. See, for example, Margaret Gibson's description of accommodation strategies used by Sikh immigrants in California in *Accommodation without Assimilation: Sikh Immigrants in an American High School* (Ithaca, N.Y.: Cornell University Press, 1988).

8. Edward Spicer, "Persistent Identity Systems," *Science,* no. 4011 (1971): 795–800.

9. Robert C. Christopher has framed the Japanese approach to change this way: "Since their primary commitment is to the well-being of their tribe rather than to ideology or religion, Japanese find it easier than most peoples to accept change. . . . [I]n the philosophic sense, it is not really possible to speak of an un-Japanese society; a truly Japanese society—like truly Japanese behavior—is whatever the Japanese consensus holds it to be at any given period." *The Japanese Mind* (New York: Fawcett Columbine, 1983), 55.

10. Harumi Befu notes how *nihonjinron,* as a discursive symbol of identity with minimal emotive content, has been altered over the years from emperor-centered ideology to discussion of Japan's unique cultural, linguistic, and racial traits; see "Symbols of Nationalism and *Nihonjinron,*" in *Ideology and Practice in Modern Japan,* ed. Roger Goodman and Kirsten Refsing (New York: Routledge, 1992), 42–43.

11. Ronald Dore, "Cultures Don't Meet: People Do," *Japan Foundation Newsletter* 26, no. 3 (1997): 9.

EPILOGUE: MIRROR ON MULTICULTURALISM
IN THE UNITED STATES

1. Francine Ruskin and Hervé Varenne, "The Production of Ethnic Discourse: American and Puerto Rican Patterns," in *The Sociogenesis of Language and Human Conduct,* ed. Bruce Bain (New York: Plenum, 1983), 567.

2. I am indebted to Thomas Rohlen for this insight.

3. Michael Olneck, "The Recurring Dream: Symbolism and Ideology in Intercultural and Multicultural Education," *American Journal of Education* 98 (1990): 161–62.

4. James Banks, *Multiethnic Education: Theory and Practice,* 2nd ed. (Boston: Allen and Bacon, 1988).

5. Diane Hoffman, "Culture and Self in Multicultural Education: Reflections on Discourse, Text, and Practice," *American Educational Research Journal* 33 (1996): 548.

6. See David Kertzer, *Ritual, Politics, and Power* (New Haven: Yale University Press, 1988).

7. Clifford Geertz, "The Uses of Diversity," in *Assessing Cultural Anthropology*, ed. Robert Borofsky (New York: McGraw-Hill, 1994), 465.

Bibliography

Abegglen, James. "Japan's Ultimate Vulnerability." In *Inside the Japanese System: Readings on Contemporary Society and Political Economy*, edited by Daniel I. Okimoto and Thomas P. Rohlen, 257–64. Stanford: Stanford University Press, 1988.

Aiga, Yoshie. "Is Japanese English Education Changing?" *Cross Currents* 17, no. 2 (1990): 139–45.

Bailey, Jackson. "Student Exchanges and the Use of Technology." In *Between Understanding and Misunderstanding: Problems and Prospects for International Cultural Exchange*, edited by Yasushi Sugiyama, 94–115. New York: Greenwood Press, 1990.

Banks, James. *Multiethnic Education: Theory and Practice*. 2nd ed. Boston: Allyn and Bacon, 1988.

Barth, Fredrik, ed. *Ethnic Groups and Boundaries: The Social Organization of Culture Differences*. Boston: Little, Brown, 1969.

Beasley, W. G. *Japan Encounters the Barbarian: Japanese Travellers in America and Europe*. New Haven: Yale University Press, 1995.

Befu, Harumi. "An Ethnography of Dinner Entertainment in Japan." In *Japanese Business: Cultural Perspectives*, edited by Subhash Durlabhji and Norton E. Marks, 123–36. Albany: State University of New York Press, 1993.

———. "The Internationalization of Japan and *Nihon Bunkaron*." In *The Challenge of Japan's Internationalization: Organization and Culture*, edited by Hiroshi Mannari and Harumi Befu, 232–66. Tokyo: Kodansha, 1983.

———. "Symbols of Nationalism and *Nihonjiron*." In *Ideology and Practice in Modern Japan*, edited by Roger Goodman and Kirsten Refsing, 26–46. New York: Routledge, 1992.

Befu, Harumi, and Kazufumi Manabe. "An Empirical Study of Nihonjinron: How Real Is the Myth?" *Kwansei Gakuin University Annual Studies* 36 (1987): 97–111.

Bellah, Robert, et al. *Habits of the Heart: Individualism and Commitment in American Life*. Berkeley: University of California Press, 1985.

Bennett, John, Herbert Passin, and R. K. McKnight. *In Search of Identity: The Japanese Overseas Scholar in America and Japan.* Minneapolis: University of Minnesota Press, 1958.

Bestor, Theodore. *Neighborhood Tokyo.* Stanford: Stanford University Press, 1989.

Blaker, Michael. "Evaluating Japanese Diplomatic Performance." In *Japan's Foreign Policy After the Cold War: Coping with Change,* edited by Gerald Curtis, 1–42. New York: M. E. Sharpe, 1993.

Campbell, John Creighton. "Japan and the United States: Games That Work." In *Japan's Foreign Policy After the Cold War: Coping with Change,* edited by Gerald Curtis, 43–61. New York: M. E. Sharpe, 1993.

———. "Policy Conflict and Its Resolution within the Governmental System." In *Conflict in Japan,* edited by Ellis Kraus, Thomas P. Rohlen, and Patricia G. Steinhoff, 295–334. Honolulu: University of Hawai'i Press, 1984.

Christopher, Robert C. *The Japanese Mind.* New York: Fawcett Columbine, 1983.

Cummings, William. *Education and Equality in Japan.* Princeton: Princeton University Press, 1980.

DeVos, George. *Social Cohesion and Alienation: Minorities in the United States and Japan.* Boulder, Colo.: Westview Press, 1992.

DeVos, George, and Hiroshi Wagatsuma. *Japan's Invisible Race.* Berkeley: University of California Press, 1966.

Dore, Ronald. "Cultures Don't Meet: People Do." *Japan Foundation Newsletter* 26, no. 3 (1997): 9.

———. "The Internationalisation of Japan." *Pacific Affairs* 52 (1979): 595–611.

Edwards, Walter. "Buried Discourse: The Toro Archaeological Site and Japanese National Identity in the Early Postwar Period." *Journal of Japanese Studies* 17 (1991): 1–23.

———. "Internationalization, *Nihonjinron,* and the Question of Japanese Identity." Paper presented at the annual conference of the Japan Association of Language Teachers, Kobe, November 1988.

Fallows, James. "Getting Along with Japan." *Atlantic,* December 1994, pp. 60–62.

Feiler, Bruce S. *Learning to Bow: Inside the Heart of Japan.* New York: Ticknor and Fields, 1991.

Fine, Michelle. *Framing Dropouts: Notes on the Politics of an Urban Public High School.* Albany: State University of New York Press, 1991.

Fishman, Joshua. *Language and Nationalism: Two Integrative Essays.* Rowley, Mass.: Newbury House, 1972.

Foucault, Michel. *Discipline and Punish: The Birth of the Prison.* Translated by A. Sheridan. New York: Pantheon Books, 1977.

Fujitani, Takashi. *Splendid Monarchy: Power and Pageantry in Modern Japan.* Berkeley: University of California Press, 1996.

Fukui, Haruhiro. "State in Policymaking: A Review of the Literature." In *Policymaking in Contemporary Japan,* edited by T. J. Pempel, 22–59. Ithaca, N.Y.: Cornell University Press, 1977.

Fukuzawa, Rebecca Erwin. "The Path to Adulthood According to Japanese Middle Schools." In *Teaching and Learning in Japan*, edited by Thomas Rohlen and Gerald LeTendre, 295–320. New York: Cambridge University Press, 1996.

Gaikoku Seinen Shōchi Jigyō Ukeiredantai yō Manyuaru (JET Program host organization's orientation manual).Tokyo: Council of Local Authorities for International Relations, 1988.

Geertz, Clifford. "From the Natives' Point of View: On the Nature of Anthropological Understanding." In *Meaning in Anthropology*, edited by Keith Basso and Henry Selby, 221–238. Albuquerque: University of New Mexico Press, 1976.

———. "The Integrative Revolution: Primordial Sentiments and Civil Politics in the New States." In *The Interpretation of Cultures*, 255–310. New York: Basic Books, 1973.

———. "The Uses of Diversity." In *Assessing Cultural Anthropology*, edited by Robert Borofsky, 454–65. New York: McGraw-Hill, 1994.

George, Aurelia. "Japan's America Problem: The Japanese Response to U.S. Pressure." *Washington Quarterly* 14, no. 3 (1991): 5–19.

Gibson, Margaret. *Accommodation without Assimilation: Sikh Immigrants in an American High School*. Ithaca, N.Y.: Cornell University Press, 1988.

Giddens, Anthony. *Central Problems in Social Theory: Action, Structure, and Contradiction in Social Analysis*. Berkeley: University of California Press, 1979.

Gluck, Carol. *Japan's Modern Myths: Ideology in the Late Meiji Period*. Princeton: Princeton University Press, 1985.

Goodman, Roger. *Japan's "International Youth": The Emergence of a New Class of Schoolchildren*. Oxford: Clarendon Press; New York: Oxford University Press, 1990.

Haley, John O. "Governance by Negotiation: A Reappraisal of Bureaucratic Power in Japan." *Journal of Japanese Studies* 13 (1987): 343–57.

Hamada, Tomoko, and Willis E. Sibley, eds. *Anthropological Perspectives on Organizational Culture*. Lanham, Md.: University Press of America, 1994.

Hannerz, Ulf. *Cultural Complexity*. New York: Columbia University Press, 1992.

Harasawa, Masayoshi. "A Critical Survey of English Language Teaching in Japan: A Personal View." *English Language Teaching Journal* 29, no. 1 (1974): 71–72.

Haraway, Donna. *Primate Visions: Gender, Race, and Nature in the World of Modern Science*. New York: Routledge, 1989.

Hardacre, Helen. *Shinto and the State, 1868–1988*. Princeton: Princeton University Press, 1989.

Heginbotham, Stanley J. *Cultures in Conflict: The Four Faces of Indian Bureaucracy*. New York: Columbia University Press, 1975.

"Heisei 4–5 Nendo Teimu Teichingu Kenkyū Shinshinkō Kenkyū Shūroku" (Summaries of reports from the 1990–92 team-teaching research schools). *Chūtō Kyōiku Shiryo* (Curriculum Materials for Secondary Education) 4, no. 651 (1994).

Henrichsen, Lynn Earl. *Diffusion of Innovation in English Language Teaching: The ELEC Effort in Japan, 1956–1968.* New York: Greenwood Press, 1989.

Hoffman, Diane. "Culture and Self in Multicultural Education: Reflections on Discourse, Text, and Practice." *American Educational Research Journal* 33 (1996): 545–69.

Hood, Christopher P. "Nakasone Yasuhiro and Japanese Education Reform: A Revisionist View." Ph.D. diss., University of Sheffield, 1998.

Hori, G. Victor Soogen. "Teaching and Learning in the Rinzai Zen Monastery." In *Teaching and Learning in Japan*, edited by Thomas Rohlen and Gerald LeTendre, 20–49. New York: Cambridge University Press, 1996.

Horio, Teruhisa. *Educational Thought and Ideology in Modern Japan.* Translated by Steven Platzer. Tokyo: University of Tokyo Press, 1988.

Horsley, William. "An Outsider's View of CLAIR's Activities." *Jichitai Kokusaika Forāmu* (Forum on Internationalization for Local Governments), no. 11 (November 1989): 21.

Huang, Bao zhong. "Working for Friendship between China and Japan." In *The JET Programme: Ten Years and Beyond*, 335–36. Tokyo: Council of Local Authorities for International Relations, 1997.

Inoguchi, Takashi. "The Legacy of a Weathercock Prime Minister." *Japan Quarterly* 34, no. 3 (1987): 363–70.

The Japan Exchange and Teaching Programme General Information Handbook. Tokyo: Council of Local Authorities for International Relations, 1995.

"Japan Welcomes More JETers." *Japan Pictorial* 12, no. 1 (1989).

Japan-U.S. Friendship Commission. "Commission Funds Center to Promote Study Abroad in Japan." *The Commissioner*, spring/summer 1997, pp. 1–2.

The JET Program(me): Five Years and Beyond. Tokyo: Council of Local Authorities for International Relations, 1992.

The JET Programme: Ten Years and Beyond. Tokyo: Council of Local Authorities for International Relations, 1997.

Johnson, Chalmers. *Japan: Who Governs?* New York: W. W. Norton, 1995.

Jones, H. J. *Live Machines: Hired Foreigners in Meiji Japan.* Vancouver: University of British Columbia Press, 1980.

Juppé, Robert, Jr. "Time to Structurally Develop Team-Teaching." *Tsukuba Women's University Research Bulletin* 2 (1998): 1–17.

Kanter, Rosabeth Moss. *Men and Women of the Corporation.* New York: Basic Books, 1977.

Kato, Hidetoshi. "Soybean Curd and Brine." In *Listening to Japan: A Japanese Anthology*, edited by Jackson Bailey, 3–6. New York: Praeger, 1973.

Kazukimi Ebuchi. "Kokusaika no bunseki shiten to daigaku Shihyō settei no kokoromi" (The concept of internationalization: A semantic analysis with special reference to the internationalization of higher education). *Daigaku Ronshū* (Research in Higher Education) 18 (1989): 29–52.

Kertzer, David. *Ritual, Politics, and Power.* New Haven: Yale University Press, 1988.

Kim, Chishyku. "Looking Back upon a Bygone Year and Four Months." In *The JET Programme: Ten Years and Beyond*, 294. Tokyo: Council of Local Authorities for International Relations, 1997.

Kim, Choong Sun. *Japanese Industry in the American South*. New York: Routledge, 1995.

Knight, Paul. "Thoughts on an Annual Marathon." In *The JET Programme: Ten Years and Beyond*, 350. Tokyo: Council of Local Authorities for International Relations, 1997.

Kobayashi, Tetsuya. "Educational Problems of 'Returning Children.'" In *Japanese Schooling: Patterns of Socialization, Equality, and Political Control*, edited by James J. Shields, Jr., 185–93. University Park: Pennsylvania State University Press, 1989.

Kottak, Conrad, and Elizabeth Colson. "Multilevel Linkages: Longitudinal and Comparative Studies." In *Assessing Cultural Anthropology*, edited by Robert Borofsky, 396–412. New York: McGraw-Hill, 1994.

LaBrack, Bruce. "Is an International Identity Possible for the Japanese?" Forum address presented at the International Education Center, Tokyo, 21 May 1983.

Lebra, Takie Sugiyama. *Japanese Patterns of Behavior*. Honolulu: University of Hawai'i Press, 1976.

———. *Japanese Women: Constraint and Fulfillment*. Honolulu: University of Hawai'i Press, 1984.

Lee, Changsoo, and George DeVos, eds. *Koreans in Japan*. Berkeley: University of California Press, 1981.

LeTendre, Gerald K. "Shidō: The Concept of Guidance." In *Teaching and Learning in Japan*, edited by Thomas Rohlen and Gerald LeTendre, 275–94. New York: Cambridge University Press, 1996.

Levy, Robert. "Person-Centered Anthropology." In *Assessing Cultural Anthropology*, edited by Robert Borofsky, 180–89. New York: McGraw-Hill, 1995.

Lewis, Catherine. *Educating Hearts and Minds: Reflections on Japanese Preschool and Elementary Education*. New York: Cambridge University Press, 1995.

Lincoln, Edward. *Japan's New Global Role*. Washington, D.C.: Brookings Institution, 1993.

Mannari, Hiroshi, and Harumi Befu, eds. *The Challenge of Japan's Internationalization: Organization and Culture*. Tokyo: Kodansha, 1983.

Miller, Roy Andrew. *Japan's Modern Myth: The Language and Beyond*. New York: Weatherhill, 1982.

Minoura, Yasuko. "Life in Between: The Acquisition of Cultural Identity among Japanese Children Living in the United States." Ph.D. diss., University of California at Los Angeles, 1979.

Miyamoto, Masao. *Straightjacket Society: An Insider's Irreverent View of Bureaucratic Japan*. Translated by Juliet Winters Carpenter. Tokyo: Kodansha International, 1994.

Miyoshi, Masao. *Off Center: Power and Culture Relations between Japan and the United States*. Cambridge, Mass.: Harvard University Press, 1991.

Montgomery, John D. "Beyond Good Policies." In *Great Policies: Strategic Innovations in Asia and the Pacific Basin*, edited by John D. Montgomery and Dennis Rondinelli, 1–13. London: Praeger, 1995.

Nachtsheim, Suzy. "Bull's Eye: Keeping Your One-Shot Visits on Target." *Language Teacher* 12, no. 9 (1988): 25–26.

Nakamura, Hajime. "The Tendency to Emphasize a Limited Social Nexus." In *Ways of Thinking of Eastern Peoples: India, China, Tibet, and Japan*, edited by Philip P. Wiener, 496–513. Honolulu: University of Hawai'i Press, 1964.

Nakane, Chie. *Japanese Society*. Berkeley: University of California Press, 1970.

Nakanishi Akira. "Ibunka rikai to kaigai shijo kyōiku/kikokushijo kyōiku" (Intercultural understanding and education for overseas and returning children). *Ibunkakan Kyōiku* (Intercultural Education) 2 (1988): 16–24.

Nitobe, Inazo. "The Teaching and Use of Foreign Languages." *Sewanee Review* 31 (1923): 338–39.

O'Dowd, Gregory V. G. "Australia—Don't Miss the JET!" *Japanese Studies: Bulletin of the Japanese Studies Association of Australia* 12, no. 1 (1992): 37–41.

Olneck, Michael. "The Recurring Dream: Symbolism and Ideology in Intercultural and Multicultural Education." *American Journal of Education* 98 (1990): 147–83.

Passin, Herbert. *Education and Society in Japan*. New York: Teachers' College Press, 1965.

Pyle, Kenneth. "Japan and the Future of Collective Security." In *Japan's Emerging Global Role*, edited by Danny Unger and Paul Blackburn, 99–120. Boulder, Colo.: Lynne Rienner, 1993.

———. *The Japanese Question: Power and Purpose in a New Era*. Washington, D.C.: AEI Press, 1992.

Reed, Steven R. *Japanese Prefectures and Policymaking*. Pittsburgh: University of Pittsburgh Press, 1985.

Reischauer, Edwin. *The Japanese Today: Change and Continuity*. Cambridge, Mass.: Belknap Press of Harvard University Press, 1988.

"Research on the Situation of Foreign Teachers of English in Japanese Schools." *IRLT Bulletin*, no. 2 (1988): 1–108.

Robertson, Jennifer. *Native and Newcomer: Making and Remaking a Japanese City*. Berkeley: University of California Press, 1991.

Rohlen, Thomas P. "Conflict in Institutional Environments: Politics in Education." In *Conflict in Japan*, edited by Ellis Krauss, Thomas P. Rohlen, and Patricia G. Steinhoff, 136–73. Honolulu: University of Hawai'i Press, 1984.

———. *Japan's High Schools*. Berkeley: University of California Press, 1983.

———. "Learning: The Mobilization of Knowledge in the Japanese Political Economy." In *Cultural and Social Dynamics*, edited by Shumpei Kumon and Henry Rosovsky, 321–63. Vol. 3 of *The Political Economy of Japan*, edited by Yasusuke Murakami and Hugh T. Patrick. Stanford: Stanford University Press, 1992.

———. "Order in Japanese Society: Attachment, Authority, and Routine." *Journal of Japanese Studies* 15 (1989): 5–40.

Rohlen, Thomas, and Gerald LeTendre. "Introduction: Japanese Theories of Learning." In *Teaching and Learning in Japan,* edited by Thomas Rohlen and Gerald LeTendre, 1–15. New York: Cambridge University Press, 1996.

Ruskin, Francine, and Hervé Varenne. "The Production of Ethnic Discourse: American and Puerto Rican Patterns." In *The Sociogenesis of Language and Human Conduct,* edited by Bruce Bain, 553–568. New York: Plenum, 1983.

Saito Eiji. "AET o mukaete akirakani natta nihon no eigokyōiku no mondaiten" (The problems of English education in Japan as illuminated by the arrival of AETs). *IRLT Newsletter,* no. 104 (1989): 1.

Samuels, Richard. *The Politics of Regional Policy in Japan: Localities Incorporated?* Princeton: Princeton University Press, 1983.

The Sasakawa Peace Foundation. Tokyo: Sasakawa Peace Foundation, 1991.

Sato, Nancy. "Honoring the Individual." In *Teaching and Learning in Japan,* edited by Thomas Rohlen and Gerald LeTendre, 119–53. New York: Cambridge University Press, 1996.

Schoolland, Ken. *Shogun's Ghost: The Dark Side of Japanese Education.* New York: Bergin and Garvey, 1990.

Schoppa, Leonard J. *Education Reform in Japan: A Case of Immobilist Politics.* New York: Routledge, 1991.

Singleton, John. "Japanese Folkcraft Pottery Apprenticeship: Cultural Patterns of an Educational Institution." In *Apprenticeship: From Theory to Method and Back Again,* edited by Michael Coy, 13–30. Albany: State University of New York Press, 1989.

Smith, Robert. "The Cultural Context of the Japanese Political Economy." In *Cultural and Social Dynamics,* edited by Shumpei Kumon and Henry Rosovsky, 13–31. Vol. 3 of *The Political Economy of Japan,* edited by Yasusuke Murakami and Hugh T. Patrick. Stanford: Stanford University Press, 1992.

———. "Gender Inequality in Contemporary Japan." *Journal of Japanese Studies* 13 (1987): 1–25.

———. *Japanese Society: Tradition, Self, and the Social Order.* New York: Cambridge University Press, 1983.

Sōseki, Natsume. *Botchan.* Translated by Umeji Sasaki. Tokyo: Charles Tuttle, 1968.

Spicer, Edward. "Persistent Identity Systems." *Science,* no. 4011 (1971): 795–800.

Sproull, Lee S. "Response to Regulation: An Organizational Process Framework." *Administration and Society* 12 (1981): 447–70.

Sugimoto, Yoshio. *An Introduction to Japanese Society.* New York: Cambridge University Press, 1997.

Tamamoto, Masaru. "The Japan That Wants to Be Liked: Society and International Participation." In *Japan's Emerging Global Role,* edited by Danny Unger and Paul Blackburn, 37–54. Boulder, Colo.: Lynne Rienner, 1993.

Thayer, Nathaniel. "Japanese Foreign Policy in the Nakasone Years." In *Japan's Foreign Policy After the Cold War: Coping with Change,* edited by Gerald Curtis, 90–104. London: M. E. Sharpe, 1993.

Titus, David. "Accessing the World: Palace and Foreign Policy in Post-Occupation Japan." In *Japan's Foreign Policy After the Cold War: Coping with Change*, edited by Gerald Curtis, 62–89. London: M. E. Sharpe, 1993.

Todhunter, Maureen. "International Cultural Exchange in Japan's Foreign Policy Today." In *Japan and the World*, 98–105. Vol. 1 of *Proceedings of the Seventh Biennial Conference of the Japanese Studies Association of Australia*. Canberra: Australia Japan Research Centre, 1991.

Uehara Shuichi. *AET to tsukiau jūhassho* (Eighteen steps for interacting with an AET). Tokyo: Sankaisha Shuppan, 1988.

Unger, Danny. "Japan's Capital Exports: Molding East Asia." In *Japan's Emerging Global Role*, edited by Danny Unger and Paul Blackburn, 155–70. Boulder, Colo.: Lynne Rienner, 1993.

Upham, Frank K. *Law and Social Change in Postwar Japan*. Cambridge, Mass.: Harvard University Press, 1987.

Varenne, Hervé. *Americans Together: Structured Diversity in a Midwestern Town*. New York: Teachers' College Press, 1977.

Vogel, Ezra. *Japan as Number One: Lessons for America*. Cambridge, Mass.: Harvard University Press, 1979.

Wagatsuma, Hiroshi. "The Social Perception of Skin Color in Japan." *Daedalus* 96, no. 2 (1967): 407–43.

Weick, Karl. "Educational Organizations as Loosely Coupled Systems." *Administrative Science Quarterly* 21 (1976): 1–19.

White, Merry. *The Japanese Educational Challenge: A Commitment to Children*. New York: Free Press, 1987.

———. *The Japanese Overseas: Can They Go Home Again?* New York: Free Press, 1988.

———. *The Material Child: Coming of Age in Japan and America*. Berkeley: University of California Press, 1993.

Whiting, Robert. *You Gotta Have Wa*. New York: Vintage Books, 1989.

Wolcott, Harry. *The Man in the Principal's Office*. Prospect Heights, Ill.: Waveland Press, 1974.

Wolferen, Karel van. *The Enigma of Japanese Power: People and Politics in a Stateless Nation*. New York: Vintage Books, 1990.

Yamazumi, Masami. "State Control and the Evolution of Ultranationalistic Textbooks." In *Japanese Schooling: Patterns of Socialization, Equality, and Political Control*, edited by James J. Shields, Jr., 234–42. University Park: Pennsylvania State University Press, 1989.

Yoo, Se Hee. "Sino-Japanese Relations in a Changing East Asia." In *Japan's Foreign Policy After the Cold War: Coping with Change*, edited by Gerald Curtis, 303–22. New York: M. E. Sharpe, 1993.

Yoshida, Teigo. "The Stranger as God: The Place of the Outsider in Japanese Folk Religion." *Ethnology* 20, no. 2 (1981): 87–99.

Yoshino, Kosaku. *Cultural Nationalism in Contemporary Japan*. New York: Routledge, 1992.

Index

Abe, Shintaro, 303n
Abegglen, James, 1
ACT (assistant Chinese teacher), 256
AET (assistant English teacher), 2, 45, 283n
Affluence, 14, 35–36
Africa, 9, 199, 234
African Americans, 79–83, 187, 293n
AFT (assistant French teacher), 73–74, 283n, 292n
Age: differential between ALTs and Japanese hosts, 75–76, 219, 293n; limit for JET Program, 76–77
AGT (assistant German teacher), 73–74, 283n, 292n
AIDS, 84, 88
Aiga, Yoshie, 212, 302n
The Ainu, 277
AJET (Association of JET Participants): appropriation of initiatives by CLAIR, 246–248, 291n; and attempts to improve national-level conferences, 238–239; and conflict with CLAIR, 304n; and criticism of one-shot system, 126; gay support group of, 87–88; membership of, 248; minority support group of, 81, 293n; name, in Japanese, 76; and pension rebate, 237; and prefectural liaisons, 158–159; and standardization, 144; as a pressure group, 66–68; and support for Japanese

language training, 263; and Women's Support Network, 149
AJET Magazine, 72, 238, 292n, 293n, 303n, 304n
AKT (assistant Korean teacher), 256
Alien Registration Card, 200
Allied Occupation of Japan, 6, 13, 19, 112, 258, 269
ALTs (assistant language teachers): adjustment difficulties of, 90; background characteristics of, 57–60; as "boys and girls," 75–76, 219, 293n; conspiracy theories of, 196–197; as "cultural ambassadors," 64; and elementary schools, 257; employment contracts of, 36; extracurricular activities of, 176–178, 201, 256; irresponsible behavior of, 242–246, 304n; Japanese language abilities of, 54–55, 57, 59–60, 65, 291n; living conditions of, 142–145; marital status of, 59, 249–250; motivations of, 60–62; nationalities of, 50–51, 230–236, 283n; personal appearance of, 136, 186; prefectural vs. municipal, 138–142; premature departures of, 295n; and privacy, 85–86, 90, 98, 223; racial and ethnic backgrounds of, 60; renewal rate of, 258, 295n; salary and working conditions of, 51–52, 85; satisfaction level of, 4, 258; and school switching, 153–155;

317

Text:	10/13 Aldus
Display:	Aldus
Composition:	Impressions Book and Journal Services, Inc.
Printing and binding:	Edwards Brothers, Inc.